Register of the Confederate Debt

REGISTER OF THE CONFEDERATE DEBT

Raphael P. Thian

QUARTERMAN PUBLICATIONS, INC.
Boston

Originally published in 1880 under the title *Register of Issues of Confederate States Treasury Notes Together with Tabular Exhibits of the Debt, Funded and Unfunded of the Confederate States of America 1861–1865.* The present republication has been enlarged to include a foreword.

ISBN 0 88000 002 3
Library of Congress catalog card number: 70-189169

Printed in the United States of America

Quarterman Publications, Inc.
61 Park Drive
Boston, Massachusetts 02215

FOREWORD

For years Americans have been fascinated by their Civil War with all its political, social, military, legal, and economic ramifications. Yet it is true that despite this interest, many key areas of that struggle remain neglected, and the books necessary to provide the source material for their resuscitation are out of print. Thian's *Register of Issues of Confederate States Treasury Notes Together with Tabular Exhibits of the Debt, Funded and Unfunded of the Confederate States of America 1861–1865* Appendix II (hereafter referred to as Thian's *Register of the Confederate Debt*) is a classic example of a rare book, there being only five copies extant. It was originally intended to be part of a ten-volume series of which it was to be the statistical portion. Only five of the ten volumes reached the printer and constitute the obscure monument to Raphael Prosper Thian, soldier, Chief Clerk of the Adjutant General's Office, and, in his spare time, over a forty-year period, an avid student of Confederate monetary and economic history.

To fit Thian's *Register of the Confederate Debt* into its proper perspective as an important contribution to any study of Confederate financial policy, I shall discuss first, Thian's life in brief and antecedents; second, the history of the Confederate Archives in United States hands; third, Thian's connection and work with those records; fourth, Thian's publications from those records; and fifth, the merits and use of this book itself.

A Brief Biography of Raphael P. Thian

According to Prosper E. Thian, his father Raphael Prosper Thian was born in Paris, France in 1829. But the official records of the War Department, which I shall take as authoritative, state that the older Thian was born on April 5, 1830, at Denil in the Department of Seine et Oise. His father was Antoine Louis Thian, formerly a soldier in the French army. We know little of his father except that he reached the rank of Captain and served with Napoleon in all the latter's campaigns except those in Spain and Russia.

Having been fortunately absent from those disasters, Captain Thian, with approximately twenty years' service behind him, was kept in the army following the Bourbon restoration in the spring of 1814. He evidently was cooperative or an individual whom someone thought worth cultivating, for on October 10, 1814, he was among those honored with the Order of the Lily, which consisted of a white ribbon powdered with fleur-de-lis, the royalist insignia. (This order was abolished in 1830 with the overthrow of Charles X.)

As a member of the 5th Regiment of Light Infantry, Captain Thian might have been among those to accompany Marshal Ney on his ill-fated trip to arrest Napoleon. The regiment went over to the Emperor, and Captain Thian must have had to do some fast talking when the royalists came back in July of 1815 hell-bent on the reign of "White Terror" which liquidated so many Bonapartists. He managed to stay on in the army until February 25, 1817, when he retired.

His retirement may have been motivated by a variety of factors. As a veteran, he could probably get a small pension. Service with the growingly reactionary Bourbons could not have been comfortable for a soldier of the Revolution. Moreover, Captain Thian was not of noble birth and was probably politically suspect. His chances for promotion in a peacetime army could not have been encouraging. On the other hand, he may have belatedly taken a wife of adequate means or received a small but timely inheritance. Whatever the reason, he settled down in Denil where he raised a family.

As a younger child of a retired soldier of modest means, Raphael P. Thian had his own way to make. Moreover, France in 1848 convulsed with Revolutionary disorders and unemployment probably looked less promising than America where comparatively good times prevailed. Thian therefore sailed to America, probably going to Canada first where his lack of English would be less of a handicap. He evidently learned English quickly, for in 1850 he decided to try his luck across the border. Harkening to the family military tradition, he enlisted in the United States Army for a five-year tour on November 13, 1850.

His first assignment was with Company C of the Fourth Artillery Battalion in Buffalo, New York. Subsequently, he passed by way of the Carlisle General Depot (in Pennsylvania) to Fort Leavenworth, Kansas, arriving on March 8, 1851. By a subsequent order (November 22, 1851), Thian was detached for duty with the Headquarters of the Sixth Department (Order number 131, Headquarters Fort Leavenworth) and remained in that desk job until March 1853.

On March 23, 1853, he was transferred to Company B, First Dragoons (effective April 1, 1853) under Special Order 55 of the Adjutant General's Office. But at the last moment, March 31, 1853, these orders were suspended and a new directive issued ordering him to report to New York where he would join the General Recruiting Service at the Headquarters of the Army at Fort Jay. While there, he came to the attention of the General-in-Chief, old "Fuss and Feathers" Winfield Scott. Scott persuaded the young Frenchman to give up his active duty career (Thian resigned on September 1, 1853, as a sergeant) and to take instead a position with the general's civilian staff. In due course, Thian was appointed a Clerk second class and remained with his aging mentor until November 1, 1861, when General Scott retired.

It was here that Thian showed some of the same cat-like ability to land on his feet that his father had shown earlier. Certainly Thian would never have survived in a patronage and intrigue-ridden Washington bureaucratic jungle without some elementary skills in lifesmanship. Whatever the source of his good luck, Thian found a new job with the Adjutant General's Office (AGO). The vast military operations in progress put a premium on skilled personnel, and Thian advanced rapidly, making Clerk fourth class by April 1, 1864. He also survived the postwar cutbacks, becoming Chief Clerk of the AGO on July 1, 1871. He was destined to hold that position, or its equivalent, for the next forty years.

For those whose knowledge of the military is limited, Thian's duties with the Adjutant General's Office put him at the heart of the Army. For the Adjutant of any unit, whatever its size, is the communications center and right-hand man for his chief. From his office go personnel orders, such as appointments to command, and also unit orders. Personnel records and career planning are done at this level, and during this period the AGO trenched on some of the functions of the G-2 and G-3 by taking part in intelligence operations and drawing up operations orders. An Adjutant General who can't make up his mind on regulations and who makes poor command appointment recommendations (like Samuel

Cooper did for Jefferson Davis) or one who writes obscurely worded orders with double meanings (like Marshal Soult at Waterloo) can be the cause of a total disaster. It says something for more than just Thian's fence-mending technique that he was able to win the favor of so many chiefs or that they should retain him until he was eighty-one, when so many younger men were doubtless anxious to get his post.

In 1904, under the impact of President Roosevelt's taste for military reforms, the AGO and the military pension office were merged under the new title of the Military Secretary's Office. While his division was under that title, Thian received his final promotion to Clerk fifth class. The Military Secretary's Office went back to being the Adjutant General's Office in 1907. Four years later, on December 19, 1911, Thian died. He had been in Federal service sixty-one years, fifty of them in the Adjutant General's Office. He left behind his wife, his children, and his dream that sometime someone would think his work sufficiently important to publish on an adequate scale.

A History of the Confederate Archives

To understand how Thian came to make his lifelong commitment to the study of the Confederate Archives, it is necessary to understand what those archives consisted of during his labors with them and where they were deposited.

At the end of the Civil War, the Confederate Government had fled from Richmond, taking with it such records as the limited transportation facilities would permit. Such records as were left behind were burned in the ensuing fires, trampled in the mud, and thrown away or willfully destroyed by Federal troops who were determined to extirpate every remnant of their fallen foe. This attitude changed swiftly when Major General Halleck arrived in Richmond under orders from Secretary of War Stanton. The Secretary was convinced that Jefferson Davis was implicated in the Lincoln-Seward asassination plot. He therefore ordered that the Rebel Archives be gathered up and shipped to Washington so that Federal investigators could locate the documentary evidence for his contention. Moreover, Stanton was under pressure from the Treasury Department. The latter had sent agents south to gather in all the defeated government's assets. With the Southerners trying to recoup their own losses by pocketing Confederate cotton, and with Federal agents stealing right and left, little money was reaching the Treasury. Secretary McCulloch hoped to reverse this trend by using the rebels' own archives to back up his claims to the Produce Loan cotton.

The materials seized in Richmond, amounting to four hundred and ninety boxes and barrels of documents and one hundred and twenty bags of undelivered mail, reached Washington in the early summer of 1865. Under AGO General Order 127, dated July 21, 1865, the documents were placed in a "Rebel Archives Bureau" for "collection, safe-keeping and publication." Francis Lieber and his son Lieutenant Colonel G. Norman Lieber were put in charge of the bureau. After two years' hard work, the Liebers finally reduced the chaos to the point where they were able to report to the Secretary of War regarding the materials in hand. From that report it was apparent that what they had were mostly quartermasters' accounts and the parallel documents of the Second Auditor who was responsible for reviewing such accounts. More pertinent to our discussion, there were also Congressional, Post Office, and Treasury Department documents.

When the Confederate Archives failed to produce the evidence needed to hang Jeff Davis, interest in them subsided for the time. Congress was in an economy mood, and the time when such documents would appear in the *Record of the Rebellion* was far in the future. The Secretary of War therefore decided to downgrade the bureau (order August 19, 1867) to the status of a small office with five clerks. Working under the Adjutant General, these men struggled on without much outside assistance until 1881, when interest revived. In the meantime, more records were accessioned while some were transferred to other departments. Valuable time was also consumed in answering a growing volume of inquiries from the Treasury.

Following the Produce Loan cotton fiasco, the Treasury lost interest in the Confederate Treasury records. But in the late 1860s and 1870s there arose a mass of claims of *soi-disant* Southern unionists for real or fictitious losses suffered at the hands of the contending armies. To say that the Treasury was unwilling to pay these claims would be an understatement. And to say that the loyal Republican Treasury officers had forgotten or forgiven their Democratic foes' revolt would be a misstatement. But they could not base their refusal to pay on mere partisan prejudices. Something more substantial was required. And that something could often be procured from the Confederate Treasury records in the form of proof of voluntary subscription to the various rebel loans. What better way could be found to frustrate a claimant than to riposte with a charge of treason and aiding of rebellion?

The years 1867 to 1881 are also significant in the genesis of Thian's *Register of the Confederate Debt.* With few officials to interfere, and with the records open to the inspection of anyone possessing the time and patience to look through them, Thian had little difficulty in pursuing his research. How much more work he might have done remains a moot point. For, in 1881, these records were moved to the Records Office of the Secretary of War and did not come back until 1888. By that time Congress had belatedly come forward with publication funds, and Thian, discouraged by his failures to induce Congress to print his work, was not disposed to renew his efforts.

One wishes that one could say that the documents that Thian worked with during those years were safe and well-secured against loss. But such was not in fact the case. In fact, there is a good deal of evidence to show that during this period the government lost control of a large number of Confederate notes and bonds, printed documents, letters, and even correspondence books. In fairness to the government, these items at the time had little material value and existed with so many duplicates that few discerned any need to protect them. Moreover, there were many officially or semiofficially authorized losses. Several Civil War generals, including General Sherman, were recipients of gift scrapbooks filled with choice Confederate notes, bonds, and even correspondence. The Adjutant General, sometimes at the behest of the Secretary of War, also presented similar materials to chapters of the GAR (Grand Army of the Republic). As the Adjutant General's chief clerk, Thian had to spend many hours sifting through notes and documents to find what was needed. To aid him in his own researches for his *Register of the Confederate Debt* he made up two scrapbooks of bonds and four books of notes for his personal use. These are happily now on deposit with the Duke University Library, which purchased them from Thian's son in 1944.

The contents of the Thian scrapbooks, those in both public and private hands, suggest that the half million notes and bonds contained a complete cross section of the Confederate currency. Yet the collection today is missing many types. An examination of several large collections formed in the late 19th and early 20th centuries provides an answer to this anomaly. Several of these collections have been kept in government department stamped envelopes current during the 1870s and 1880s. Such collections contain not one or two rarities of each separate variety, but frequently several such. A few duplicates would obviously have sufficed for trading purposes. Yet these collectors held so many of these notes that either this stock was accumulated for investment purposes or the cost of acquisition was zero, or both. Moreover, as government clerks earning at most $1400 to $1800 per annum, such men would be hard pressed to support themselves and their families along with a two- to five-thousand-dollar hobby. Thian was among the largest of these collectors, disposing of over twelve Montgomeries and thousands of other notes, many high-priced for the time, in December of 1885. He may, as the issuer of a catalog, have also pursued a side business as a note dealer. But the problem of the government's losses remains.

The return of the Confederate Archives to the control of the Adjutant General's Office seems to have brought some tightening of the security precautions. Confederate imprints and bonds had a red "Rebel Archives" stamp placed on them while various publications were in process of preparation. Yet even some of these items leaked out of the Archives and are readily met with today. One hopes that someday the Smithsonian Institution will take custody of its share of these collections and so preserve from further harm a valuable portion of our national heritage.

Thian's Publications

On January 7, 1887, Thian wrote to his retired Chief, former Adjutant General E. D. Townsend, reporting on the completion of his labors and asking General Townsend's support in securing the publication of his work. In this letter he noted:

"It is now nearly twelve years since you suggested to me that my leisure hours be given to preparing a history of the several issues of paper money emitted from the Treasury of the Confederate States, and that, for this purpose, you afforded me special facilities for examining the many books and papers which the War Department, in accordance with your singularly far-sighted suggestion, caused to be carefully collected and preserved from possible destruction.

"A preliminary general view of these records soon made me recognize their great historical value, and, after full consideration of the subject and consultation with you, I determined to make a careful and exhaustive examination, with a view to determine and illustrate the financial, fiscal, and commercial measures of the Confederate States; and it is with sincere pleasure that I add, that in this arduous undertaking I have had the advantage of your constant support and valuable aid in securing me access to other records of the same class but not embraced in the Archive Division of your office.

"This work, to which I have for so long a time devoted almost my entire leisure, is at last in such a state of completion that the only possible contingency is that the printers will not be able to keep up with the editor. I enclose, herewith, a description in brief of the several parts composing the history of 'The Treasury of the Confederate States' which it is estimated will be comprised in ten volumes, octavo, of some seven hundred pages each; and I shall be profoundly grateful if you will take such steps as you may deem proper to bring the work to the attention of the Government, with a view to securing its publication by the Government Printer under the authority of Congress, with a provision that I shall edit the volumes, correct proofs, etc., at such a compensation therefore as Congress may deem just and proper."

After making some remarks on various aspects of Confederate finance, Thian continued with the statement:

". . . the history of the *purse* is as valuable as that of the *sword*; and deeply impressed with this fact, my energies and best ability have been devoted to securing the future historian positive and authentic *data* which possibly, without my labors, would have remained for an indefinite period in the domain of the unknown.

"Another product of my leisure, and one which I would be glad to have considered in connection with my labors in the field above indicated, is a 'Documentary History of the Flag and Seal of the Confederate States,' a short description of which is also enclosed herewith, under its appropriate title."

This letter is important for a variety of reasons. First, Thian was absolutely right when he noted that his labors had placed much important information at the disposal of the historians. No history of Confederate finance or history of the Civil War which touches on economic events in the South can ignore these works. The reason for this is simple, as I discovered after nine months' work in going through the same papers. (In my ignorance I did not know the Thian books existed.) The mass of papers is beyond the patience of any single individual except one who is mad about Confederate finance. After I made copies of the Thian works I found that I had only 300 letters of importance which he did not have, and of these fully 200 were not available to him at the time.

Thian's letter is important for another reason. From his comments about the printers, and also his description of his proposed ten-volume series, which will be covered shortly, there arise a number of unanswerable questions. All the printed works of Raphael P. Thian are dated between 1878 and 1880. Yet here he mentions the printers as being still at work. If they were at work, where are the missing five volumes? If, on the other hand, the books he printed were made up in the late 1880s, why were they predated ten years earlier? Surely, if as Thian asserted, and there he was backed up by General Townsend, all this work was done on his own time and not on the government's, what was there to hide? The only conclusion that I can come to is that the work was started on the dates indicated but not completed at the time Thian wrote his letter.

Just what was it that Thian proposed to do? As he noted in his letter to General Townsend, he wanted the Congress to authorize his work under the title of "The Treasury of the Confederate States" being a "Documentary History of the Financial, Fiscal, and Commercial Measures of the Confederate States of America, 1861–'65," with an Appendix, "The Treasury-Note Bureau." This book in turn was divided in his prospectus into six subsections:

First, "Extracts from the Journals of the Provisional Congress and of the First and Second Congresses of the Confederate States of America on Legislation affecting Finance, Revenue, and Commerce." This last is one of the printed volumes appearing under the same name, but with the addition of the dates 1861–1865. As Appendix I, it was evidently intended to be the first volume of the series. This book, by the way, is now missing from the Archives and is the subject of extended inquiry. Its loss would be most unfortunate as it was a unique copy.

Second, Thian planned a volume entitled "Public and Secret

Laws of the Confederate States of America affecting Finance, Revenue, and Commerce." This probably was intended to be the second volume, but Thian's *Register of the Confederate Debt* usurped that place in the actual printing.

Third, Thian proposed a volume entitled "Reports of the Secretary of the Treasury of the Confederate States of America." Such a volume, with the dates 1861–1865 added, was published in 1878 as Appendix III.

Fourth, Thian proposed for his fourth volume the "Correspondence of the Treasury Department of the Confederate States of America." This volume was in fact published in 1879 as Appendix IV. A sister series of volumes, *Correspondence with the Treasury Department,* representing the incoming mail, was published the next year as Appendix V, with the years 1861–2 being Part I and the years 1863–5 appearing in a second volume called Part II. These works, outside the *Register of the Confederate Debt,* represent the heart of Thian's work, as the *Reports of the Secretary* are readily available, admittedly in scattered form, elsewhere. They are also, so far as is now known, the last of his work, the other proposed volumes never having been found, even in manuscript form.

Those volumes consisted of "Miscellaneous Papers concerning the Financial and Commercial Measures of the Confederate States of America, embracing Governor's Messages, Resolves of Legislatures, and General Correspondence." From the prospectus, it was evident that Thian intended that this volume would do for Congressional speeches and State affairs what the compilations of laws, Secretary of the Treasury reports, and Treasury correspondence had done in the earlier volumes. Various military matters were added along with minor foreign operations and other miscellaneous business which Thian might have placed elsewhere but decided to include here.

Finally, Thian turned his attention to the Fourth Estate in his proposed ". . . Spirit of the Press; or, Editorials, Communications, &c., on the Financial and Commercial Measures of the Confederate States of America." This last volume represented Thian's work outside the Archives and if it is ever found will be the first comprehensive collection of Southern newspaper articles organized by subject.

It is in what Thian contemplated as the "Appendix, The Treasury Note Bureau" that his work, *Register of the Confederate Debt,* was intended to appear. As originally conceived, this supplementary volume was to include the correspondence with the Treasury-note engravers and printers and other such matters as pertained to the production of the Confederate securities. In addition to this, there was also to be a "full register of issues of Treasury notes, tabular exhibits of the funded and unfunded debt . . ." along with descriptions of the several designs used for the notes.

So far as is known, the printer correspondence was integrated among the Treasury correspondence in Appendices IV and V mentioned above and never appeared separately. The descriptions of the notes were left in one of the four scrapbooks in Thian's personal possession and now rest with his other things in the Duke University Library. The *Register of the Confederate Debt* was printed separately as Appendix II in the five printed Thian volumes.

The only remaining Thian publishing scheme was his "Illustrated Documentary History of the Flag and Seal of the Confederate States of America, 1861–'65." Two copies of this volume remain: one in the Library of Congress and the other at Duke. Both were made entirely by hand and must have occupied many months of work, for they contain not merely documents but Thian's painstaking reconstruction of written proposals for Confederate flags and seals. The designs are done with surprising artistry and provide living proof of Chairman of the Confederate Congressional Committee on Flag and Seal Mr. William Porcher Miles' contention that most of the proposed designs were inferior editions of the United States flag or designs that were "elaborate, complicated or fantastical." The seals were much the same with only the final product appearing in the form in which it was submitted by its maker. The other entries had to be drawn on the basis of some none-too-clear verbal descriptions.

The Failure of the Government to Print Thian's Work

The story of Thian's efforts to get his various works published is soon told. Using an endorsement given to him by General Townsend, Thian approached the Secretary of War with his prospectus. For some reason, there was a hiatus of nearly a year before Secretary of War William C. Endicott forwarded the materials to Congress. In his letter of January 20, 1888, the Secretary urged Senator Daniel C. Voorhees to introduce a joint resolution for the books' publication. But his letter lacked any sense of urgency, and there was a notable lack of a vigorous personal appeal which such things need if they are to come to fruition. There were other problems which I shall describe in Thian's own words:

"The request of Mr. Secretary Endicott that the subject be referred to the Committee on Printing instead of the proper one (the Committee on the Library) was unfortunate, as the former Committee, whose principal duty was to reduce expenses of printing, pigeon-holed the paper after a *pro forma* report of inadvisability to print."

There is no evidence that the matter was brought up again, and with the completion of Series IV of the *Rebellion Record* which included a smattering of the more important material in Thian, the incentive to publish disappeared. Thus the Thian books are remnants that might have become part of the *Rebellion Record* but didn't make it.

Thian's Register of the Confederate Debt

It is probable that Thian, as one of the earlier collectors of Confederate currency and bonds, should have wondered about the rarity (and therefore value) of the items which he possessed in his ample collection. His position as a dealer with a published catalog dictated the need for adequate information rather than the crude guesses made by other collectors. Finally, Thian must have realized that some quantification was needed in his proposed history of the Confederate finances. The result was his *Register of the Confederate Debt* published in 1880.

At first sight it might seem that to write a book with detailed information about the dates of issue of interest-bearing securities, the signers of them, and the quantities issued would involve a comparatively simple task of consulting the available Confederate records. That this task was not simple can be discovered by anyone who has had occasion to consult with those records, for there are a number of problems one encounters—the number varying with the nature of the inquiry.

First, the Confederate records were never housed under one roof. Even today, the books in which the issues of currency are listed are located in the military side of the National Archives. So, for that matter, are some of the loan books. But the bulk of the loan books are housed in Record Group 56 over in the Diplomatic, Legal and Fiscal Branch. Some of these books are duplicates; some appear to be so but then turn out to contain some curious discrepancies. And there are a variety of addenda regarding bond issues that were hurriedly entered in the wrong volume.

Second, in addition to the external and internal chaos of these records, there is also a problem of missing records. Confederate law required the Register and Treasurer to keep a record of all issues, and, in the case of the interest-bearing notes, to record their date of issue, the interest paid, and their date of cancellation. Some books with this information are missing today. For instance, the books with the cancellation information on those notes issued under the Act of March 9, 1861, as amended August 3, 1861, exist only for the denomination of $50. From the number of $50 notes left, we can subtract that total sum from the Register's reports of what was outstanding, but that still doesn't give an exact number for the uncanceled $1000, $500, and $100 notes. Likewise, while there are reports of the number of notes issued by month in 1863, the signature books for April and part of May are missing. Had the Government carried out a project first proposed in 1967 to organize the Smithsonian collection, this information could have been reconstructed from the extant notes. But the rejection of that scheme has compelled the deferral of the publisher's original plan to include the new tables in an addendum to the reprint.

Third, to the above problems must be added the steady deterioration in the quality of the information provided by the records. In the early days, when the notes were issued under the Act of May 16, 1861, and only $200,000 a day was being printed in large denomination notes, the clerks kept good records. So meticulous were they that Philip H. Chase was able to do much of his detective work on the plating of that issue merely by using the journal entries. But with the notes issued under the Act of August 19, 1861, a certain sloppiness crept in. Helpful side comments become ever rarer. Issues appear more and more often out of their chronological order, with dates of issue jumping around according to the speed with which the reports reached the entry clerks. With the March 23, 1863 issue, confusion set in. Overwhelmed with daily issues of $2 million, the clerks contented themselves with merely entering the month issue stamp, the denomination, the signers, and the note numbers. No distinctions were made between the work of various printers; indeed even the various series (First, Second, Third, etc.) were totally ignored. Fortunately, with the notes issued under the

Act of February 27, 1864, some semblance of order returns. Books are kept for the various series of notes, but here there are many missing books. Where such was the case, Thian could not, of course, provide the signer lists. He could, however, look for and put down the highest numbered note of a series that he had any information on. These numbers are noted by an asterisk. In the intervening ninety years some higher numbered notes have been found, but the total issue figures are changed by the comparatively small amount of $8 million. Most of the difference lies in the large number of $500 notes issued.

Organization of the Book

As originally conceived and executed by Thian, this book was organized to meet certain objectives.

First, he wanted to summarize the total issues of each type of note: first by series, if any, and second by serial letters or numbers in their various combinations. Where this information was not available, as in the 1863 issues, monthly figures are given. This summary table can be found just before the section on the bonds on pages 173 to 178.

Second, Thian tried to compile a complete list of those who signed for the Treasurer and those who signed for the Register. Up to 1863 his list is remarkably accurate, but problems set in during and after that date. Thian obviously couldn't know who had signed the notes in the missing books. The best he could do was to spot sample such notes in the hope of finding any new names. I, myself, have found at least a dozen new signers, some of them transfers from the other section. Such temporary shifts were probably necessitated when absenteeism among too many members from one section threatened to cut back production. Then clerks would be shifted over to the Register's office or the Treasurer's, as the case might be, until the missing workers reported for duty.

Third, Thian decided to give the signature series for all the Treasury notes he could, dividing them first into series and then by serial letter or number. For the interest-bearing notes he added the date of issue information. This information, as shall be seen in the last section, is a useful tool for counterfeit detection. It should also be noted that such face issue dates may not be the real date of the note's issue from the Treasury. This can often be found on the back of the note either in handwritten or stamped form. The differences in date represent the time between the dispatch of the note from the signers to the time it was paid out by the Treasury agents. Such a precaution was necessary to prevent the payment of unnecessary interest to the noteholders. Thian could have included date of issue information on the non-interest-bearing notes had he wished to. However, he evidently didn't feel this was of sufficient interest to include in his book. He did keep records of this information which appeared in his scrapbooks for both types and their attendant varieties. Those interested in such matters are referred to Philip H. Chase's article in the 1962 *Numismatist* where a fine graphic chart covers the issues of 1861–1862.

Fourth, Thian decided to treat the bonds in much the same way. Where the bonds were coupon bonds of fixed denomination, he gives the number issued and the date spread between the first and last issued. Sometimes intermediate number-date information is provided. With registered bonds he provided the same information, only his task was complicated by the greater variety of denomination. He tends to give more date of issue information on the stock certificates (registered bonds) than for the coupon bonds. Date and number information, when available, provides first echelon protection against the few counterfeits on the market.

How to Use Thian's Register of the Confederate Debt

Despite its seemingly complex character, Thian's *Register of the Confederate Debt* is an absolute must, particularly for the less experienced dealer and collector of Confederate securities. The reason for this apparent paradox lies in the fact that the experienced collectors can usually identify counterfeit notes when they see them, for they often have reference collections of such material in their possession. The newcomer is not so advantageously placed. Some of the Confederate counterfeits are very dangerous and have fooled even experts. One has only to look into two well-known catalogs issued in the last 25 years to see painful proof of this. Moreover, many collectors and dealers have lost substantial sums due to the purchase at high prices of genuine notes fraudulently overprinted with real or imaginary series numbers. To demonstrate the use of this book, I shall therefore go through the procedure used in testing a suspected note for fraud or counterfeiting.

First take your note and go to the summary pages. There you

will find under the notes with the date of the one in your hand a list of denominations and a brief description of each. Find the note that fits the description of the item in your hand. Check the total number issued against the number of your note. If your note has a higher number it is probably counterfeit, unless of course it is one of those series where Thian was making a footnoted guess. This is a particularly useful tool in dealing with false overprints of the second series type 26 and the third series type 36 which have high numbered fakes.

Second, if the total number issued indicates nothing amiss, turn to the front of the book in the section devoted to the signatures. Look on the right side of the note to see who signed for Treasurer. If you can't make it out, look under the Treasury signers in the very front to see if you can find a name that looks like it. If you still can't make it out, try the Register's signer on the left. It is generally helpful to use the former, not the latter, as the Treasurer's signer appears in the left column of Thian. When you find the Treasurer's signer (if you don't, you have a counterfeit), then look to see who signed for the Register. When you find the right combination of signers look at the number of the note. Most counterfeiters, by looking at the notes, could tell which signers were partners. But they couldn't, without procuring many notes, tell which groups of two hundred or three hundred sheets the signers had filled up. If the signers are not proper partners, if the number isn't right for those partners, then you very probably have an altered or counterfeit note. With the interest notes of types 39–41 (those bearing two cents per day interest on $100) one has the added protection of dates of issue. Some of the notes were issued out of order. That is, some notes while having a higher number than others were dated before. Since the normal order meant the higher the number the later the date, the counterfeiters frequently blundered here. And if these tests are passed, one can fall back upon such telltale items as printed numbers and signatures, poor paper, and bad engraving or lithography. With time, an experienced collector gets to know the common signatures as well as his own. And when that time comes, it is easy to detect even traced or freehand forgeries.

When one utilizes Thian's book this way, one uses it exactly as the Confederates used their own records. Their hope of keeping the number of signers sufficiently small so that the public would be able to identify forgeries swiftly came to naught under the growing volume of notes. It was then that the original records, from which Thian drew his book, came to their own. The correspondence published in his books shows again and again that the Confederate Treasury note books were an important element in the government's efforts to stop counterfeiting. That these books were not more useful was not entirely the Treasury's fault. There were simply too many kinds of notes with too many different signers for the public to get to know either well enough to stop the evil at its source.

Acknowledgments

I would like to express my sincere appreciation to the many persons who made the Foreword to this reprint possible. I particularly wish to thank Miss Mattie Russell of the Duke University Manuscript Division for making available the Thian family correspondence and photographs and Dr. Elmer O. Parker, Assistant Chief of the Old Military Branch of the National Archives, who made available the Thian biographical materials.

With this book the historian of the Confederacy, and the collector of its paper securities, obtains an important tool for his studies. May it never again sink back into its ninety-year obscurity.

New York
January 1972

Douglas B. Ball

Register of the Confederate Debt

NAMES OF SIGNERS OF TREASURY NOTES.

FOR TREASURER.

Adams, Miss S. J.
Allen, Miss Maria
Allen, William G.
Ambler, Mrs. Jennie
Angel, Mrs. J. H.
Archer, Miss Lizzie *
Armstrong, Miss L.
Ashby, F. Westwood
Ashford, Craven
Bagby, P. C. * †
Bain, R.
Baker, Miss E. A.
Balaguer, Mrs. H. M.
Baldwin, C. A
Ball, Miss R. F.
Banks, Miss M.
Bartlett, Miss H.
Bass, N. A.
Beall, Miss E. O.
Bell, Miss E. M.
Bell, Thomas W.
Benton, Miss Ida
Berry, B. H.
Boyd, Miss M.
Breeden, Miss Louise
Bridges, Miss V.
Bridges, Clifford C.
Briggs, Mrs. Virginia B.
Brown, T. W. *
Bunting, J.
Caldwell, Mrs. A.
Capron, Miss Annie B.
Carr, John H.
Carrington, Miss M. J.
Carter, Mrs. L.
Christian, Mrs. M. B.
Clark, Miss S.*
Clarke, Miss Bettie J. *
Cone, Mrs Hattie Berrien
Cooper, Miss Mary E.
Darby, Miss Mary
Dargan, Miss M. A.
Davies, Miss Virginia K. *
Dennison, Miss E. A.
Dewees, Miss M. A.
Dickins, Miss Fannie M.
Dimity, J. B. S.
Dinkins, T. Waties
Dix, John S.
Douglas, Miss Joan *
Douglass, Miss H. M. *
Dudley, Mrs. Mary E.
Doyle, Walter J.
Ellery, Mrs. Julia
Fauntleroy Miss E. H.
Faxon, J. W.
Fort, Miss H.
Fuller, Miss Sallie G.
Gale, Thomas C.
Garnett, Miss Mary W.
Garrett, Miss W. A.
Giles, Miss F. G. *
Giles, Miss N.
Gill, Miss Isabel L.
Gilliam, Robert
Gills, E. W.
Gist, Mrs. M. S.
Goddin, Edward C.
Godwin, Miss Missouri
Goodloe, Harrel H.
Goodwin, Miss Nannie
Gott, Miss Julia F.
Graham, Miss H.
Grattan, Miss Sallie G.
Gray, Albert W.
Gray, Mrs. A. E.
Green, Mrs. E. C.
Gwynn, Mrs. M.
Hamilton, Miss M. E. *
Harrison, Miss A.
Harvey, William L. *
Hatch, Thomas J.
Haynes, Miss Riché
Henderson, John E. *
Heth, Miss Kitty
Hix, A. P.
Hix, Mrs. C.
Hoge, W. T.
Holmes, Mrs. L. L.
Hooe, Philip B.
Irvine, Mrs. M. C.
Jacobs, Mrs. J. A.
Jacobs, S. B.
Jones, E. W.
Jones, John A.
Jones, John W.
Jones, Mrs. Mary *
Joplin, James C.
Keesee, Thomas O.
Kelly, Miss Etta A.
Kepler, H.
Kingman, Miss Mary M.
Knox, Mrs. Mary S.
Korff, Miss Kate.
Lambert, Miss Sally
Layne, Mrs. E. D.
Leigh, C.
Levin, L. J.
Lewis, John S.
Link, Frank H.
Logan, Miss J.
Loughborough, Mrs. M.
Loyd, Miss Georgia
Lyon, D.
Marshall, O. M.
Macmurdo, Miss Rosa
Marshall, Miss M. L.
Mason, Miss Eva *
Maurice, C. S.
Mayo, Miss Martha T.
McCants, Miss S.
McCully, Mrs. Eliza M.
McGowan, Miss O. R.
Miller, Miss Alice M.
Minor, Mrs. Lucy C.
Moise, Mrs. H. L.
Moore, Miss H.
Morris, Miss C. S.
Morris, Miss M. J. *
Mumford, Miss C. C.
Neill, Miss Sophia
Nelson, Miss Kate
Nethers, J.
Newton, Miss M.
Nicholas, Miss Mary S.
Ott, John.
Overton, Mrs. Rebecca
Palmer, Miss Nellie *
Patton, Anthony
Payne, R. M.
Pellet, Miss A. P. *
Points, Miss Adele
Porter, Miss E. P. *
Quarles, Mrs. Mary L.
Read, Miss Emma S. *
Reeves, Miss M. C.
Rind, Miss Virginia M.
Ringgold, Mrs. Mary
Sanxay, Miss Sophia G.
Savage, Miss M. L.
Scott, Miss S.
Selden, Miss Maria
Semple, Miss Nannie
Shaver, Miss Sally F.
Shook, H. C.
Sieker, Miss Emma
Simons, Miss S. R.
Sims, Miss L.
Skinner, Miss C.
Smalley, Mrs. W. L.
Sommers, Mrs. M.
Sparnick Henry
Stalnaker, Miss C.
Stanard, Miss Virginia M.
Starke, Miss H.
Stocker, Miss F.
Stuart, Miss A. S.
Tennent, John C.
Tighe, R. H. L.
Todd, William R.
Tompkins, James H.
Trescot, Miss E. C.
Tyler, Miss V. M.
Wade, Mrs. M. F. *
Walford, T. D.
Waller, Mrs. M. C.
Waties, Mrs. Fannie
Watkins, Mrs. Hortense
Watts, A. S.
Weisiger, F. C.
Wells, Mrs. S. K. *
West, A.
White, Miss C. P.
White, William H.
Williams, Hampton C.
Willis, Miss Elvira
Wilson, Mrs. Josephine
Wise, Miss S.
Wray, Mrs. Fannie
Young, M. M.

* Transferred. † Ladies.

Names of Signers of Treasury Notes—Continued.

FOR REGISTER.

Abbott, Mrs. B. M.
Acosta, Mrs. Julia A.
Adams, Mrs. E. A.
Alexander, Miss H. E.
Allen, William H.
Apperson, Miss M. S.
Archer, Miss Lizzie *
Arthur, Miss L.
Bagby, P. C. * †
Bailey, Miss M. W.
Barnwell, Miss H.
Bernard, Miss Fannie E.
Black, Miss M. J.
Boykin, Miss Nannie
Boykin Robert V.
Brady, Miss M. E.
Brisbane, Miss N.
Brown, T. W. *
Bryan, Mrs. H. E.
Caldwell, W. P.
Cary, Mrs. M. F.
Clark, Miss S. *
Clarke, Miss Bettie J. *
Cocke, William Archer
Coffin, Miss Eliza M.
Connor, Miss Julia M.
Cooke, Mrs. Isabella A.
Cooke, Miss Hattie L.
Cooke, James H.
Courtney, Mrs. L.
Crouch, T. L.
Cullen, Miss M. E.
Dabney, Miss Bettie
Davies, Miss Virginia K. *
Davis, Miss Ella.
De Leon, Miss Isabel
Delony, Robert J.
Devine, Miss Lizzie
De Witt, Bennet M.
Dickson, J. T.
Dixon, Mrs. M.
Doar, Miss S. A.
Dorsey, R. J.
Douglas, Miss Joan *
Douglass, Miss H. M. *
Downman, W. Y.
Dunbar, W. G.
Dutcher, S.
Eggleston, J. W.
Ellett, Temple
Ellett, Miss S. C.
Elliott, Miss L. W.
Forde, L. †
Foran, Mrs. A. M.
French, W. T.
Gaither, Mrs. M. S.
Garlick, Miss Elizabeth
Garrett, G. W.
Gay, Miss M.
Gibb, Miss M. A.
Gibson, J.
Gifford, Mrs. M. A.
Giles, Miss F. G. *
Gilliam, Miss M. E.
Gilman, William S.
Grayson, T. Fitzhugh
Hamilton, Miss M. E. *
Hancock, William
Harper, Mrs. M. E.
Harris, J. H.
Harvey, William L. *
Hayes, S. C.
Henderson, John E. *
Henry, Miss L.
Herbert, Mrs. H.
Heriot, Miss H. P.
Hill, jr., R.
Holt, John T.
Howell, Miss K. P.
Huard, Miss S. L.
Huger, Mrs. Caroline P.
Hughes, Mrs. S. E.
Hunt, J. H.
Hunter, Miss L. M.
Jackson, J. T.
Jarvis, Miss M. F.
Johnson, C. H.
Johnson, Mrs. M. S.
Johnson, Miss S.
Johnston, Gabriel
Johnston, Mrs. J. L.
Jones, Miss Fannie C.
Jones, Mrs. Mary *
Jones, R. S.
Keim, C. W.
Kelly, Miss E. *
Kennedy, Miss A.
King, Miss R. B.
Kinney, J. M.
Kirby, Mrs. Mary B.
Kirk, Mrs. Martha A.
Lathrope, Miss M. C.
Laurens, Mrs. Eliza B.
Laval Miss S. E.
Lyon, Miss Bella T.
Macon, Miss Lydia
Marks, Mrs. F. H.
Mason, Miss Eva *
Massie, E. L.
Matthews, J. J.
Matthews, Miss Emily
McCarthy, Miss Jane
McGarr, Miss Jennie
McRae, Miss B.
McRae, Richard
Meade, Miss Charlotte R.
Michel, Miss L. G.
Miller, Thomas J.
Miller, W.
Mills, R. A.
Mobley, Miss M. A.
Morris, Miss M. J. *
Morrison, Miss Mary W.
Morton, Miss M. C.
Nelson, J. †
Newman, Miss Ada
Norris, Mrs. L. A.
Norton, Mrs. Mary E.
Nott, William
Nulty, E.
Orr, Henry E.
Pace, Miss M. E.
Palmer, Miss Nellie *
Parry, Mrs. A. S.
Payne, Miss Betty M.
Pellet, Miss A. P. *
Pelot, Mrs. S. L.
Pendleton, Miss Emma W.
Penrifoy, Mrs. V. M.
Percival, Miss C. E.
Pleasants, Mrs. M.
Pleasants Miss P.
Porter, Miss E. P. *
Proctor, Mrs. E. S.
Randolph, Miss S. A.
Read, Miss Emma S. *
Rhett, Mrs. F. M.
Richardson, Miss Nannie
Riggs, Myron C.
Robinson, W. R.
Rogers, Louis P.
Rothrock, William
Royster, Mrs. L. C.
Sale, John O.
Sands, Johnson
Saunders, Miss Margaret A.
Savage Miss Parkie
Sessions, Mrs. C.
Sinton, Samuel
Slade, W. O.
Smith, E. H.
Smith, Herbert
Snead, W. T.
Snyder, John O.
Southall, Miss Sallie
Spottswood, Miss Lucy
Stanard, Miss E.
Stevens, Mrs. M. F.
Swords, Joseph P.
Talley, Miss Susan A.
Taylor, Charles S.
Taylor, Mrs. Miriam
Thayer, C. C.
Thomas, Miss H. C.
Tiffey, Miss Julia B.
Tinsley, S. G.
Treadwell, Mrs. J. D.
Tyler, Miss Betty W.
Upshur, Mrs. Mary E.
Veal, Miss C. C.
Via, Miss Josephine
Wade, Mrs. M. F. *
Wade, William A.
Walker, Miss Kate
Waller, William
Walston, William B.
Walthall, C.
Warren, G. N.
Watkins, A. S.
Watson, Miss Virginia C.
Wells, S. K. * †
Windle, Mrs. C. F.
Wingate, Mrs. N. E.
Winston, Meriwether
Winston, Miss E. C.
Woodward, Miss M.
Yates, Mrs. M. A.
Zealy, Miss Anna W.

* Transferred. † Ladies.

Synopsis of Issues of Confederate States Treasury Notes.

Issue.	Number of clerks.			Sets of signatures.			Highest number of partners.	Average per set.	Total.
	Male.	Female.	Total.	Male.	Female.	Total.			
Act of March 9, 1861.*									
General currency	......	......	......	......	......	......	......	......	$2,021,100 00
Act of May 16, 1861.									
General currency	16	......	16	22	......	22	6	$788,543 40	17,347,955 00
Act of August 19, 1861.									
General currency	97	35	132	100	18	118	9	2,475,439 23	292,101,830 00
Act of April 17, 1862.									
7-30 $100 notes	49	......	49	29	......	29	3	2,509,387 75	122,960,000 00
Twos and ones	2	71	73	1	40	41	2	76,712 33	5,600,000 00
Act of October 13, 1862.									
General currency	61	112	173	34	59	93	2	1,484,473 11	138,056,000 00
Twos and ones	......	80	80	......	42	42	2	55,885 71	2,347,200 00
Act of March 23, 1863.									
General currency	58	103	161	99	548	649	28	784,534 56	510,832,000 00
Twos and ones	......	101	101	......	137	137	11	22,069 48	3,023,520 00
Fifty cents†	......	......	......	......	......	......	......	......	912,962 50
Act of February 17, 1864.									
General currency	20	181	201	29	1,589	1,618	40	203,757 72	453,376,200 00
Twos and ones	......	......	......	......	......	......	......	......	2,243,184 00
Fifty cents†	......	......	......	......	......	......	......	......	523,606 50
Grand total	......	......	......	......	......	......	......	......	1,549,324,458 00

* The notes issued under this act were signed by the register and treasurer.
† Fractional currency has engraved fac-simile signatures of the register and treasurer.

Register of Confederate States Treasury Notes.

ACT OF MARCH 9, 1861.

A.—(MONTGOMERY.)

Date of issue.	$1,000.		$500.		$100.		$50.	
	From—	To—	From—	To—	From—	To—	From—	To—
April 5, 1861					1	19	1	5
April 8, 1861			1	14	20	101	6	101
April 9, 1861			15	19	102	156	102	161
April 25, 1861	1	17	20	54	157	261	162	261
May 1, 1861	18	29	55	86				
May 2, 1861							262	265
May 3, 1861					262	561	266	465
May 4, 1861			87	122	562	809	466	809
May 14, 1861					810	984	810	959
May 16, 1861			123	131	985	1237	960	1253
May 20, 1861							1254	1256
May 21, 1861					1238		1257	1259
May 22, 1861	30	39	132	171	1239	1450	1260	1436
May 23, 1861	40	69	172	211	1451	1545	1437	1586
May 25, 1861					1546	1560		
May 28, 1861	70	369						
June 11, 1861					1561	1570		
June 17, 1861	370	403	212	231				
June 18, 1861	404	462	232	290				
June 19, 1861	463	477	291	305	1571	1573	1587	1590
June 20, 1861							1591	1592
June 21, 1861			306	331	1574	1606	1593	1606
June 22, 1861			332	333				
June 24, 1861	478	607	334	473				
June 28, 1861			474	537				
July 8, 1861			538	540				
July 18, 1861			541	576				
July 23, 1861			577	607				

B.—(RICHMOND.)

Date of issue.	$1,000. From—	$1,000. To—	$500. From—	$500. To—	$100. From—	$100. To—	$50. From—	$50. To—
Aug. 27, 1861					1	133	1	134
Aug. 28, 1861					134	1800	135	1800
Aug. 31, 1861					1801	2100	1801	2100
Aug. 12, 1861					2101	2109	2101	2102
Sept. 3, 1861					2110	2500	2103	2500
Sept. 5, 1861					2501	2800	2501	2800
Sept. 6, 1861					2801	3000	2801	3000
Sept. 7, 1861					3001	3300	3001	3300
Sept. 9, 1861					3301	3600	3301	3600
Sept. 10, 1861					3601	4100	3601	4099
Sept. 11, 1861					4101	4500	4100	4500
Sept. 12, 1861					4501	4900	4501	4900
Sept. 13, 1861					4901	5300	4901	5300
Sept. 14, 1861					5301	5700	5301	5699
Sept. 23, 1861					5701	5798	5700	5798

Register of Confederate States Treasury Notes.

ACT OF MAY 16, 1861.

For Treasurer.	For Register.	Numbers of the notes signed.
		$100—B.
Jno. Ott	C. C. Thayer	1–4695.
		$100—C.
Jno. Ott	C. C. Thayer	1–256, 1501–2200, 3801–4000, 6801–7200, 9601–10200, 11001–11800, 13601–14400, 15001–15600, 17401–20000, 22401–23400, 25801–26600, 27401–28600.
H. H. Goodloe	T. Ellett	257–700, 3001–3400, 4001–4800, 7201–8800, 11801-12400, 13201–13600, 14401–15000, 15601–16400, 16601–17000, 20201-20800, 23401–23800, 29801–30200, 31001–31400.
R. H. L. Tighe	R. J. Delony	701–1100, 2201–2600, 12401–13200.
Do	Tho. J. Miller	16401–16600, 17001–17400, 20801–22400, 24201–25000, 28601–29800, 31401–31800.
Do	E. L. Massie	31801–32200.
R. M. Payne	Tho. J. Miller	1101–1500, 2601–3000, 3401–3800, 5201–6800, 8801-9600, 10201–11000.
Do	R. Hill, jr	23801–24200, 25001–25800, 30601–31000, 32201–32460.
L. J. Levin	do	4801–5200.
Do	R. J. Delony	26601–27400, 30201–30600.
		$50—B.
Jno. Ott	C. C. Thayer	1–29800, 32201–33000, 34601–35400, 36201–38200, 43001-45800.
R. H. L. Tighe	R. J. Delony	29801–31400, 33001–33800, 39001–39800, 46601–47400, 48201–49000, 49025–49800.
Do	C. C. Thayer	38201–39000, 41401–42200.
Do	T. Ellett	49001–49024.
L. J. Levin	R. Hill, jr	31401–32200, 35401–36200, 40601–41400, 47401–48200, 50601–51400.
H. H. Goodloe	T. Ellett	33801–34600, 39801–40600, 42201–43000, 45801–46600, 49801–50600.
		$50—Bb.
Jno. Ott	C. C. Thayer	1–800, 4001–5200, 6401–7200, 12801–13600, 17681-18480, 19281–19880, 23081–23880, 39481–39704.
L. J. Levin	R. Hill, jr	801–1600, 3201–4000, 7201–8000, 9601–11200, 14401–15480, 23881–25080, 29081–29880.
Do	C. C. Thayer	33081–33880.
H. H. Goodloe	T. Ellett	1601–2400, 5201–5584, 8001–9600, 16881–17680, 18481–19280, 19881–21480, 25881–26680, 27481–29080, 29881-31480, 35481–37080, 37881–39480.
R. H. L. Tighe	R. J. Delony	2401–3200, 5585–6400, 11201–12800, 13601–14400, 15481-16880, 21481–23080, 25081–25880, 26681–27480, 31481–33080.
R. M. Payne	Tho. J. Miller	33881–35480, 37041–37880.
		$50—C.
Jno. Ott	C. C. Thayer	1–256, 1501–2200, 3801–4000, 6801–7200, 9601–10200, 11001–11800, 13601–14400, 15001–15600, 17401–20200, 22401–23400, 25801–26600, 27401–28600.
H. H. Goodloe	T. Ellett	257–700, 3001–3400, 4001–4800, 7201–8800, 11801-12400, 13201–13600, 14401–15000, 15601–16400, 16601–17000, 20201-20800, 23401–23800, 29801–30200, 31001–31400.
R. H. L. Tighe	R. J. Delony	701–1100, 2201–2600, 12401–13200.
Do	Tho. J. Miller	16401–16600, 17001–17400, 20801–22400, 24201–25000, 28601–29800.
Do	E. L. Massie	31401–32200.
R. M. Payne	Tho. J. Miller	1101–1500, 2601–3000, 3401–3800, 5201-6800, 8801-9600, 10201–11000.
Do	R. Hill, jr	23801–24200, 25001–25800, 30601–31000, 32201–32460.
L. J. Levin	do	4801–5200.
Do	R. J. Delony	26601–27400, 30201–30600.
		$20—B.
Jno. Ott	C. C. Thayer	1–400, 801–940, 1341–2780, 3181–3580, 3981–4780, 5181–5680, 6081–6880, 7281–7680, 8081–9980. *
H. Sparnick	T. Ellett	401–800, 941–1340, 2781–3180, 3581–3980, 4781–5180, 5681–6080, 6961–6970, 7147–7280, 7681–8080.
Do	R. McRae	6881–6960, 6971–7146.

* Nos. 8781–9980 have the words "for Treas'r" printed twice.

Register of Confederate States Treasury Notes—Continued.

ACT OF MAY 16, 1861—Continued.

For Treasurer.	For Register.	Numbers of the notes signed.
		$20—C.
H. S. Sparnick	T. Ellett	1-400, 4101-4900, 8101-8900.
Do	R. McRae	9701-10100, 12501-12900, 15301-15700.
Jno. Ott	C. C. Thayer	401-1200, 1301-4100, 4901-7300, 8901-9700, 10501-12500, 12901-15300, 15701-16500, 16901-17300, 17701-18500.
H. H. Goodloe	R. McRae	1201-1300.
Do	T. Ellett	7301-8100, 10101-10500, 16501-16900, 17301-17700, 18501-18900.
L. J. Levin	R. J. Delony	18901-19300.
Do	R. Hill, jr	19301-19660.
		$20—Cc.
Jno. Ott	C. C. Thayer	1-2800, 3601-4400, 5201-6000, 7601-8400, 9201-10800, 13201-15600, 17201-17600, 20001-20800, 21601-23200, 26401-27200, 28001-28800, 31201-32800, 36001-39000.
H. H. Goodloe	T. Ellett	2801-3600, 6801-7600, 8401-9200, 10801-11600, 19201-20000, 25601-26400, 27201-28000, 29601-30400, 35201-36000.
L. J. Levin	R. J. Delony	4401-5200, 6673-6800, 15601-16400, 17601-19200, 20801-21600, 23201-25600, 28801-29600, 30401-31200, 32801-35200.
Do	R. Hill, jr	39001-39536.
R. H. L. Tighe	R. J. Delony	6001-6672, 11601-13200, 16401-17200.
		$20—Ccc.
Jno. Ott	C. C. Thayer	1-2000, 2801-4400, 6001-10000, 13201-14000, 30001-30800, 32401-33200, 40401-41200, 62501-63300, 64101-64820, 70421-71620, 83429-84228.
Do	R. Hill, jr	57721-58500, 61701-62500.
L. J. Levin	R. McRae	2001-2800.
Do	R. J. Delony	10001-11600, 19601-21200.
Do	R. Hill, jr	14001-14800, 17201-18000, 24401-26000, 27601-29200, 30801-32400, 36401-38000, 39601-40400, 42001-42800, 45201-47600, 51201-52000, 55201-56000, 58501-59300, 63301-64100, 67221-69620, 73221-74020, 75621-76420, 78021-78820, 85829-86012.
H. H. Goodloe	T. Ellett	4401-6000, 15601-16400, 18801-19600, 21201-22800, 29201-30000, 33201-34800, 47601-48400, 50401-51200, 52801-55200, 64821-65620, 72421-73220, 79429-80228, 81829-82628, 84229-85028.
R. H. L. Tighe	R. J. Delony	11601-13200, 14801-15600, 16401-17200, 18001-18800, 22801-24400, 26001-27600, 34801-36400, 38001-39600, 41201-42000, 42801-45200, 48401-50400, 52001-52800, 56001-57200, 60101-61700, 65621-67220, 69621-70420, 71621-72420, 74021-75620, 76421-78020, 78821-79428, 80229-81028, 85029-85828.
Do	T. Ellett	57201-57720.
Do	R. Hill, jr	59301-60100.
R. M. Payne	Tho. J. Miller	81029-81828, 82629-83428.
		$20—D.
Jno. Ott	C. C. Thayer	1-2400, 3201-4000, 9001-9800, 11401-12200, 13001-14600, 17001-17800, 19401-21000, 22601-23400, 24201-25000, 29001-29800, 36201-37000, 41001-41800, 42601-44200, 58601-60200, 63401-65000, 69801-71400, 73001-73800, 96201-99400.
Do	R. Hill, jr	39401-41000, 44201-45000, 54601-55400.
L. J. Levin	R. J. Delony	2401-3200, 38601-39400, 61801-62600, 78601-79400, 99401-100200, 103401-104200, 106601-107400.
H. H. Goodloe	T. Ellett	4001-6000, 8401-9000, 23401-24200, 33001-33800, 34601-35400, 49001-50600, 60201-61800, 73801-74600, 77801-78600, 83401-85000, 87401-88200, 89001-89800, 100201-101800, 105001-106600.
Do	R. Hill, jr	16201-17000, 25801-27400, 30601-31400, 32201-33000.
R. H. L. Tighe	R. J. Delony	6001-8400, 9801-11400, 14601-16200, 17801-19400, 25001-25800, 27401-29000, 29801-30600, 33801-34600.
Do	Tho. J. Miller	35401-36200, 37001-38600, 41801-42600, 47401-49000, 52201-54600, 65001-65800, 68201-69800, 79401-80200, 81001-82600, 88201-89000, 89801-90600, 93001-94600, 107401-109000.
R. M. Payne	do	12201-13000, 21001-22600, 31401-32200, 77001-77800.
Do	R. Hill, jr	55401-56200, 62601-63400, 71401-73000, 91401-93000, 94601-96200, 101800-103400.
H. Kepler	E. L. Massie	45000-47400, 50601-52200, 56201-58600, 65801-68200, 74601-77000, 80201-81000, 82601-83400, 85001-87400, 90601-91400, 104201-105000, 109001-109800.

Register of Confederate States Treasury Notes—Continued.

ACT OF MAY 16, 1861—Continued.

For Treasurer.	For Register.	Numbers of the notes signed.
		$10—A.
Jno. Ott	C. C. Thayer	1–800, 17401–18200, 33441–34200, 37441–38240, 56041–56840, 62041–62840, 91841–93440.
L. J. Levin	R. Hill, jr	801–15200, 19001–20600, 22761–25160, 26561–28160, 30241–32640, 34241–35840, 36641–37440, 38241–42020, 42841–45640.
Do	R. J. Delony	45641–56040, 56841–60440, 62841–65240, 69841–73040, 82241–83840, 95041–97440, 111041–112640, 115041–116640.
R. M. Payne	Tho. J. Miller	15201–17400, 18201–19000, 21401–21960, 25161–25760, 28161–28960, 35841–36640, 66041–66840.
Do	R. Hill, jr	75841–77440, 85441–86240, 89441–91800, 94241–95040, 117441–119840.
R. H. L. Tighe	R. J. Delony	20601–21400, 21961–22760, 25761–26560, 28961–29760, 32641–33440, 42041–42840.
Do	Tho. J. Miller	79041–79840, 93441–94240, 98241–99840, 100641–101440, 106241–107840, 112641–113440, 116641–117440, 122241–124640.
H. H. Goodloe	T. Ellett	29761–30240, 68241–69840, 74241–75840, 83841–85440, 88641–89440, 103841–105440, 107841–109440, 119841–122240.
H. Kepler	E. L. Massie	60441–62040, 65241–66040, 66841–68240, 73041–74240, 77441–79040, 79841–82240, 86241–88640, 97441–98240, 99841–100640, 101441–103840, 105441–106240, 109441–111040, 113441–115040, 124641–126240.
E. W. Jones	R. J. Delony	126241–126776.
		$10—B.
Jno. Ott	C. C. Thayer	1–400, 801–940, 1341–2780, 3181–3580, 3981–4780, 5181–5680, 6081–6880, 7281–7680, 8081–9280, 10281–10780, 11281–11780.
H. Sparnick	T. Ellett	401–800, 941–1340, 2781–3180, 3581–3980, 4781–5180, 5681–6080, 6961–6970, 7147–7280, 7681–8080, 9781–10280.
Do	R. McRae	6881–6960, 6971–7146.
H. H. Goodloe	do	9281–9780, 10781–11280, 11781–12180.
		$10—C.
H. Sparnick	T. Ellett	1–400, 2501–3000, 4001–4500, 5001–5500.
Do	R. McRae	6501–6900, 12901–13800, 14201–15000, 19501–20000.
Jno. Ott	C. C. Thayer	401–1200, 1301–2500, 3001–3500, 5501–6000, 7301–7700, 8501–10400, 10901–12900, 15001–17400, 19001–19500, 20001–21400, 21801–23200, 23701–24200, 25501–25900, 26901–27300, 30701–31200.
H. H. Goodloe	R. McRae	1201–1300, 3501–4000, 4501–5000, 6001–6500.
Do	T. Ellett	6901–7300, 7701–8500, 10401–10900, 13801–14200, 17401–19000, 21401–21800, 23201–23700, 24201–25500, 26401–26900, 28701–29200, 29701–30200, 31201–31700.
L. J. Levin	R. J. Delony	25901–26400, 27301–28700, 29201–29700.
Do	R. Hill, jr	31701–32038.
R. H. L. Tighe	R. J. Delony	30201–30700.
		$5—B.
Jno. Ott	C. C. Thayer	1–3485, 5486–6485, 8486–8985, 9486–9985, 13486–13985, 22486–22985.
H. Sparnick	T. Ellett	3486–3985.
Do	R. McRae	7986–8485, 9986–10485, 12486–12985, 15986–17485.
H. H. Goodloe	do	3986–5485, 6486–6985.
Do	T. Ellett	6986–7985, 8986–9485, 10486–12485, 12986–13485, 13986–15985, 17486–19485, 19986–20485, 20986–21985, 22986–23455.
L. J. Levin	R. J. Delony	19486–19985, 20486–20985, 21986–22485.
		$5—Bb.
Jno. Ott	C. C. Thayer	1–500, 1001–2000, 4001–4500, 5501–7500, 10001–10500, 11001–12500, 13001–13500, 17001–17500, 19501–20500, 25001–26000, 29001–29500, 33001–34500, 35501–36500, 41001–41500.
H. H. Goodloe	T. Ellett	501–1000, 3001–4000, 4501–5500, 9001–10000, 10501–11000, 12501–13000, 14501–15500, 16001–17000, 17501–19500, 20501–25000, 28001–29000, 30001–30500, 31001–33000, 36501–38000, 42501–45500.
L. J. Levin	R. J. Delony	2001–3000, 7501–9000, 13501–14500, 15501–16000.
Do	R. McRae	26001–27000.
Do	R. Hill, jr	34501–35500, 39001–39500, 47001–48000, 48501–49000.
R. H. L. Tighe	R. J. Delony	27001–28000, 29501–30000, 30501–31000, 38001–39000, 39501–41000, 41501–42500, 45501–47000, 48001–48500, 49001–49900.

Register of Confederate States Treasury Notes—Continued.

ACT OF MAY 16, 1861—Continued.

For Treasurer.	For Register.	Number of the notes signed.
		$5—F to I.
Jno. Ott	C. C. Thayer	1–800.
L. J. Levin	do	801–1200.
R. H. L. Tighe	do	1201–2400.
Do	R. J. Delony	2401–3800.
H. Kepler	M. C. Riggs	3801–3889.

ACT OF AUGUST 19, 1861.

For Treasurer.	For Register.	Number of the notes signed.
		$100—A.
Jno. Ott	C. C. Thayer	1–800, 3601–4000, 4801–9600, 10801-12000, 12801-15200, 16001–20400, 21601–25600, 28001–29600.
R. M. Payne	R. Hill, jr	801–1600, 2001–2800, 3201–3600, 4001–4800, 29601–30400.
H. Kepler	E. L. Massie	1601–2000, 10001–10400, 12001–12400, 20401–21200, 30401–32000, 32800–33200.
L. J. Levin	R. J. Delony	2801–3200.
H. H. Goodloe	T. Ellett	9601–10000, 15201–16000, 21201–21600.
R. H. L. Tighe	Tho. J. Miller	10401–10800, 12401–12800.
J. W. Jones	R. J. Delony	25601–28000.
R. Gilliam	M. C. Riggs	32001–32800, 33201–34000.
		$100—B, C, D, E.
H. H. Goodloe	T. Ellett	1–100.
J. W. Jones	R. J. Delony	101–600, 801–1000, 1801–2200, 3901–4000, 4901–5200.
Jno. Ott	C. C. Thayer	601–800, 1001–1800, 2201–3900, 4201–4900.
J. C. Tennent	R. S. Jones	4001–4200.
H. Kepler	E. L. Massie	5201–5202, 5203 (B, C, D).
		$100—cA to oA.
Jno. Ott	C. C. Thayer	1–7626, 9301–9344 (cA to kA), 9345–9410 (gA to kA).
J. W. Jones	R. J. Delony	7627–8100 (cA to kA).
J. C. Tennent	H. E. Orr	8101–8500 (cA to kA).
R. M. Payne	R. Hill, jr	8501–8900 (cA to kA).
R. H. L. Tighe	Tho. J. Miller	8901–9300 (cA to kA).
		**$100**—$A^C$ to A^K.
Jno. Ott	C. C. Thayer	1–7800, 9401–9800, 10201–11000, 12001–12600, 13001–16000, 17501–18100, 19501–20100, 20901–21500, 21900–22918.
L. J. Levin	M. C. Riggs	7801–8200, 8701–8900, 9001–9400, 18101–18500, 18801–19100, 21501–21900.
H. Kepler	E. L. Massie	8201–8700, 8901–9000, 9801–10200, 11500–12000, 12601-13000.*
J. C. Tennent	C. C. Thayer	11001–11300.
Do	H. E. Orr	11301–11500, 16001–16300, 18501–18800, 19101–19500.
J. W. Jones	R. J. Delony	16301–16700, 20501–20900.
H. H. Goodloe	T. Ellett	16701–17100, 20101–20500.
R. H. L. Tighe	Tho. J. Miller	17101–17500.
		**$100**—$A^1$ to A^8.
F. W. Ashby	T. L. Crouch	1–400.
Do	S. G. Tinsley	5301–5400. 11101–11900, 15701–17300, 18101–18900, 19701–20500, 21301–22100, 22701–23600, 24401–24800, 26401-27200, 29601–29700.
Jno. Ott	C. C. Thayer	401–1100, 2001–2600, 3001–3600, 4001–4500, 4801–5300, 5401–5500, 8001–8700, 12801–13500.
L. J. Levin	M. C. Riggs	1101–1500, 4501–4800, 6301–8000, 11901–12400.
J. W. Jones	R. J. Delony	1501–2000.
Do	C. C. Thayer	29701–29800, 32701–32946.
H. H. Goodloe	T. Ellett	2601–3000, 3601–4000, 5501–6300.

*A^C to A^K 12901–12973, A^C to A^F 12974, A^G to A^K 12975, A^C to A^K 12976–12986, and A^C to A^K 12988–13000, never issued.

Register of Confederate States Treasury Notes—Cotinued.

ACT OF AUGUST 19, 1861—Continued.

For Treasurer.	For Register.	Numbers of the notes signed.
		**$100**—$A^1$ to A^8—Continued.
E. W. Gills	Wm. Nott	8701–9500, 10301–11100.
R. M. Payne	R. Hill, jr	9501–10300, 14301–15200, 17301–18100, 18901–19700, 20501–21300, 22101–22700, 23601–24400, 24801–26400, 27201–29600, 30401–31200, 31501–31700.
T. O. Keesee	T. Ellett	12401–12800, 15201–15700.
R. H. L. Tighe	Tho. J. Miller	13501–14300, 29801–30400.
H. Kepler	R. J. Delony	31201–31500, 31701–32000.
J. C. Tennent	M. Winston	32001–32400.
A. W. Gray	C. C. Thayer	32401–32700.
		$50—A.
Jno. Ott	C. C. Thayer	1–800, 3601–4000, 4801–9600, 10801–12000, 12801-15200, 16001-20400, 21601–25600, 28001–29600.
R. M. Payne	R. Hill, jr	801–1600, 2001–2800, 3201–3600, 4001–4800, 29601–30400.
H. Kepler	E. L. Massie	1601–2000, 10001–10400, 12001–12400, 20401–21200, 30401–32000, 32801–33200, 34001–34008.
L. J. Levin	R. J. Delony	2801–3200.
H. H. Goodloe	T. Ellett	9601–10000, 15201–16000, 21201–21600.
R. H. L. Tighe	Tho. J. Miller	10401–10800, 12401–12800.
J. W. Jones	R. J. Delony	25601–28000.
R. Gilliam	M. C. Riggs	32001–32800, 33201–34000.
		$50—B, C, D, E.
H. H. Goodloe	T. Ellett	1–100.
J. W. Jones	R. J. Delony	101–600, 801–1000, 1801–2200, 3901–4000, 4901–5200.
Jno. Ott	C. C. Thayer	601–800, 1001–1800, 2201–3900, 4201–4900.
J. C. Tennent	R. S. Jones	4001–4200.
H. Kepler	E. L. Massie	5201–5202, 5203 (B, C, D).
		**$50**—$A^D$.
J. C. Tennent	R. S. Jones	1–4200, 5401–7800.
Do	H. E. Orr	48601–55800, 58201–61800, 75001–76200, 78601–79800, 83401–87000, 100201–101400, 105001–106200.
R. M. Payne	R. Hill, jr	4201–5400, 27001–30600, 45001–48600, 55801–58200, 72601–75000, 76201–77400, 79801–83400, 90601–93000, 95401–97800, 99001–100200, 102601–105000, 108601–112200, 114601–115473.
R. H. L. Tighe	Tho. J. Miller	7801–13800, 61801–65400.
H. Kepler	E. L. Massie	13801–23400, 34201–45000.
J. W. Jones	R. J. Delony	23401–27000, 30601–34200, 65401–69000, 77401–78600, 93001–95400, 97800–99000, 101401–102600, 106201–108600, 112201–114600.
L. J. Levin	M. C. Riggs	69001–72600, 87001–90600.
Jno. Ott	C. C. Thayer	115474–116207.
		**$50**—$A^E$ to A^L.
Jno. Ott	C. C. Thayer	1–734.
		$50—A (Southern Bank-Note Company).
H. H. Goodloe	T. Ellett	1–1900, 2301–3900, 4401–5600.
Do	C. C. Thayer	1901–2300, 3901–4400, 7201–8400.
R. H. L. Tighe	Tho. J. Miller	5601–6400, 9701–11300.
A. W. Gray	S. G. Tinsley	6401–7200, 14401–14860.
R. M. Payne	R. Hill, jr	8401–9200.
F. W. Ashby	T. L. Crouch	9201–9700.
J. C. Tennent	M. Winston	11301–12000.
T. O. Keesee	T. Ellett	12001–14400.
		**$50**—$A^1$ to A^8.
R. M. Payne	R. Hill, jr	1–4500, 5401–6800, 8801–9200, 97001–10100.
J. C. Tennent	H. E. Orr	4501–5000.
Do	M. Winston	10501–10900, 11901–12700, 14201–15000, 16801–17600, 19201–20200, 23101–23400, 23501–23600.
R. H. L. Tighe	Tho. J. Miller	5001–5400, 10101–10500, 20201–21000.
J. W. Jones	R. J. Delony	6801–7200, 7301–8300, 13101–14200, 18201–19200.
A. W. Gray	S. G. Tinsley	7201–7300.
Do	T. L. Crouch	9201–9700, 10901–11900, 15801–16800.
F. W. Ashby	do	8301–8600.

Register of Confederate States Treasury Notes—Continued.

ACT OF AUGUST 19, 1861—Continued.

For Treasurer.	For Register.	Numbers of the notes signed.
		**$50**—A^{1} to A^{8}—Continued.
F. W. Ashby	S. G. Tinsley	8601–8800, 15001–15800.
L. J. Levin	M. C. Riggs	12701–13100.
Jno. Ott	C. C. Thayer	17601–18200, 22401–23100.
T. O. Keesee	T. Ellett	21001–21600, 23401–23500, 23601–26800, 27601–28400, 29201–33145.
H. Kepler	R. J. Delony	26801–27600, 28401–29200.
E. W. Gills	Wm. Nott	21601–22400.
		**$50**—A^{9} to A^{16}.
H. Kepler	R. J. Delony	1–800.
T. O. Keesce	T. Ellett	801–3542.
		$50—wA to zA.
T. O. Keesee	T. Ellett	1–3200, 5601–29300, 29701–30500, 31001–32100.
Do	T. L. Crouch	32101–45500, 46301–47100, 48701–49500, 50301–51100, 51901–52700, 53501–55300, 57701–59300, 60401-63800, 64701-73800, 75401–76400,* 81201–81247.
H. Kepler	R. J. Delony	3201–5600.
R. Bain	J. H. Harris	29301–29700, 30501–31000.
D. Lyon	J. T. Dickson	45501–46300, 47101–48700, 49501–50300, 52701–53500, 55301–57700, 59301–60400, 63801–64700, 77001–77800.
T. C. Gale	E. H. Smith	51101–51900.
H. C. Shook	C. Walthall	73801–75400, 76401–77000, 77801–81200.
		$50—wA to zA (2d series).
D. Lyon	J. T. Dickson	1–900.
T. O. Keesee	T. L. Crouch	901–14700.
A. W. Gray	W. Hancock	14701–16500, 17301–18300, 19901–20800, 21601–23600.
W. G. Allen	C. S. Taylor	16501–17300, 18301–19900, 20801–21600, 23601–25000.
		$50—1A to 4A.
T. O. Keesee	T. Ellett	1–239.
		$20—A (green).
Jno. Ott	C. C. Thayer	1–43732.
		$20—A.
Jno. Ott	C. C. Thayer	1–3200, 28001–29600, 30401–32000, 47201–48500, 84801–85600, 86401–88000, 96001–98400.
H. Kepler	E. L. Massie	3201–4800, 12001–15200, 21601–24800, 36001–36800, 40001–43200, 51201–54400, 68801–70400, 81601–83200, 85601-86400, 94401–96000, 106401–107638.
H. H. Goodloe	T. Ellett	4801–6400, 10401–12000, 33601–35200, 39201–40000, 54401–56000, 67201–68800, 76801–79200, 104001–106400.
R. H. L. Tighe	Tho. J. Miller	6401–7200, 15201–16800, 29601–30400, 36801–376000, 45601–47200, 59201–60800, 74401–75200, 98401–100800.
Do	C. C. Thayer	60801–61600, 83201–84400.
Do	R. J. Delony	75201–76800.
Do	E. L. Massie	103201–10400.
L. J. Levin	R. J. Delony	7201–8000, 16801–21600, 32001–33600, 35201–36000, 37601–39200.
R. M. Payne	R. Hill, jr	8001–10400, 24801–28000, 43201–45600, 48801–51200, 64801–67200, 79201–81600, 92001–94400, 100801–103200.
J. W. Jones	R. J. Delony	56001–59200, 61601–64800, 70401–74400, 88001–92000, 107639–107878.
		$20—B to E and K to N.
H. Kepler	E. L. Massie	1–100, 501–600, 1601–1900.
R. H. L. Tighe	Tho. J. Miller	101–200, 601–800, 1301–1500, 3701–4000, 4201–4300.
J. C. Tennent	R. S. Jones	201–400, 901–1000, 1101–1200.
Do	H. E. Orr	2101–2200.
R. M. Payne	R. Hill, jr	401–500, 801–900, 1001–1100.
R. Gilliam	M. C. Riggs	1201–1300, 1501–1600, 1901–2100, 2601–2700.
J. W. Jones	R. J. Delony	2201–2600.

* Notes lettered wA and numbered 76201–76400 never issued.

Register of Confederate States Treasury Notes—Continued.

ACT OF AUGUST 19, 1861—Continued.

For Treasurer.	For Register.	Numbers of the notes signed.
		$20—B to E and L to O.
R. Gilliam	M. C. Riggs	2701–2900.
J. W. Jones	R. J. Delony	2901–3300, 5701–6400.
H. Kepler	E. L. Massie	3301–3700.
R. H. L. Tighe	Tho. J. Miller	4001–4200, 4301–5700.
J. C. Tennent	H. E. Orr	6401–6458.
		$20—F to J and O to R.
R. H. L. Tighe	Tho. J. Miller	1–100, 1201–1300.
J. W. Jones	R. J. Delony	101–200, 401–500, 601–700, 901–1000, 1101–1200, 1501–1800, 2001–2100, 3701–4000.
R. Gilliam	M. C. Riggs	201–300, 701–900.
H. Kepler	E. L. Massie	301–400, 1301–1400, 2101–2200, 2601–2900.
R. M. Payne	R. Hill, jr	501–600.
J. C. Tennent	R. S. Jones	1001–1100, 1401–1421.
Do	H. E. Orr	1422–1500, 1801–2000, 2201–2600.
		$20—F to K and P to R.
H. Kepler	E. L. Massie	2901–3000, 4001–4100.
R. Gilliam	M. C. Riggs	3001–3300, 4601–5200.
R. H. L. Tighe	Tho. J. Miller	3301–3500, 5801–6200.
Do	M. C. Riggs	3501–3600.
J. W. Jones	R. J. Delony	3601–3700, 4101–4200, 5201–5400.
R. M. Payne	R. Hill, jr	4201–4600.
L. J. Levin	M. C. Riggs	5401–5800.
J. C. Tennent	H. E. Orr	6201–6353.
		$20—S and T.
Jno. Ott	C. C. Thayer	1–3264.
		$20—bA.
R. H. L. Tighe	Tho. J. Miller	1–2400, 19201–24000, 34401–37600, 49601–50400, 56001–58400, 64801–67200, 82401–83200, 85601–86400, 99201–100000.
R. M. Payne	R. Hill, jr	2401–4800, 12801–15200, 24001–26400, 40001–42400, 62401–64800, 72001–72800, 84001–84800, 92001–92800.
H. H. Goodloe	T. Ellett	4801–6400, 10401–12800, 32001–34400, 48001–48800, 52801–54400.
J. W. Jones	R. J. Delony	6401–8800, 50401–52800, 54401–55200, 60001–62400, 68001–69600, 72801–76000, 84801–85600, 87201–88000, 90401–91200, 93601–94400, 95201–96000, 100001–101600, 102401–103644.
H. Kepler	M. C. Riggs	8801–10400.
Do	E. L. Massie	15201–19200, 26401–28800, 45601–48000, 48801–49600, 67201–68000, 71201–72000, 80801–82400, 88801–89600, 92801–93600, 96001–96800, 98401–99200, 101601–102400.
R. G. Gilliam	M. C. Riggs	28801–30400, 37601–40000, 55201–56000, 58401–60000, 88001–88800, 94401–95200, 96801–97600.
J. C. Tennent	R. S. Jones	30401–32000, 42401–45600, 69601–71200, 76001–79200, 83201–84000, 86401–87200, 89601–90400, 91201–92000, 97601–98400.
Jno. Ott	C. C. Thayer	79201–80800.
		$20—aC to aF.
R. H. L. Tighe	Tho. J. Miller	1–400, 1401–1600, 2801–3400, 5001–5800, 6001–6800.
R. Gilliam	M. C. Riggs	401–600, 1801–2000, 2601–2800.
R. M. Payne	R. Hill, jr	601–800, 1601–1800, 7601–7800.
J. W. Jones	R. J. Delony	801–1200, 3401–4200, 5801–6000.
J. C. Tennent	R. S. Jones	1201–1400, 2201–2400.
Do	H. E. Orr	7801–7893.
H. Kepler	E. L. Massie	2001–2200, 2401–2600, 4201–5000.
L. J. Levin	M. C. Riggs	6801–7600.
		$20—BA.
H. Kepler	E. L. Massie	1–2400, 10401–12000, 13601–14400, 19201–20800, 22401–24800, 27201–28800, 29601–30400, 36801–37600.
R. Gilliam	M. C. Riggs	2401–4000, 8801–10400, 12001–13600, 16801–19200, 28801–29600, 30401–31200, 32801–34400.
J. W. Jones	R. J. Delony	4001–7200, 31201–32800, 35201–36000, 38401–40328.
R. M. Payne	R. Hill, jr	7201–8800, 21601–22400, 24801–27200, 34401–35200, 37601–38400.
R. H. L. Tighe	Tho. J. Miller	14401–15200, 20801–21600, 36001–36800.
J. C. Tennent	R. S. Jones	15201–16800.

Register of Confederate States Treasury Notes—Continued.

ACT OF AUGUST 19, 1861—Continued.

For Treasurer.	For Register.	Numbers of the notes signed.
		$20—cA.
R. Gilliam	M. C. Riggs	1–4000.
J. C. Tennent	H. E. Orr	4001–5600, 15201–18400, 28801–32000, 42785–43484.
Do	M. Winston	43485–43584.
L. J. Levin	M. C. Riggs	5601–8000, 18401–21600, 25601–28800, 38401–42784.
Do	H. E. Orr	8001–8800.
R. H. L. Tighe	Tho. J. Miller	8801–12000, 32001–35200.
J. W. Jones	R. J. Delony	12001–15200, 35201–38400.
R. M. Payne	R. Hill, jr	21601–25600.
Jno. Ott	C. C. Thayer	43585–43819.
		$20—dA to lA.
J. W. Jones	R. J. Delony	1–400, 1701–2100, 3401–3800, 6001–6600, 7401–7800, 8801-9500, 12101–12600, 14701–15200, 18601–19400, 21001–21400.
L. J. Levin	M. C. Riggs	401–900, 10001–10400, 13601–14300, 17401–17500, 18201-18600, 20201–20600, 22601–23000.
H. Kepler	E. L. Massie	901–1300, 2101–2600, 4601–4627.
Do	S. G. Tinsley	4628–5000.
R. H. L. Tighe	Tho. J. Miller	1301–1700, 3001–3400, 3801–4200, 5201–6000, 7001–7400, 8401–8800, 11701–12100, 16601–17000, 17801–18200, 20601–21000, 25701–26100.
J. C. Tennent	H. E. Orr	2601–2700, 2801–3000, 4201–4600, 5001–5200, 10401–10800, 13001–13400, 15801–16200, 21801-22200, 24201-24600, 26701-26822, 26823–27522 (dA to kA).
Do	R. J. Delony	2701–2800.
Do	M. Winston	27523–27622 (dA to kA).
H. H. Goodloe	T. Ellett	6601–7000, 8001–8400, 11201–11600, 14301–14700, 17701-18000, 19801–20200, 23001–23400, 25401–25700.
A. W. Gray	S. G. Tinsley	7801–8000, 10801–11200, 11601–11700, 12601–13000, 16201–16600, 21401–21800, 23801–24200, 26101–26500.
R. M. Payne	R. Hill, jr	9501–10000, 15201–15800, 19401–19800, 23401–23800, 25001–25400.
Jno. Ott	C. C. Thayer	13401–13600, 17001–17400, 17501–17700, 22201–22600, 24601–25000, 27623–27857 (dA to kA).
		$20—bB to tT.
J. W. Jones	R. J. Delony	1–300, 1101–1300.
R. H. L. Tighe	Tho. J. Miller	301–500. *
R. M. Payne	R. Hill, jr	501–700, 1301–1500.
L. J. Levin	M. C. Riggs	701–900.
J. C. Tennent	H. E. Orr	901–1100, 1501–1511.
		**$20**—$A^D$ to A^L.
R. H. L. Tighe	Tho. J. Miller	1–300, 701–1100, 2001–2400, 4401–5200, 6201–6600, 8301–8700, 8801–9200, 9701–10100, 11201–11600, 12501–12900, 14001–14400, 15901–16300, 17601–18000, 18901–19300, 19501-19900, 21001–21300, 24701–25100.
J. C. Tennent	H. E. Orr	301–400, 1801–2000, 3501–3900, 5401–5700, 6901–7300, 7901–8300, 9401–9700, 10101–10600, 20801–21000, 21301–21800, 24601–24700.
Do	E. L. Massie	12901–13400, 14401–14900, 16701–17100.
Do	C. C. Thayer	17101–17200.
L. J. Levin	M. C. Riggs	401–700, 1501–1800, 3201–3500, 5701–6100, 10901-11200, 11801-12000, 13401–13800, 15301–15700, 17201–17600, 18501-18900, 19901–20400, 21801–22200, 23001–23400.
R. M. Payne	R. Hill, jr	1101–1300, 2401–2800, 5301–5400, 6101–6200, 7301–7500, 8701–8800, 10801–10900, 24201–24600.
J. W. Jones	R. J. Delony	1301–1500, 2801–3200, 3901–4400, 5201–5300, 6601-6900, 7501-7900, 9201–9400, 12101–12500, 14901–15300, 16301–16700, 19301–19500, 20401–20800, 23801–24200.
H. Kepler	E. L. Massie	10601–10800, 11601–11800, 13801–14000, 15701–15900, 18001–18500,
H. H. Goodloe	T. Ellett	22201–22600, 23401–23800.
A. W. Gray	S. G. Tinsley	22601–23000, 25101–25516.
		**$20**—$A^C$ and A^M to A^U.
Jno. Ott	C. C. Thayer	1–544.

* Note lettered fF and numbered 478 was canceled and not issued.

Register of Confederate States Treasury Notes—Continued.

ACT OF AUGUST 19, 1861—Continued.

For Treasurer.	For Register.	Numbers of the notes signed.
		**$20**—$A^{1-4}$ and A^{10-13}, A^{5-9} and A^{14-18}.
R. M. Payne	R. Hill, jr	1–200, 1501–1600, 2101–2300.
L. J. Levin	M. C. Riggs	201–400, 1601–1700, 2501–2600.
H. Kepler	E. L. Massie	401–500, 801–900.
J. C. Tennent	C. C. Thayer	501–800, 901–1100, 1701–1800, 2301–2500.
J. W. Jones	R. J. Delony	1101–1200, 1401–1500, 1801–1900, 2601–2700.
R. H. L. Tighe	Tho. J. Miller	1201–1400, 1901–2100.
Jno. Ott	C. C. Thayer	2701–2834 (A^{17} and A^{18}).
		**$20**—$A^{1-4}$, A^{9-12}.
J. W. Jones	R. J. Delony	2701–3100, 3701–3900.
Do	C. C. Thayer	15001–15800.
H. H. Goodloe	T. Ellett	3101–3300, 4101–4300, 5501–5700, 6201–6400, 6801–7000, 7401–7600.
R. H. L. Tighe	Tho. J. Miller	3301–3500, 5101–5500, 6601–6800, 7001–7200, 10701–11000, 12601–13400, 14201–15000.
Do	W. H. Brown	18801–19600.
A. W. Gray	S. G. Tinsley	3501–3700, 4701–4900, 9801–10200.
Do	T. L. Crouch	9201–9800, 11801–12600.
L. J. Levin	M. C. Riggs	3901–4100, 4901–5100, 5701–6200.
J. C. Tennent	M. Winston	4301–4500, 8001–8200, 10201–10700, 13401–14200, 18001–18800, 21201–21700.
Jno. Ott	C. C. Thayer	4501–4700.
R. M. Payne	R. Hill, jr	6401–6600, 7601–7800, 8401–9200, 17301–18000.
Do	M. Winston	21701–21706.
F. W. Ashby	S. G. Tinsley	7201–7400, 7801–8000, 8201–8400, 11001–11800.
T. O. Keesee	T. Ellett	15801–16600.
E. W. Gills	Wm. Nott	16601–17300.
C. L. Maurice	Tho. J. Miller	19601–20400.
T. C. Gale	E. H. Smith	20401–21200.
		**$20**—$A^{5-8}$ and A^{13-16}.
J. W. Jones	R. J. Delony	2701–3100, 3701–3900, 10801–11800.
Do	C. C. Thayer	16301–16500.
H. H. Goodloe	T. Ellett	3101–3300, 3501–3700, 4101–4300, 4701–4900, 5501–5700, 6201–6400, 6801–7000, 7401–7600, 8401–9200, 11801–12000, 12401–12600.
R. H. L. Tighe	Tho. J. Miller	3301–3500, 5101–5500, 6601–6800, 7001–7200.
Do	W. H. Brown	17301–18100.
L. J. Levin	M. C. Riggs	3901–4100, 4901–5100, 5701–6200.
J. C. Tennent	M. Winston	4301–4500, 8001–8200, 9201–10000, 13401–13900, 18501–19100, 20401–21200.
Jno. Ott	C. C. Thayer	4501–4700, 12001–12400.
R. M. Payne	R. Hill, jr	6401–6600, 7601–7800, 14701–15500, 19101–19600, 21201–21700.
F. W. Ashby	S. G. Tinsley	7201–7400, 7801–8000, 8201–8400, 10001–10800.
H. Kepler	R. J. Delony	12601–13400, 16501–17300.
T. O. Keesee	T. Ellett	13901–14700.
E. W. Gills	Wm. Nott	15501–16300.
C. L. Maurice	Tho. J. Miller	18101–18500, 19601–20400.
		**$20**—$A^{19}$ to A^{26}.
R. H. L. Tighe	Tho. J. Miller	1–800, 3101–3900, 7201–8000, 12001–12800, 14401-15200, 16801-17700, 24401–25200, 26601–27400, 32401–33200, 35601–36400, 38001–38400, 39201–40000, 42001–43500.
Do	T. L. Crouch	43501–43600.
Do	W. H. Brown	50001–50800, 53201–54000, 60401–62000, 66901–67700, 71101–71900, 76301–77100, 82601–83200, 90601–91400, 95401–96200, 101801–102600, 104201–105000, 106901–107000.
H. Kepler	R. J. Delony	801–1600, 5601–7200, 9601–10400, 13601–14400, 16001–16800, 23601–24400, 28001–28800, 30801–31600, 34801–35600, 37201-38000, 40401–40500, 41201–42000, 45601–46400, 47601-48400, 51601–52400, 56401–57200, 59601–60400, 65301–66100, 72701-73500, 79901–80300, 86801–86900, 87801–88600, 97801–98600, 101001–101800.

Register of Confederate States Treasury Notes—Continued.

ACT OF AUGUST 19, 1861—Continued.

For Treasurer.	For Register.	Numbers of the notes signed.
		**$20**—$A^{19}$ to A^{26}—Continued.
J. C. Tennent	M. Winston	1601–2600, 10401–11200, 18501–19300, 22601–23100, 25201–26000, 29401–30200, 31601–32400, 36401–37200, 38401–39200, 44401–45200, 47201–47600, 48401–49200, 54001–54800, 64501–65300, 70101–70900, 75501–76300, 80701–81400, 83601–84000, 86001–86800, 89401–90200, 96201–97000.
J. W. Jones	C. C. Thayer	2601–3100.
E. W. Gills	Wm. Nott	3901–4000, 4801–5600, 8801–9600, 12801–13600, 15201–16000, 20101–20900.
T. O. Keesee	T. Ellett	4001–4800, 8001–8800, 11201–12000, 19301–20100, 40501–40800, 93801–94600, 99401–100200, 105801–106400.
H. H. Goodloe	W. G. Dunbar	17701–18500, 21501–22200 (A^{19} to A^{24}).
Do	T. Ellett	21401–21500, 21501–22200 (A^{25} and A^{26}).
Do	W. A. Wade	57201–58000, 73501–74300, 78701–78900, 79001–79100.
Do	Wm. Rothrock	78901–79000, 79101–79500, 82201–82600, 84001–84400, 90201–90600, 92201–93000, 97001–97800, 102601–103400.
Jno. Ott	E. H. Smith	20901–21400, 22201–22600, 23101–23600, 26001–26600, 27401–28000, 28801–29400, 30201–30800, 33201–34800, 40001–40400, 40801–41200, 45201–45600, 46401–46800.
J. S. Lewis	W. G. Dunbar	43601–44400, 46801–47200, 49201–50000, 54801–55600, 67701–68500, 74301–74700, 77101–77900, 81801–82200, 84401–85200, 93001–93800, 100201–101000.
T. C. Gale	E. H. Smith	50801–51600, 55601–56400, 58801–59600, 62801–63600, 66101–66900, 69301–70100, 74701–75800, 79501–79900, 81401–81800, 83201–83600.
C. L. Maurice	Tho. J. Miller	52401–53200, 58001–58800, 62001–62800, 68501–69300, 71901–72700, 77901–78700, 80301–80700, 85201–86000, 88601–89400, 91401–92200, 98601–99400, 103401–104200, 105001–105800.
R. M. Payne	R. Hill, jr	63601–64500, 70901–71100, 86901–87800, 94601–95400, 106401–106900, 107001–107053.
		$20—A (Southern Bank-Note Company).
H. H. Goodloe	T. Ellett	1–1900, 2301–3900, 4401–5600.
Do	C. C. Thayer	1901–2300, 3901–4400.
R. H. L. Tighe	Tho. J. Miller	5601–6400, 9701–11300.
A. W. Gray	S. G. Tinsley	6401–7200.
Do	T. L. Crouch	14401–14860.
Jno. Ott	C. C. Thayer	7201–8400.
R. M. Payne	R. Hill, jr	8401–9200.
F. W. Ashby	T. L. Crouch	9201–9700.
J. C. Tennent	M. Winston	11301–12000.
T. O. Keesee	T. Ellett	12001–14400.
		$20—19A to 26A.
A. W. Gray	T. L. Crouch	1–800, 2401–3200, 7401–8200, 15201–16000, 20001–20700.
J. C. Tennent	M. Winston	801–1600, 3201–4000, 12301–13100, 19401–20000, 21201–21700.
R. M. Payne	R. Hill, jr	1601–2400, 10701–11500, 14301–15100, 21701–22200.
F. W. Ashby	S. G. Tinsley	4001–4800, 10101–10700, 16001–16600, 18601–19400.
Jno. Ott	C. C. Thayer	4801–5500, 6301–6600, 8201–8900, 18001–18600.
J. W. Jones	R. J. Delony	5501–6300, 11501–12300.
Do	C. C. Thayer	15101–15200, 16601–17400, 23801–24000.
R. H. L. Tighe	Tho. J. Miller	6601–7400, 13501–14300, 20701–21200.
L. J. Levin	M. C. Riggs	8901–9300, 13101–13500.
E. W. Gills	Wm. Nott	9301–10100, 23001–23800.
T. O. Keesee	T. Ellett	17401–18000, 22201–23000, 24001–24097.
		**$20**—$A^{1}$ to A^{8} (2d series).
R. H. L. Tighe	W. H. Brown	1–800.
J. C. Tennent	M. Winston	801–1300, 3301–4100, 4901–7100, 7501–8000.
R. M. Payne	R. Hill, jr	1301–3300, 4101–4900, 7101–7500.
Do	M. Winston	8701–8723.
D. Lyon	J. T. Dickson	8001–8200.
H. C. Williams	J. M. Kinney	8201–8300.
W. H. White	R. J. Dorsey	8301–8700.

Register of Confederate States Treasury Notes—Continued.

ACT OF AUGUST 19, 1861—Continued.

For Treasurer.	For Register.	Numbers of the notes signed.
		$20—1 to 8 (1st series).*
J. C. Tennent	M. Winston	1–2100, 2501–2900, 3301–3700, 4101–4600, 5001–6100, 7301–8300.
R. M. Payne	R. Hill, jr	2101–2500, 2901–3300, 3701–4100, 4601–5000.
Do	M. Winston	6101–6700, 8701–9100, 13101–13500, 14701–15100, 17201-17600.
T. O. Keesee	T. Ellett	6701–6900.
A. S. Watts	W. T. Snead	6901–7300, 8301–8700, 9501–9900, 11101–11500, 12701–13100.
D. Lyon	J. T. Dickson	9101–9500, 10301–10700, 11901–12300, 13501–13900, 14301–14700.
C. S. Maurice	Tho. J. Miller	9901–10300, 11501–11900, 12301–12700, 13901–14300, 15101–15500, 16401–16800, 17601–18000.
T. O. Keesee	T. L. Crouch	10701–11100, 18001–18100.
H. C. Shook	C. Walthall	15501–16000.
J. B. S. Dimitry	Wm. Nott	16001–16400, 16801–17200.
		$20—1 to 8 (1st series—duplicates).
R. M. Payne	M. Winston	1–400, 1601–2000, 2401–3200, 3601–4000, 4801–5200.
C. S. Maurice	Tho. J. Miller	401–800, 1201–1600, 4401–4800, 5201–6000.
T. W. Bell	W. B. Walston	801–1200.
A. S. Watts	W. T. Snead	2001–2400, 4001–4400.
D. Lyon	J. T. Dickson	3201–3600.
		$20—1 to 10 (1st series). *
T. O. Keesee	T. L. Crouch	18101–18200, 20601–21800.
J. B. S. Dimitry	Wm. Nott	18201–18600, 19001–19200, 19301–19400, 92801–93100, 102701–103100, 118601–118900, 124501–124900, 135101–135500, 142701–143000.
C. S. Maurice	Tho. J. Miller	18601–19000, 19201–19300, 19401–19800, 20201–20600, 22301–22600.
R. M. Payne	M. Winston	19801–20200, 20801–21100.
J. W. Faxon	R. J. Delony	21101–21900, 22601–23000, 23401–23800, 24101–24300, 25101–25200, 25601–26000, 27401–27800, 29001–29400, 30701-31100, 32301–32700, 42201–42600, 45201–45600, 47501-47800, 49401-49800, 50901-51300, 54501–54900, 56601-57000, 62901–63300, 63901–64200, 68201–68300, 69101–69500, 72601-73000, 77601-78000, 83201–83600, 90101–90500, 91701–92100, 97801-98200, 105901-106300, 110601-111000, 146001-146400, 150301-150700.
J. W. Jones	J. O. Snyder	21901–22300, 23001–23400, 23801–24100, 24301–24700, 26701–27100, 28601–29000, 30001–30300, 31601–32000, 33101-33500, 33801–34200, 34601–35000, 36601–37000, 38101-38400, 39401-39800, 40501–40900, 43301–43700, 45601–45900, 47801-48200, 49801–50200, 52001–52400, 56101–56400, 56501-56600-58001-58400, 60901–61300, 65201–65600, 69901–70300, 74101–74500, 80201–80600, 84301–84700, 87701–88100, 95601-95900, 99401-99800, 107401-107800, 112301-112700, 118901-119300, 123001-123400, 128601–129000, 133901–134300, 137501–137900, 141201–141600, 147601–148000, 151101–151500.
D. Lyon	J. T. Dickson	24701–25100, 26001–26400, 28001–28300, 29601–30000, 31301–31600, 35001–35400, 50201–50600, 52801–53100, 55701-56100, 61301–61700, 67501–67900, 70301–70700, 80601-81000, 84001-84300, 89301–89700, 102301–102700, 109601–110000, 113401-113800, 117801–118200.
E. C. Goddin	E. Nulty	25201–25600, 27101–27400, 28301–28600, 30301–30700, 32001–32300, 32701–33100, 34201–34600, 36201–36600, 37701-38100, 40901–41300, 42901–43300, 45901–46300, 55301-55700, 57601-58000, 62101–62500, 79101–79500.
Do	J. M. Kinney	75901–76300, 85101–85500, 89701–90100, 92101–92400, 101901–102300, 108901–109300, 118401–118600, 123801–124100, 135601–135700, 135801–135900, 138301–138700.
H. C. Shook	C. Walthall	26401–26700, 27801–28000, 29401–29600, 31101–31300, 33501–33800, 122701–123000.
Do	G. N. Warren	107801–108100, 113801–114200, 128201–128600, 133201-133600, 140201–140600, 150701–151100.

* Series of 1 to 8 proper ends at 18100; series of 1 to 10 commences at 18101, being a continuation of series 1 to 8, numbers 9 and 10 being an addition to the 1st series. First number of 9 and 10 is 18101—from 1 to 18100 not issued.

Register of Confederate States Treasury Notes—Continued.

ACT OF AUGUST 19, 1861—Continued.

For Treasurer.	For Register.	Numbers of the notes signed.
		$20—1 to 10 (1st series)—Continued.
C. C. Bridges	W. Hancock	35401–35800, 37001–37300, 38401–38700, 39801–40100, 41601–41900, 43701–44000, 44901–45200, 47201–47500, 48201–48800, 51301–51600, 53401–53800, 59201–59500, 60201–60500, 66001–66400, 72101–72400, 82801–83200.
Do	W. S. Gilman	74501–74800, 79501–79800, 95301–95600, 99101–99400, 108501–108900, 115601–116000, 120501–120900, 137901–138300, 140901–141200, 144901–145300, 150001–150300, 155101–155400.
F. C. Weisiger	W. P. Caldwell	35801–36200, 38701–39100, 40201–40500, 42601–42900, 44601–44900, 46901–47200, 48801–49100, 50601–50900, 53101–53400, 57001–57300, 59501–59800, 64201–64500, 68701–69100, 73401–73700, 77001–77300. 81401–81700, 86601–87000, 90801–91100, 96701–97100, 104801–105100, 112701–113000, 117401–117800, 119301–119700, 124901–125200, 126201–126500, 131101–131400, 138701–139000, 143401–143800, 149301–149600, 154101–154400.
C. Leigh	G. N. Warren	37301–37700, 40101–40200, 41301–41600, 44001–44300, 46301–46600, 56401–56500, 63701–63900, 67901–68200, 71801–72000.
Do	E. Nulty	72001–72100, 76301–76600, 77301–77600, 85901–86200.
B. H. Berry	J. T. Holt	39101–39400, 41901–42200, 44301–44600, 46601–46900, 48201–48400, 49101–49400, 51601–52000, 53801–54100, 57301–57600, 59801–60200, 64901–65200, 68301–68700, 75201–75500, 78001–78300, 82101–82500, 90501–90800, 91401–91700, 97501–97800, 104701–104800, 110001–110300, 114901–115200, 132801–133200, 139001–139300, 144601–144900.
T. W. Bell	W. B. Walston	52401–52800, 54101–54500, 58401–58800, 61701–62100, 66801–67200, 70701–71100, 78701–79100, 85501–85900, 88501–88900, 93101–93500, 100801–101200, 111301–111700.
W. G. Allen	C. S. Taylor	54901–55300, 58801–59200, 63301–63700, 72401–72600, 74801–75200, 81001–81400, 81701–82100, 87001–87400, 120901–121300, 127901–128200, 132401–132800, 139601–139900, 146801–147200, 152601–152900.
J. C. Joplin	S. Dutcher	60501–60900, 65601–66000, 71501–71800, 73001–73400, 76601–77000, 82501–82800, 86201–86600, 91101–91400, 97101–97500, 105101–105500, 110301–110600, 116301–116700, 120101–120500, 144201–144600, 148000–148400–152901–153300.
A. W. Gray	W. S. Gilman	62501–62900, 66401–66800, 71101–71300.
Do	W. Hancock	71301–71500, 75501–75900, 79801–80200, 84701–85100, 88101–88500, 93501–93900, 101201–101600, 108101–108500, 115201–115600, 124201–124500, 129601–130000, 134701–135100, 136701–137100, 142301–142700, 147201–147600, 152201–152600.
H. H. Goodloe	W. Rothrock	64501–64900, 93901–94300, 98501–98800, 109301–109600, 116101–116300, 124101–124200, 130001–130300, 135501–135600, 135701–135800.
W. R. Todd	J. H. Cooke	67201–67500, 69501–69900, 73701–74100, 78301–78700, 83601–84000, 87401–87700, 92401–92800, 98201–98500, 106301–106700, 113001–113400, 121601–122000, 129301–129600, 131701–132100, 135901–136300, 140601–140900, 145601–146000, 151501–151800.
C. Ashford	S. Sinton	88901–89300, 96201–96400, 103901–104200, 111701–112000, 116001–116100, 119701–120100, 125601–126200, 132101–132400.
P. B. Hooe	Tho. J. Miller	94301–94700, 103101–103500.
J. H. Carr	R. A. Mills	94701–95000, 100401–100800, 106701–107100, 114301–114900, 118201–118400, 122301–122700, 127201–127600, 133601–133900, 141901–142300, 145301–145600, 149601–150000, 154801–155100, 155401–155640, 155641–155726 (No. 6), 155641–155732 (No. 7), 155641–155734 (Nos. 1 and 3), 155641–155738 (No. 2), 155641–155739 (No. 4), 155641–155742 (No. 8).
F. W. Ashby	S. G. Tinsley	95001–95300, 95901–96000, 101601–101900.
T. W. Dickins	A. S. Watkins	96001–96200.
F. H. Link	L. P. Rogers	96401–96700, 104301–104500, 116701–117100.
J. Bunting	J. H. Hunt	98801–99100, 104501–104600, 105501–105900, 112001–112300, 114201–114300, 117101–117400, 126901–127200, 130301–130700, 139301–139600, 143001–143400, 149001–149300, 154401–154800.

Register of Confederate States Treasury Notes—Continued.

ACT OF AUGUST 19, 1861—Continued.

For Treasurer.	For Register.	Numbers of the notes signed.
		$20—1 to 10 (1st series)—Continued.
J. S. Lewis	J. P. Swords	99801–100100, 104601–104700, 107101–107400, 111001–111300, 151801–152200.
T. D. Walford	T. F. Grayson	100101–100400, 104201–104300.
W. F. Hoge	C. W. Keim	103501–103900.
N. A. Bass	A. S. Watkins	121301–121600, 122001–122300, 125201–125600, 126501–126900, 127601–127900, 130701–131100, 131401–131700, 137101–137500, 139901–140200, 141601–141900, 143801–144200, 146401–146800, 148401–149000, 153301–154100.
T. C. Gale	E. H. Smith	123401–123800, 129001–129300, 134301–134700, 136301–136700.
		$20—1 to 10 (2d series).
T. W. Bell	W. B. Walston	1–400, 8401–8800, 14601–15000, 21901–22300, 37401–37800, 43901–44200, 58901–59200.
C. Ashford	S. Sinton	401–700, 7401–7700, 12901–13000, 14301–14600, 19001–19400, 26301–26600, 34301–34700, 43601–43900, 47901–48000, 73901–74300, 80401–80700, 90601–91000, 98301–98600.
B. H. Berry	J. T. Holt	701–1100, 8801–9100, 14001–14300, 32801–33200, 40801–41100, 46201–46400, 51801–52100, 52501–52800, 58601–58900, 64901–65300, 81301–81400, 82001–82100, 87701–88100, 91801–92100, 92401–92800, 97601–97900.
H. C. Shook	G. N. Warren	1101–1500, 10401–10800, 13001–13400, 22301–22700, 27901–28200, 33901–34300, 55501–55900, 59301–59700, 66201–66600, 70001–70400, 74701–75100, 80001–80400, 86901–87300, 92801–93200.
J. W. Jones	J. O. Snyder	1501–1900, 11201–11500, 17001–17500, 23801–24100, 30001–30400, 40101–40500, 45201–45600, 50101–50500, 56601–57000, 62001–62500, 65701–65900, 71601–72000, 79201–79600, 81401–81800, 86501–86900, 89301–89700, 95301–95700.
J. W. Faxon	R. J. Delony	1901–2300, 5201–5600, 28501–28900, 36601–37000, 46001–46200.
N. A. Bass	A. S. Watkins	2301–2600, 6701–7100, 15701–16000, 22701–23100, 28201–28500, 35801–36200, 44201–44300, 48601–49000, 53701–53800, 54401–54800, 59201–59300, 66901–67200, 76801–77200, 98601–99400.
E. C. Goddin	E. Nulty	2601–2700.
Do	J. M. Kinney	4001–4200, 8001–8400, 16601–17000, 24101–24400, 30401–30800, 38701–39100, 56201–56600, 63301–63700, 68201–68600, 72001–72400, 78401–78700, 82401–82800, 85301–85700, 90101–90600,* 96001–96300, 100401–100600.
H. H. Goodloe	W. Rothrock	2701–3000, 9801–10100, 16001–16300, 19401–19700, 28901–29200, 43001–43300, 48301–48600, 54101–54400.
W. R. Todd	J. H. Cooke	3001–3300, 10101–10400, 17501–17900, 23301–23400, 29201–29600, 37801–38100, 42601–43000, 49701–50100, 55901–56200, 60901–61300, 67501–67800, 70401–70800, 75801–76100, 83901–84300, 87301–87700, 91401–91800, 97901–98300.
C. C. Bridges	W. S. Gilman	3301–3600, 12301–12600, 18701–19000, 23401–23800, 27601–27900, 34701–35100, 44301–44600, 51001–51400, 62501–62900, 66601–66900, 75101–75500, 94901–95300, 99401–99700.
P. B. Hooe	Tho. J. Miller	3601–4000, 9101–9500, 24401–24800, 31501–31900, 39501–39800, 61601–62000, 77601–78000, 81801–82000,
A. W. Gray	W. Hancock	4201–4600, 11501–11900, 18301–18700, 24801–25200, 30801–31200, 39101–39500, 45601–46000, 51401–51800, 57001–57400, 62901–63300, 68801–69000, 72401–72800, 78001–78400, 83501–83900, 86101–86500, 89701–90100, 96701–97100.
W. G. Allen	C. S. Taylor	4601–4900, 9501–9800, 17901–18300, 21301–21600, 32101–32500, 38301–38700, 76101–76500, 85701–86100, 100001–100400.
J. S. Lewis	J. P. Swords	4901–5200, 7701–8000, 19701–20100, 23101–23300, 32501–32800, 40501–40800, 46401–46800, 50801–51000.
F. H. Link	L. P. Rogers	5601–5900, 13701–14000, 21601–21900.
J. C. Joplin	S. Dutcher	5901–6300, 15001–15400, 20101–20500, 26601–27000, 33501–33900, 41101–41500, 46801–47200, 52101–52500, 57401–57800, 64501–64900, 69601–70000, 73101–73500, 79601–80000, 84601–85000, 88501–88900, 91001–914000.
J. Bunting	J. H. Hunt	6301–6700, 13401–13700, 20901–21300, 27001–27300, 35101–35500, 42301–42600, 47201–47600, 52801–53100, 57801–58200, 65901–66200, 73501–73900, 81101–81300, 94701–94800.

* Notes numbered 90501–90600 never issued.

Register of Confederate States Treasury Notes—Continued.

ACT OF AUGUST 19, 1861—Continued.

For Treasurer.	For Register.	Numbers of the notes signed.
		$20—1 to 10 (2d series)—Continued.
F. C. Weisiger	W. P. Caldwell	7101–7400, 15401–15700, 20501–20900, 27301–27600, 35501–35800, 41901–42300, 47601–47900, 53101–53400, 65301–65700, 74301–74700.
J. B. S. Dimitry	Wm. Nott	10801–11200, 25501–25900, 31201–31500, 39801–40100, 44901–45200, 50501–50800, 64101–64500, 69101–69300, 72801–73100, 78901–79200, 97101–97400.
D. Lyon	J. T. Dickson	11901–12300, 25201–25500, 29601–30000, 36201–36600, 41501–41900, 49401–49700, 55101–55500, 61301–61600, 69301–69600, 71201–71600, 75501–75800, 80701–81100, 84301–84600, 88901-89300, 93601–93900.
J. H. Carr	R. A. Mills	12601–12900, 16301–16600, 37001–37400, 44601–44900, 49001–49400, 54801–55100, 60101–60500, 67201–67500, 70801–71200, 76501–76800, 82801–83200, 85001–85300, 88101–88500, 94201-94500.
T. D. Walford	T. F. Grayson	25901–26300, 33201–33500, 43301–43600, 53401–53700, 58201–58600.
H. C. Williams	C. Walthall	31901–32100, 38101–38300, 94501–94700, 94801–94900, 99701–100000.
F. W. Ashby	S. G. Tinsley	48001–48300, 53801–54100, 60501–60900, 93901–94200, 97501–97600.
N. A. Bass	A. S. Watkins	59701–60100.
T. C. Gale	E. H. Smith	63701–64100, 67801–68200, 77201–77600, 83201–83500, 96301–96700.
T. O. Keesee	T. L. Crouch	78701–78900, 82101–82400.
R. M. Payne	M. Winston	92101–92400.
T. J. Hatch	E. Nulty	93201–93600.
O. M. Marshall	J. W. Eggleston	95701–96000, 97401–97500.
		$20—1 to 10 (3d series).
C. Ashford	S. Sinton	1–100, 5001–5400, 11101–11400, 16401–16800, 22201–22500.
J. C. Joplin	S. Dutcher	101–500, 7001–7400.
N. A. Bass	A. S. Watkins	501–900, 5401–5700, 6001–6300, 10701–11100, 11401–11800, 17501–17800, 18001–18300, 23801–24200.
C. C. Bridges	W. S. Gilman	901–1300, 10301–10700, 24901–25000.
B. H. Berry	J. T. Holt	1301–1700, 12501–12900, 18301–18600, 22801–23100.
W. G. Allen	C. S. Taylor	1701–2000, 9201–9600, 14901–15300, 15701–16000, 24201-24600, 25401–25800.
W. R. Todd	J. H. Cooke	2001–2400, 12901–13300, 19001–19300, 25801–25900.
J. H. Carr	R. A. Mills	2401–2700, 6301–6700, 12201–12500, 18601–19000, 23101–23400, 25901–26036 (Nos. 2 and 8), 25901–26038 (No. 5), 25901–26039 (Nos. 1, 3, 4, 7, and 10), 25901–26040 (No. 6), 25901–26041 (No. 9).
J. Bunting	J. H. Hunt	2701–3100, 6701–7000, 11801–12200, 16801–17100, 21801–22200.
J. W. Jones	J. O. Snyder	3101–3500, 8401–8800, 13301–13700, 20401–20800.
E. C. Goddin	J. M. Kinney	3501–3900, 14501–14900, 20801–21200.
A. W. Gray	W. Hancock	3901–4300, 8801–9200, 13701–14100, 19301–19700.
T. C. Gale	E. H. Smith	4301–4700, 8101–8400, 14101–14900, 19701–20000.
J. B. S. Dimitry	Wm. Nott	4701–5000, 9601–9900, 15301–15700, 21201–21500, 24601–24900.
F. C. Weisiger	W. P. Caldwell	5701–6000, 9901–10300, 16001–16400, 21501–21800.
R. M. Payne	M. Winston	7401–7700, 17801–18000, 22501–22800.
T. D. Walford	T. F. Grayson	7701–8100.
H. C. Shook	G. N. Warren	17101–17500, 23401–23800.
H. C. Williams	C. Walthall	20001–20400.
J. W. Faxon	R. J. Delony	25001–25400.
		$20—W to Z.
J. C. Tennent	M. Winston	1–15600, 16001–16700.
M. M. Young	M. C. Riggs	15601–16000.
H. Kepler	R. J. Delony	16701–17800.
W. F. Hoge	C. W. Keim	17801–18600.
H. C. Shook	W. Y. Downman	18601–19400.
Do	C. Walthall	31301–31900, 32701–33500.
D. Lyon	J. T. Dickson	19401–19800, 31901–32700, 33501–34300, 37901–38300.
C. S. Maurice	Tho. J. Miller	19801–21400, 22201–23000, 23801–24600.
R. M. Payne	M. Winston	21401–22200, 23001–23800, 24601–31300, 36301–37100, 38301–38700, 39501–40300.
T. O. Keesee	T. L. Crouch	34301–36300, 37101–37900, 38701–39500, 40301–41062.

Register of Confederate States Treasury Notes—Continued.

ACT OF AUGUST 19, 1861—Continued.

For Treasurer.	For Register.	Numbers of the notes signed.
		$10—A and B (number *black*)—Southern Bank Note Company.
H. H. Goodloe	T. Ellett	1-14700, 16301-16900.
R. H. L. Tighe	Tho. J. Miller	14701-15500.
L. J. Levin	M. C. Riggs	15501-16300.
J. W. Jones	R. J. Delony	16901*-18900.
F. W. Ashby	S. G. Tinsley	18901-19000, 19101-19400, 21101-21200, 21301-21500, 21801-21900.
T. O. Keesee	T. Ellett	19001-19100, 19401-19700, 20301-20500, 21901-22000.
A. W. Gray	T. L. Crouch	19701-20100.
R. M. Payne	R. Hill, jr	20101-20300, 20501-20600, 21201-21300, 21601-21800.
J. C. Tennent	M. Winston	20601-21100, 21501-21600.
		$10—C (number *black*)—Southern Bank Note Company.
H. H. Goodloe	T. Ellett	1-1900, 2301-3900, 4401-5600.
Do	C. C. Thayer	1901-2300.
Jno. Ott	do	3901-4400, 7201-8400.
R. H. L. Tighe	Tho. J. Miller	5601-6400, 9701-11300.
A. W. Gray	S. G. Tinsley	6401-7200.
R. M. Payne	R. Hill, jr	8401-9200.
F. W. Ashby	T. L. Crouch	9201-9700.
J. C. Tennent	M. Winston	11301-12000.
T. O. Keesee	T. Ellett	12001-14860.
		$10—A (number *red*).
H. H. Goodloe	T. Ellett	1-10000.
		$10—A1.
H. H. Goodloe	T. Ellett	1-10333.
		$10—Ab.
H. H. Goodloe	T. Ellett	1-7160.
		$10—A9 to A16.
J. W. Jones	R. J. Delony	1-400, 10601-11100, 13001-14000.
Do	C. C. Thayer	30301-31400, 34201-34500, 35001-35600, 36801-37400, 37801-38000, 39601-40200, 43401-44500, 45301-45900, 46701-47900, 48701-49100, 49901-50500.
Do	S. G. Tinsley	50501-50700.
Do	J. O. Snyder	93901-94200, 102701-103200, 109001-109500.
L. J. Levin	M. C. Riggs	401-800, 6901-7300, 10201-10600, 11101-11300, 11801-12200.
R. M. Payne	R. Hill, jr	801-1200, 4601-4900, 8501-8900, 14801-15600, 16401-17000, 21501-22300.
Do	M. Winston	88801-89200, 118301-118700, 122901-123300, 124101-124500, 126501-126900, 128201-128600, 130001-130400.
J. C. Tennent	H. E. Orr	1201, 1600, 3801-4200, 6101-6500.
Do	M. Winston	18901-19700, 27701-27900.
H. H. Goodloe	T. Ellett	1601-2400, 4901-5300, 17001-17900.
Do	W. Rothrock	72901-73700, 130801-131200.
Jno. Ott	C. C. Thayer	2401-3000, 4201-4600, 6501-6900, 7901-8500, 18201-18900, 20001-20700, 25901-26100, 27101-27700.
R. H. L. Tighe	Tho. J. Miller	3001-3400, 5301-5700, 9801-10200, 12201-13000, 15601-16400, 20701-21500, 25101-25900.
Do	W. H. Brown	81801-82400, 102401-102700.
A. W. Gray	S. G. Tinsley	3401-3800, 5701-6100-7301-7600, 11301-11800.
Do	T. L. Crouch	7601-7700, 8901-9800, 17901-18200, 19701-20000, 26101-27100.
Do	W. S. Gilman	132401-132800, 133801-134200.
F. W. Ashby	T. L. Crouch	7701-7900.
Do	S. G. Tinsley	14001-14800, 23901-24700, 34901-35000, 100401-100800, 133201-133400.
E. W. Gills	Wm. Nott	22301-23900.
L. J. Levin	M. C. Riggs	24701-25100.
M. M. Young	do	27901-29500, 31401-31800, 32201-32600, 33001-33400, 34501-34900, 35601-36800, 38801-39600, 40201-41000, 42601-43400, 44501-45300, 49101-49900, 52201-52600, 60301-61100, 64701-65500, 69901-70500, 82401-82800, 87701-88100, 92601-92800, 94201-94400, 103201-103600, 114301-114700.

* Notes A and B, Nos. 16901-18200, were numbered in *red*.

Register of Confederate States Treasury Notes—Continued.

ACT OF AUGUST 19, 1861—Continued.

For Treasurer.	For Register.	Numbers of the notes signed.
		$10—A9 to A16—Continued.
T. O. Keesce	T. Ellett	29501–30300, 31801–32200, 32601–33000, 33401–34200.
Do	T. L. Crouch	89201–89600.
C. A. Baldwin	J. M. Kinney	37401–37800, 38001–38800, 41001–42600, 45901–46700, 47901–48700, 50701–51800, 52601–53000, 53401–54100.
J. S. Lewis	W. G. Dunbar	51801–52200, 53001–53400, 54101–54900, 63501–64700, 80601–81000, 90401–90900, 95201–95600, 100801–101200, 103601–104000, 105701–106100, 108601–109000, 111901–112300.
Do	J. P. Swords	117101–117500, 118701–119100, 119501–119900, 120301–120500, 121301–121700, 123301–123700, 124501–124900, 126101–126500, 126901–127300, 127801–128200, 129201–129600, 134201–134400.
W. H. White	R. J. Dorsey	54901–55700, 61901–62300, 69101–69900.
Do	W. B. Walston	75801–76200, 78301–78700, 83601–84000.
H. C. Williams	J. M. Kinney	55701–56500, 57701–58500, 76601–77000, 82801–83200, 96601–97000, 110301–110700, 115901–116300, 125301–125700.
C. S. Maurice	J. H. Harris	56501–57300.
Do	Tho. J. Miller	62301–63100, 66501–67500, 68301–69100, 72101–72900, 75001–75800, 88101–88500, 89601–90000, 108201–108600, 115501–115900.
T. D. Walford	T. F. Grayson	57301–57700, 61501–61900, 105301–105700, 106501–106800, 110701–111100, 129001–129200.
W. F. Hoge	C. W. Keim	58501–59300, 73701–74400, 78501–79400, 100001–100400, 129601–130000, 133401–133800.
D. Lyon	J. T. Dickson	59301–59500, 65501–65900, 67501–68300, 74401–75000, 86301–86800, 90901–91300, 92801–93400, 94401–94800, 95601–95800, 96201–96600, 102001–102400, 104901–105300, 107101–107600, 111501–111900, 113901–114300.
H. Kepler	R. J. Delony	59501–60300, 65901–66500, 78001–78300, 81001–81800, * 85601–86300, 88501–88800.
A. S. Watts	W. T. Snead	61101–61500, 84801–85200, 107601–10800, 111101–111500, 114701–115100, 131201–131600.
R. Bain	J. H. Harris	63101–63500, 98201–98800, 115101–115500.
P. B. Hooe	C. H. Johnson	70501–71300, 98801–99200.
Do	Tho. J. Miller	132001–132400.
W. G. Allen	C. S. Taylor	71301–72100, 77201–77600, 83201–83600, 87301–87700, 90001–90400, 92201–92600, 95801–96200, 101601–102000, 104501–104900, 106801–107100, 109901–110300, 113501–113900, 116701–117100, 117901–118300, 120501–120900, 122501–122900, 123701–124100, 124901–125300, 125701–126100, 127301–127800, 128601–129000, 132801–133200.
T. C. Gale	E. H. Smith	76201–76600, 80201–80600, 85201–85600, 91801–92200, 99201–99600, 131601–132000.
H. C. Shook	W. Y. Downman	77001–77200, 77601–78000, 79801–80200, 84001–84400, 86801–87300, 91301–91800, 93401–93900, 94801–95200, 97001–97400, 101201–101600, 104001–104500, 106101–106500, 108001–108200, 109501–109900, 112301–112700.
Do	C. Walthall	130401–130800.
E. C. Goddin	E. Nulty	79401–79800, 84401–84800, 99601–100000.
J. B. S. Dimitry	Wm. Nott	97401–97800.
T. W. Bell	W. B. Walston	97801–98200, 112701–113100.
J. W. Faxon	R. J. Delony	113101–113500.
O. M. Marshall	J. W. Eggleston	116301–116700, 117501–117900, 119101–119500, 119901–120300, 120901–121300, 121701–122500.
C. Ashford	S. Sinton	134401–134588, 134589 (A9), 134589–134591 (A 16), 134589–134593 (A11, 13, and 14), 134589–134594 (A10), 134589–134597 (A15).
		$10—H to K.
Jno. Ott	C. C. Thayer	1–1600, 2201–4700.
L. J. Levin	M. C. Riggs	1601–2200, 4701–11900, 13101–13400.
J. W. Jones	C. C. Thayer	11901–13100, 13901–16900, 17201–33000.
M. M. Young	M. C. Riggs	13401–13900, 16901–17200, 33301–55400.
Do	W. R. Robinson	55401–60000.
Do	S. Dutcher	60601–61400, 62601–63200.
R. M. Payne	M. Winston	60001–60600, 63201–65400, 68401–69200.
J. S. Lewis	J. P. Swords	61401–62600.
W. R. Todd	J. H. Cooke	65401–66100.
J. B. S. Dimitry	Wm. Nott	66101–68400, 69201–69600.

* Notes numbered 81006–81025 abstracted, therefore not regularly issued.

Register of Confederate States Treasury Notes—Continued.

ACT OF AUGUST 19, 1861—Continued.

For Treasurer.	For Register.	Numbers of the notes signed.
		$10—A to H.
J. W. Jones	C. C. Thayer	1–4200, 7201–7800, 9001–9800, 20701–21200.
Do	S. G. Tinsley	12201–12900, 14501–14900, 15301–15700, 16501–18100, 20501–20700.
J. C. Tennent	M. Winston	4201–5000, 29701–30500, 34501–34900, 35301–35800.
T. O. Keesee	T. Ellett	5001–5800.
A. W. Gray	T. L. Crouch	5801–6300, 6701–7200.
Jno. Ott	E. H. Smith	6301–6700.
E. W. Gills	W. Nott	7801–8200.
M. M. Young	M. C. Riggs	8201–9000, 9801–10600, 12901–13700, 14901–15300, 15701–16500, 18101–18900, 21201–22000, 23601–24000, 25701–26500, 27301–28100, 30501–31300, 34101–34500.
C. A. Baldwin	J. M. Kinney	10601–12200, 13701–14500, 18901–20500, 23001–23600, 24001–25700, 26501–27300, 28101–28900, 32101–32900.
F. W. Ashby	S. G. Tinsley	22001–22800, 35801–35826.
H. Kepler	R. J. Delony	22801–23000.
H. H. Goodloe	W. Rothrock	28901–29700, 31301–32100, 34901–35300.
J. S. Lewis	W. G. Dunbar	32901–33300.
R. M. Payne	R. Hill, jr	33301–34100.
W. L. Harvey	G. Johnston	35827 (H), 35827–35828 (E and F), 35827–35829 (A), 35827–35830 (B and G), 35827–35831 (C).
		$10—W to Z (number *red*).
J. W. Jones	C. C. Thayer	1–44679.
		$10—W to Z (number *black*).
J. W. Jones	C. C. Thayer	1–3800.
Do	J. O. Snyder	3801–5800, 36401–37000, 37401–38400, 45001–46000, 47901–49700, 52901–53900, 54701–55700, 56501–58500, 65901–66900, 68501–70800, 72401–73400, 74201–75200, 77401–80600, 81101–81900.
T. O. Keesee	T. Ellett	5801–6500, 17101–17900.
Do	T. L. Crouch	19501–20300, 24901–25700, 93701–94500, 104401–105200.
W. G. Allen	C. S. Taylor	6501–7300, 16301–17100, 24101–24900, 46201–47000, 49701–50500, 62701–63500, 89701–90500, 91301–92100.
A. S. Watts	W. T. Snead	7301–7700, 13501–13900, 25701–26300, 29501–30300, 44001–45000, 61901–62700.
T. C. Gale	E. H. Smith	7701–8500, 39201–40000.
H. Kepler	R. J. Delony	8501–9300, 30301–31200.
C. S. Maurice	Tho. J. Miller	9301–10100, 17901–19500, 27901–28700, 50501–51100, 51901–52100, 53901–54700, 55701–56500, 59101–59900, 76001–76600.
J. S. Lewis	W. G. Dunbar	10101–10900, 28701–29500, 40001–40800.
Do	J. P. Swords	90501–91300, 103401–103600, 124901–125700.
W. H. White	W. B. Walston	10901–11700.
H. C. Shook	W. Y. Downman	11701–12500, 23301–24100, 32801–33400, 38401–39200, 60701–61100, 63501–64300.
F. W. Ashby	S. G. Tinsley	12501–13500, 21101–22300, 35401–36400, 41601–42400, 114901–115700, 118301–119100, 120901–121700, 127701–128500.
E. C. Goddin	E. Nulty	13901–14300, 33401–34200.
M. M. Young	M. C. Riggs	14301–14700, 20301–21100, 26301–27100, 37001–37400, 47201–47900, 67701–68500.
Do	W. R. Robinson	81901–85300.
Do	S. Dutcher	87201–87800, 88701–88900, 92101–93700, 95301–95500, 97201–98000, 98801–99600, 102601–103400, 105201–106000, 106801–107400, 110401–111400.
H. C. Williams	J. M. Kinney	14701–15500, 64301–65100, 98001–98800, 99601–100400, 101401–102600, 106001–106800, 107401–110400, 111401–114900.
R. H. L. Tighe	W. H. Brown	15501–16300, 40801–41600, 47001–47200.
D. Lyon	J. T. Dickson	22301–23300, 31201–32000, 42401–43200, 61101–61900, 73401–74200, 76601–77400, 80601–81100, 85301–86200, 87801–88700, 96301–97200, 127301–127600.
T. D. Walford	T. F. Grayson	27101–27900, 125701–126500.
J. B. S. Dimitry	W. Nott	32001–32800, 88901–89700, 127601–127700, 128501–128600.
W. F. Hoge	C. W. Keim	34201–35000, 43201–44000, 51101–51900, 66901–67700, 115701–117300, 119101–119900, 121701–122500, 123501–124100, 126501–127300.
P. B. Hooe	C. H. Johnson	35001–35400, 46001–46200.
Do	Tho. J. Miller	117301–118300, 119901–120900, 122501–123300.

Register of Confederate States Treasury Notes—Continued.

ACT OF AUGUST 19, 1861—Continued.

For Treasurer.	For Register.	Numbers of the notes signed.
		$10—W to Z (number *black*)—Continued.
T. W. Bell	W. B. Walston	52101–52900, 71601–72400.
R. M. Payne	M. Winston	58501–59100, 70801–71600, 75201–76000, 94501–95300, 95501–96300, 100401–101400, 103601–104400.
J. W. Faxon	R. J. Delony	59901–60700, 65101–65900, 86201–87200.
J. Bunting	J. H. Hunt	124101–124900.
		$10—W to Z (number *black*), 2d series.
F. W. Ashby	S. G. Tinsley	1–800, 6101–6900, 8601–9400, 10201–11000.
J. B. S. Dimitry	W. Nott	801–1300, 7701–8500, 11801–12100.
F. H. Link	L. P. Rogers	1301–2100, 8501–8600.
T. J. Hatch	E. Nulty	2101–2900.
B. H. Berry	J. T. Holt	2901–3700.
C. Ashford	S. Sinton	3701–4500.
H. H. Goodloe	W. Rothrock	4501–5300.
O. M. Marshall	J. W. Eggleston	5301–6100.
T. C. Gale	E. H. Smith	6901–7700, 9401–10200, 11001–11800.
		$10—1 to 8 (1st series).
C. A. Baldwin	J. M. Kinney	1–500, 2201–2600, 2701–3100.
M. M. Young	M. C. Riggs	501–600, 1401–2200, 2601–2700, 3501–3900, 4701–5100, 6701–7100, 12001–12800, 14401–15200, 29101–29300, 33501–33900, 40901–41300, 45301-45700, 50101-50400, 52001-52300.
J. S. Lewis	W. G. Dunbar	601–1400, 3101–3500, 4301–4700, 5901–6300, 8401–8800, 16001-16800, 20801–21600, 31901–32700, 40501–40900, 55101-55500, 60901–61300.
P. B. Hooe	C. H. Johnson	3901–4300, 9201–9600, 41701–42100, 61301–61700.
C. S. Maurice	J. H. Harris	5101–5500, 7601–8000, 10801–11600.
Do	Tho. J. Miller	19201–20000, 25901–26700, 30901–31100, 43301–44100, 47501–48300, 50401–50900, 51701–52300, 59601–60000.
H. Kepler	R. J. Delony	5501–5900, 8001–8400, 10001–10800, 23401–24200, 49301-49400, 53701–54500.
W. H. White	R. J. Dorsey	6301-6700, 9601-10000, 27101-27500, 28301-29100, 46201–46300.
A. S. Watts	W. T. Snead	7101–7600, 12801–13600, 27501–27900, 29701–30000, 30801–30900, 34301–34600, 38401–38900, 41301–41700, 45701-46200, 58001–58400, 60501–60900.
H. C. Williams	J. M. Kinney	8801–9200, 18401–18800, 25501–25900, 30001–30800, 34601–35400, 42101–42500, 46601–47000, 48901–49300, 60001-60400.
D. Lyon	J. T. Dickson	11601–12000, 15201–16000, 20001–20800, 24601–25000, 31101–31900, 39701–40500, 44501–45300, 46301–46600, 48301-48900, 51301–51700, 52501–52700, 53101–53700, 55901-56500, 57201-57600, 60401–60500, 61701–61900.
T. D. Walford	T. F. Grayson	13601–14400.
W. G. Allen	C. S. Taylor	16801–17600, 23001–23400, 24201–24600, 29301–29700, 33901–34300, 42501–43300, 49401–49700, 54501–55000, 58801-59200.
H. C. Shook	W. Y. Downman	17601–18400, 21601–22400, 25001–25500, 27901–28300, 32701–33500, 37601–38400, 47001–47500, 49701–50100, 50901-51300, 52301–52500, 52701–53100, 56901–57200, 57601–58000.
R. M. Payne	R. Hill, jr	18801–19200, 22401–22600, 26701–27100, 36201–36800.
Do	M. Winston	44101–44500, 55501–55900.
E. C. Goddin	E. Nulty	22601–23000.
R. H. L. Tighe	W. H. Brown	35401–36200.
T. C. Gale	E. H. Smith	36801–37600, 59201–59600, 61900–61976.
R. Bain	J. H. Harris	38901–39700.
T. O. Keesee	T. Ellett	55001–55100, 56501–56900.
Do	T. L. Crouch	58401–58800.
W. L. Harvey	G. Johnston	91976 (duplicate), Nos. 1, 2, 3, 6, 7, and 8.
		$10—1 to 8 (2d series).
W. G. Allen	C. S. Taylor	1–400, 2001–2400, 3501–3600, 4401–4800, 9801–10200, 10801–11200, 12001–12400, 15101–15500, 17401–17800, 22301-22700, 25201-25600, 27401-27800, 28601-29000, 31601–32000, 33201–33600, 37201–37600, 40001–40400, 41101–41900, 43101-43500, 44701-45100, 46401–46800, 47901–48300, 51101–51500, 52301-53100, 55801–56200, 57801–58200, 59801–60200, 61801-62200, 63701–64100, 65701–66000, 66801–67200, 110901–111300.

Register of Confederate States Treasury Notes—Continued.

ACT OF AUGUST 19, 1861—Continued.

For Treasurer.	For Register.	Numbers of the notes signed.
		$10—1 to 8 (2d series)—Continued.
H. C. Shook	W. Y. Downman	401–800, 2401–2800, 5601–6000, 8001–8200, 8601–9000, 11201–11500, 12401–12800, 43901–44200.
Do	C. Walthall	15501–15800, 17801–18200, 21101–21400, 26901–27300, 28101–28600, 31301–31600, 32801–33200, 35201–35600, 37601-38000, 38901–39300, 40401–40700, 42301–42700, 48701–49000, 49901-50300, 51501–51900, 53501–53900, 54301–54700, 54901-55300, 55501–55800, 57401–57800, 68201–68600, 71201-71600, 74201-74600, 77401–77800, 79401–79800, 83001-83200.
Do	G. N. Warren	83201–83400, 86501–87000.
D. Lyon	J. T. Dickson	801–1200, 1801–2000, 6801–7200, 21401–21900.
J. W. Jones	J. O. Snyder	1201–1700, 10201–10400, 15001–15100, 23401–24000, 25601–26000.
T. D. Walford	T. F. Grayson	1701–1800, 2801–3200, 6401–6800, 15801–16200, 67801–68200, 70801–71200, 73801–74200, 76601–77000, 79801–80200, 84201-84600, 87401–87800, 90201–90600, 94501–94900, 101101–101400, 103001–103400, 104601–105000, 108601–108900, 115401–115500, 115801–116200, 119101–119400, 121401–121800.
A. S. Watts	W. T. Snead	3201–3500, 3601–4000, 12801–13200, 19001–19400, 21901-22300, 24801–25200, 29001–29400, 34401–34800, 36001–36400.
J. W. Faxon	R. J. Delony	4001–4400, 8201–8600, 10401–10800, 13201–13600, 16601-17000, 27301–27400, 27801–28100, 29401–29800, 30401-30900, 33601-34000, 36801–37200, 38401–38900, 41901–42300, 43501-43900, 44601–44700, 45501–46000, 46801–47300, 49401-49900, 54701-54900.
J. S. Lewis	W. G. Dunbar	4801–5200, 7601–8000, 16201–16600, 18601–19000.
Do	J. P. Swords	30201–30400, 30901–31300, 34001–34400, 36401–36800, 38001–38400, 39301–39700, 40701–41100, 42701–43100, 44201-44600, 46001–46400, 47301–47700, 49001–49400, 50701-51100, 51901-52300, 53901–54300, 55301–55500, 56601–57000, 58201–58600, 59401–59800, 60601–61000, 62201–62500, 62901-63700, 64901-65300, 64401–64800, 69401–69600, 72401–72800, 75401-75800, 78201–78600, 80201–80600, 85001–85400, 91001-91400, 95301-95700, 106201-106600, 107601-108000, 110101-110500, 116201-116600.
T. W. Bell	W. B. Walston	5201–5600, 19401–19800, 23001–23400.
H. C. Williams	J. M. Kinney	6001–6400, 11501–12000, 20201–20600, 24401–24800, 26401–26800, 32401–32800, 34801–35200, 73201–73400, 74601-75000, 79001–79400, 82601–82900.
Do	C. Walthall	82901–83000, 86201–86500, 89801–90200, 94101–94500, 99801–100200, 103801–104200, 105001–105400, 119401–119800.
M. M. Young	M. C. Riggs	7201–7600, 14601–15000.
F. W. Ashby	S. G. Tinsley	9001–9200, 70401–70800, 82201–82600, 85801–86200, 89401–89800, 93401–93800, 97701–98100, 101801–102100, 107201–107600, 109701–110100, 113701–114100, 114901–115300.
E. C. Goddin	E. Nulty	9201–9400, 14201–14600, 19801–20200.
W. F. Hoge	C. W. Keim	9401–9800, 14001–14200, 88201–88600, 91801–92200, 95701–96100.
C. S. Maurice	Tho. J. Miller	13601–14000, 17001–17400, 21001–21100.
T. C. Gale	E. H. Smith	18201–18600, 69601–70000, 72801–73200, 75801–76200, 77801–78200, 80601–81000, 120601–121000.
P. B. Hooe	C. H. Johnson	20601–21000, 26001–26400, 26801–26900, 29801–30200, 32001–32400.
Do	Tho. J. Miller	64501–64900, 66001–66400, 70001–70400, 85401–85800, 87801–88200, 92601–93000, 96501–96900, 100701–101100.
T. O. Keesee	T. L. Crouch	22701–23000, 39701–40000, 61001–61800, 108001–108200.
R. H. L. Tighe	W. H. Brown	24001–24400.
R. M. Payne	M. Winston	35601–36000, 57001–57400, 60201–60600, 62501–62900, 64101–64500, 65301–65700, 67201–67400, 69001–69400, 75001-75400, 77001–77400, 81001–81400, 83801–84200, 91401-91800, 96101-96500, 99401–99800, 102601–103000, 106601–107000, 108901–109300, 113301–113700, 115301–115400, 117401–117800, 122201-122300, 122489-122490 (No. 1), 122489-122491 (No. 4), 122489–122492 (No. 7), 122489–122493 (No. 2), 122489–122494 (No. 5), 122489–122495 (No. 3), 122489–122496 (No. 6).
W. L. Harvey	G. Johnston	45101–45500, 47701–47900, 48301–48700, 50301–50700, 53101–53500.

Register of Confederate States Treasury Notes—Continued.

ACT OF AUGUST 19, 1861—Continued.

For Treasurer.	For Register.	Numbers of the notes signed.
		$10—1 to 8 (2d series)—Continued.
O. M. Marshall	J. W. Eggleston	56201–56600, 58601–59400, 111301–111400, 112501–112900, 117001–117400, 118201–118600.
H. H. Goodloe	W. Rothrock	67401–67800, 71601–72000, 73401–73800, 76201–76600, 81401–81800, 83401–83800, 88601–89000, 92201–92600, 97301–97700, 110501–110900.
J. B. S. Dimitry	W. Nott	68601–69000, 96901–97300, 102101–102400, 104201–104600, 105401–105800, 120201–120600.
A. W. Gray	W. S. Gilman	72001–72400.
J. Bunting	J. H. Hunt	78601–79000, 81801–82200, 84601–85000, 87001–87400, 90601–91000, 94901–95300, 111801–112200.
T. W. Dickins	A. S. Watkins	89001–89400, 93801–94100.
J. H. Carr	R. A. Mills	93001–93400, 98101–98500.
F. H. Link	L. P. Rogers	98501–99000, 100201–100500, 100601–100700, 103501–103800, 111401–111800.
C. Leigh	E. Nulty	99001–99400, 100501–100600, 101401–101800, 102401–102600, 103401–103500, 105801–106200, 107001–107200, 108201–108600.
C. Ashford	S. Sinton	109301–109700, 112901–113300.
B. H. Berry	J. T. Holt	112201–112500, 114501–114900, 116601–117000, 121801–122200.
C. C. Bridges	W. S. Gilman	114101–114500, 117801–118200, 118601–119000.
F. C. Weisiger	W. P. Caldwell	115501–115800.
N. A. Bass	A. S. Watkins	119801–120200.
T. J. Hatch	E. Nulty	121001–121400, 122301–122488.
		$10—1 to 8 (3d series).
F. H. Link	L. P. Rogers	1–300, 2201–2600, 5801–6100, 6101 (Nos. 3, 4, 5, 6, 7, and 8), 6101–6106.
H. H. Goodloe	W. Rothrock	301–600, 3401–3800.
O. M. Marshall	J. W. Eggleston	601–900, 3801–4200.
B. H. Berry	J. T. Holt	901–1200, 4201–4600.
F. W. Ashby	S. G. Tinsley	1201–1500, 3001–3400.
R. M. Payne	M. Winston	1501–1900, 4601–5000.
J. S. Lewis	J. P. Swords	1901–2200, 5001–5400.
T. J. Hatch	E. Nulty	2601–3000.
C. Ashford	S. Sinton	5401–5800.
		$10—1 to 10 (4th series).*
H. C. Shook	G. N. Warren	1–400, 5601–5900, 9501–9800.
J. C. Joplin	S. Dutcher	401–800, 7001–7400, 10601–11000, 13801–14200, 18101–18500, 24901–25300, 30801–31200, 35301–35700, 40301–40700, 44501–44900, 49401–49800, 52401–52800.
F. H. Link	L. P. Rogers	801–1200, 17401–17800.
C. Ashford	S. Sinton	1201–1600, 7701–8000, 18801–19200, 26101–26400, 31601–31900.
N. A. Bass	A. S. Watkins	1601–1900, 9101–9500, 12001–12300, 14601–15000, 21301–21600, 25301–25700, 30201–30500, 36101–36500, 41001–41300, 46801–47200, 49801–50100, 52801–53100, 53101–53133 (No. 10), 53101–53140 (Nos. 1, 2, 3, 4, 5, and 9), 53101–53141 (Nos. 6, 7, and 8).
F. C. Weisiger	W. P. Caldwell	1901–2300, 6701–7000, 11001–11300, 13401–13800, 18501–18800, 26401–26700, 31201–31600.
J. Bunting	J. H. Hunt	2301–2600, 8001–8400, 11701–12000, 14201–14600, 20301–20600, 25701–26100, 30501–30800, 37101–37500.
B. H. Berry	J. T. Holt	2601–3000, 21601–22000, 40701–41000, 44901–45300, 49101–49400.
T. J. Hatch	E. Nulty	3001–3400, 17801–18100, 27001–27300, 36801–37100.
J. S. Lewis	J. P. Swords	3401–3800, 21001–21300, 24801–24900.
O. M. Marshall	J. W. Eggleston	3801–4200, 20601–21000.
J. H. Carr	R. A. Mills	4201–4500, 7401–7700, 12301–12700, 22001–22400, 26701–27000, 32301–32600, 39801–40000, 41601–41900, 47201–47500, 51001–51300.
C. C. Bridges	W. S. Gilman	4501–4800, 8701–9100, 15801–16200, 24101–24400, 28001–28400, 34301–34600, 38201–38600, 43801–44100, 45301–45700, 51301–51600.
H. H. Goodloe	W. Rothrock	4801–5200, 36001–36100, 40001–40300.

* Notes numbered 37801–38200, 43401–43800, and 46401–46800 were neither signed nor issued.

Register of Confederate States Treasury Notes—Continued.

ACT OF AUGUST 19, 1861—Continued.

For Treasurer.	For Register.	Numbers of the notes signed.
		$10—1 to 10 (4th series)—Continued.
J. W. Faxon	R. J. Delony	5201–5600, 10201–10600, 11301–11700, 15401–15800, 24401–24800, 29801–30200, 32801–33200.
J. W. Jones	J. O. Snyder	5901–6300, 9801–10200, 12701–13100, 17001–17400, 23401–23800, 28401–28800, 32601–32800, 39001–39400, 42601–43000, 47901–48300, 51601–52000.
W. R. Todd	J. H. Cooke	6301–6600, 8401–8700, 13101–13400, 23101–23400, 27301–27600, 33201–33600, 36501–36800, 41901–42300, 46101–46400, 50401–50700.
H. C. Williams	C. Walthall	6601–6700.
R. M. Payne	M. Winston	15001–15400, 19601–19900.
J. B. S. Dimitry	W. Nott	16201–16600, 23801–24100, 29101–29400, 35001–35300.
T. C. Gale	E. H. Smith	16601–17000, 22801–23100, 28801–29100, 33601–33900.
E. C. Goddin	J. M. Kinney	19201–19600, 22401–22800, 27601–28000, 33901–34300, 35701–36000, 38601–39000, 43001–43400, 47501–47900.
F. W. Ashby	S. G. Tinsley	19901–20300, 31901–32300.
A. W. Gray	W. Hancock	29401–29800, 34601–35000, 39401–39800, 44101–44500, 48701–49100, 52001–52400.
T. D. Walford	T. F. Grayson	37501–37800, 41301–41600, 45701–46100, 50101–50400.
W. G. Allen	C. S. Taylor	42301–42600, 48301–48700, 50701–51000.
		$10—I to P.
T. W. Dinkins	A. S. Watkins	1–400.
H. C. Williams	C. Walthall	401–800, 1201–1600, 4601–5000, 6601–7000, 10901–11300, 13801–14000, 18001–18400, 21001–21300, 21601–22400, 26701–27100, 28301–28700, 34701–35100, 46101–46500, 56101–56500, 59501–59900, 63901–64200, 70601–70700, 71901–72100, 74401–74600.
C. Leigh	E. Nulty	801–1200, 1601–1900, 5001–5400, 7001–7200, 7601–8400, 12201–12600, 15201–15600, 19201–19400, 21301–21600, 25001–25400.
C. Ashford	S. Sinton	1901–2200, 19801–20200, 31101–31500, 65401–65800, 67801–68200, 73401–73800, 77801–78200.
N. A. Bass	A. S. Watkins	2201–2700, 23001–23400, 27901–28300, 33901–34300, 36401–36800.
P. B. Hooe	Tho. J. Miller	2701–3100, 5801–6300, 10501–10900, 15601–16000, 18401–18800, 24201–24600.
E. C. Goddin	J. M. Kinney	3101–3600, 9701–10100, 77401–77800.
R. M. Payne	M. Winston	3601–3800, 4201–4600, 14001–14400, 16801–17200, 19401–19800, 32701–33000, 38001–38100, 39201–39600, 42101–42500, 44901–45300, 50501–50900, 53801–54200, 56501–56900, 59301–59500, 79401–79405, 79406–79409 (L), 79406–79410 (I, M), 79406–79411 (J, K, N, O), 79406–79412 (P).
T. D. Walford	T. F. Grayson	3801–4200, 5401–5800, 7201–7600, 12601–13000, 37601–38000, 42501–42900, 43701–44100, 49601–49700, 51301–51500, 52301–52700, 56901–57300, 58101–58500, 61501–61900, 74201–74400.
J. B. S. Dimitry	W. Nott	6301–6600, 18801–19200, 29101–29500, 35401–35600, 54201–54500, 67101–67500.
H. H. Goodloe	W. Rothrock	8401–8800, 20201–20600, 23801–24200, 25901–26300, 36801–37200, 39601–40000, 41301–41700, 45701–46100, 46801–47200, 50901–51300, 51501–51900, 55301–55700, 57701–58100, 59901–60300, 63501–63900, 66201–66600, 68201–68600, 71601–71900, 74601–75000.
T. C. Gale	E. H. Smith	8801–9200, 11301–11700, 14401–14800, 17601–18000, 24601–25000, 33401–33500, 35101–35400, 66601–67000, 69401–69800, 75801–76200.
F. W. Ashby	S. G. Tinsley	9201–9300, 10101–10500, 14801–15200, 47201–47600, 49701–50100, 67001–67100, 69001–69400, 77401–77800.
W. G. Allen	C. S. Taylor	9301–9700, 13401–13800, 16001–16400, 23401–23800, 28701–29100, 29501–29900, 37201–37600, 40001–40300, 41701–42100, 43301–43700.
H. C. Shook	G. N. Warren	11701–12200.
O. M. Marshall	J. W. Eggleston	13001–13400, 16401–16800, 20601–21000, 25501–25900, 26301–26700, 33501–33900, 42901–43300, 45301–45700, 47601–48000, 50101–50500, 53001–53400, 54501–54900, 58501–58900, 60301–60700, 62701–63100, 65801–66200, 69801–70200, 72101–72400, 79001–79400.
J. S. Lewis	J. P. Swords	17201–17600, 22401–22700, 25401–25500, 27101–27500, 31501–31900, 33001–33400, 36001–36400, 38801–39200, 40901–41300, 44501–44900, 48401–48800, 49201–49600, 53401–53800, 55701–56100, 58901–59300, 61101–61500, 61901–62300, 64201–64600, 70701–71000, 72701–73000, 75401–75800, 78601–79000.

Register of Confederate States Treasury Notes—Continued.

ACT OF AUGUST 19, 1861—Continued.

For Treasurer.	For Register.	Numbers of the notes signed.
		$10—I to P—Continued.
F. C. Weisiger	W. P. Caldwell	22701–23000, 30301–30700, 31901–32300, 35601–36000, 38101-38500.
T. J. Hatch	E. Nulty	27501–27900, 29901–30300, 32301–32700, 40301–40900, 44101-44500, 48001–48400, 48801–49200, 51901–52300, 54901-55300, 57301–57700, 60701–61100, 63101–63500, 64601-65000, 70201-70600, 72401–72700, 73801–74200, 76601–77000.
J. Bunting	J. H. Hunt	30701–31100.
C. C. Bridges	W. S. Gilman	34301–34700.
B. H. Berry	J. T. Holt	38501–38800, 46501–46800, 52701–53000, 68601–69000, 71301-71600, 75001–75400, 78201–78600.
F. H. Link	L. P. Rogers	62301–62700, 65001–65400, 67501–67800, 71001–71300, 73001-73400, 76201–76600.
		$5—A and B (number *black*)—Southern Bank Note Company.
H. H. Goodloe	T. Ellett	1–14700, 16301–16900.
R. H. L. Tighe	Tho. J. Miller	14701–15500.
L. J. Levin	M. C. Riggs	15501–16300.
J. W. Jones	R. J. Delony	16901*–18900.
F. W. Ashby	S. G. Tinsley	18901–19000, 19101–19400, 21101–21200, 21301–21500, 21801-21900.
T. O. Keesee	T. Ellett	19001–19100, 19401–19700, 20301–20500, 21900–22000.
A. W. Gray	T. L. Crouch	19701–20100.
R. M. Payne	R. Hill, jr	20101–20300, 20501–20600, 21201–21300, 21601–21800.
J. C. Tennent	M. Winston	20601–21100, 21501–21600.
		$5—C (number *black*)—Southern Bank Note Company.
H. H. Goodloe	T. Ellett	1–1900, 2301–3900, 4401–5600.
Do	C. C. Thayer	1901–2300, 3901–4400.
R. H. L. Tighe	Tho. J. Miller	5601–6400, 9701–11300.
A. W. Gray	S. G. Tinsley	6401–7200.
Jno. Ott	C. C. Thayer	7201–8400.
R. M. Payne	R. Hill, jr	8401–9200.
F. W. Ashby	T. L. Crouch	9201–9700.
J. C. Tennent	M. Winston	11301–12000.
T. O. Keesee	T. Ellett	12001–14860.
		$5—A (number *red*).
H. H. Goodloe	T. Ellett	1–10000.
		$5—Aa.
H. H. Goodloe	T. Ellett	1–10333.
		$5—Ab.
H. H. Goodloe	T. Ellett	1–7160.
		$5—H to K (number *black*).
A. W. Gray	T. L. Crouch	1–34189. †
		$5—H to K (number *red*).
A. W. Gray	T. L. Crouch	1–4400.
Do	W. S. Gilman	6001–6800, 8001–12000, 15101–16300, 18701–25300.
F. W. Ashby	S. G. Tinsley	4401–5200, 12801–13600, 17901–18700.
R. H. L. Tighe	W. H. Brown	5201–6000.
W. F. Hoge	C. W. Keim	6801–7600, 14401–15100.
E. C. Goddin	E. Nulty	7601–8000, 12001–12800.
H. H. Goodloe	W. Rothrock	13601–14400.
T. C. Gale	E. H. Smith	16301–17100.
P. B. Hooe	B. M. De Witt	17101–17900.
C. C. Bridges	W. S. Gilman	25301–25344.

* Notes A and B, Nos. 16901–18200, were numbered in *red*.

† From March 25, 1862 (No. 7801), the letters L, M, N, and O, were substituted for H, I, J, and K, and so continued through the series; but the letters H, I, J, and K, were kept upon the records.

Register of Confederate States Treasury Notes—Continued.

ACT OF AUGUST 19, 1861—Continued.

For Treasurer.	For Register.	Numbers of the notes signed.
		$5—W to Z.
A. W. Gray	T. L. Crouch	1-13900.
Do	W. S. Gilman	13901-21400, 21501-22600, 23401-24200, 25801-31800.
W. F. Hoge	C. W. Keim	21401-21500, 22601-23400, 25001-25800.
P. B. Hooe	B. M. De Witt	24201-25000.
C. C. Bridges	W. S. Gilman	31801-31822.
		$5—9A to 16A.
E. W. Gills	W. Nott	1-800, 901-2100, 2501-3300, 4501-9300, 10401-11200, 16701-17500, 20501-21600, 22101-22300, 23101-23300, 23401-23700, 24901-25000, 27301-27700.
A. W. Gray	T. L. Crouch	801-900, 2101-2500, 3301-4500, 9301-9600, 11201-12000, 15201-15900, 17501-18500, 22301-22500, 22801-23000, 26501-26900, 28901-29000, 40901-41700, 43701-44700, 54001-54200, 56001-56300, 79901-80300.
Do	W. S. Gilman	90201-90600, 93001-93200, 99901-100300.
W. H. White	W. H. Allen	9601-10400, 12001-12800.
Do	R. J. Dorsey	13601-14400.
Do	W. B. Walston	76301-76700, 81201-81600.
T. C. Gale	E. H. Smith	12801-13600, 14401-15200, 18501-19300, 22501-22800, 23701-24100, 25001-25500, 27701-28100, 29801-30200, 35701-36500, 47101-47900, 53201-53600, 57401-58200, 63801-64600, 72301-72700, 77901-78300, 89001-89400, 91801-92200, 95501-95900, 98701-99100, 102401-102800, 106101-106500, 109601-110000, 114001-114400, 117301-117700, 120201-120600, 123001-123400, 124501-124900, 131601-132000, 135601-136000, 138701-139100, 143901-144300, 148301-148700, 151901-152300, 160601-161000, 161901-162400, 165901-166300.
F. W. Ashby	S. G. Tinsley	15901-16700, 19301-19700, 33401-34200, 44701-45500, 49401-50700, 70601-71100, 85501-85900, 86601-87000, 89801-90200, 92601-93000, 97501-97900, 101101-101500, 117701-118100, 120601-121000, 123801-124100, 133201-133600, 139901-140100, 146701-147100, 149901-150300, 156601-156900, 164001-164300, 167201-167400.
J. C. Tennent	M. Winston	19701-20500, 21601-21900.
P. B. Hooe	C. H. Johnson	21901-22100, 23001-23100, 23301-23400, 24501-24900, 28101-28500, 30201-31000, 34901-35700, 41701-42500, 56301-56700, 57201-57400, 61301-61700, 63401-63800, 67401-67800, 68601-69000, 84701-85100, 87401-87800, 91401-91800, 94801-95100, 97101-97500, 99501-99900, 107301-107700, 149501-149900.
Do	B. M. De Witt	163601-164000, 166301-166700.
R. H. L. Tighe	W. H. Brown	24101-24500, 25501-25700, 26101-26500, 29001-29400, 52801-53200, 58501-59200, 62501-63000, 65401-66200, 72701-73500, 79101-79900, 82601-83100, 100701-101100, 104201-104600, 107701-108100, 110801-111200, 113101-113600, 116601-117000, 118501-119000, 121001-121400, 125201-125600, 130801-131200, 133601-134000, 139501-139900, 140501-140900, 145501-145900.
Do	G. Johnston	152301-152700, 153501-153900, 155801-156200.
H. H. Goodloe	W. Rothrock	25701-26100, 28501-28900, 42501-43300, 48201-48600, 52001-52800, 54201-55200, 64601-65400, 75101-75500, 97901-98300, 103601-103800, 105001-105300, 108901-109200, 114401-114700, 115101-115400, 118101-118500, 121401-121800, 125601-126000, 132401-132800, 134401-134800, 138301-138700, 141301-141700, 142701-143100, 146301-146700, 147101-147500, 151501-151900, 153101-153500, 154601-155000, 156901-157300, 158901-159300, 159501-159800, 161501-161900, 164301-164700, 166701-167100, 167401-167800.
E. C. Goddin	E. Nulty	26901-27300, 29401-29800, 31001-31400, 33001-33400, 37301-37800, 43301-43700, 46301-47100, 57101-57200, 61001-61300, 63001-63400, 67001-67400, 73501-73900, 76701-77100, 83901-84300, 85901-86200, 88601-89000, 91001-91400, 94401-94800, 95901-96300, 99101-99500, 103801-104200, 106501-106900, 110401-110800, 114701-115100, 115801-116200, 119801-120200, 122601-123000, 124901-125200, 128501-128900, 132001-132400, 136401-136600, 139101-139500, 144301-144700, 149101-149500, 152701-153100, 156201-156600, 158501-158900, 159801-160200, 163201-163600, 165501-165900.

Register of Confederate States Treasury Notes—Continued.

ACT OF AUGUST 19, 1861—Continued.

For Treasurer.	For Register.	Numbers of the notes signed.
		$5—9A to 16A—Continued.
H. C. Shook	W. Y. Downman	31401–32200, 38801–39600, 53601–54000, 69401–69700, 75501–75900, 129401–129800, 138201–138300.
D. Lyon	J. T. Dickson	32201–33000, 37801–38000, 59201–59800, 112101–112300.
W. F. Hoge	C. W. Keim	34201–34900, 39601–40100, 45501–46300, 50701–51200, 55201–56000, 59801–60600, 66201–67000, 70001–70600, 82201–82600, 84301–84700, 88201–88600, 96701–97100, 103201–103600, 110001–110400, 112701–113100, 115401–115800, 119001–119400, 122201–122600, 128101–128500, 137001–137400, 142101–142700, 144701–145100, 147901–148300, 150701–151100, 154301–154600, 155401–155800, 157701–158100, 160201–160600, 162801–163200, 164701–165100, 167101–167200, 168001–168100.
R. Bain	J. H. Harris	36501–37300, 40101–40900, 47901–48200, 48601–49400, 51201–52000, 56701–57100, 67801–68100, 81601–82200, 85101–85500, 86201–86600, 89401–89800, 92201–92600, 93601–94400, 96301–96700, 108101-108500, 111301-111700, 113601-114000, 116201–116600, 123401–123800, 131201–131600, 135201–135600, 137801–138200, 141701–142100, 143501–143900, 145901–146300, 147501–147900, 151101–151500, 153901–154300, 155001–155400, 158101–158500.
A. S. Watts	W. T. Snead	38001–38800, 58201–58500, 69701–70000, 74701–75100, 100301–100700, 102801–103200, 106901–107300, 111201–111300.
H. Kepler	R. J. Delony	60601–61000, 61701–62500, 74301–74700, 78301–78700.
H. C. Williams	J. M. Kinney	68101-68600, 78701-79100, 81101-81200, 101601-102000, 105701–106100, 111701–112100.
J. S. Lewis	W. G. Dunbar	69001–69400, 75901–76300, 80701–81100, 83101–83500, 87801–88200, 105301-105700, 108501-108900, 126001,126400, 129801–130000, 134801–135200, 136601–137000, 140101–140500.
W. G. Allen	C. S. Taylor	71101–71900, 112301–112700, 126801–127200, 132801–133200.
T. O. Keesee	T. Ellett	71901–72300, 77101–77500.
C. S. Maurice	Tho. J. Miller	73901–74300, 77501–77900, 136001–136400.
J. B. S. Dimitry	W. Nott	80301–80700, 83501–83900, 87001–87400, 90601–91000, 93201–93600, 95101–95500, 98301–98700, 102001–102400, 104601–105000, 109201–109600, 117001–117300, 119401–119800, 121801–122200, 130401–130800, 134001–134400, 137401–137800, 140901–141300, 143101–143500, 145101–145500, 148701–149100, 150301–150700, 157301–157700, 159301–159500, 161001–161500, 162401–162800, 165101–165500, 167801–16800.
T. D. Walford	T. F. Grayson	101501–101600, 124101–124500, 128901–129200.
J. W. Faxon	R. J. Delony	126401–126800.
T. W. Bell	W. B. Walston	127201–127600.
J. W. Jones	J. O. Snyder	127601–128100.
M. M. Young	M. C. Riggs	129201–129400.
R. M. Payne	M. Winston	130001–130400.
W. L. Harvey	G. Johnston	168101 (12A and 14A), 168102 (13A and 16A), 168103 (9A, 10A, 11A, and 15A).
		$5—9A to 16A (2d series).
W. F. Hoge	C. W. Keim	1–100, 3401–3800, 7101–7500, 10301–10700, 11901-12200, 14001–14400, 16901–17200, 20501–20900, 25301–25700, 26501-26900, 30401–30700, 30801–31300, 34501–34900, 37301–37700, 40101–40500, 43301–43700, 45701–46100, 48501–48900, 51501-51900, 54101–54500, 58101–58500, 61701–62100, 64401–64800, 67001–67400, 72401–72800, 76001–76400, 78801–79200, 81601-82000.
E. C. Goddin	E. Nulty	101–500, 4401–4800, 7501–7900, 10701–11100, 12201-12600, 15501–15900, 18501–18900, 19701–20100, 21401-21800, 23001–23400, 24901–25300, 27301–27700, 30001–30400, 32101-32500.
Do	J. M. Kinney	260601–261000, 275501–276000, 282301-282700, 287501–287900.
P. B. Hooe	C. H. Johnson	501–900, 4001–4400, 5201–5600.
Do	B. M. De Witt	8301–8700, 13001–13400, 14401–14800, 16101–16500, 18101–18500, 23701–24100, 25701–26100, 27701–28100, 29601-30000, 32901–33300, 36101–36500, 38901–39300, 41701-42100, 43701–44100, 47301–47700, 49701–50100, 52301–52700. 56101-56500, 59701–60100.
Do	Tho. J. Miller	62501–62900, 81201–81600.

Register of Confederate States Treasury Notes—Continued.

ACT OF AUGUST 19, 1861—Continued.

For Treasurer.	For Register.	Numbers of the notes signed.
		$5—9A to 16A (2d series)—Continued.
F. W. Ashby	S. G. Tinsley	901–1400, 2501–2800, 4801–5200, 5601–6000, 8701–9100, 11101-11500, 13401–13800, 16501–16900, 18901–19300, 21801-22200, 26101–26500, 28501–28800, 30701–30800, 33301-33700, 36501-36900, 39301–39700, 42101–42500, 44501–44900, 47701-48100, 50501–50700, 53101–53500, 56501–56900, 63301-63600, 65901-66200, 69001–69100, 71601–72000, 278201–278600, 284801-285200, 288601–289000.
J. B. S. Dimitry	W. Nott	1401–1700, 2801–3000, 6401–6700, 9101–9500, 11501–11900, 13801–14000, 15201–15500, 22601–23000, 53501-53700, 54901-55300, 58501–58900, 60901–61300, 65801–65900, 66601-67000, 69801–70200, 73201–73600, 76801–77200, 78401-78800, 83601-84000, 84401–84600, 246101–246500, 249601–250000, 252701-253100, 255901–256300, 263201–263600, 270401–270800.
H. C. Williams	J. M. Kinney	1701–2100.
T. C. Gale	E. H. Smith	2101–2500, 3001–3400, 7901–8300, 9901–10300, 12601–13000, 14801–15200, 15901–16100, 17601–18100, 20901-21400, 23401-23700, 24501–24900, 28101–28500, 29201–29600, 31301-31700, 35301–35700, 38101–38500, 41301–41700, 44901-45300, 46101-46500, 48901–49300, 51901–52300, 55301–55700, 58901-59300, 62101–62500, 64801–65000, 68201–68600, 70601-71000, 74801-75200, 78001-78400, 80801-81200, 84001-84400, 245701-246100, 249201–249600, 255501–255900, 261901–262300, 267801-268200, 276901–277300, 281001–281400, 286601–287000.
R. Bain	J. H. Harris	3801–4000.
C. S. Maurice	Tho. J. Miller	6001–6400.
H. H. Goodloe	W. Rothrock	6701–7100, 9501–9900, 17201–17600, 19301–19700, 20101-20500, 22201–22600, 24101–24500, 26901–27300, 28801-29200, 32501-32900, 33701–34100, 37701–38100, 39701–40100, 42501-42900, 46901–47300, 48101–48500, 50701–51100, 53701–54100, 56901-57300, 60101–60500, 63601–64000, 67401–67800, 69101-69400, 72001–72400, 75201–75600, 250401–250800, 255101–255500, 257101–257500, 267401–267800, 272501–272700.
A. W. Gray	W. S. Gilman	31701–32100, 34901–35300, 71001–71200, 74001–74400, 77201-77600, 80001–80400, 83201–83600.
Do	W. Hancock	262301–262800, 269901–270400.
T. D. Walford	T. F. Grayson	34101–34500, 36901–37300, 40901–41300, 42901–43300, 45301-45700, 49301–49700, 51101–51500, 54501–54900, 57301-57700, 61301–61700, 64001–64400, 66201–66600, 69401-69800, 72801-73200, 75601–76000, 79201–79600, 82001–82400, 84601-84800.
T. W. Bell	W. B. Walston	35701-36100, 38501–38900, 40501–40900, 44101–44500, 46501-46900, 50101–50500, 52701–53100, 55701–56100, 59301-59700, 62901–63300, 65401–65800, 68601–69000, 70201-70600, 74401-74800, 77601–78000, 80401–80800, 82401–82800.
A. S. Watts	W. T. Snead	57701–58100, 60501–60900, 65001–65400, 67801–68200, 71201–71600, 73601–74000, 76401–76800, 79601–80000, 82801-83200.
M. Allen	M. A. Gibb	84801-85600, 86401-87200, 93301-93700, 104701-105000, 105301-105700, 108001–108400, 111101–111300, 113501–113900, 116001–116400, 119301–119700, 123301–123700, 126101-126500, 129001–129100, 131301–131600.
Do	B. T. Lyon	140401–140800, 144201–144600, 148301–148700, 151601-152000, 155201–155600, 158601–159000, 161101–161500, 163701-164100, 167101–167600, 172301–172700, 174601–174900, 178701–179100, 183001–183400, 186601–187000, 190801-191200, 196301–196700, 220701–221100, 223901–224300, 227601–228000, 231301–231700, 235201–235600, 239101-239500, 243301–244000.
E. Mason	M. C. Lathrop	85601–86400, 87201–87600, 88401–88800, 89701–90100, 91401–91800, 94101–94500, 96301–96700, 98101–98500, 100901-101300, 103701–104100, 106701–107100, 109001–109400, 111301–111700, 114501–114900, 116401–116800, 119701-120100, 124601–125000, 127201–127600, 130001–130400, 133401–133800, 135701–136100, 138701–139100, 141401-141800, 144901–145300, 148701–149100, 152401–152800, 157901–158300, 159701–160100, 165401–165800, 168901-169300, 174201–174600, 174901–175300, 179801–180200, 185101–185500, 187301–187700, 191301–191700, 195401-195800, 201401–201800, 202801–203200, 206601–207000,

Register of Confederate States Treasury Notes—Continued.

ACT OF AUGUST 19, 1861—Continued.

For Treasurer.	For Register.	Numbers of the notes signed.
		$5—9A to 16A (2d series)—Continued.
E. Mason	M. C. Lathrop	212401-212800, 213701-214100, 217601-218000, 223101-223400, 225701-225800, 228401-228800, 233801-234200, 236001-236400, 239501-239900.
V. M. Rind	V. K. Davies	87601-88000, 88901-89300, 92401-93000, 98501-99100, 104101-104400, 107101-107400, 109401-109700, 112301-112600, 114901-115200, 118301-118600, 120101-120400, 123701-124000, 126901-127200, 129701-130000, 132701-133000, 136101-136400, 139401-139700, 141101-141400, 146701-147000, 165801-166100, 170601-170900, 172701-173000, 177801-178100, 181601-181900, 183401-183700, 189901-190200, 190501-190800, 197001-197300, 199701-200000, 203501-203800, 208001-208300, 213401-213700, 214401-214700, 219801-220100, 222001-222300, 225001-225300, 229401-229700, 231901-232200, 241401-241800.
A. Points	M. Gay	88001-88400, 89301-89700, 90901-91400, 93701-94100, 95901-96300, 97401-97800, 100201-100600, 103001-103400, 106001-106400, 110001-110400, 110701-111100, 115501-115700, 116801-117300, 118901-119300, 122601-123000, 125001-125500, 128401-128800, 132301-132700, 134401-134800, 139701-140100, 142101-142500, 145901-146300, 152001-152400, 155901-156300, 159001-159400, 162301-162700, 164701-165100, 168501-168900, 171601-172000, 176601-177000, 180601-181000, 184401-184800, 188301-188700, 193401-193800, 208601-209000, 211101-211500, 215101-215500, 218301-218700, 223401-223600, 232201-232600, 238601-238800, 240601-241000.
H. Bartlett	M. Taylor	88801-88900, 90501-90900, 91801-92000, 94501-94800, 96701-97100, 99401-99600, 101701-102400, 107401-107700, 108401-108700, 112001-112300, 113201-113500, 117901-118300, 121201-121500, 121901-122300, 126501-126900, 129401-129700, 133001-133400, 135101-135400, 137301-137700, 142801-143100, 145301-145600, 149701-150100, 153901-154200, 157201-157500, 157801-157900, 160501-160800, 161501-161900, 164401-164700, 167001-167100, 167901-168200, 172001-172300, 176201-176600, 179501-179800, 183701-184100, 189301-189600, 191701-192200, 196701-197000, 199301-199700, 204801-205100, 207001-207400, 212101-212400, 214701-215100, 218001-218300, 221601-222000, 225301-225700, 228101-228400, 233501-233800, 236601-236700, 236801-237100, 240201-240600.
R. F. Ball	L. M. Hunter	90101-90500, 92001-92400, 101301-101700, 104401-104700, 107701-108000, 109701-110000, 112601-112900, 115201-115500, 118601-118900, 121501-121800, 124301-124600, 127801-128100, 130401-130700, 133801-134100, 136401-136700, 138401-138700, 143701-144000, 148001-148300, 151001-151300, 154901-155200, 157501-157800, 160801-161100, 163401-163700, 166101-166400, 169901-170200, 173001-173300, 177501-177800, 181301-181600, 184101-184400, 188001-188300, 194101-194500, 198701-199000, 200601-200700, 201801-202000, 205101-205400, 209001-209300, 213101-213400, 216401-216700, 220101-220400, 222601-222900, 226401-226700, 230901-231100, 234501-234900, 238801-239100, 242701-243000.
E. C. Green	B. McRae	93001-93300, 95001-95300, 99101-99400, 99601-99900, 102401-102700, 105001-105300, 108701-109000, 110401-110700, 112901-113200, 115701-116000, 120601-120800, 121801-121900, 123001-123300, 125801-126100, 128801-129000, 130701-130800, 131901-132200, 134101-134400, 137701-138000, 144001-144200, 147701-148000, 149101-149400, 152801-153100, 155601-155900, 164101-164400, 168201-168500, 171301-171600, 175901-176200, 179101-179500, 185501-185700, 188701-189000, 192201-192400, 196001-196300, 200201-200600, 205701-206000, 209701-209900, 217401-217600, 223601-223900, 227201-227400.
S. F. Shaver	M. Dixon	94801-95000, 95601-95900, 97101-97400, 114201-114500, 117601-117900, 120401-120600, 121101-121200, 124001-124300, 127601-127800, 129101-129400, 131601-131900, 134801-135100, 137001-137300, 141801-142100, 145601-145900,

Register of Confederate States Treasury Notes—Continued.

ACT OF AUGUST 19, 1861—Continued.

For Treasurer.	For Register.	Numbers of the notes signed.
		$5—9A to 16A (2d series)—Continued.
S. F. Shaver	M. Dixon	146601–146700, 150101–150400, 153701–153900, 156601–156900, 163101–163400, 166701–167000, 169301–169500, 169601–169700, 173901–174200, 178101–178400, 182701–183000, 186001–186300, 189601–189900, 194501–194800, 198201–198400, 200701–201100, 202601–202800, 206001–206300, 210201–210500, 212801–213100, 215801–216100, 218701–218900, 221401–221600, 226101–226400, 229101–229400, 234201–234500, 237101–237400, 241801–242100.
R. Haynes	B. Dabney	95301–95600, 99901–100200, 103401–103700, 106401–106700, 130801–131000, 132201–132300, 140101–140400, 143101–143400, 147401–147700, 150401–150700, 153101–153400, 169501–169600, 169701–169900, 173601–173900, 178401–178700, 182401–182700, 186301–186600, 190201–190500, 194801–195100, 202301–202600, 205401–205700, 209301–209600, 217101–217400, 220401–220700, 226701–226900, 228001–228100, 231101–231300, 234901–235200, 238301–238600, 243001–243300.
L. C. Minor	B. M. Abbott	97801–98100, 100601–100900, 102701–103000, 105701–106000, 111701–112000, 113901–114200, 117301–117600, 120801–121100, 122301–122600, 125501–125800, 128101–128400, 131001–131300, 135401–135700, 140801–141100, 144601–144900, 149401–149700, 154601–154900, 156901–157200, 159401–159700, 161901–162300, 165101–165400, 167601–167900, 170901–171300, 175301–175600, 181001–181300, 184801–185100, 187701–188000, 192801–193100, 197301–197600, 206301–206600, 209601–209700, 210501–210800, 224401–224700, 242101–242400.
E. P. Porter	A. P. Pellet	136701–137000, 138001–138400, 142501–142800, 147001–147400, 151301–151600, 154201–154600, 156301–156600, 160101–160500, 162701–163100, 166401–166700, 170201–170600, 173301–173600, 175601–175900, 180201–180600, 189001–189300, 192401–192800, 197601–198200, 200001–200200, 204501–204800, 207401–207700, 211801–212100, 216101–216400, 219201–219500, 221101–221400, 224701–225000, 229701–230100, 232601–232900, 237401–237700, 241101–241400.
H. M. Douglass	F. C. Jones	139101–139400, 143401–143700, 146301–146600.
E. A. Dennison	J. L. Johnston	150701–151000, 153401–153700, 158301–158600, 177001–177500, 181901–182400, 185701–186000, 191201–191300, 193801–194100, 199001–199300, 204101–204500, 207701–208000, 211501–211800, 215501–215800, 219501–219800, 222901–223100, 225801–226100, 228801–229100, 233201–233500, 236401–236600, 242401–242700.
H. Graham	M. B. Kirby	187001–187300, 195101–195400, 198401–198700, 202001–202300, 203801–204100, 209901–210200, 216701–217100, 226901–227200, 230101–230600, 231701–231900, 235601–236000, 238001–238300.
M. S. Nicholas	J. McCarthy	193101–193400, 195801–196000, 201101–201400, 203201–203500, 208301–208600, 210801–211100, 214101–214400, 218901–219200, 222301–222600, 227401–227600, 230601–230900, 232901–233200, 237701–238000, 239901–240200.
S. G. Sanxay	L. Macon	224301–224400.
V. B. Briggs	J. B. Tiffey	236701–236800.
F. H. Link	L. P. Rogers	244001–244100, 247301–247600, 252001–252300, 253101–253500, 256301–256700, 264901–265300, 271301–271700, 279401–279800, 283601–284000, 288201–288600.
J. S. Lewis	J. P. Swords	244101–244500, 248001–248400, 252301–252700, 272701–272900, 277301–277700, 280601–281000, 287901–288100, 291101–291400.
B. H. Berry	J. T. Holt	244501–244900, 248401–248800, 250801–251200, 254301–254700, 257501–257900, 268701–269100, 273301–273800, 275101–275500, 278601–279000, 284001–284400, 289001–289400.
W. G. Allen	C. S. Taylor	244901–245300, 246501–246900, 247601–248000, 251601–252000, 253901–254300, 259201–259600, 262801–263200, 264501–264900, 272901–273300, 288101–288200.
R. M. Payne	M. Winston	245301–245700, 285601–285700, 291447–291464 (13A), 291447–291466 (12A), 291447–291469 (9A), 291447–291470 (10A, 11A, and 16A), 291447–291472 (15A), 291447–291473 (14A).

Register of Confederate States Treasury Notes—Continued.

ACT OF AUGUST 19, 1861—Continued.

For Treasurer.	For Register.	Numbers of the notes signed.
		$5—9A to 16A (2d series)—Continued.
C. Ashford	S. Sinton	246901-247300, 250001-250400, 254701-255100, 256701-257100, 266901-267400, 271701-272100, 279801-280200, 284401-284800, 289401-289800.
T. J. Hatch	E. Nulty	248801-249200, 251201-251600, 253501-253900, 258801-259200, 265301-265700, 274701-275100.
N. A. Bass	A. S. Watkins	257901-258000, 266501-266900, 274301-274700, 279001-279400, 286201-286600.
F. C. Weisiger	W. P. Caldwell	258001-258400, 265701-266100, 272101-272500, 282701-283100.
J. H. Carr	R. A. Mills	258401-258800, 269501-269900, 276501-276900, 281401-281800, 285701-286200, 289801-290200, 291401-291446.
W. R. Todd	J. H. Cooke	259601-260100, 266101-266500, 273801-274300, 280201-280600, 285201-285600, 290201-290600.
J. Bunting	J. H. Hunt	260101-260600, 264101-264500.
J. W. Jones	J. O. Snyder	261001-261500, 268201-268700, 276001-276500, 281801-282300, 287001-287500, 290601-291100.
C. C. Bridges	W. S. Gilman	261501-261900, 269101-269500.
J. C. Joplin	S. Dutcher	263601-264100, 270801-271300, 277701-278200, 283101-283600.
		$5—9A to 16A (3d series).
J. S. Lewis	J. P. Swords	1-100, 1801-1900.
T. C. Gale	E. H. Smith	101-500.
F. H. Link	L. P. Rogers	501-900.
B. H. Berry	J. T. Holt	901-1300, 1901-2200.
F. W. Ashby	S. G. Tinsley	1301-1800.
J. H. Carr	R. A. Mills	2201-2289.
		$5—A to H.
A. W. Gray	T. L. Crouch	1-500, 10001-11000, 14201-15200, 20301-20700, 22301-22800, 24401-25200, 51701-51800, 53201-53300, 58101-58300, 62701-63100.
E. W. Gills	W. Nott	501-8400, 15201-15700, 19901-20300, 21501-22300, 28801-29600, 35401-36200, 47601-48000, 50601-51000, 53301-53700, 56901-57300, 59501-59900, 63501-63900, 65101-65500.
F. W. Ashby	S. G. Tinsley	8401-9000, 9075-9100, 71901-73500, 82901-82973.
C. S. Maurice	do	9001-9074.
C. A. Baldwin	J. M. Kinney.	9101-9200, 34601-35400, 46801-47200, 51201-51400.
P. B. Hooe	R. V. Boykin	9201-10000, 12601-13400, 18701-19500.
Do	C. H. Johnson	25601-26400, 32201-33000, 49201-49600, 53701-54100, 57701-58100, 59901-60300, 61901-62300, 64701-65100, 67101-67900, 76701-77500, 81901-82700.
W. H. White	R. J. Dorsey	11001-11800, 17901-18700, 26401-27200, 37001-37800, 44701-45100, 48001-48400, 52001-52400, 75901-76700.
T. C. Gale	E. H. Smith	11801-12600, 16501-17300, 19501-19900, 23201-23600, 29601-30400, 36201-37000, 43901-44300, 47201-47600, 51401-51700, 57301-57700, 59101-59500, 61501-61900, 64301-64700, 66201-66600, 77501-78300, 82701-82900.
R. H. L. Tighe	R. V. Boykin	13401-14200.
Do	W. Nott	15701-16500.
Do	W. H. Brown	20701-21500, 42301-43100, 51801-52000, 54101-54500, 55701-56100, 58701-59100, 61101-61500, 63101-63500, 68701-69100, 75101-75900.
T. O. Keesee	T. Ellett	17301-17900, 24001-24400, 30601-31400, 38201-39000, 46501-46800, 52401-52700.
J. S. Lewis	W. G. Dunbar	22801-23200, 28001-28800, 37801-38200, 48401-48800, 51001-51200, 56101-56500.
H. Kepler	R. J. Delony	23601-24000, 39501-40000, 46101-46500, 50401-50600, 52901-53200.
H. H. Goodloe	W. Rothrock	25201-25600, 27201-28000 (A and B), 33801-34600, 43101-43900, 54901-55700, 60301-60700, 62301-62700, 65501-65800, 66601-67100, 69501-69900, 71101-71900, 78301-79100.
Do	T. Ellett	27201-28000 (C, D, E, F, G, and H).
M. M. Young	M. C. Riggs	30401-30600, 31401-32200, 40001-40800.
A. S. Watts	W. T. Snead	33001-33800, 41501-42300, 50001-50400, 52701-52900, 80701-81100.
R. M. Payne	R. Hill, jr	39001-39500, 49601-50000.
J. C. Tennent	M. Winston	40801-41500, 45101-45700.

Register of Confederate States Treasury Notes—Continued.

ACT OF AUGUST 19, 1861—Continued.

For Treasurer.	For Register.	Numbers of the notes signed.
		$5—A to H—Continued.
T. D. Walford	T. F. Grayson	44301–44700, 48801–49200, 73501–74300.
E. C. Goddin	E. Nulty	45701–46100, 54501–54900, 56501–56900, 58301–58700, 60701-61100, 63901–64300, 65801–66200, 69101–69500, 69901–70700, 79101–79900.
D. Lyon	J. T. Dickson	67901–68700.
W. F. Hoge	C. W. Keim	70701–71100, 79901–80700.
H. C. Williams	J. M. Kinney	74301–75100.
W. L. Harvey	G. Johnston	82974–83081 (D), 82974–83088 (A), 82974–83095 (B, E, and G), 82974–83096 (F), 82974–83097 (C).
		$5—1 to 8 (2d series).
T. C. Gale	E. H. Smith	1–600, 6201–6600, 8601–9400, 13401–13800, 17301-17700, 20201-21000, 31501–31900, 38401–38800, 42201–42333.
R. H. L. Tighe	W. H. Brown	601–1400, 5201–5800, 9801–10600, 16501–17300, 22001–22800, 33501–33800, 40101–40500, 41301–41500.
H. H. Goodloe	W. Rothrock	1401–2400, 26401–27200, 31301–31400, 39401–39700.
W. H. White	R. J. Dorsey	2401–2800.
Do	W. B. Walston	15301–15700.
A. S. Watts	W. T. Snead	2801–3600, 17901–18300.
W. F. Hoge	C. W. Keim	3601–4000, 6601–7000, 12101–12500, 16101–16500, 27201-27700, 34601–35000, 37601–38000, 40501–40900.
R. Bain	J. H. Harris	4001–4400, 9401–9800, 10601–10900, 12501–13400, 15701-16100, 18301–19100, 21801–22000, 23901–24500, 30101-30700, 36201-36300, 40901–41300.
E. C. Goddin	E. Nulty	4401–4800, 7801–8600, 19601–20000, 21001–21400, 25601–26000, 32301–32700, 37201–37600.
W. G. Allen	C. S. Taylor	4801–5200, 10901–11300, 23501–23900, 29701–30100.
P. B. Hooe	C. H. Johnson	5801–6200, 7001–7800, 14501–15300, 20001–20200, 21401-21800, 28501–28900, 33101–33500, 38001–38400, 39201–39400.
D. Lyon	J. T. Dickson	11301–12100.
H. Kepler	R. J. Delony	13801–14500, 22801–23200, 28901–29700, 31901–32300.
F. W. Ashby	S. G. Tinsley	17701–17900, 25001–25600, 33801–34200, 35801–36200, 38801-39200.
A. W. Gray	T. L. Crouch	19101–19600.
Do	W. S. Gilman	30901–31300, 35001–35400.
H. C. Williams	J. M. Kinney	23201–23500, 32701–33100.
R. M. Payne	M. Winston	24501–24600, 31401–31500, 41501–41600.
H. C. Shook	W. Y. Downman	24601–25000, 30701–30900.
J. S. Lewis	W. G. Dunbar	26001–26400, 35401–35800.
T. O. Keesee	T. Ellett	27701–28100.
C. S. Maurice	Tho. J. Miller	28101–28500.
J. B. S. Dimitry	W. Nott	34201–34600, 36301–37200, 39701–40100, 41601–42000.
M. M. Young	M. C. Riggs	42001–42200.
W. L. Harvey	G. Johnston	42334 (Nos. 2, 5, 6, 7, and 8).

ACT OF APRIL 17, 1862.

Date of issue.		Numbers of the notes signed.
1862.		**$100**—A, and Ab to Ah.
May	5	1–200, 401–500, 701–800.
	6	201–400, 601–700, 1101–1200.
	7	501–600, 901–1000, 1201–1300.
	8	801–900, 1001–1100, 1401–1500, 1901–2000.
	9	1301–1400, 1501–1900, 2001–2500.
		$100—Aa to Ah.
June	4	3501–3900.
	5	2701–2900, 3901–4300.
	6	2901–3000, 4301–4400.
	7	2501–2700, 3001–3500.

Register of Confederate States Treasury Notes—Continued.

ACT OF APRIL 17, 1862—Continued.

Date of issue.	Numbers of the notes signed.
1862.	**$100**—Aa to Ah—Continued.
June 9	4401–4700.
13	5501–5800.
14	5301–5500, 6701–6900.
16	5201–5300, 7701–7900, 8601–8800.
17	4701–5000, 5801–6200, 6601–6700, 6901–7300, 7401–7500, 11101–11200.
18	7501–7700, 7901–8200, 9001–9300, 9801–10000.
19	7301–7400, 8201–8300, 8801–9000, 9301–9400, 10001–10100, 10301–10500, 11301–11400.
20	10601–10700, 10801–10900, 11000–11100, 11401–11500, 11801–12100, 12201–12400, 12501-12600, 12901–13000.
21	9601–9800, 10100–10200, 10701–10800, 11501–11800, 12801–12900, 13901–14000.
23	13301–13400, 14101–14200, 14501–14600.
24	8301–8600, 9401–9600, 10201–10300, 10901–11000, 12401–12500, 12601–12800, 13001–13100, 13201–13300.
25	6301–6500, 13401–13800, 14201–14300, 14401–14500.
26	5001–5100, 6501–6600, 11201–11300, 12101–12200, 13101–13200, 14701–14800.
27	10501–10600, 13801–13900, 14001–14100, 14301–14400, 14601–14700, 14801–15100.
28	15101–15300.
29	15601–15700, 16001–16100, 16801–16874.
30	15301–15600, 15701–15800, 16101–16400, 16875–17100, 17201–17900.
July 2	15801–15900, 16601–16700, 17101–17200, 18101–18200.
3	15901–16000, 16401–16500, 18401–18500.
4	5101–5200, 6201–6300, 16501–16600.
5	16701–16800, 18001–18100, 18201–18300, 18701–18900.
7	19101–19200.
8	19701–19800.
9	18501–18600, 19301–19600, 19801–19900.
10	18301–18400, 18601–18700, 19201–19300, 19601–19700, 20301–20400.
11	22301–22400.
14	18901–19100, 19901–20300, 20401–20600, 20901–21000.
21	21301–21500, 21601–21700, 22701–22800, 23201–23300, 24701–24900, 25101-25400, 26101-26200.
22	21101–21200, 21701–21900, 25701–25800.
24	17901–18000, 20801–20900, 21501–21600, 23301–23400, 23901–24000, 25401–25600, 26001-26100, 26701–26900.
25	21001–21100, 21201–21300, 22101–22200, 22901–23000, 25801-26000, 26301-26400, 26501-26700.
28	20601–20800, 21901–22000, 22201–22300, 22401–22500, 22801–22900, 25601-25700, 26201-26300, 26401–26500, 26901–27200.
August 1	22001–22100, 22501–22700, 23001–23200, 23401–23900, 24001–24200, 24901–25100.
2	27201–27400, 27601–28000, 28301–28400, 28501–28600.
4	28001–28300, 28401–28500, 29201–29600.
5	27401–27600.
8	24201–24700, 28601–28900.
9	28901–29200, 30001–30400.
12	29601–29900, 30401–30700, 30801–30900, 31301–31400, 31801–32000, 32101–32200.
13	29901–30000, 30701–30800, 30901–31300, 31401–31800, 32001–32100, 32201–32300.
14	32301–32400, 32501–32900, 33001–33300, 33501–33700, 33801–34000.
15	32401–32500, 32901–33000, 33301–33500, 33701–33800.
16	34001–34800.
18	34801–35600.
19	35601–35900, 36001–36400.
20	35901–36000, 36401–37500.
23	37501–38300.
24	38301–39100.
28	39101–39500.
September 1	39501–40000, 40101–41000.
2	40001–40100, 41001–41200, 41201–41600 (Aa to Af).
6	41201–41600 (Ag and Ah).
8	41601–42700.
11	42701–43700, 43801–44300.
12	43701–43800, 44301–46300.
15	46301–47500.
18	47501–49300.
20	49301–50100, 50501–50900.
23	50101–50500, 51501–51600, 51701–51800, 51901–52000.
25	51101–51500, 51601–51700.
October 1	50901–51100, 51801–51900, 53201–53500, 53601–54000, 54401–54500.

Register of Confederate States Treasury Notes—Continued.

ACT OF APRIL 17, 1862—Continued.

Date of issue.	Numbers of the notes signed.
	$100—Aa to Ah—Continued.
1862.	
October 2	53501–53600, 54001–54400, 54501–59100.
6	59101–59900.
11	59901–61900.
15	61901–62600.
18	62601–63000, 63501–64300.
22	63001–63400, 64301–65000.
25	63401–63500.
1863.	
January 6	65001–65700, 66101–67300, 67401–67800.
8	65701–66100, 67301–67400, 68201–69900.
	$100—W to Z.
1862.	
August 26	1–1800.
28	2201–3800.
30	1801–2200, 3801–7200.
September 1	7201–8000.
2	8001–8400.
6	8401–11600.
8	11601–11900.
12	11901–12700.
18	12701–13700, 49101–49300.
23	14701–15600, 51501–51600, 51701–51800, 51901–52300.
24	15601–16400.
25	16401–19800, 51601–51700.
27	13701–14500, 19801–21500.
29	14501–14700, 21501–21800, 21901–23000, 23101–23700, 23801–24000.
October 1	51801–51900.
2	21801–21900, 23001–23100, 23701–23800, 24001–24700.
17	30901–31100.
22	24701–25400.
25	25401–29300.
29	29301–30900, 31101–36300.
November 3	37101–42700.
5	36301–37100, 42701–44300.
6	44301–47500.
10	49301–49900, 50401–50600.
20	53901–55500, 55601–58400, 60301–67600, 69201–69400.
24	47501–49100, 49901–50400, 50601–51500, 68401–69200, 69401–73400.
27	52301–53900, 55501–55600, 58401–60300, 67601–68000, 73401–78200, 79001–80600.
29	83001–84100.
December 1	78201–79000, 80601–83000, 84601–86200, 87001–88600.
4	89401–92600.
8	92601–96900, 97001–99800.
11	99801–103200, 103801–105400.
15	96901–97000, 103201–103800, 105401–116800, 117701–118500.
18	116801–117700, 118501–126600, 126901–127700.
20	135001–135200.
22	84101–84600, 86201–87000, 88601–89400, 126601–126900, 127701–134600, 135201–137700.
23	137701–140900.
26	134601–13500, 140901–143600.
27	147401–150100.
29	143601–147400.
30	150101–152500, 153301–154300.
31	152501–153300, 154301–155700, 155901–156000.
1863.	
January 1	156801–158400.
2	159401–161000.
3	155701–155900, 158401–159400.
5	156001–156800, 161001–164200, 165801–166600.
6	164201–165800, 166601–167600.
—	68001–68400.

Register of Confederate States Treasury Notes—Continued.

ACT OF APRIL 17, 1862—Continued.

For Treasurer.	For Register.	Numbers of the notes signed.
		$100—A and Ab to Ah.
R. M. Payne	R. Hill, jr	1–400, 1501–1900.
J. C. Tennent	M. Winston	401–500, 1101–1500.
H. Kepler	R. J. Delony	501–700, 1001–1100, 2101–2500.
C. S. Maurice	Tho. J. Miller	701–1000, 1901–2100.
		$100—Aa to Ah.
H. Kepler	R. J. Delony	2501-2700, 4301-4700, 7401–7800, 8601-9000, 9801-10500, 11301-12100, 12901–13300.
A. S. Watts	W. T. Snead	2701–3500, 4701–5000, 5901–6100, 7001–7400, 8201-8600, 10501-11200, 13301–13700, 14501–15200, 15601–16000, 17201-17600, 19101–19500, 20701–21100, 22001–22500, 22801–23000, 23601-24000, 26601–26900, 29201–29600, 30001–30800, 31801-32200, 33701–34000, 35201–35600, 40501–40900, 64701-65000, 65701-66100, 67801–68200. *
T. O. Keesee	T. Ellett	3501–4300, 5201–5500, 5801–5900, 11201–11300, 12501–12900, 13701–14100.
Do	J. T. Dickson	66101–66500, 68601–69000.
T. D. Walford	T. F. Grayson	5001–5200, 6201–6600, 16001–16400, 17601–18000, 28401-28600, 37201–37900, 39101–39500, 39701–40100, 40901-41600, 42301-42700, 43101–43900, 44701–45500, 47101–47900, 49101-49700, 50501–50900, 51501–51800, 51901–52300, 52701-53600, 54401-54800, 66501–66900, 68201–68600.
W. H. White	R. J. Dorsey	5501–5800, 6101–6200, 6601–7000, 7801–8200, 9001-9800, 12101-12500, 14101–14500, 15201–15600, 16801–17200, 18701-19100, 19901–20300.
H. C. Williams	J. M. Kinney	16401–16800, 18001–18700, 20301–20700, 21101–21600, 22501-22800, 23301–23400, 24001–24200, 25701–26100, 26301–26600, 26901–27200, 28801–29200, 29601–30000, 33301-33700, 34001-34400, 36001–36400, 38301–38700, 44301–44700, 45501-45900, 46701–47100, 48301–48700, 50901–51100, 51801–51900, 54001-54400, 55901–56300.
W. F. Hoge	C. W. Keim	19501–19900, 32901–33300.
P. B. Hooe	C. H. Johnson	21601–22000, 27601–28000.
Do	Tho. J. Miller	63901–64700.
W. G. Allen	C. S. Taylor	23001–23300, 24701–24900, 25401–25700, 31201–31600, 32201-32600, 67401–67800, 69501- 69900.
R. Bain	J. H. Harris	23401–23600, 24901–25400, 26101–26300.
R. M. Payne	M. Winston	24201–24700.
E. C. Goddin	E. Nulty	27201–27600, 57101–57500, 63501–63900.
T. C. Gale	E. H. Smith	28001–28400, 28601–28800.
A. W. Gray	W. S. Gilman	30801–31200, 31601–31800, 34801–35200.
Do	W. Hancock	65001–65300, 66901–67400, 69001–69500.
J. W. Jones	J. O. Snyder	32601–32900.
T. W. Bell	W. B. Walston	34401–34800, 35601–36000, 36401–37200, 37901–38300, 38701-39100, 39501–39700, 41601–42300, 42701–43100, 43901-44300, 45901–46700, 47901–48300, 48701–49100, 49701-50500, 51101-51500, 53601–54000, 55501–55900.
M. M. Young	M. C. Riggs	40101–40500.
W. L. Harvey	G. Johnston	52301–52700, 55101–55500, 56301–56700, 57501–63500.
D. Lyon	J. T. Dickson	54801–55100.
H. C. Shook	C. Walthall	56701–57100.
O. M. Marshall	W. B. Walston	65301–65700.
		$100—W to Z.
T. W. Bell	W. B. Walston	1–800, 1801–2200, 10001–10800, 11601–12700, 19001–19800, 22301–23100.
H. C. Williams	J. M. Kinney	801–1600, 3001–4600, 5601–6400, 10801–11600, 13101–14700, 24901–25700.
T. D. Walford	T. F. Grayson	1601–1800, 5401–5600, 7201–10000, 12701–13100, 15601–16400, 94201–95000, 96601–97400, 99001–99800, 101401–102200, 104601–105400, 107001–107800, 111101–111900, 114401-115200, 117701–118500, 119301–120100, 123601–124400, 126901–127700, 130101–130900, 133401–134200, 135201-136000, 138501–139300, 141701–142500, 145701–146500, 149301–150100, 150901–151500, 154101–155000, 157601-158400, 160201–161000, 163401–164200, 166601–167400.

* Notes numbered 67801–68200 were destroyed January 24, 1863.

Register of Confederate States Treasury Notes—Continued.

ACT OF APRIL 17, 1862—Continued.

For Treasurer.	For Register.	Numbers of the notes signed.
		$100—W to Z—Continued.
A. S. Watts	W. T. Snead	2201–3000, 4601–5400, 6401–7200, 24701–24900, 25701–26500, 27301–28100, 28501–29300, 30901–32500, 33301-34100, 34701-35500, 36301–37100, 38701–39500, 40301–41100, 41901-42700, 43501–44300, 45101–45900, 46701–47500, 48301-49100, 49901-50700, 51501–52300, 54701–55500, 56301–57100, 57901-58700, 59501–60300, 61101–61900, 62701–63500, 64901-65700, 66001-66800, 68401–69200, 72601–73400, 74201–75000, 75801-76600, 79001–79800, 81401–82200, 83001–83800, 85401-86200, 87801-88600, 90201–91800, 92601–93400, 95001–95800, 97401-98200, 100601–101400, 103801–104600, 105401–106200, 109501-110300, 111901–112700, 116001–116800, 118501–119300, 122001–122800, 125201–126000, 129301–130100, 132601-133400, 136001–136800, 139301–140100, 140901–141700, 144101–144900, 147501–148300, 150101–150900, 153301-154100, 156001–157600.
D. Lyon	J. T. Dickson	14701–15600, 16401–17300, 18101–19000, 19801–20700, 23101-24300, 32501–33300.
W. L. Harvey	G. Johnston	17301–18100, 20701–22300, 26501–27300, 28101–28500, 29301-30900, 34101–34700, 35501–36300, 37101–38700, 39501-40300, 41101–41900, 42701–43500, 44301–45100, 45901-46700, 47501-48300, 49101–49900, 50701–51500, 52301–54700, 55501-56300, 57101–57900, 58701–59500, 60301–61100, 61901-62700, 64101-64900, 66801–68400, 69401–70200, 71001–71800, 73401-74200, 76601–77400, 78201–79000, 80601–81400, 84601-85400, 87001-87800, 89401–90200, 91801–92600, 93401–94200, 95801-96600, 98201–99000, 99801–100600, 102201–103000, 106201–107000, 110301–111100, 112701–113500, 115201–116000, 120101-120900, 122801–123600, 124401–125200, 128501–129300, 131801–132600, 136801–137600, 137701–138500, 143301-144100.
T. O. Keesee	T. L. Crouch	24301–24700, 63501–64100, 65701–66000, 69201–69400, 70201-71000, 71801–72600, 75001–75800, 77401–78200, 79801-80600, 82201-83000, 83801-84600, 86201-87000, 88601-89400, 135001-135200, 137601–137700, 140101–140900, 142501–143300, 144901–145700.
Do	J. T. Dickon	162601–163400, 165001–165800.
N. A. Bass	A. S. Watkins	103001–103800, 107801–109500, 113501–114400, 116801-117700, 121101–122000, 126001–126900, 127701–128500, 130901-131800, 134201–135000.
W. G. Allen	C. S. Taylor	120901–121100, 147401–147500, 148301–149300, 151501-153300, 155001–155700, 155901–156000, 159401–160200, 161001-161800, 164201–165000.
A. W. Gray	W. Hancock	146501–147400, 155701–155900, 158401–159400, 167401-167600.
O. M. Marshall	W. B. Walston	161801–162600, 165801–166600.
		$2—1 to 10 (1st series).
H. Graham	M. B. Kirby	1–100, 1001–1100, 1401–1500, 2601–2800, 5801–5900, 6001-6100, 7501–7600, 7701–7800, 10701–10800, 11401–11500, 11901-12000, 15701–15900, 17501–17600, 17701–17800, 19101-19300, 19401–19500, 20301–20500, 20601–20700, 21601-21700, 21801-22000, 22501–22600, 23101–23300, 25001–25100, 26901-27000, 28901–29100, 30401–30500, 31201–31400, 36701-37200, 39301-39700, 41301–41500, 41801–42100, 42701–43000, 44201-44500.
M. S. Nicholas	M. A. Saunders	101–200, 1201–1300, 1701–1900, 3801–3900, 5301–5500, 6401-6500, 7801–7900, 8301–8400, 10301–10500, 12601–12700, 13101–13200, 14501–14600, 15001–15200, 23301-23400, 25101-25200, 25301–25400, 26801–26900, 27301–27500, 29101-29400, 33501–33700, 42301–42500, 43501–43700, 44601–44800.
E. D. Layne	V. C. Watson	201–300, 1501–1600, 3101–3200, 4201–4300, 5701–5800, 7201-7300, 8001–8100, 8801–8900, 12901–13000, 13801–13900, 15201–15300, 16101–16200, 16801–17000, 17601-17700, 18301-18500, 19801–20000, 21401–21600, 22801–23000, 24901-25000.

Register of Confederate States Treasury Notes—Continued.

ACT OF APRIL 17, 1862—Continued.

For Treasurer.	For Register.	Numbers of the notes signed.
		$2—1 to 10 (1st series)—Continued.
K. Heth	M. E. Gilliam	301–400, 1101–1200, 2301–2500, 3601–3700, 4901–5100, 7301-7500, 8401–8500, 9401–9500, 9601–9700, 11301–11400, 12401-12600, 13901–14000, 15501–15700, 16201–16300, 18601-18900, 20001–20300, 24701–24900, 26501–26700, 27801-28100, 30101-30400, 31001–31200, 32001–32200, 32701–33300, 34101-34300, 34801–35000, 35401–35600, 36301–36500, 38001-38200, 39001-39200, 40601–40700, 42501–42700, 43301–43500, 45101-45300.
M. T. Mayo	M. C. Lathrop	401–500, 2001–2200, 3401–3500, 3901–4200, 6701–7000, 9101-9200, 9501–9600, 10501–10700, 10901–11000, 11701–11900, 13201–13400, 15301–15500, 16301–16400, 23701-23900, 26101-26300, 28501–28800, 45401–45600.
H. Bartlett	S. A. Randolph	501–600, 1301–1400, 2201–2300, 3001–3100, 3701–3800, 5101-5300, 7001–7200, 8501–8600, 9201–9300, 11001–11100, 12201-12400, 13401–13600, 14601–14800, 21001–21200, 22301-22400, 24501–24700, 26301–26500, 27501–27800, 29901-30100, 30801-31000, 31801–32000, 32501–32700, 33701–33900, 34601-34800, 35001–35200, 36101–36300.
Do	M. Taylor	37601–37800, 38801–39000, 40301–40500, 40701–41000, 41601-41800, 43901–44200.
V. M. Rind	V. K. Davies	601–700, 1601–1700, 3201–3300, 4501–4700, 6501–6700, 8101-8200, 9301–9400, 9801–9900, 11201–11300, 12701–12900, 14301–14500, 16401–16601, 23901–24100, 25701-25900, 28101-28300, 35201–35400, 35701–35900, 37801–38000, 45301-45400.
R. F. Ball	L. M. Hunter	701–800, 2501–2600, 3301–3400, 4701–4900, 6101–6200, 7601-7700, 8601–8700, 10801–10900, 12001–12200, 14001–14200, 16001–16100, 18901–19100, 21201–21400, 22601–22800, 24101-24300, 25201–25300, 25901–26100, 28301–28500, 33001-33200, 33901–34100, 36501–36700, 38201–38400, 39701–39900.
M. Allen	M. A. Gibb	801–900, 1901–2000, 2801–2900, 3501–3600, 4301–4500, 5901-6000, 6201–6400, 7901–8000, 8701–8800, 9001–9100, 9701-9800, 9901–10100, 11101–11200, 11501–11700, 13601–13800, 14801–15000, 16601–16800, 17101–17400, 17801-17900, 18001-18300, 19301–19400, 19601–19800, 20701–21000, 22001-22300, 23401–23700, 25401–25700, 27001–27300, 29401-29700, 30501-30800, 31501–31800, 32201–32500, 33201–33500, 34301-34600, 35601–35700, 35901–36100, 37301–37600, 38501-38800, 39901-40200, 43001–43300, 43701–43900, 44801–45100, 45601-47000.
R. Overton	C. R. Meade	901–1000, 2901–3000, 5501–5700, 8201–8300, 8901-9000, 10101-10300, 13001–13100, 14201–14300, 15901–16000, 17001-17100, 17401–17500, 17901–18000, 18501–18600, 19501-19600, 20501-20600, 21701–21800, 23001–23100, 24301–24500, 26701-26800, 28801–28900, 29701–29900, 31401–31500, 37201-37300, 38401-38500, 39201–39300, 40201–40300, 40501–40600, 41201-41300, 41501–41600, 42101–42300, 44501–44600.
E. H. Fauntleroy	J. L. Johnston	22401–22500, 41001–41200.
		$2—1 to 10 (2d series).
H. Bartlett	M. Taylor	1–200, 701–800, 2501–2700, 3301–3500, 4201–4500, 5401–5600, 6401–6600, 7401–7600, 8501–8700, 9601–9800, 15201–15300, 46301–47000, 50701–50900, 54401–54600, 54801-55000, 57201-57500, 58601–58800.
R. F. Ball	L. M. Hunter	201–400, 2101–2300, 2901–3100, 4801–4900, 5001–5200, 6901-7100, 8001-8100, 9201–9400, 11301-11500, 12701-12900, 14001-14300, 15801–16000, 17101–17300, 18401–18600, 20401-20600, 20801–21100, 22201–22400, 24001–24200, 25301–25500, 26701-26900, 29701–29900, 31201–31400, 34001–34200, 43601-43800, 49201–49700, 54001–54400.
E. D. Layne	V. C. Watson	401–600, 2301–2500, 3101–3300, 4501–4700, 5201–5400, 6201-6400, 7101–7300, 8301–8500, 9401–9600, 9801–10000, 11201-11400, 12101–12300, 12901–13100, 13501–13700, 13801-14000, 14701–15000, 16201–16400, 16601–16800, 17501-17700, 18101-18300, 19601–19800, 20601–20800, 22401–22600, 23801-24000, 25101–25300, 27301–27500, 29901–30100, 31401-31600, 34201-34400, 35801–36000, 37401–37600, 40801–41200, 62801-62940.

Register of Confederate States Treasury Notes—Continued.

ACT OF APRIL 17, 1862—Continued.

For Treasurer.	For Register.	Numbers of the notes signed.
		$2—1 to 10 (2d series)—Continued.
R. Overton	C. R. Meade	601–700, 801–1000, 3501–3600, 4701–4800, 4901–5000, 5601–5700, 6801–6900, 7301–7400, 8101–8300, 8901–9000, 11001–11200, 11901–12100, 13301–13500, 13701–13800, 14501–14700, 15601–15800, 16801–17100, 18301–18400, 19301–19600, 21801–21900, 22901–23200, 26001–26100, 28501–28800, 33001–33300, 36001–36100, 38501–38800, 41501–41800, 44501–44700.
M. Allen	M. A. Gibb	1001–1300, 10601–11000, 19801–20400, 21901–22200, 23201–23800, 26101–26700, 30201–30800, 34601–35200, 38801–39400, 41801–42400, 44201–44500, 44701–45900, 48201–48800, 50901–51500, 55001–55600, 58801–59400, 61301–61900, 62201–62800.
M. S. Nicholas	M. A. Saunders	1301–1500, 45901–46300, 48801–49200, 51901–52300, 56201–56400, 58201–58400.
M. T. Mayo	M. C. Lathrop	1501–1700.
V. M. Rind	V. K. Davies	1701–1900, 9001–9200, 18901–19300, 21101–21500, 24201–24600, 27501–27700, 29301–29700, 33601–34000, 36301–36800, 51501–51900, 60301–60800.
K. Heth	M. E. Gilliam	1901–2100, 24901–25000, 26901–27100, 29001–29300, 31001–31200, 33301–33600, 35601–35800, 37101–37400, 39901–40300, 43201–43600, 43901–44200, 47601–48200, 53501–54000, 58101–58200, 58401–58600, 60101–60300, 60801–61000, 61901–62200.
H. Graham	M. B. Kirby	2701–2900, 3601–4200, 5701–6200, 7601–8000, 10001–10400, 11401–11900, 15301–15600, 17701–18100, 18601–18900, 21501–21800, 22601–22900, 24601–24900, 25701–26000, 27701–28300, 32101–32700, 37601–38500, 49901–50700, 57501–58100, 61001–61300.
E. A. Dennison	S. A. Randolph	6601–6800, 15001–15200, 16001–16200, 16401–16600, 17301–17500, 25001–25100, 27101–27300, 28801–29000, 30801–31000, 54601–54800.
E. H. Fauntleroy	J. L. Johnston	8701–8900, 10401–10600, 12501–12700, 13101–13300, 14301–14500, 25501–25700, 28301–28500, 32701–33000, 36801–37100, 41201–41500, 52301–52600.
V. M. Stanard	S. C. Ellett	30101–30200, 31901–32100, 34401–34500, 35201–35600, 39401–39900, 42401–42800.
M. S. Knox	M. W. Bailey	31601–31900, 34501–34600, 40301–40800, 43801–43900, 52601–53000, 56801–57200.
L. C. Minor	B. M. Abbott	36101–36300, 42801–43200, 47001–47600, 49701–49900, 53001–53500, 55601–56200, 59401–59700.
M. L. Quarles	F. G. Giles	56401–56800, 59701–60100.
		$2—1 to 12 (3d series).
M. S. Nicholas	M. A. Saunders	1–200, 501–700, 3401–3600, 5701–5900, 6401–6600, 7701–7900, 10201–10400, 12201–12400, 13601–13800, 15501–15700, 16501–16700, 18601–18800, 19201–19400, 20401–20600, 21001–21200, 24801–25000, 26101–26300, 29401–29600, 31901–32100, 33701–33900.
Do	J. McCarthy	53501–53700.
E. Mason	M. C. Lathrop	201–500, 2101–2400.
M. Allen	M. A. Gibb	501–1100.
E. D. Layne	V. C. Watson	1101–1500, 8401–8700, 11901–12200, 14801–15200, 16701–17100, 19601–20000, 25201–25600, 29201–29400, 29801–30000, 32101–32200, 32301–32400, 35501–35700, 40201–40300, 41201–41400, 43001–43200, 45201–45600, 47101–47300, 49201–49400, 50201–50400, 51201–51400.
V. M. Stanard	S. C. Ellett	1701–2100, 4401–4700, 6601–7000, 18201–18600, 24001–24400, 28601–28800, 30001–30200, 38001–38200, 39301–39500, 41801–42000, 43401–43600, 45601–45800, 46901–47100.
M. S. Knox	M. W. Bailey	2401–2700, 4701–5000, 5901–6200, 9201–9400, 11501–11700, 12601–12800, 15201–15400, 15901–16100, 17101–17300, 18801–19000, 20001–20200, 22801–23000, 25801–25900, 26301–26500, 28001–28200, 30401–30600, 32501–32700, 35101–35300, 35901–36000, 37601–37700, 39901–40100, 43201–43400, 45101–45200.
E. A. Dennison	S. A. Randolph	2701–2900, 3801–4000, 13401–13600, 16301–16500.
Do	J. L. Johnston	53001–53300, 54001–54200.
H. Graham	M. B. Kirby	2901–3400, 17301–18000, 23001–23300, 25601–25800, 28201–28400, 31201–31400, 33501–33700, 35701–35900.

Register of Confederate States Treasury Notes—Continued.

ACT OF APRIL 17, 1862—Continued.

For Treasurer.	For Register.	Numbers of the notes signed.
		$2—1 to 12 (3d series)—Continued.
K. Heth	M. E. Gilliam	3601–3800, 5401–5700, 7901–8100, 9401–9600, 11001–11200, 13001–13200, 14401–14600, 16101–16300, 19001–19200, 20201–20400, 20801–21000, 22001–22200, 23301–23500, 26701–26900, 28401–28600, 30801–31000, 32901–33100, 34301–34500, 44901–45100, 47301–47500, 48801–49000, 49801–50000, 51001–51200.
V. M. Rind	V. K. Davies	4001–4400.
R. Macmurdo	J. McCarthy	5001–5200, 8701–8800, 10001–10200, 12801–13000, 14601–14800, 22201–22400, 23501–23600, 26501–26700, 27601–27800, 30201–30400, 33101–33200, 34501–34700, 37901–38000.
S. G. Sanxay	L. Macon	5201–5400, 6201–6400, 8101–8400, 11701–11900, 13201–13400, 25001–25200, 27401–27600, 33201–33400, 35301–35500, 36401–36600, 38501–38700, 47601–48000, 49401–49600, 51401–51600.
A. Points	M. Gay	7001–7200, 51901–52100.
L. C. Minor	B. M. Abbott	7201–7700, 11201–11500, 13801–14200, 52801–53000.
R. Haynes	B. Dabney	8801–9000, 10601–10800, 12401–12600, 22601–22800.
M. A. Dewees	H. L. Cooke	9001–9200, 10801–11000, 15401–15500, 24601–24800, 37401–37600, 39591–39700, 40701–40900, 42801–43000, 43801–44000, 48201–48400, 50001–50200, 53301–53500.
M. V. Tyler	H. Herbert	9601–9800, 21601–21800, 23601–23800, 25901–26100, 27001–27200, 31001–31200.
Do	S. A. Talley	36201–36400.
S. F. Shaver	M. Dixon	9801–10000, 52501–52800.
M. Godwin	E. A. Adams	10401–10600, 14201–14400, 15701–15900, 22401–22600, 24401–24600, 32201–32300, 32401–32500, 34701–34900, 36601–36800, 39701–39900, 41401–41600, 42401–42600, 44201–44400, 45801–46000, 48401–48600, 49601–49800, 50901–51000, 53701–54000.
M. L. Quarles	F. G. Giles	18001–18200, 19401–19600, 20601–20800, 21201–21600, 21801–22000, 23801–24000, 26901–27000, 34101–34300, 37201–37400, 38901–39100, 40501–40700, 42201–42400, 44701–44900, 46001–46500, 48001–48200.
W. A. Garrett	J. McGarr	27201–27400, 31701–31900, 37001–37200, 40301–40500, 44001–44200, 48601–48800.
C. Skinner	S. E. Hughes	27801–28000, 30601–30800, 32701–32900, 34901–35100, 36801–37000, 38701–38900, 40901–41200, 42601–42800, 44401–44700, 50601–50800.
M. Newton	M. E. Pace	28801–29000, 29601–29800, 31501–31700, 36001–36200, 38301–38500, 52101–52500.
H. Watkins	M. L. Savage	29001–29200, 31401–31500, 33401–33500, 33901–34100, 38201–38300, 40101–40200, 42001–42200, 43601–43800, 47501–47600, 49001–49200, 50801–50900.
L. Breeden	L. C. Royster	37701–37900, 39101–39300, 41601–41800, 46501–46900, 50401–50600.
H. Bartlett	M. Taylor	51601–51800.
V. B. Briggs	J. B. Tiffey	51801–52100.
		$1—1 to 10 (1st series).
E. D. Layne	V. C. Watson	1–100, 501–600, 1501–1700, 10601–10800, 11601–11800, 13101–13200, 13801–14000, 14301–14500, 15101–15300, 16501–16700, 17801–18000, 18401–18600, 19301–19500, 20001–20100, 21001–21200, 45301–45700, 50301–50700, 51201–51340.
H. Graham	M. B. Kirby	101–200, 701–800, 1701–1800, 2901–3100, 3301–3400, 4801–4900, 10801–10900, 12501–12900, 14001–14300, 16701–17100, 24901–25300, 46701–47100.
H. Bartlett	S. A. Randolph	201–300, 901–1100, 2301–2500, 4201–4500, 5201–5400, 6601–6800, 7201–7500, 8001–8200, 9101–9400.
Do	M. Taylor	22101–22400, 23801–24100, 26601–26800, 28401–28600, 29901–30300, 33101–33300, 34701–34900, 36501–36700, 38701–39200, 40901–41200, 42001–42300, 43601–43800, 45201–45300, 47101–47300.
M. S. Nicholas	M. A. Saunders	301–400, 801–900, 2101–2300, 3601–3800, 4901–5200, 6301–6400, 7001–7200, 8201–8400, 8901–9000, 9901–10000, 11001–11300, 12001–12300, 14901–15100, 16301–16500, 17301–17500, 18201–18400, 18601–18800, 19501–19700, 20501–20700, 21601–21800.
R. F. Ball	L. M. Hunter	401–500, 601–700, 1101–1300, 2501–2700, 3201–3300, 4501–4700, 5601–5700, 6801–7000, 8501–8600, 10201–10400, 10901–11000, 11801–12000, 12901–13100, 15801–16100, 17101–17300, 19901–20000, 21201–21400, 21801–22000, 22901–23200, 26301–26600, 29401–29600, 48401–48900.

Register of Confederate States Treasury Notes—Continued.

ACT OF APRIL 17, 1862—Continued.

For Treasurer.	For Register.	Numbers of the notes signed.
		$1—1 to 10 (1st series)—Continued.
K. Heth	M. E. Gilliam	1301–1500, 2701–2900, 4001–4200, 4701–4800, 7901–8000, 9401–9700, 22001–22100, 24701–24900, 25901–26100, 27001–27200, 29201–29400, 30301–30500, 32601–32800, 34401–34600, 35801–36000, 38301–38500, 39401–39600, 40001–40100, 46401–46700, 48901–49200.
V. M. Rind	V. K. Davies	1801–1900, 3101–3200, 3801–4000, 5401–5600, 6001–6100, 6401–6600, 7701–7900, 8601–8700, 9701–9900, 10401–10600, 13201–13500, 14701–14900, 15301–15500, 19101–19300, 20101–20500, 21401–21600, 22701–22900, 23201–23300, 23501–23800, 26101–26300, 26801–27000, 29601–29800, 47701–48100, 49201–49600.
M. T. Mayo	M. C. Lathrop	1901–2100, 3401–3600, 5701–6000, 6101–6300, 7501–7700, 8401–8500, 8701–8900, 9001–9100, 10001–10200, 11301–11600, 12301–12500, 13501–13800, 14501–14700, 15501–15800, 16101–16300, 17501–17800, 18001–18200, 18801–19100, 19701–19900, 20701–21000, 22401–22700, 23301–23500, 24101–24700, 27401–28000, 31101–31700, 33501–34100, 36801–37400, 40101–40700, 42601–43200.
M. Allen	M. A. Gibb	25301–25900.
L. C. Minor	B. M. Abbott	27201–27400, 28601–28800, 30501–30800, 32101–32400, 34101–34400, 36701–36800, 37701–37900, 44001–44800.
E. C. Green	B. McRae	28001–28200, 29001–29200, 30801–31100, 33301–33500, 35301–35500, 36201–36400, 37401–37700, 39801–40000, 41401–41600, 42301–42600, 43201–43400, 43801–44000.
M. L. Quarles	F. G. Giles	28201–28400, 29801–29900, 31701–31900, 33001–33100–34601–34700, 35501–35600, 36401–36500, 38101–38300, 39601–39800, 41201–41400, 41601–41800, 43401–43600, 47301–47700, 49601–49900.
E. A. Dennison	S. A. Randolph	28801–29000, 31901–32100, 32801–33000, 35101–35300, 36001–36200, 38501–38700.
M. S. Knox	M. W. Bailey	32401–32600, 34901–35100, 35601–35800, 37901–38100, 39201–39400, 40701–40900, 41801–42000, 46001–46400, 50701–50900.
V. M. Stanard	S. C. Ellett	44801–45200, 49901–50300.
E. Mason	M. C. Lathrop	45701–46000, 48101–48400, 50901–51200.
		$1—1 to 10 (2d series).
M. Allen	M. A. Gibb	1–300, 1201–1500, 2501–2800, 3701–4300, 6301–6600, 7401–8000, 9701–9900, 11601–12200.
V. M. Rind	V. K. Davies	301–500, 1801–2000, 3301–3500, 4301–4600, 5901–6100, 6601–6800, 9601–9700, 9901–10100, 13801–14100, 15101–15400, 23201–23600, 25901–26300, 34201–34600, 37401–37800, 40401–40800, 44901–45300, 49701–50100.
E. A. Dennison	S. A. Randolph	501–800, 2201–2500, 6101–6300, 7201–7400, 8601–8900, 11001–11200, 14401–14500, 14701–14900, 16401–16600, 18401–18600, 19101–19300, 22401–22600, 23601–23800, 25701–25900, 28401–28600, 31501–31900, 37001–37400.
M. T. Mayo	M. C. Lathrop	801–1200, 2801–3300, 5401–5900, 8001–8500, 10101–10600, 12501–13100, 15601–15900, 16701–17300, 20001–20600, 22601–23200, 28101–28400, 32501–33100, 37801–38400, 41101–41400, 42601–42900, 43001–43300, 44601–44900.
K. Heth	M. E. Gilliam	1501–1800, 3501–3700, 4601–5000, 6801–7000, 8501–8600, 8901–9100, 10601–10800, 14901–15100, 15901–16100, 31901–32500.
R. F. Ball	L. M. Hunter	2001–2200, 5001–5200, 7001–7200, 9101–9300, 10801–11000, 13601–13800, 15401–15600, 18601–18801, 19301–19600, 21601–22000, 26601–27000, 33701–34200, 39701–40100, 46101–46500, 48201–48600, 50901–51400.
E. H. Fauntleroy	J. L. Johnston	5201–5400, 26301–26600, 34601–34900, 36701–37000, 40801–41100.
H. Bartlett	M. Taylor	9301–9500, 11201–11600, 12201–12500, 14101–14400, 14501–14700, 16101–16400, 18801–19100, 19601–20000, 22001–22400, 25201–25700, 34901–35300, 48601–48800, 49001–49200, 52101–52300, 53601–53800.
R. Overton	C. R. Meade	9501–9600, 29701–30000.
H. Graham	M. B. Kirby	13101–13600, 25001–25200, 27201–27800, 35901–36500, 52301–52900.
M. L. Quarles	F. G. Giles	16601–16700, 17301–17600, 20601–21000, 23801–24200, 28801–29000, 33301–33700, 39301–39700, 42201–42600, 43301–43700, 52901–53300.

Register of Confederate States Treasury Notes—Continued.

ACT OF APRIL 17, 1862—Continued.

For Treasurer.	For Register.	Numbers of the notes signed.
		$1—1 to 10 (2d series)—Continued.
E. C. Green	R. McRae	17601–18100, 21001–21200, 24201–24600, 27801–28100, 30001-30400, 41401–41800, 43701–44200, 45701–46100, 46901-47300, 53801–54200.
M. S. Knox	M. W. Bailey	18101–18400, 27001–27200, 29501–29700, 33101–33300, 36501-36700, 39201–39300, 40101–40400, 42901–43000, 47801-48200, 50501–50900.
L. C. Minor	B. M. Abbott	21201–21600, 29001–29300, 30801–31100, 35301–35900, 49201-49700.
E. D. Layne	V. C. Watson	24601–25000, 28601–28800, 30401–30800, 38801–39200, 46501-46900, 48801–49000, 51401–51800, 54201–54300.
V. M. Stanard	S. C. Ellett	29301–29500, 31101–31500, 38401–38800, 41801–42200, 44201-44600, 45301–45700, 47301–47800, 50101–50500.
E. Mason	M. C. Lathrop	51801–52100.
		$1—1 to 12 (3d series). *
L. C. Minor	B. M. Abbott	1–400, 22801–23000, 78401–78600, 80101–80300, 85101–85300.
E. C. Green	B. McRae	401–600, 1801–2200, 6001–6400, 7901–8300, 11701-12100, 14801-15200.
K. Heth	M. E. Gilliam	601–800, 3501–4100, 24201–24400, 26401–26600, 29201–29400, 31601–31800, 34101–34300, 40401–40600, 42301-42500, 45501-45700, 47701–47900, 49901–50100, 55001–55200, 57601-57800, 60801–61000, 71501–71700, 73601–73800, 74901-75100, 77801-78000, 82901–83000, 86201–86400.
E. A. Dennison	S. A. Randolph	801–1000, 5101–5300, 5501–5700, 10601–10800, 13701–13900, 14501–14600, 15301–15500, 19701–19900, 25901-26000, 26301-26400.
Do	J. L. Johnston	78201–78400, 82101–82300, 86401–86600.
R. F. Ball	L. M. Hunter	1001–1200, 5301–5500, 5701–6000, 7301–7700, 11201–11300, 12901–13300, 18001–18200, 84001–84100.
E. Mason	M. C. Lathrop	1201–1400, 4101–4400, 7101–7300, 77101–77300.
E. D. Layne	V. C. Watson	1401–1800, 9301–9700, 24801–25100, 29401–29800, 34701-35000, 36301–36700, 39401–39700, 45301–45500, 48101-48300, 50101-50300, 53001–53200, 57001–57200, 59601–59800, 62101-62300, 64901–65100, 68601–68800, 69801–70000, 71901-72100, 73501-73600, 75101–75300, 79101–79300, 84101–84300.
V. M. Rind	V. K. Davies	2201–2600, 6401–6800, 76201–76500, 80301–80600, 83501-83700, 85901–86100.
V. M. Stanard	S. C. Ellett	2601–3000, 22001–22200, 22401–22800, 27101–27400, 33201-33600, 36701–37100, 39901–40100, 42901–43100, 44501-44700, 48601–48700, 53601–53800, 57401–57600, 59801-60000, 62701-62900, 66701–66900, 70401–70500, 71701–71900.
H. Graham	M. B. Kirby	3001–3500, 23601–23800, 25701–25900, 28401–28600, 31401-31600, 34301–34500, 35201–35400, 37301–37500, 46901-47100, 50701–50900, 52501–52700, 54001–54200, 58101-58300, 60201-60400, 63301–63400, 79601–79700, 82701–82900, 84301-84700.
M. S. Knox	M. W. Bailey	4401–4700, 24001–24200, 24401–24500, 29001–29200, 30601-30800, 33701–33900, 35001–35200, 40201–40400, 42701-42900, 44701–44900, 47601–47700, 50901–51100, 52701-52800, 54201-54400, 58501–58600, 61001–61200, 63401–63600, 66101-66300, 82501–82700, 83701–83900.
M. L. Quarles	F. G. Giles	4701–5100, 8501–8800, 12101–12500, 15201–15300, 16601-16800, 17301–17500, 17901–18000, 18701–18900, 26001-26100, 28601-28800, 31001–31200, 35701–35900, 37501–37700, 39201-39400, 42101–42300, 44901–45100, 53401–53600, 57201-57400, 59401-59600, 61901–62100, 65901–66100, 69201–69500, 70701-70900, 72901–73100.
E. H. Fauntleroy	J. L. Johnston	6801–7100, 9701–9900, 13301–13500, 14601–14800, 16801-17000, 17701–17900, 19301–19500, 21101–21300, 24501–24600.
M. V. Tyler	H. Herbert	7701–7900, 10901–11000, 11501–11700, 15701–15900, 17101-17200, 17501–17700, 18201–18300, 18901–19100, 20001-20200, 21001–21100, 21701–21900, 23001–23200, 26601-26700, 26901-27100, 30201–30400, 32801–33000, 41201–41400, 43501-43700, 43701–43800 (duplicates), 46301–46500, 48501–48600, 55801-56000, 61201–61400, 61501–61641.
Do	S. A. Talley	61642–61700, 63901–64100.

* Notes numbered 46001–46100 missing—never signed.

Register of Confederate States Treasury Notes—Continued.

ACT OF APRIL 17, 1862—Continued.

For Treasurer.	For Register.	Numbers of the notes signed.
		$1—1 to 12 (3d series)—Continued.
R. Haynes	B. Dabney	8301–8500, 10301–10500, 12701–12900, 16201–16400, 23201-23400, 25301–25500, 28001–28200, 30001–30200, 32401-32600, 33901–34100, 38201–38400, 49701–49900, 78801–79100.
S. F. Shaver	M. Dixon	8801–9000, 10501–10600, 11301–11400, 13501–13700, 15501-15700, 17001–17100, 17201–17300, 76901–77100, 79901-80100, 84901–85100.
M. A. Dewees	I. A. Cooke	9001–9200, 10001–10300, 11001–11200, 13901–14300, 15901-16200, 19101–19300, 20201–20400, 22201–22400, 23801-24000, 26101–26300, 28201–28400, 30801–31000, 32201-32400, 33001-33200, 63101–63300, 65101–65300, 81201–81400, 86101-86200.
M. Godwin	E. A. Adams	9201–9300, 9901–10000, 12501-12700, 14301-14500, 16401-16600, 18501–18700, 19501–19700, 20601–20800, 21301–21500, 25501-25700, 27601–27800, 31201–31400, 35501–35700, 37701-37800, 38001–38200, 39701–39900, 45701–45900, 48301-48400, 49501-49700, 51101–51300, 53801–54000, 57801–58000, 60401-60600, 62501–62700, 65301–65500, 68001–68200, 70001-70200, 73901-74100, 74501–74700, 79301–79500, 81501–81700, 82301-82500, 83901–84000, 85701–85900.
E. C. Goddin	E. Nulty	10801–10900.
R. Macmurdo	J. McCarthy	11401–11500, 18301–18500, 19901–20000, 20801–21000, 21901-22000, 24601–24800, 28801–29000, 30401–30600, 33601-33700, 35401–35500, 37101–37300, 40101–40200, 42501-42700, 44401-44500, 47101–47200, 49401–49500, 51501–51700, 54701-54800, 56601–56800, 58601–58800, 63601–63700, 64701–64900.
S. G. Sanxay	L. Macon	20401–20600, 21501–21700, 23401–23600, 25101–25300, 27801-28000, 29801–30000, 32001–32200, 32601–32800, 36101-36300, 38401–38600, 39001–39200, 41901–42100, 44001-44200, 46701-46900, 50301–50500, 51901–52100, 55201–55500, 56201-56400, 60001–60200, 61401–61500, 64101–64300, 67201-67400, 68801-69000, 70501–70700, 72301–72700, 74301–74500, 76701-76900, 84701–84900.
M. S. Nicholas	M. A. Saunders	26701–26900, 27401–27600, 31801–32000, 34501–34700, 35901-36100, 38801–39000, 43301–43500, 43801–44000, 47401–47600, 49201–49400, 54801–55000, 59001–59200, 65701–65900.
Do	J. McCarthy	76501–76700, 81801–82100.
W. A. Garrett	J. McGarr	37801–38000, 41001–41200, 43101–43200, 46101–46200, 49001-49200, 52101–52300, 55501–55700, 58301–58500, 65501–65700, 67401–67600, 71101–71300, 75601–75800, 79701–79900, 83301-83500, 86801–87000.
C. Skinner	S. E. Hughes	38601–38800, 41401–41700, 44201–44400, 46501–46700, 48701-49000, 51301–51500, 54401–54700, 56401–56600, 59201-59400, 62301–62500, 66301–66500, 67101–67200–67601–67800, 69501-69800, 70901–71100, 73301–73500, 74701–74900, 77501-77800, 81001–81200.
H. Watkins	M. L. Savage	40601–40800, 43701–43800, 45901–46000, 47201–47400, 50501-50700, 52301–52500, 55701–55800, 58001–58100, 62901-63100, 66901–67100, 72101–72300, 73801–73900, 75401–75500, 79501-79600, 81401–81500, 83001–83100.
M. Newton	M. E. Pace	40801–41000, 41701–41900, 45101–45300, 47901–48100, 53201-53400, 56001–56200, 58801–59000, 61701–61900, 64301-64700, 67801–68000, 69001–69200, 72701–72900, 74101–74300, 75801-76000, 85501–85700.
S. G. Grattan	M. A. Gifford	43201–43300, 46201–46300, 48401–48500.
L. Breeden	L. C. Royster	51701–51900, 52801–53000, 56801–57000, 60601–60800, 63701-63900, 66501–66700, 68201–68400, 70201–70300, 71301-71500, 73101–73300, 75301–75400, 75501–75600, 78601–78800.
F. Wray	E. Garlick	68401–68600, 70301–70400.
A. Points	M. Gay	76001–76200, 80601–81000, 85301–85500.
H. Bartlett	M. Taylor	77301–77500, 81701–81800.
A. P. Pellet	E. P. Porter	78001–78200, 83101–83300, 86601–86800.

Register of Confederate States Treasury Notes—Continued.

ACT OF OCTOBER 13, 1862—Continued.

For Treasurer.	For Register.	Numbers of the notes signed.
		$100—A to D (1st series).
W. L. Harvey	S. G. Tinsley	1–3300.
A. W. Gray	W. Hancock	3301–6400, 7201–8000, 9201–10000, 12001–12800, 14401–16100, 18701–19500, 21101–21900, 24401–25200, 26801-27600, 31601-32400, 35401–36200, 37801–38600, 40801–41600, 43201-44000, 44801–45600, 47801–48600, 50201–52700, 54301-55100, 56701-57500, 58301–59100, 61101–61900, 63501–64300, 66401-67200, 69601–70400, 72001–72800, 74401–75200, 76801-77600, 79001-79800, 81401–82200, 85001–85800, 87401–88200, 90601-91400, 93001–93800, 96001–96800, 98801–99600, 101201–102000, 104401–105200, 106801-107600, 110801–111600, 113301-114300, 117201–118300, 120701–121700.
T. D. Walford	T. F. Grayson	6401–7200, 8001–8800, 10401-11200, 12801–13600, 16101–16600, 17101–17900, 18501–20300, 21901–22800, 29201-30000, 33201-34000, 37001–37800, 38601–39200, 41601–42400, 44001-44800, 47001–47800, 49401–50200, 52701–53500, 55101-55900, 57501-58300, 60301–61100, 62701–63500, 65601–66400, 68001-68800, 71201-72000, 76001-76800, 78401-79000, 79801-80600, 100401-101200, 102801–103600, 106001–106800, 109201–110000, 112401–113200, 115301–116100, 119901–120700, 123501-124400.
R. M. Payne	M. Winston	8801–9200, 10001–10400, 11201–12000, 13601–14400, 16601-17100, 17901–18700, 20301–21100, 22801–23600, 25201-26000, 30801–31600, 34801–35400, 39201–40000, 42401-43200, 45601-46200, 73601–74400, 80601–81400, 84201–85000, 89001-89800, 92201–93000, 95401–96000, 97601–98400.
W. R. Todd	J. H. Cooke	23601–24400, 27601–28400, 30001–30800, 32401–33200, 36201-37000, 40001–40800, 46201–47000, 48601–49400, 53501-54300, 59101–60300, 61901–62700, 64301–65100, 67201-68000, 70401-71200, 72801–73600, 75201–76000, 77601–78400, 82201-83400, 86601–87400, 88201–89000, 93801–94600, 98401-98800, 99601-100400, 102001–102800, 105201–106000, 108401–109200, 111601–112400, 113201–113300, 118301–119900, 122701-123500.
W. G. Allen	C. S. Taylor	26001–26800, 28401–29200, 34001–34800, 55901–56700, 65101-65600, 68801–69600.
A. S. Watts	W. S. Gilman	83401–84200, 85801–86600, 89801–90600, 91401–92200, 94601-95400, 96801–97600.
J. W. Jones	J. O. Snyder	103601–104400, 107601–108400, 110001–110800, 114301-115300, 116101–117200, 121701–122700.
		$100—A to D (2d series).
* * * *	* * * *	* * * * * * * *
		$50—wA to zA (3d series).*
T. O. Keesee	J. T. Dickson	1–3000, 3801–4600, 5401–6200, 7001–7800, 9601–12300, 13701-14500, 16101–16900, 17701–18500, 21901–25100, 25901-26700, 27501–28100, 28601–29400, 30301–31100, 31901-35900, 36701-37300, 38101–38900, 40501–42100, 42901–43700, 45001-45400, 46001–47200, 48001–49600, 50401–51200, 51501–52300, 53901-54700, 56301–57100, 57901–59500, 60301–61100, 61701-62500, 64101–64900, 67301–68100, 70501–71300, 73701-74500, 77701-78500, 80101–80900, 83331–84100, 87901–88700.
A. W. Gray	W. Hancock	3001–3800, 4601–5400, 6201–7000, 7801–9600, 12301–13100, 14501–15300, 16901–17700, 18501–21900.
W. G. Allen	C. S. Taylor	13101–13700, 15301–16100, 25101–25900, 26701–27500, 28101-28600, 29401–30300, 31101–31900, 35901–36700, 37301-38100, 38901–40500, 42101–42900, 43701–45000, 45401-46000, 47201-48000, 49601–50400, 51201–51500, 52301–53900, 54701-56300, 57101–57900, 59501–60300, 61101–61700, 62501-63300, 68101-68900, 69701–70500, 72901–73700, 76101–76900, 79301-80100, 84101–85000, 86201–87000, 90401–91200.
H. C. Shook	G. N. Warren	63301–64100, 65701–66500, 68901–69700, 72101–72900, 75301-76100, 78501–79300, 82501–83300, 85001–86200, 88701-89500.
T. C. Gale	E. H. Smith	64901–65700, 66501–67300, 71301–72100, 74501–75300, 76901-77700, 80901–82500, 87001–87900, 89501–90400.

* Third series, but commencement of issue under this act.

Register of Confederate States Treasury Notes—Continued.

ACT OF OCTOBER 13, 1862—Continued.

For Treasurer.	For Register.	Numbers of the notes signed.
		$20—A to H (1st series).
J. C. Joplin	S. Dutcher	1-400, 1901-2300, 3101-3500, 4701-5100, 7901-8300, 9601-10000, 11901-12600, 14701-15100, 16301-16600, 18301-18500, 18901-19700, 20901-21300, 22101-22500, 22901-23100, 23301-23700, 25101-25500, 27101-27500, 28701-29100, 29901-30200, 30701-31100, 32001-32400, 34101-34500, 35701-36100, 36901-37300, 38901-39300, 40101-40500, 41701-42100, 43301-43700, 44901-45300, 46501-47300, 48101-48500, 48701-50100, 51301-51700, 53301-53700, 54501-54900, 56201-56600, 57401-57800, 59001-59400, 60601-60700, 61101-61500, 62701-63100, 63901-64300, 65501-65900, 67601-68000, 68801-69200, 70401-70800, 71601-72000, 73101-73500, 74301-74700, 76001-76100, 76501-77000, 78501-79200, 80801-81300, 84801-85300, 88001-88200.
E. C. Goddin	J. M. Kinney	401-800, 1501-1900, 3901-4300, 5501-5900, 6101-6300, 7101-7500, 9101-9600, 10801-11200, 13401-13800, 15101-15500, 16901-17200, 21301-21700, 23701-24100, 25901-26300, 27901-28300, 29101-29500, 30501-30700, 31501-32000, 33301-33701, 34901-35300, 36501-36900, 38101-38500, 39701-40100, 40901-41300, 42901-43300, 44501-44900, 46101-46500, 47301-47700, 48301-48700, 50501-50900, 52101-52500, 54101-54500, 55301-55400, 56601-57000, 58601-59000, 59801-60200, 61501-61900, 63101-63500, 64701-65100, 66301-66700, 67501-67600, 68001-68400, 69601-70000, 71201-71600, 72801-73100, 73901-74300, 75501-76000, 77801-78300, 79601-79900, 83101-83600, 86701-87200.
J. W. Jones	J. O. Snyder	801-1100, 2301-2700, 3501-3900, 5101-5500, 5901-6100, 6701-7100, 8701-9100, 11201-11600, 13101-13400, 15501-15900, 17601-17800, 19701-20100, 21701-22100, 23101-23300, 24501-24900, 26301-26700, 27501-27900, 29501-29900, 30201-30500, 31101-31500, 32901-33300, 34501-34900, 36101-36500, 37701-38100, 39301-39700, 41301-41700, 42501-42900, 43701-44100, 45301-45700, 47701-48100, 48901-49300, 50901-51300, 52501-52900, 53701-54100, 55401-55800, 57001-57400, 58201-58600, 60201-60600, 61901-62300, 63501-63900, 65101-65500, 66701-67100, 68401-68800, 70001-70400.
J. H. Carr	R. A. Mills	1101-1500, 2701-3100, 4301-4700, 7501-7900, 10001-10400, 11601-11900, 12601-13000, 14301-14700, 16601-16900, 18501-18900, 20101-20500, 22501-22900, 24101-24500, 25501-25900, 26701-27100, 28301-28700.
Do	W. O. Slade	72401-72800, 73501-73900, 75101-75500, 77001-77400, 79201-79600, 82101-82600, 85801-86300.
W. G. Allen	C. S. Taylor	6301-6700, 8301-8700, 20501-20900, 24901-25100, 32501-32900, 48501-48900.
T. O. Keesee	J. T. Dickson	10401-10800, 32401-32500, 50101-50500.
A. W. Gray	W. Hancock	13801-14300, 15901-16300, 17401-17600, 18101-18300.
W. F. Hoge	Tho. J. Miller	17201-17400.
J. W. Faxon	W. Waller	17801-18100.
Do	W. B. Walston	77401-77800, 79901-80300, 82601-83100.
O. M. Marshall	do	33701-34100, 35301-35700, 37301-37700, 38501-38900, 40501-40900, 42101-42500, 51701-52100, 52901-53300, 54901-55300, 55801-56200, 57801-58200, 59401-59800, 60701-61100, 62301-62700, 64301-64700, 65901-66300, 67101-67500, 69201-69600, 70801-71200, 72001-72400.
W. R. Todd	J. H. Cooke	44101-44500, 45701-46100.
T. J. Hatch	J. P. Swords	74701-75100, 76101-76500, 78301-78700, 81301-81700, 83601-83700, 85301-85800.
F. C. Weisiger	W. P. Caldwell	80301-80800, 83801-84300.
S. B. Jacobs	H. C. Hayes	81701-82100, 86301-86700.
W. L. Harvey	T. Ellett	83701-83800.
N. A. Bass	A. S. Watkins	84301-84800.
F. H. Link	L. P. Rogers	87201-87500, 88201-88400.
C. Ashford	S. Sinton	87501-87800.
B. H. Berry	J. T. Holt	87801-88001.
		$10—A to H (1st series).
J. C. Joplin	S. Dutcher	1-400, 2401-2800, 7201-7600, 11801-12200, 35001-35200, 37201-37300, 38001-38400, 45501-45700, 54301-54700, 61901-62200, 108801-109200, 116101-116500, 136601-137000.

Register of Confederate States Treasury Notes—Continued.

ACT OF OCTOBER 13, 1862—Continued.

For Treasurer.	For Register.	Numbers of the notes signed.
		$10—A to H (1st series)—Continued.
R. M. Payne	M. Winston	401–800, 3601–4000, 9301–9700, 13401–13800, 17801–18200, 20201–20600, 25401–25800, 37001–37200, 42501–42900, 49601-50000, 54701–55100, 61401–61600, 65701–66100, 69701-69900, 75401–75600, 77601–77800, 82401–82800, 87601–87900, 91301-91500, 95901–96200, 103001–103300, 110901–111300, 118501-118900, 124901–125300, 141001–141400, 143301–143700.
F. C. Weisiger	W. P. Caldwell	801–1200, 2801–3200, 19401–19800, 23801–24200, 28601–29000, 34201–34400, 37301–37400, 42101–42500, 43801–43900, 48401-48800, 53901–54300, 59001–59300, 64501–64900, 69501-69700, 74001–74200, 78001–78200, 80001–80400, 86001–86200, 89901-90100, 94101–94500, 101101–101500, 109201–109600, 114901-115300, 122501–122900, 130401–130800, 133401–133800, 135801–136200, 142501–142900.
N. A. Bass	A. S. Watkins	1201–1600, 4001–4400, 8001–8400, 12201–12600, 16101–16600, 20601–21000, 26201–26600, 31401–31800, 42901-43300, 47201-47600, 52701–53100, 59901–60200, 66501–66900, 72201-72500, 75801–76000, 78401–78600, 80401–80800, 86801-87000, 91501-91700, 97001–97400, 102601–103000, 111701–112100, 117301-117700, 126901–127600, 131601–131800, 135401–135800, 139401–139800.
T. C. Gale	E. H. Smith	1601–2000, 5201–5600, 10101–10500, 14701–15100, 17401-17800, 22601--23000, 25801–26200, 31001–31400, 36001-36200, 37501-37600, 40001–40400, 44901–45100, 50001–50300, 58201-58600, 61601–61900, 63601–63900, 67301–67700, 70801-71100, 75201-75400, 77201–77400, 84801–85200, 88101–88300, 90501-90700, 97601–97800, 99601–99800, 105601–106000, 113701–114100, 120101–120500, 125701–126100, 129201–129600, 135001-135400, 140601–141000, 143701–143900.
O. M. Marshall	W. B. Walston	2001–2400, 3201–3600, 31801–32200, 34401–34600, 41301-41700, 44001–44100, 46801–47200, 56301–56700, 59301-59600, 66901-67300, 69901–70100, 73801–74000, 77001–77200, 92301-92500, 94501–94900, 104001–104400, 132201–132600, 137001-137400.
Do	J. W. Eggleston	24201–24600.
J. H. Carr	R. A. Mills	4401–4800, 8801–9300, 15101–15300, 34801–35000, 40401-40900, 53501-53900, 60401-60700, 92101-92300, 95001-95100, 102301-102600, 107201–107600, 114501–114900.
J. W. Jones	J. O. Snyder	4801-5200, 9701-10100, 14201–14700, 35601–35800, 37601-37700, 57801–58200, 71701–72000, 93101–93300, 98601-98800, 99401-99600, 112101–112500, 119301–119700.
W. R. Todd	J. H. Cooke	5601–6000, 10501–10900, 35201–35400, 37901–38000, 43301-43700, 49201–49600, 56701–57100, 61101–61400, 67701-68100, 70501–70800, 83601–84000, 86201–86500, 89701-89900, 95101-95500, 101901-102300, 108001-108400, 116501-116900, 123701-124100, 139001–139400.
E. C. Goddin	J. M. Kinney	6001–6400, 8401–8800, 13801–14200, 36601–36800, 37701-37800, 57101–57400, 63001–63300, 72801–73000, 92501-92700, 98401-98600, 100201-100400, 104801-105200, 111301-111700, 121301-121700, 142201–142500.
F. H. Link	L. P. Rogers	6401–6800, 11401–11800, 15301–15700, 19001–19400, 23001-23400, 27801–28200, 34001–34200, 39201–39600, 45701-45800, 46401–46800, 51901–52300, 60701–61100, 64401-64500, 69301-69500, 73601–73800, 79001–79200, 80801–81200, 87001-87200, 91901–92100, 93301–93700, 101501–101900, 108401–108800, 115301–115700, 122901–123300, 130001–130400, 131801-132200, 136201–136600.
T. J. Hatch	J. P. Swords	6801–7200, 11001–11400, 15701–16100, 19801–20200, 25001-25400, 28201-28600, 34601–34800, 37401–37500, 38401-38800, 45801–46000, 47601–48000, 53101–53500, 59601-59900, 79601-80000, 86501–86800, 90301–90500, 93701–94100, 100701-101100, 107601–108000, 115701–116100, 123301–123700, 131201–131600, 132601–133000, 137801–138200.
C. Ashford	S. Sinton	7601–8000, 12601–13000, 17001–17400, 21401–21800, 24601-25000, 29801–30200, 35401–35600, 43901–44000, 44101-44500, 50701–51100, 55101–55500, 66101–66500, 70301-70500, 74601-74800, 77801–78000, 84001–84400, 87401–87600, 90701-90900, 96601–97000, 103601–104000, 110501–110900, 118901-119300, 125301-125700, 128801–129200, 133801–134200, 138601-139000, 142901–143300.

Register of Confederate States Treasury Notes—Continued.

ACT OF OCTOBER 13, 1862—Continued.

For Treasurer.	For Register.	Numbers of the notes signed.
		$10—A to H (1st series)—Continued.
F. W. Ashby	S. G. Tinsley	10901-11000, 13001-13400, 16601-17000, 21001-21400, 27001-27400, 29001-29400, 36201-36400, 40901-41300, 48801-49200, 57401-57800, 60201-60400.
H. C. Shook	G. N. Warren	18201-18600, 22201-22600, 26601-27000, 30201-30600, 35801-36000, 37801-37900, 38801-39200, 45101-45300, 50301-50700, 55501-55900, 62501-62800, 68101-68500, 71401-71700, 76601-77000, 82801-83200, 88301-88500, 91701-91900, 97801-98000, 99201-99400, 106001-106400, 114101-114500, 120501-120900, 126101-126500, 128001-128400, 134201-134600, 140201-140600.
W. F. Hoge	Tho. J. Miller	18601-19000, 21801-22200, 23401-23800, 30601-31000, 41701-42100, 48001-48400, 63301-63600, 64901-65300, 73001-73300, 76001-76200, 78801-79000, 85601-86000, 90901-91100, 98001-98200, 99801-100000, 104401-104800, 113301-113700, 122101-122500, 126501-126900, 128401-128800, 134601-135000, 141801-142200.
J. B. S. Dimitry	W. Nott	27401-27800, 32601-33000, 36801-37000, 46001-46400, 51501-51900, 58601-59000, 63901-64100, 68901-69300, 72001-72200, 75601-75800, 79201-79400, 83201-83600, 89001-89500, 98201-98400, 100001-100200, 106401-106800, 112501-112900, 121701-122100, 129601-130000.
W. G. Allen	C. S. Taylor	29401-29800, 52301-52700, 62201-62500, 68501-68900, 72501-72800, 74401-74600, 79401-79600, 84401-84800, 88801-89000, 90101-90300, 97401-97600, 100401-100700, 116901-117300, 138201-138600.
T. D. Walford	T. F. Grayson	32201-32600, 36401-36600, 39601-40000, 45301-45500, 51101-51500, 55901-56300, 62801-63000, 65301-65700, 70101-70300, 74801-75000, 78601-78800, 81601-82000, 87901-88100, 89501-89700, 96201-96600, 105201-105600, 110101-110500, 119701-120100, 124501-124900, 141401-141800.
A. W. Gray	W. Hancock	33001-33400, 73301-73600.
W. L. Harvey	S. G. Tinsley	33401-34000, 75001-75200, 78201-78400, 82001-82400, 88501-88800, 94901-95000, 109601-109700, 118101-118500.
A. S. Watts	W. T. Snead	43701-43800.
B. H. Berry	J. T. Holt	44501-44900, 74201-74400, 77401-77600, 81201-81600, 87201-87400, 92701-92900, 95501-95900, 103301-103600, 109701-110100, 117701-118100, 124101-124500, 127601-128000, 130801-131200, 133001-133400, 137401-137800.
T. O. Keesee	J. T. Dickson	71101-71400, 91101-91300, 139801-140200.
J. W. Faxon	W. Waller	76201-76600, 85201-85600, 92901-93100, 98801-99200, 106801-107200, 112901-113300, 120901-121300.
		$10—A to H (2d series).
T. J. Hatch	J. P. Swords	1-400, 7201-7500, 12401-12600, 13201-13600, 20601-21000, 26601-27000, 32501-32900, 38701-39100, 41501-41900, 48901-49000, 51601-51700, 52901-53000, 55001-55400, 58101-58200, 58801-59200, 63201-63600.
F. H. Link	L. P. Rogers	401-800, 6901-7200, 14201-14600, 19001-19200, 19801-20200, 26201-26600, 38301-38700, 43501-43900, 49401-49500, 51701-51800, 52301-52400, 53401-53800, 58301-58800, 62801-63200.
N. A. Bass	A. S. Watkins	801-1100, 6601-6900, 14001-14200, 14901-15200, 19601-19700, 22701-23100, 29701-30100, 32101-32500, 33701-34100, 39501-39900, 45101-45500, 49601-49700, 50801-50900, 52101-52200, 55401-55800, 57901-58000, 59201-59600, 64001-64400.
W. R. Todd	J. H. Cooke	1101-1500, 10401-10700, 11401-11600, 15401-15600, 19401-19600, 21001-21400, 29301-29700, 34101-34500, 39901-40300, 45501-45900, 50401-50500, 51201-51300, 51501-51600, 55801-56000, 57401-57700, 60001-60400.
F. C. Weisiger	W. P. Caldwell	1501-1900, 6301-6600, 11801-12000, 14601-14900, 18701-18800, 20201-20600, 25401-25800, 33301-33700, 37901-38300, 42301-42700, 49001-49100, 63601-64000, 65201-65600.
C. Ashford	S. Sinton	1901-2300, 8001-8200, 12801-13000, 16001-16300, 18801-18900, 23101-23500, 28901-29300, 34501-34900, 37101-37500, 46201-46600, 49701-49800, 51401-51500, 52601-52700, 54601-55000, 58201-58300, 59601-60000, 64401-64800.
W. G. Allen	C. S. Taylor	2301-2700, 8801-9100, 13801-14000, 18401-18600, 23901-24300, 28101-28500, 43901-44300, 49901-50000.

Register of Confederate States Treasury Notes—Continued.

ACT OF OCTOBER 13, 1862—Continued.

For Treasurer.	For Register.	Numbers of the notes signed.
		$10—A to H (2d series)—Continued.
T. C. Gale	E. H. Smith	2701-3100, 9901-10100, 13601-13800, 16901-17200, 18901-19000, 21801-22300, 27801-28100, 35501-35900, 36701-37100, 46601-47000, 50301-50400, 51901-52000, 52401-52500, 56201-56400, 57001-57200, 62401-62800.
E. C. Goddin	J. M. Kinney	3101-3500, 8201-8500, 11201-11400, 30901-31300, 45901-46200, 52501-52600.
R. M. Payne	M. Winston	3501-3800, 9101-9400, 12201-12400, 16301-16600, 18601-18700, 22301-22700, 44701-45100, 50601-50700.
T. D. Walford	T. F. Grayson	3801-4200, 9701-9900, 13001-13200, 15201-15400, 19201-19400, 44301-44700, 50001-50100.
B. H. Berry	J. T. Holt	4201-4600, 7801-8000, 11001-11200, 15601-16000, 21401-21800, 27001-27400, 32901-33300, 39101-39500, 43101-43500, 49801-49900, 51801-51900, 52801-52900, 54201-54600, 60401-60800.
H. C. Shook	G. N. Warren	4601-5000, 9401-9700, 11601-11800, 16601-16900, 19701-19800, 23501-23900, 30501-30900, 35101-35500, 40301-40700, 47401-47800, 49501-49600, 52701-52800, 53201-53400, 56001-56200, 56801-57000, 61601-62000, 64801-65200.
J. W. Jones	J. O. Snyder	5001-5400, 8501-8800, 31301-31700, 47001-47400, 50501-50600.
T. O. Keesee	J. T. Dickson	5401-5600, 10101-10400, 47801-48200.
W. F. Hoge	Tho. J. Miller	5601-6000, 10701-11000, 12001-12200, 18001-18400, 25001-25400, 28501-28900, 34901-35100, 40701-41100, 49201-49300, 50701-50800, 52001-52100, 53001-53100, 56601-56800, 57201-57400, 61201-61600.
J. C. Joplin	S. Dutcher	6001-6300, 27401-27800, 42701-43100, 49301-49400.
J. H. Carr	R. A. Mills	7501-7800, 12601-12800, 25801-26200.
Do	W. O. Slade	41901-42300, 49101-49200, 50901-51000, 53101-53200.
J. B. S. Dimitry	W. Nott	17201-17600, 24701-25000, 30101-30500, 35901-36300, 37501-37900, 48201-48600, 51001-51200, 56401-56600, 57701-57900, 62001-62400.
J. W. Faxon	W. Waller	17601-18000, 24301-24700, 31701-32100.
Do	W. B. Walston	36301-36700, 41101-41500.
A. W. Gray	W. Hancock	48601-48900, 50101-50200.
O. M. Marshall	W. B. Walston	50201-50300, 51301-51400, 52201-52300, 53801-54200, 58001-58100, 60801-61200.
		$10—A to H (3d series).
W. F. Hoge	Tho. J. Miller	1-400, 3601-4000, 7401-7800, 11801-12200, 15801-16200, 28601-29000, 36301-36700.
F. H. Link	L. P. Rogers	401-800, 5001-5400, 8201-8600, 12201-12600, 17401-17800, 21001-21400, 25801-26200, 31901-32300, 40701-41100, 43101-43500, 46301-46700, 55001-55400, 57801-58200, 63401-63800, 69201-69600, 71601-72000, 98601-99000, 101801-102200, 103801-104200, 105901-106300.
T. J. Hatch	J. P. Swords	801-1200, 4601-5000, 9001-9400, 13401-13800, 18201-18600, 22201-22600, 26601-27000, 34701-35100, 39501-39900, 48301-48700, 90401-90800, 93001-93400, 95001-95400, 96201-96600, 99801-100200.
N. A. Bass	A. S. Watkins	1201-1600, 6201-6600, 9801-10200, 14601-15000, 17001-17400, 23801-24200, 28201-28600, 33901-34300, 43901-44300, 47101-47500, 51901-52300, 55401-55800, 59801-60200, 62201-62600, 65401-65800, 68401-68800, 70401-70800, 74501-74900, 76901-77300, 81601-82000, 83601-84000, 84901-85300, 88401-88800, 89601-90000, 91401-91800, 93401-93800, 95401-95800, 97001-97400, 100201-100600, 103001-103400, 104201-104700, 106701-107000.
B. H. Berry	J. T. Holt	1601-2000, 5801-6200, 9401-9800, 13001-13400, 17801-18200, 21801-22200, 27401-27800, 34301-34700, 41501-41900, 46701-47100, 51501-51900, 54201-54600, 59401-59800, 63001-63400, 80101-80500, 83201-83600, 85301-85700, 88001-88400, 89201-89600, 90801-91200, 92201-92600, 94601-95000, 97401-97800, 99001-99400, 102201-102600, 104701-105100.
F. C. Weisiger	W. P. Caldwell	2001-2400, 4201-4600, 8601-9000, 12601-13000, 16601-17000, 20601-21000, 26201-26600, 32301-32700, 39101-39500, 45501-45900, 50301-50700, 54601-55000, 58201-58600, 62601-63000, 67201-67600, 70001-70400, 72001-72400, 73701-74100, 76101-76500, 78901-79300, 82801-83200, 84501-84900, 86801-87200, 91201-91400, 91801-92200, 93801-94200, 106301-106700.

Register of Confederate States Treasury Notes—Continued.

ACT OF OCTOBER 13, 1862—Continued.

For Treasurer.	For Register.	Numbers of the notes signed.
		$10—A to H (3d series)—Continued.
C. Ashford	S. Sinton	2401–2800, 5401–5800, 10201–10600, 13801–14200, 20201-20600, 23401–23800, 27801–28200, 35101–35500, 40301-40700, 47501-47900, 52301–52700, 53801–54200, 59001–59400, 61801-62200, 66601–67000, 69601–70000, 72401–72800, 74901-75300, 77301-77700, 79701–80100, 82401–82800, 86101–86500, 87201-87600, 90001–90400, 92601–93000, 94201–94600, 96601-97000, 99401-99800, 101401–101800, 105101–105500.
T. C. Gale	E. H. Smith	2801–3200, 7001–7400, 11401–11800, 14201–14600, 19001-19400, 24201–24600, 29801–30200, 37501–37900, 43501-43900, 49501-49900, 53501–53800, 57001–57400, 60601–61000, 64601-65000, 67001–67200, 67601–68000, 71201–71600, 73201-73600, 78501-78900, 84401–84500, 86501–86800, 88801–89200.
H. C. Shook	G. N. Warren	3201–3600, 6601–7000, 10601–11000, 15001–15400, 19401-19800, 22601–23000, 29401–29800, 36701–37100, 65801-66200, 68001-68400, 72801–73200, 74101–74500, 80801–81200, 84001-84400, 85701–86100, 87601–88000.
J. B. S. Dimitry	W. Nott	4001–4200, 7801–8200, 11001–11400, 15401–15800, 16201-16600, 19801-20200, 24601-25000, 30601–31400, 38701-39100, *44701-45100, 49901–50300, 53101–53500, 57401–57800, 61401-61800, 65001–65400, 66201–66600, 68801–69200, 70801-71200, 73601-73700, 95801–96100, 98201–98600, 101001–101400, 103401-103800, 105501–105900.
O. M. Marshall	W. B. Walston	18601–19000, 21401–21800, 27001–27400, 33101–33500, 39901-40300, 41901–42300, 47901–48300, 51101–51500, 52701-53100, 55801–56600, 58601–59000, 60201–60600, 63801-64200, 75701-76100, 79301–79700.
J. W. Jones	J. O. Snyder	23001–23400, 29001–29400, 31501–31900, 37901–38300, 45101-45500, 49101–49500, 78101–78500, 82001–82400.
E. C. Goddin	J. M. Kinney	25001–25400, 30201–30600, 31401–31500, 38301–38700, 42701-43100, 48701–49100, 77701–78100, 81201–81600.
J. C. Joplin	S. Dutcher	25401–25800, 32701–33100, 41101–41500, 45901–46300, 76501-76900, 80501–80800.
T. O. Keesee	J. T. Dickson	33501–33900.
T. D. Walford	T. F. Grayson	35501–35900.
W. R. Todd	J. H. Cooke	35901–36300, 42301–42700.
R. M. Payne	M. Winston	37101–37500, 44301–44700, 50701–51100, 56601–57000, 61001-61400, 64201–64600, 75301–75700, 97801–98200, 100601-101000, 102601–103000.
J. H. Carr	W. O. Slade	96101–96200.
		$10—A to H (4th series).
E. Mason	M. C. Lathrop	1–400, 4901–5300, 7301–7700, 9501–9900, 11201–11600, 13601-14000, 16201–16600, 17601–18000, 24601–25100, 45301-45600, 64101–64500.
V. Bridges	E. W. Pendleton	401–700, 1601–1900, 2201–2600, 3101–3800, 4301–4600, 6501-6800, 8501–8800, 10701–11000, 13001–13300, 14901–15200, 16901–17200, 21001–21100.
A. Harrison	M. S. Johnson	701–1000, 1901–2200, 7001–7300, 9101–9500.
M. W. Garnett	N. Boykin	1001–1300, 2601–2800, 4101–4300, 5601–5900, 7701–7800, 9901-10200, 11901–12200, 14001–14300, 18301–18500, 23501-23900, 43801–44200, 57901–58100.
P. C. Bagby	J. Douglas	1301–1600, 2801–3100, 5901–6100, 7801–8100, 12201–12500, 14301–14700, 16601–16900, 19101–19200, 20001-20300, 26201-26700, 51001–51400.
M. V. Tyler	B. M. Payne	3801–4100, 4601–4900, 6801–7000, 8801–9100, 11001–11200, 13301–13600, 15201–15500, 17401–17600, 20701-21000, 40601-40900, 53301–53600.
M. Allen	B. T. Lyon	5301–5600, 6101–6500, 8101–8200, 8301–8500, 10201–10700, 12501–13000, 15501–15900, 19701–20000, 20301-20700, 28101-28600, 37001–37500, 65601–65800.
M. S. Nicholas	J. McCarthy	8201–8300, 61101–61500, 62001–62100.
C. Stalnaker	E. C. Winston	11601–11900, 14701–14900, 15901–16200, 17201–17400, 21701-22000, 43401–43800, 56601–57100.
N. Palmer	E. S. Read	18001–18300, 22001–22300, 44601–45000, 60501–60900.
H. Starke	M. C. Morton	18501–18800, 23901–24200, 47301–47700.

* The first three letters in package numbered 44701–44800 being duplicated, an x was added—thus, A, B, C, D, E, Ax, Bx, Cx—the series remaining.

Register of Confederate States Treasury Notes—Continued.

ACT OF OCTOBER 13, 1862—Continued.

For Treasurer.	For Register.	Numbers of the notes signed.
		$10—A to H (4th series)—Continued.
N. Giles	M. F. Cary	18801–19100, 22701–23100, 46501–46900, 64801–65200.
L. Archer	M. J. Morris	19201–19500, 22301–22700, 45601–46000, 62801–63200.
S. Sieker	M. F. Jarvis	19501–19700, 21401–21700, 42401–42800, 54001–54300.
L. Breeden	L. C. Royster	21101–21400, 27601–28100, 36301–36500, 37501–37800, 48501–48900, 64001–64100.
H. Bartlett	M. Taylor	23101–23500, 28601–29100, 36501–37000, 64501–64800.
S. G. Sanxay	L. Macon	24201–24600, 40001–40400, 51801–52200.
E. C. Green	B. McRae	25101–25500.
E. A. Dennison	J. L. Johnston	25501–25900, 63601–64000.
F. Wray	E. Garlick	25901–26200, 40201–40600, 52901–53300, 56201–56600, 65901–66000.
A. B. Capron	K. Walker	26701–27100, 59101–59500.
R. F. Ball	L. M. Hunter	27101–27600, 36101–36300, 65201–65400.
V. M. Rind	V. K. Davies	29101–29600, 51401–51800.
M. A. Dewees	S. E. Hughes	29601–30000, 52201–52600, 55101–55200.
N. A. Bass	A. S. Watkins	30001–30100, 31701–32200.
C. Ashford	S. Sinton	30101–30500, 33001–33400, 34801–35000.
B. H. Berry	J. T. Holt	30501–30900, 32601–33000, 35001–35200.
S. B. Jacobs	S. C. Hayes	30901–31300.
J. B. S. Dimitry	W. Nott	31301–31700, 33801–34200, 35201–35700.
F. H. Link	L. P. Rogers	32201–32600, 34601–34800.
R. M. Payne	M. Winston	33401–33800.
A. P. Hix	J. T. Jackson	34201–34300, 34501–34600.
J. H. Tompkins	J. E. Henderson	34301–34400.
J. Bunting	T. L. Crouch	34401–34500.
H. Watkins	M. L. Savage	35701–35900.
M. S. Knox	M. W. Bailey	35901–36100, 58301–58700.
M. B. Christian	M. S. Apperson	37801–37900, 43201–43400, 49901–50200.
E. H. Fauntleroy	M. A. Saunders	37901–38200, 65401–65600.
R. Overton	C. R. Meade	38201–38500, 52601–52900.
V. M. Dickins	F. E. Bernard	38501–39000, 55201–55600, 58101–58200.
A. Points	M. Gay	39001–39500, 55601–56200.
L. C. Minor	B. M. Abbott	39501–40000, 57501–57900.
V. B. Briggs	J. B. Tiffey	40401–40600, 54701–55000.
M. Loughborough	E. Stanard	40901–41200, 53601–54000.
C. C. Mumford	L. Spottswood	40601–42000, 57101–57500.
H. M. Douglass	F. C. Jones	42001–42400, 54301–54700, 58201–58300.
M. Godwin	E. A. Adams	42801–43200.
Do	M. S. Apperson	60101–60500.
K. Heth	M. E. Gilliam	44201–44600, 59501–59900.
M. L. Marshall	M. Woodward	45001–45300, 60901–61100.
S. F. Shaver	M. Dixon	46001–46500, 50201–50700, 55001–55100.
S. G. Grattan	H. L. Cooke	46901–47300, 63201–63600.
M. L. Quarles	F. G. Giles	47701–48100, 62101–62500.
E. O. Beall	M. Morrison	48101–48500, 61501–62000.
V. M. Stanard	S. C. Ellett	48901–49300.
R. Haynes	B. Dabney	49301–49700, 58701–59100, 65801–65900.
M. Wade	N. Richardson	49701–49900, 62501–62800.
I. Benton	C. F. Windle	50701–51000.
M. E. Dudley	M. E. Norton	59901–60100.
		$5—A to H (1st series).
M. Allen	B. T. Lyon	1–400, 801–1100, 1501–1900, 3101–3500, 5501–5900, 14801–14900, 15201–15600, 23101–23500, 32401–32900, 40701–40900, 44001–44400, 50401–50800, 55101–55300, 57101–57500, 60501–60800, 68401–68600, 70501–70900, 75601–76000, 81801–82200, 86901–87300, 93701–94100, 107401–107700, 110101–110500, 116501–116900, 119401–119800, 121801–122200, 122701–123800.
E. Mason	M. C. Lathrop	401–800, 1101–1500, 1901–3100, 3501–4600, 4901–5300, 6501–6900, 12201–12500, 18501–18900, 25101–25600, 36701–37200, 39801–40000, 46001–46300, 51701–52100, 55301–55600, 64001–64400, 68801–69000, 78801–79200, 83901–84300, 90901–91300, 95301–95700, 100001–100400, 106601–106900, 109201–109500, 113901–114300, 117501–117900.
L. C. Minor	B. M. Abbott	4601–4900, 6901–7200, 13701–13900, 22401–22600, 26501–26800, 34401–34700, 40901–41200, 44401–44700, 52101–52400, 57501–57800, 61801–62200, 69901–70200, 76001–76300, 83401–83700, 89101–89400, 95001–95300, 99101–99400, 112301–112600, 118701–119000.

Register of Confederate States Treasury Notes—Continued.

ACT OF OCTOBER 13, 1862—Continued.

For Treasurer.	For Register.	Numbers of the notes signed.
		$5—A to H (1st series)—Continued.
K. Heth	M. E. Gilliam	5301-5400, 8101-8400, 21701-21900, 29801-30100, 45001-45400, 49801-50300, 67401-67700, 73001-73300, 79501-79800, 85401-85700, 89701-90000, 97201-97500, 102201-102500, 105601-105900, 114301-114600.
V. M. Stanard	S. C. Ellett	5401-5500, 9401-9700, 14401-14600, 17301-17600, 27601-27900, 35401-35700, 46301-46600, 54601-54800, 59901-60100, 64401-64700, 70201-70500, 77601-77900, 112701-112900.
E. P. Porter	A. P. Pellet	5901-6200, 11701-12000, 16201-16500, 23901-24200, 36401-36700, 40201-40400, 61101-61400, 68201-68400, 72101-72400, 79201-79500, 81501-81800, 87601-87900, 92701-93000, 98801-99100, 104301-104600, 109501-109800, 112001-112300, 115901-116200, 120801-121000, 121101-121800.
E. C. Green	B. McRae	6201-6500, 10801-11100, 17901-18200, 24201-24500, 31501-31900, 46601-46900, 58101-58400, 62201-62500, 71201-71500, 77301-77600, 84401-84700, 88201-88500, 99701-99800, 111001-111100, 120401-120800.
R. F. Ball	L. M. Hunter	7201-7500, 13201-13400, 14701-14800, 21001-21300, 29001-29300, 37801-38100, 48101-48400, 53601-53900, 66201-66500, 75101-75300, 81001-81300, 86201-86500, 91601-91900, 98001-98400, 102501-102700, 105301-105600, 114601-114900.
E. D. Layne	V. C. Watson	7501-7800, 14201-14400, 17601-17900, 27001-27300, 35101-35400, 44701-45000, 52401-52700, 59601-59900, 65901-66200, 72701-73000, 78201-78500, 84701-85000, 88501-88800, 96001-96300, 101001-101300, 104601-104900, 119801-120100, 124101-124400.
M. S. Nicholas	J. McCarthy	7801-8100, 12501-12800, 18201-18500, 28201-28500, 38101-38400, 53901-54200, 59001-59300, 68601-68800, 72401-72700, 76701-77000, 82501-82800, 90601-90900, 94701-95000, 100701-101000, 104001-104300, 108601-108900, 113601-113900, 118401-118700, 124401-124600.
A. Points	M. Gay	8401-8800, 13901-14200, 23501-23900, 32001-32400, 42301-42600, 49401-49800, 61401-61800, 69501-69900, 93301-93700, 98401-98800, 115101-115600, 119001-119400.
H. Bartlett	M. Taylor	8801-9100, 11101-11400, 16901-17300, 30101-30400, 34701-35100, 54401-54600, 76301-76700, 83101-83400, 89401-89700, 96601-96900, 99401-99700, 103701-104000, 110501-110800, 117901-118400, 122501-122700.
S. F. Shaver	M. Dixon	9101-9400, 13401-13700, 18901-19200, 25901-26200, 33801-34100, 40001-40200, 51101-51400, 62801-63100, 85101-85400, 86701-86900, 87301-87600, 92201-92400, 94401-94700, 95701-96000, 101901-102200, 103001-103200, 105901-106100, 112601-112700, 122201-122500.
R. Haynes	B. Dabney	9701-10000, 12801-13200, 21901-22200, 28701-29000, 39301-39400, 42601-42900, 48701-49000, 54201-54400, 66501-66800, 74201-74500, 80701-81000, 86501-86700, 90001-90300, 104901-105200, 121001-121100.
L. Breeden	L. C. Royster	10001-10300, 27901-28200, 37501-37800, 42901-43200, 46901-47200, 53001-53300, 65301-65600, 74501-74800, 79801-80100, 106101-106400.
V. M. Bind	V. K. Davies	10301-10500, 11401-11700, 14901-15200, 24501-24800, 33201-33500, 40401-40700, 45401-45700, 51401-51700, 64701-65000, 74801-75100, 78501-78800, 85701-86000.
E. A. Dennison	J. L. Johnston	10501-10800, 14601-14700, 22601-22900, 34101-34400, 45701-46000, 53301-53600, 63701-64000, 71801-72100, 77901-78200, 85001-85100, 90301-90600, 96301-96600, 100401-100700, 106901-107100, 112901-113200.
H. Graham	M. B. Kirby	12001-12200, 20701-21000, 29601-29800, 30401-30700, 49001-49200, 54801-55000, 65601-65900, 75301-75600, 92401-92700, 97501-98000, 102701-103000, 105201-105300, 107101-107400, 113201-113600.
S. G. Sanxay	L. Macon	15601-15900, 69001-69200, 73301-73600, 82801-83100, 88801-89100, 93001-93300, 108901-109200, 111101-111400, 116201-116500, 120101-120400.
M. E. Dudley	M. E. Norton	15901-16200, 29301-29500, 31901-32000, 38601-38800, 41801-42100, 43801-44000, 50301-50400, 57801-58100, 66801-67100, 73601-73900, 81301-81500, 83701-83900, 84301-84400, 91901-92200, 101301-101600, 103501-103700, 107701-108000, 114901-115100, 116901-117200.

Register of Confederate States Treasury Notes—Continued.

ACT OF OCTOBER 13, 1862—Continued.

For Treasurer.	For Register.	Numbers of the notes signed.
		$5—A to H (1st series)—Continued.
M. Godwin	E. A. Adams	16501–16700.
W. A. Garrett	J. McGarr	16701–16900, 22901–23100, 31001–31200, 35701–36000, 58701–59000, 67101–67400, 70901–71200, 77001–77300, 82201–82500, 87901–88200, 94101–94400, 99801–100000, 103201–103500, 108301–108600, 109801–110100, 110801–111000, 115601–115900.
A. B. Capron	K. Walker	19201–19600, 30701–31000, 39101–39300, 43201–43500, 47801–48100, 56401–56800, 67701–67900.
F. Wray	E. Garlick	19601–19800, 26801–27000, 31301–31500, 38401–38600, 42101–42300, 60101–60300.
M. A. Dewees	H. L. Cooke	19801–20100, 24801–25100, 41201–41500.
Do	S. E. Hughes	47201–47500.
M. S. Knox	M. W. Bailey	20101–20400, 28501–28700, 37201–37500, 41501–41800, 47501–47800, 52701–53000, 60301–60500, 65001–65300, 73901–74200, 80401–80700, 86001–86200, 91301–91600, 96901–97200, 101601–101900, 106401–106600, 123801–124100.
S. G. Grattan	M. A. Gifford	20401–20700, 26201–26500, 43501–43800, 58401–58700, 80101–80400.
C. Skinner	S. E. Hughes	21301–21700, 25601–25900, 36001–36400, 39401–39800, 48401–48700, 50801–51100, 55001–55100, 59301–59600, 62501–62800, 69201–69400, 108001–108300, 111701–112000.
V. B. Briggs	J. B. Tiffey	22201–22400, 29501–29600, 31201–31300, 33501–33800, 55901–56400, 56801–57100, 63101–63400, 67901–68200, 71501–71800.
M. B. Christian	M. S. Apperson	27301–27600, 38801–39100.
M. V. Tyler	S. A. Talley	32901–33200, 53601–55900, 60801–61100, 111401–111700, 117201–117500.
H, Watkins	M. L. Savage	49201–49400.
F. M. Dickins	F. E. Bernard	63401–63700, 69401–69500.
		$5—A to H (2d series).
L. Breeden	L. C. Royster	1–300, 5301–5600, 11601–11900, 15701–15800, 18801–19100, 23901–24200, 29701–29900, 37401–37700, 47001–47300, 68401–68700, 76001–76200, 80501–80800, 86801–87100, 91301–91600, 100701–101000, 106401–106600, 130801–131200, 139701–140100, 148001–148200, 162401–162700, 171601–172000.
K. Heth	M. E. Gilliam	301–600, 20201–20500, 23601–23900, 27401–27700, 29101–29400, 33301–33600, 37701–38000, 42701–43000, 47601–47900, 51901–52200, 56301–56600, 63001–63300, 69001–69100, 69301–69500, 82301–82600, 86501–86800, 92501–92800, 96701–97000, 100101–100400, 105801–106100, 112901–113200, 119001–119400, 130101–130400, 141201–141600, 145701–146100, 147001–147400, 152301–152600, 164501–164800, 169001–169400.
E. A. Dennison	J. L. Johnston	601–800, 68101–68400, 74101–74400, 79001–79300, 85501–85600, 96401–96700, 101601–101900, 104701–105000, 110901–111200, 118401–118700, 138301–138600, 173001–173400.
H. M. Douglass	F. C. Jones	801–900, 5601–5900, 9501–9800, 136201–136500, 150201–150500.
R. F. Ball	L. M. Hunter	901–1200, 6201–6500, 10701–11000, 13901–14200, 18501–18800, 24201–24500, 28001–28300, 29401–29700, 34501–34800, 38501–38800, 43301–43600, 47301–47600, 52901–53200, 56001–56300, 75201–75400, 81701–82000, 87401–87700, 92901–93200, 100401–100700, 106901–107200, 113201–113500, 119401–119700, 124201–124500, 128001–128400, 140901–141200, 147801–148000, 155001–155200, 156801–157100, 163001–163300, 172401–173000.
R. Haynes	B. Dabney	1201–1500, 4701–5000, 11001–11300, 14401–14700, 19301–19600, 24501–24800, 28301–28500, 46801–47000, 57701–57900, 62501–62800, 69101–69300, 72901–73200, 81401–81700, 87101–87400, 91001–91300, 102401–102700, 113501–113800, 121901–122200, 126401–126700, 134501–134900, 143901–144200, 154701–155000, 163601–163900.
V. M. Stanard	S. C. Ellett	1501–1800, 4501–4700, 9801–10100, 15201–15400, 17001–17300, 26501–26800, 33601–33900, 42001–42300, 48101–48400, 53201–53400, 54701–55000, 63901–64100, 69501–69800, 76301–76500, 81101–81400, 93201–93400, 93901–94200, 101901–102200, 107201–107500, 112301–112600, 132001–132300, 138001–138300, 149101–149400, 157301–157600, 158501–158800, 166701–167100.

Register of Confederate States Treasury Notes—Continued.

ACT OF OCTOBER 13, 1862—Continued.

For Treasurer.	For Register.	Numbers of the notes signed.
		$5—A to H (2d series)—Continued.
H. Graham	M. B. Kirby	1801–2100, 6501–6800, 11301–11600, 15401–15700, 30301-30600, 111501–111900, 119901–120200.
M. V. Tyler	S. A. Talley	2101–2300, 6801–7100, 13001–13200.
S. G. Sanxay	L. Macon	2301–2600, 22701–23000, 32001–32300, 35001–35300, 39701-40000, 44701–45000, 50101–50400, 54101–54400, 58501-58800, 66001–66200, 66301–66400, 78401–78700, 83901-84200, 88001-88300, 94601–94900, 102701–103000, 108701–109100, 115501-115800, 122601–122900, 126701–127000, 135901–136200, 136701–137000, 159101–159400.
M. Allen	B. T. Lyon	2601–2900, 8501–8900, 12601–13000, 17601–18000, 20801-21100, 25201–25600, 31001–31300, 35601–35900, 39201-39700, 53401-53800, 58801–59300, 64501–64900, 71001–71400, 76601-77000, 97001–97400, 107801–108300, 114701–115200, 121101-121600, 125501–126100, 139301–139700, 143601–143900.
E. P. Porter	A. P. Pellet	2901–3200, 9201–9500, 12201–12600, 16401–16700, 21701-22000, 25601–25900, 30201–30300, 36801–37100, 41701-42000, 46201-46500, 51301–51600, 56601–56900, 60301–60600, 64901-65200, 73501–73800, 77301–77600, 84201–84500, 91601-92000, 98301-98600, 105201-105500, 110301-110600, 118101-118400, 123501-123800, 129101–129400, 133501–133800, 137001–137300, 145401–145700, 148801–149100, 154001–154100.
E. C. Green	B. McRae	3201–3500, 40301–40700, 48401–48700, 53801–54100, 63601-63900, 69801–70100, 75701–76000, 82001–82300, 87701-88000, 93401–93700, 102201–102400, 103001–103400, 114101-114700, 141601–141900, 149401–149700, 155501–155900, 157601-157900, 164801–165100.
M. E. Dudley	M. E. Norton	3501–3700, 18001–18200, 21101–21400, 126101–126400, 135601-135900, 142701–143000, 158201–158500.
W. A. Garrett	J. McGarr	3701–4000, 7401–7700, 14901–15200, 17301–17600, 21401-21700, 31301–31700, 36101–36200, 49401–49700, 120201–120500, 120801–121100, 127001–127300, 131201–131500, 146701-147000, 151501–151800, 165901–166300.
M. S. Nicholas	J. McCarthy	4001–4300, 10101–10400, 16101–16400, 23301–23600, 26801-27100, 30601–30900, 32301–32700, 36501–36800, 41101-41400, 45301–45600, 51001–51300, 55701–56000, 60601-60900, 68701-69000, 72101–72400, 79601–79900, 85901–86200, 89601-89900, 99501–99800, 103401–103700, 109101–109400, 122201-122600, 131501–131800, 135201–135600, 140701–140900, 146101-146300, 146401–146700, 152001–152300, 162701–163000.
E. D. Layne	V. C. Watson	4301–4500, 8901–9200, 13601–13900, 19901–20200, 23001-23300, 26201–26500, 32701–33000, 36201–36500, 50701-51000, 61201-61500, 66401–66700, 72701–72900, 83201–83500, 88601-89000, 94901–95100, 97701–98000, 109401–109700, 117401–117700, 123201–123500, 127301–127600, 132801–133100.
M. S. Knox	M. W. Bailey	5001–5300, 10401–10700, 14201–14400, 19101–19300, 33901-34200, 38001–38200, 46501–46800, 57201–57400, 62801-63000, 67801–68100, 74401–74600, 80801–81100, 92301-92500, 92801-92900, 101301–101600, 105001–105200, 109701–110000, 116101–116400, 119701–119900, 140101–140400, 143401-143600, 162301–162400, 168401–168900.
H. Bartlett	M. Taylor	5901–6200, 8101–8500, 14701–14900, 16701–17000, 22301-22700, 27701–28000, 29901–30200, 30901–31000, 34801-35000, 37101-37400, 41401–41700, 42601–42700, 45901–46200, 50401-50700, 56901–57200, 59301–59700, 65201–65500, 73201–73500, 76201-76300, 77001–77300, 83501–83900, 92001–92300, 98601-98900, 105501–105800, 110601–110900, 117701–118100, 118901-119000, 123801–124200, 129701–130100, 133101–133500, 137301–137700, 145101–145400, 148501–148800, 153001-153400, 154101–154400, 156501–156800, 163[illegible]1–164200.
L. C. Minor	B. M. Abbott	7101–7400, 11901–12200, 18201–18500, 22001–22300, 27101-27400, 28501–28800, 31701–32000, 35901–36100, 42301-42600, 44201–44400, 49701–50100, 61501–61800, 67501-67800, 73801-74100, 79301–79600, 85201–85500, 90001–90300, 95701-96000, 98901–99200, 117101–117400, 124501–124800, 129401-129700, 134901–135200, 137701–138000, 150901–151200, 160601-160900, 167901–168400.

Register of Confederate States Treasury Notes—Continued.

ACT OF OCTOBER 13, 1862—Continued.

For Treasurer.	For Register.	Numbers of the notes signed.
		$5—A to H (2d series)—Continued.
A. Points	M. Gay	7701–8100, 13201–13600, 15801–16100, 20501–20800, 24801-25200, 38301–38500, 38801–39200, 43801–44200, 49001–49400, 64101–64500, 70601–71000, 77601–78000, 82601–82900, 89001-89300, 89901–90000, 94201–94600, 143001–143400, 150501-150900, 153701–154000, 159701–160100, 167101–167500.
S. G. Grattan	H. L. Cooke	19601–19900, 34201–34500, 43001–43300, 52201–52500, 57901-58200, 60001–60300, 67301–67500, 74901–75200, 101001-101300, 106601–106900, 118701–118900, 124801–125100, 136501–136700, 138601–138900, 148201–148500, 155201-155500, 161801–162300, 171201–171600.
S. F. Shaver	M. Dixon	25901–26200, 28801–29100, 35301–35600, 40701–41100, 44401-44700, 54401–54700, 60901–61200, 65801–66000, 71401–71700, 76501–76600, 79901–80200, 84501–84800, 88301–88600, 93801-93900, 98001–98300, 104001–104300, 108301–108700, 115801-116100, 128701–129100, 132301–132800, 142401–142700, 160101–160600, 166301–166700.
M. A. Dewees	S. E. Hughes	33001–33300, 40001–40300, 45001–45300, 51601–51900, 55001-55300, 59701–60000, 70101–70400, 72401–72700, 78701–79000, 85601–85900, 90701–91000, 95101–95400, 97401–97700, 103701–104000, 111201–111500, 116401–116700, 121601-121900, 127601–127900, 134201–134500, 140401–140700, 141901–142200, 144201–144500, 146301–146400, 151201-151500, 154401–154700, 160901–161200, 170801–171200.
H. Watkins	M. L. Savage	38201–38500, 43601–43800, 47901–48100.
M. C. Irvine	M. Upshur	45601–45900, 65501–65800, 152701–152800, 157101–157300, 161501–161800, 169401–169700.
I. Benton	C. F. Windle	48701–49000, 58201–58400, 70401–70600, 144501–144800, 149801–150000, 151801–152000, 165101–165600.
E. Mason	M. C. Lathrop	52501–52900, 55301–55700, 62101–62500, 66201–66300, 66701-67000, 71701–72100, 78001–78400, 84801–85200, 90301–90700, 96001–96400, 99801–100100, 104301–104700, 111901–112300, 116701–117100, 125101–125500, 130401–130800, 133801-134200, 138901–139300.
V. M. Rind	V. K. Davies	57401–57700, 61801–62100, 67001–67300, 75401–75700, 80201-80500, 86201–86500, 89301–89600, 95401–95700, 99201–99500, 106101–106400, 110001–110300, 122901–123200, 131801-132000, 142201–142400, 149701–149800, 152601–152700, 155901–156200, 164201–164500, 168901–169000, 169701-170100.
F. Wray	E. Garlick	58401–58500, 112601–112900, 157901–158200.
F. M. Dickins	F. E. Bernard	63301–63600, 74601–74900, 82901–83200, 128401–128700, 144801-145100, 147401–147800, 152801–153100, 159401–159700, 172001–172400.
M. Godwin	E. A. Adams	93701–93800.
A. B. Capron	K. Walker	107501–107800, 115201–115500, 120501–120800, 150001-150200, 153401–153700, 156201–156500, 167501–167900.
V. B. Briggs	J. B. Tiffey	113801–114100, 158801–159100, 165601–165900.
S. Lambert	P. Pleasants	127901–128000.
M. B. Christian	M. S. Apperson	161201–161500, 170101–170400.
M. L. Quarles	F. G. Giles	163301–163600, 170401–170800.
		$5—A to H (3d series).
S. G. Grattan	H. L. Cooke	1–100, 3301–3600, 4501–4800, 12001–12300, 14301–14600, 17501-17600, 27101–27400, 32201–32500, 47901–48200, 53501–53800.
K. Heth	M. E. Gilliam	101–400, 6301–6600, 12301–12600, 19201–19500, 23001–23300, 31501–31900.
V. M. Rind	V. K. Davies	401–700, 7001–7300, 17901–18200, 23301–23600, 26401–26500, 26601–26900, 30901–31000, 32001–32200, 40201–40500, 43201-43500, 48201–48500.
M. S. Nicholas	J. McCarthy	701–800, 4201–4500, 10501–10800, 15101–15400, 22201–22400, 26001–26100, 29301–29600, 38701–39000, 42701–42900, 47301-47600, 54601–54900.
R. F. Ball	L. M. Hunter	801–1100, 5401–5700, 10801–11100, 19501–19700, 22401–22700, 28401–28800, 48501–48800.
R. Haynes	B. Dabney	1101–1400, 2601–3000, 9201–9500, 14901–15100, 20801–21000, 29901–30300, 36901–37100, 38001–38300, 41801–42100, 47601-47900, 53201–53500, 55101–55200.

Register of Confederate States Treasury Notes—Continued.

ACT OF OCTOBER 13, 1862—Continued.

For Treasurer.	For Register.	Numbers of the notes signed.
		$5—A to H (3d series)—Continued.
H. Graham	M. B. Kirby	1401–1700, 7901–8200, 13201–13500, 17601–17900.
V. M. Stanard	S. C. Ellett	1701–1900, 7301–7600, 12901–13200, 16301–16600, 19701-20200, 27701–28000, 34301–34500, 39901–40200, 43801-44100, 49001-49300.
M. Allen	B. T. Lyon	1901–2300, 13501–13900, 18501–18800, 23901–24800, 25501-26000, 35801–36200.
S. F. Shaver	M. Dixon	2301–2600, 8201–8600, 13901–14300, 29601–29900, 34501-34800, 38301-38700, 44801–45100.
E. D. Layne	V. C. Watson	3001–3300, 8601–8900, 16001–16300.
H. M. Douglass	F. C. Jones	3601–3900, 9901-10200, 22701-23000, 34801-35100, 45401-45700, 50701–51000.
H. Bartlett	M. Taylor	3901–4200, 11101–11500, 17301–17500, 21401–21600, 33701-34000, 39601–39900, 43501–43800, 49301–49600.
L. C. Minor	B. M. Abbott	4801–5100, 10201–10500, 15701–16000, 21901–22200, 42401-42700, 47001–47300, 54301–54600.
M. A. Dewees	S. E. Hughes	5101–5400, 8901–9200, 15401–15700, 20201–20500, 30601-30900, 37401–37500, 46001–46200, 55201–55300.
E. P. Porter	A. P. Pellet	5701–6000, 11501–11800, 17001–17300, 21601–21900, 33201-33500.
M. S. Knox	M. W. Bailey	6001–6300, 11801–12000, 30301–30600, 36601–36900, 37801-38000, 40501–40800, 46501–46700, 52701–52900, 55301-55400.
E. Mason	M. C. Lathrop	6601–7000, 9501–9900, 16601–17000, 21001–21400, 25101-25500, 28001–28400, 54901–55100.
E. C. Green	B. McRae	7601–7900, 23801–23900, 28801–29000, 42101–42400, 49601-49900.
W. A. Garrett	J. McGarr	12601–12900, 18801–19200, 23601–23800, 31201–31500.
S. G. Sanxay	L. Macon	14601–14900, 20501–20800, 24801–25100, 37101–37400, 37501-37800, 41101–41400, 44101–44400, 50501–50700.
L. Breeden	L. C. Royster	18201–18500, 26101–26400, 26501–26600, 33501–33700, 39001-39300, 42901–43200.
M. Godwin	E. A. Adams	26901–27100, 32501–32800.
E. A. Dennison	J. L. Johnston	27401–27700, 31001–31200, 31901–32000, 55801–56000.
A. B. Capron	K. Walker	29001–29300, 39301–39600, 46701–47000, 50301–50500.
A. Points	M. Gay	32801–33200, 35401–35800, 41401–41800, 44401–44800, 51901-52400.
I. Benton	C. F. Windle	34001–34300, 45701–46000, 52901–53200.
M. E. Dudley	M. E. Norton	35101–35400, 40801–41100, 49901–50100, 52401–52700.
V. B. Briggs	J. B. Tiffey	36201–36600, 45101–45400, 51001–51300.
F. Wray	E. Garlick	46201–46500, 51601–51900.
M. C. Irvine	M. Upshur	48801–49000.
M. L. Quarles	F. G. Giles	50101–50200, 54001–54300.
M. B. Christian	M. S. Apperson	50201–50300, 51301–51600.
F. M. Dickins	F. E. Bernard	53801–54000, 55701–55800.
N. Palmer	E. S. Read	55401–55700.
L. Archer	M. J. Morris	56001–56200.
		$2—A.
V. M. Stanard	S. C. Ellett	1–13600, 45601–47200.
V. B. Briggs	J. B. Tiffey	13601–15200, 20001–20800, 21601–22400, 67201–68000.
H. Bartlett	M. Taylor	15201–16800, 20801–21600, 66401–67200.
C. Skinner	S. E. Hughes	16801–17600.
S. F. Shaver	M. Dixon	17601–20000, 54401–56800.
M. Godwin	E. A. Adams	22401–24800, 68001–70400.
W. A. Garrett	J. McGarr	24801–27200.
M. S. Nicholas	J. McCarthy	27201–29600, 70401–72800.
M. S. Knox	M. W. Bailey	29601–31200, 92001–94400.
K. Heth	M. E. Gilliam	31201–33600, 88001–90400.
L. Breeden	L. C. Royster	33601–36000, 76001–78400.
R. F. Ball	L. M. Hunter	36001–39200, 96801–100000.
F. M. Dickins	F. E. Bernard	39201–40800, 61601–64000.
E. D. Layne	V. C. Watson	40801–42400, 94401–96800.
R. Haynes	B. Dabney	42401–44000, 78401–80800.
A. B. Capron	K. Walker	44001–45600.
H. Graham	M. B. Kirby	47201–49600.
M. B. Christian	M. S. Apperson	49601–51200.
A. Points	M. Gay	51201–54400.
S. G. Sanxay	L. Macon	56801–60000.

Register of Confederate States Treasury Notes—Continued.

ACT OF OCTOBER 13, 1862—Continued.

For Treasurer.	For Register.	Numbers of the notes signed.
		$2—A—Continued.
M. E. Dudley	M. E. Norton	60001–61600.
M. L. Quarles	F. G. Giles	64001–66400.
H. Watkins	M. L. Savage	72801–73600.
E. P. Porter	A. P. Pellet	73601–76000.
M. A. Dewees	I. A. Cooke	80801–83200.
V. M. Rind	V. K. Davies	83201–85600.
L. C. Minor	B. M. Abbott	85601–88000.
S. G. Grattan	M. A. Gifford	90401–92000.
		$2—B to I (1st series).*
M. S. Nicholas	J. McCarthy	1–300, 7001–7300, 12101–12300, 30201–30500, 38001–38300.
A. Points	M. Gay	301–600, 6401–6700, 17301–17500, 18501–18700, 19801–20000, 30901–31100.
L. Breeden	L. C. Royster	601–900, 7301–7600, 16601–16700, 20001–20200, 23201–23500, 26901–27000, 55801–56000, 59801–59900.
E. D. Layne	V. C. Watson	901–1000, 1201–1500, 6101–6400, 10701–10900, 11501–11700, 14801–15000, 15401–15600, 16701–16900, 28601–28900, 38801–39100.
E. P. Porter	A. P. Pellet	1001–1200, 37601–37900, 40601–40900.
V. M. Rind	V. K. Davies	1501–1800, 5801–6100, 17201–17300.
R. Haynes	B. Dabney	1801–2000, 8201–8500, 20301–20400, 37001–37300, 59901–60200.
R. F. Ball	L. M. Hunter	2001–2300, 5501–5800, 13701–14000, 17901–18100, 26201–26500, 57101–57400.
M. L. Quarles	F. G. Giles	2301–2500, 49501–49800.
V. M. Stanard	S. C. Ellett	2501–2800, 18101–18300, 55201–55500.
M. A. Dewees	S. E. Hughes	2801–2900, 3001–3100, 40301–40600.
Do	I. A. Cooke	2901–3000.
A. B. Capron	K. Walker	3101–3300, 10001–10100, 20701–21100, 22001–22300, 23701–24300, 25901–26200, 27001–27100, 28301–28600, 32001–32300, 44501–44700, 44801–45000, 47501–47800.
M. S. Knox	M. W. Bailey	3301–3500, 7901–8200, 9701–9800, 11701–11900, 16101–16300, 19101–19200, 26501–26700, 27601–27900, 38301–38500, 53101–53400.
M. B. Christian	M. S. Apperson	3501–3700, 9801–9900, 10201–10300, 44401–44500.
E. C. Green	B. McRae	3701–3800, 4201–4500, 10901–11100, 15001–15200, 17701–17900, 18301–18500, 19401–19600, 39701–40000, 56401–56800.
K. Heth	M. E. Gilliam	3801–3900, 4501–4800, 11901–12100, 16301–16600, 19201–19400, 31101–31300, 56001–56400.
M. Newton	M. E. Pace	3901–4200, 8701–9000, 10301–10500, 12501–12800, 32801–33000, 34001–34300, 34901–35200, 40001–40300, 45601–45900, 48001–48300, 50801–51100, 54601–54900.
H. Bartlett	M. Taylor	4801–5200, 14601–14800, 17101–17200, 31301–31500, 37301–37600, 37901–38000, 40901–41200, 59501–59800.
M. E. Dudley	M. E. Norton	5201–5500, 8501–8700, 29701–30000, 33101–33300, 43301–43600, 45901–46200, 48701–48900, 51101–51400.
S. F. Shaver	M. Dixon	6701–7000, 27101–27200, 30501–30700, 36701–37000, 42501–42800.
F. M. Dickins	F. E. Bernard	7601–7900, 9001–9300, 10501–10700, 12901–13000, 13201–13500, 14201–14500, 24901–25300, 27301–27600, 30701–30900, 34601–34900, 35201–35500, 41201–41500, 46801–47100, 50201–50500, 51901–52200, 55501–55800, 57701–57900, 59201–59500, 61501–61775.
W. A. Garrett	J. McGarr	9301–9500, 11301–11500, 18901–19100, 26701–26900, 31501–31700, 33701–34000, 36401–36700, 45301–45600, 47101–47200, 49201–49500, 51401–51600, 54301–54600.
H. Watkins	M. L. Savage	9501–9600, 13001–13200, 14501–14600, 21401–21700, 22901–23200, 25501–25700, 27901–28100, 34301–34600, 47301–47400, 50701–50800, 52501–52800.
M. Godwin	E. A. Adams	9601–9700, 42801–43000, 46501–46800, 49801–49900, 52801–53100, 60501–60700, 61201–61500.
C. Skinner	S. E. Hughes	9901–10000, 10101–10200, 24601–24900.
S. G. Sanxay	L. Macon	11101–11300, 21701–22000, 24301–24600, 39401–39700.
V. B. Briggs	J. B. Tiffey	12301–12500, 14001–14200, 15801–16100, 20201–20300, 21101–21400, 22301–22600, 25701–25900, 28101–28300, 31701–32000, 45001–45300, 48301–48700, 53701–54000.
M. V. Tyler	S. A. Talley	13501–13700, 15201–15400, 18701–18900, 20401–20700.

* Notes numbered 12801–12900 never issued.

Register of Confederate States Treasury Notes—Continued.

ACT OF OCTOBER 13, 1862—Continued.

For Treasurer.	For Register.	Numbers of the notes signed.
		$2—B to I (1st series)—Continued.
L. C. Minor	B. M. Abbott	15601–15800, 17501–17700, 30001–30200, 41501–41800.
E. A. Dennison	J. L. Johnston	16901–17100, 42201–42500, 57001–57100, 57901–58200.
F. Wray	E. Garlick	19601–19800, 22601–22900, 23501–23700, 25301–25500, 27201–27300, 29101–29300, 43901–44100, 47801–48000, 51601–51900, 54901–55200, 58701–59000, 60701–60900.
I. Benton	C. F. Windle	28901–29100, 33501–33700, 43601–43900, 44101–44400, 48901–49200, 52201–52500.
M. C. Irvine	M. Upshur	29301–29500, 44701–44800, 47401–47500, 50501–50700, 58201–58700, 59001–59200.
H. M. Douglass	F. C. Jones	29501–29700, 39101–39400, 47201–47300, 56801–57000, 60901–61200.
S. Lambert	P. Pleasants	32301–32600, 33301–33500, 35801–36400, 43001–43300, 46201–46500, 49901–50200.
S. G. Grattan	H. L. Cooke	32601–32800, 35501–35800, 38501–38800, 53401–53700, 60201–60500.
E. Mason	M. C. Lathrop	41801–42200.
H. Graham	M. B. Kirby	54001–54300, 57401–57700.
		$2—B to I (2d series).
E. C. Green	B. McRae	1–200.
A. B. Capron	K. Walker	201–400.
M. E. Dudley	M. E. Norton	401–600.
F. M. Dickins	F. E. Bernard	601–900.
M. L. Quarles	F. G. Giles	901–1100.
		$1—A.
V. M. Stanard	S. C. Ellett	1–4800, 77601–79200.
C. Skinner	S. E. Hughes	4801–7200, 36801–40000, 100001–103200.
R. F. Ball	L. M. Hunter	7201–9600, 24801–26400, 46401–47200.
R. Haynes	B. Dabney	9601–11200, 27201–28000, 70401–72800.
H. Watkins	M. L. Savage	11201–12800, 54401–56000, 56801–57600, 92001–93600.
L. Breeden	L. C. Royster	12801–14400.
S. G. Grattan	M. A. Gifford	14401–16000, 28001–28800, 68001–70400.
M. E. Dudley	M. E. Norton	16001–17600, 76801–77600, 96001–97600.
F. M. Dickins	F. E. Bernard	17601–19200, 44001–46400.
F. Wray	E. Garlick	19201–20800, 59201–60800.
E. D. Layne	V. C. Watson	20801–23200, 72801–75200.
V. B. Briggs	J. B. Tiffey	23201–24800, 66401–68000.
M. S. Knox	M. W. Bailey	26401–27200, 47201–49600.
A. Points	M. Gay	28801–32000, 79201–82400.
E. P. Porter	A. P. Pellet	32001–34400, 93601–96000.
S. G. Sanxay	L. Macon	34401–36800, 89601–92000.
S. F. Shaver	M. Dixon	40001–41600.
L. C. Minor	B. M. Abbott	41601–44000, 87201–89600.
E. A. Dennison	J. L. Johnston	49601–52000, 106401–110400.
H. Graham	M. B. Kirby	52001–54400.
A. B. Capron	K. Walker	56001–56800, 63201–64800.
K. Heth	M. E. Gilliam	57601–59200.
M. B. Christian	M. S. Apperson	60801–63200.
V. M. Rind	V. K. Davies	64801–66400, 97601–100000.
M. Godwin	E. A. Adams	75201–76800.
M. L. Quarles	F. G. Giles	82401–84800.
M. Newton	M. E. Pace	84801–87200.
H. Bartlett	M. Taylor	103201–106400.
		$1—B to I (1st series).*
H. Bartlett	M. Taylor	1–300, 3301–3700, 9201–9500, 13301–13400, 18501–18600, 18801–19100, 23001–23200, 113401–113600.
W. A. Garrett	J. McGarr	301–600, 11501–11600, 11801–11900, 19101–19400, 21001–21300, 42401–42700, 45101–45300, 49601–49900, 52701–53000, 58001–58300, 61101–61400, 63101–63400, 65601–65900, 70501–70800, 72601–72900, 75101–75400, 77101–77400, 78901–79200, 80701–81000, 83501–83800, 84701–85000, 87201–87500, 91201–91500, 93301–93600, 96401–96700, 106001–106300, 117301–117600.

*Notes numbered 37801–37900 never issued.

Register of Confederate States Treasury Notes—Continued.

ACT OF OCTOBER 13, 1862—Continued.

For Treasurer.	For Register.	Numbers of the notes signed.
		$1—B to I (1st series)—Continued.
V. M. Stanard	S. C. Ellett	601–900, 5201–5400, 34901–35100, 46201–46400, 53601–53900, 56901–57100, 84201–84500, 102201–102500, 111601–111800, 120901–121200.
A. B. Capron	K. Walker	901–1100, 4601–4900, 10701–11000, 14501–14800, 21601–21900, 22401–22600, 27801–27900, 29801–30000, 31801-32100, 33001-33400, 37301–37600, 38501–38800, 40201–40300, 44101-44400, 47801–48100, 51301–51600, 56101–56400, 59501-59800, 62501-62800, 65101–65400, 67801–68200, 72201–72600, 74301-74500, 87001–87200, 103401–103600, 110101–110400, 115501-115800, 118001–118300, 120601–120900, 125401–126000 (B, C, D, and E).
H. Graham	M. B. Kirby	1101–1400, 6801–7100, 10301–10600, 12901–13000, 13401-13500, 14201–14300, 114601–114800.
M. B. Christian	M. S. Apperson	1401–1600, 7301–7500, 11201–11500, 12001–12200, 15201-15400, 17401–17500, 84601–84700, 86501–86700, 89401-89700, 91501-91900, 98601–98900, 123601–124000 (B, C, D, and E), 126001-126500 (B, C, D, and E).
M. E. Dudley	M. E. Norton	1601–1700, 2001–2200, 7201–7300, 8001–8300, 11601–11700, 15401–15600, 17101–17400, 18101–18200, 24201-24400, 32101-32400, 39101–39300, 40101–40200, 40801–41100, 48701-49000, 53301–53600, 63401–63700, 65901–66200, 71901-72200, 74101-74300, 75401–75700, 79601–79900, 81201–81500, 82401-82600, 82901-83200, 86801-87000, 93601-93900, 99301-99600, 107101-107400, 113601–113800, 117001–117300, 118801–119200.
Do	M. E. Pace	68901–69200.
L. C. Minor	B. M. Abbott	1701–2000, 9501–9800, 11701–11800, 24101–24300, 26101-26300, 112801–113000.
M. Newton	M. E. Pace	2201–2500, 8601–8900, 12401–12500, 25701–25900, 27401-27600, 30101–30400, 32701–33000, 36701–37000, 70201-70500, 73701-73800, 74801–75100, 78101–78400, 82101–82400, 87501-87800, 90301–90600, 94101–94400, 97001–97300, 99901–100200, 104701–105000, 111001–111200.
V. M. Rind	V. K. Davies	2501–2800, 26301-26500, 83901–84100, 109701–109900, 115001-115300.
E. P. Porter	A. P. Pellet	2801–3100, 12801–12900, 13001–13100, 56501–56700, 108801-109100, 113201–113400.
A. Points	M. Gay	3101–3300, 13101–13300, 19401–19600, 35301–35500.
S. F. Shaver	M. Dixon	3701–4000, 8301–8600, 16101–16200, 16601–16900, 17601-17700, 18201-18400, 20201-20400, 26701-26900, 35501-35700, 101901-102200.
M. A. Dewees	I. A. Cooke	4001–4300, 12501–12526, 14301–14400.
Do	S. E. Hughes	12527–12600, 18401–18500, 39801–40100, 43201–43500, 45601-45900, 50201–50500, 52201–52300, 52601–52700, 61401-61700, 107401–107700, 110801–111000.
M. Godwin	E. A. Adams	4301–4600, 7701–8000, 11001–11200, 17701–17800, 17901-18000, 85901–86200, 88101–88400, 92201–92600, 95301-95600, 97901-98100, 104101-104400, 105701-106000, 108301-108500, 112001–112200, 116401–116700.
E. D. Layne	V. C. Watson	4901–5200, 14901–15000, 27901–28000.
R. Haynes	B. Dabney	5401–5700, 13701–13900, 28401–28500, 35901–36200, 83801-83900, 84501–84600, 108501–108800, 113001–113200.
M. L. Quarles	F. G. Giles	5701–5900, 92601–92800, 94701–95000, 97601–97900, 100701-101000, 117601–117700, 124601–125200 (B, C, D, and E).
R. F. Ball	L. M. Hunter	5901–6200, 15901–16100, 23901–24100, 114401–114600.
F. M. Dickins	F. E. Bernard	6201–6500, 15001–15200, 16201–16500, 18601–18800, 20401-20700, 21901–22200, 23601–23900, 28001–28200, 28701-29000, 31001–31300, 33401–33700, 34301–34600, 36201-36400, 37701-37800, 37901–38100, 39301–39600, 41101–41400, 42901-43200, 45901–46200, 49901–50200, 54501–54700, 58601-58900, 61901-62200, 63901–64200, 66201–66500, 69201–69500, 69601-69900, 78701–78900, 81501–81800, 86201–86500, 88801-89100, 90901-91200, 95601–95900, 98101–98400, 101001–101300, 106301-106600, 117701–118000, 120301–120600, 124001-124600 (B, C, D, and E).
K. Heth	M. E. Gilliam	6501–6800, 9801-10100, 12601-12800, 16501-16600, 25901-26100, 83401–83500, 102501–102800, 112601–112800.

Register of Confederate States Treasury Notes—Continued.

ACT OF OCTOBER 13, 1862—Continued.

For Treasurer.	For Register.	Numbers of the notes signed.
		$1—B to I (1st series)—Continued.
H. Watkins	M. L. Savage	7101-7200, 10101-10300, 13501-13700, 22201-22400, 25301-25500, 26501-26700, 29501-29600, 31601-31800, 35701-35900, 37601-37700, 38401-38500, 39601-39800, 41601-41800, 44001-44100, 47001-47300, 51601-51700, 55301-55500, 57401-57700, 71501-71700, 76501-76800, 78401-78700, 86701-86800, 89101-89400, 95[illegible]1-95300, 98401-98600, 101601-101900, 106801-107100, 109901-110100, 112201-112400.
E. C. Green	B. McRae	7501-7700, 14101-14200, 14401-14500, 102801-103100, 115801-116000.
V. B. Briggs	J. B. Tiffey	8901-9200, 19901-20200, 22601-22800, 27601-27800, 29601-29800, 31301-31600, 33701-33900, 34101-34300, 34601-34900, 36401-36700, 38101-38400, 38801-39100, 41801-42100, 44401-44600, 45301-45600, 53901-54200, 60601-60900, 64801-65100, 67101-67400, 67501-67800, 70801-71100, 72901-73200, 75701-76000, 79201-79600, 81801-82100, 85001-85300, 88401-88800, 93901-94100, 98901-99100, 100201-100400, 103801-104100, 105001-105200, 105501-105700, 108001-108300, 110601-110800, 116701-117000, 119201-119500, 121801-122400 (B, C, D, and E).
E. A. Dennison	J. L. Johnston	10601-10700, 11901-12000, 27101-27300, 35101-35300.
F. Wray	E. Garlick	12201-12400, 14801-14900, 15601-15900, 19601-19900, 20701-21000, 25101-25300, 29301-29500, 30001-30100, 30701-31000, 33901-34100, 37001-37300, 47701-47800, 48401-48700, 52301-52600, 59801-60100, 62801-63100, 66801-67100, 71701-71900, 73501-73700, 73801-74100, 74501-74800, 84101-84200, 85301-85600, 89701-90000, 95901-96000, 96701-97000, 99601-99900, 105201-105400, 115301-115500, 118501-118800, 120001-120300, 121201-121800 (B, C, D, and E).
C. Skinner	S. E. Hughes	13901-14100, 22801-23000, 29001-29300, 30401-30700.
M. V. Tyler	S. A. Talley	16901-17100, 17501-17600, 17801-17900, 18001-18100, 21301-21600, 27301-27400, 28501-28700, 42101-42400, 45001-45100.
Do	B. M. Payne	44901-45000, 48101-48400, 54201-54500.
M. S. Nicholas	J. McCarthy	23401-23600, 28201-28400, 83301-83400, 107701-108000, 111801-112000.
L. Breeden	L. C. Royster	24301-24500, 57701-57900, 114201-114400.
S. G. Grattan	M. A. Gifford	24501-25100, 26901-27100.
Do	H. L. Cooke	46401-46700, 50501-50800, 55801-56100, 57101-57400, 62201-62500, 67401-67500, 80201-80500, 83201-83300, 91901-92200, 109401-109700, 112401-112600, 123001-123600 (B, C, D, and E).
S. G. Sanxay	L. Macon	25501-25700, 32401-32700, 49001-49300, 111201-111400.
H. M. Douglass	F. C. Jones	40301-40600, 43701-44000, 47501-47700, 49301-49600, 55501-55800, 58301-58600, 60301-60600, 63701-63900, 66501-66800, 68201-68500, 69901-70200, 73201-73500, 77401-77700, 82601-82900, 87801-88100, 90601-90900, 93001-93300, 96001-96400, 100401-100700, 104401-104700, 111401-111600, 116001-116400, 118301-118500, 119501-119800, 122401-123000 (B, C, D, and E).
I. Benton	C. F. Windle	40601-40800, 42701-42900, 44601-44900, 51901-52200, 56401-56500, 59201-59500, 64501-64800, 69501-69600, 76801-77100, 80501-80700, 81001-81200, 85601-85900, 92801-93000, 99101-99300, 103101-103400, 110401-110600, 114801-115000.
M. C. Irvine	M. Upshur	41401-41600, 43501-43700, 51701-51900, 53001-53300, 58901-59200, 61701-61900, 65401-65600, 71301-71500, 76301-76500, 119801-120000, 125201-125400 (B, C, D, and E).
M. S. Knox	M. W. Bailey	46701-47000, 51101-51300, 54701-55000, 57901-58000, 109101-1[illegible]9400, 114001-114200.
S. Lambert	P. Pleasants	47301-47500, 50801-51100, 55001-55300, 56701-56900, 60101-60300, 60901-61100, 64201-64500, 68501-68900, 71101-71300, 76001-76300, 77701-77800, 79901-80200, 90001-90300, 94401-94700, 97301-97600, 101301-101600, 103601-103800, 105401-105500, 106601-106800.
E. Mason	M. C. Lathrop	113801-114000.
		$1—B to I (2d series).
V. B. Briggs	J. B. Tiffey	1-300, 2001-2200.
W. A. Garrett	J. McGarr	301-600, 4501-4800.

Register of Confederate States Treasury Notes—Continued.

ACT OF OCTOBER 13, 1862—Continued.

For Treasurer.	For Register.	Numbers of the notes signed.
		$1—B to I (2d series)—Continued.
V. M. Stanard	S. C. Ellett	601-900.
F. M. Dickins	F. E. Bernard	901-1100.
H. M. Douglass	F. C. Jones	1101-1400.
S. G. Sanxay	L. Macon	1401-1700.
S. F. Shaver	M. Dixon	1701-2000.
M. A. Dewees	S. E. Hughes	2[illegible]01-2500.
V. M. Rind	V. K. Davies	2501-2800.
M. S. Knox	M. W. Bailey	2801-3100.
M. L. Quarles	F. G. Giles	3101-3400, 4201-4500.
M. S. Nicholas	J. McCarthy	3401-3600.
F. Wray	E. Garlick	3601-3900.
M. E. Dudley	M. E. Norton	3901-4200.
M. C. Irvine	M. Upshur	4801-5000.

ACT OF MARCH 23, 1863.

		MAY ISSUE.*
		$100—A to D.
* * * *	* * * *	* * * * * * *
W. R. Todd	J. H. Cooke	27301-28100, 28901-29700, 31801-32600, 33401-34400, 35201-36000, 36801-37600, 39201-40800, 41601-42400, 44001-44800, 45601-46400, 53801-54600, 55101-55900, 56701-57500, 59101-59900.
J. W. Jones	J. O. Snyder	28101-28900, 30501-31300, 32601-33400, 36001-36800, 37601-39200, 40801-41600, 42401-44000, 44801-45600, 46401-47200, 50101-50900, 52201-53000, 55901-56700, 57501-58300, 59901-60700.
T. D. Walford	T. F. Grayson	29701-30500, 31301-31800, 34401-35200.
E. C. Goddin	J. M. Kinney	47201-48000, 51401-52200, 53001-53800, 60701-61500.
W. F. Hoge	Tho. J. Miller	48001-48800.
A. W. Gray	W. Hancock	48801-50100, 50901-51400, 54601-55100, 61501-62200, 63101-64800.
J. C. Joplin	S. Dutcher	58301-59100, 62201-63100.
		$50—wA to zA.
* * * *	* * * *	* * * * * * *
W. G. Allen	C. S. Taylor	54801-54900, 58101-58900, 60501-61300, 70201-71000, 76401-78200, 81401-82200, 84601-85400, 93801-94600, 99601-100400.
T. C. Gale	E. H. Smith	54901-55700, 62101-61900, 64801-65600, 68601-69400, 74201-75000, 75801-76600, 78201-79000, 79801-80600, 83001-83800, 87001-87400, 89801-90600, 95401-96200, 97801-98800, 106301-107100.
A. W. Gray	W. Hancock	55701-56500, 58901-59700, 62901-63700, 65601-66400, 67801-68600, 71801-72600, 75001-75800, 76601-77400, 79001-79800, 80601-81400, 83801-84600, 86201-87000, 89001-89800, 101201-101600, 102701-103600, 104601-105500, 107901-108600.
T. O. Keesee	J. T. Dickson	56501-57300, 59701-60500, 63701-64500, 66401-67200, 69401-70200, 72601-73400.
T. D. Walford	T. F. Grayson	57301-58100, 64501-64800, 73401-74200.
W. R. Todd	J. H. Cooke	61301-62100, 67201-67800.
J. W. Jones	J. O. Snyder	71001-71800, 102601-102700.
E. C. Goddin	J. M. Kinney	82201-83000, 85401-86200, 88201-89000.
J. C. Joplin	S. Dutcher	87401-88200, 90601-91400, 97001-97800, 100401-101200, 101601-102600, 103601-104600, 105501-106300, 107101-107900.
T. J. Hatch	W. B. Walston	91401-92200.
C. Ashford	S. Sinton	92201-93000.
N. A. Bass	A. S. Watkins	93001-93800.
F. H. Link	L. P. Rogers	94601-95400.
S. B. Jacobs	W. O. Slade	96201-97000, 98801-99600.

* Record of April issue missing, as also part of May issue.

Register of Confederate States Treasury Notes—Continued.

ACT OF MARCH 23, 1863—Continued.

For Treasurer.	For Register.	Numbers of the notes signed.
		MAY ISSUE—Continued.
		$20—A to H.
* * * *	* * * *	* * * * * * *
R. M. Payne	M. Winston	125601-125700, 137901-138300, 143101-143500, 147101-147500.
E. C. Goddin	J. M. Kinney	125701-126100, 133601-134000, 138301-138700, 142701-143100, 147801-148200, 152201-152600, 155401-155800, 159801-160200, 176001-176400, 182901-183300, 186501-186900, 189601-190000.
J. W. Jones	J. O. Snyder	126101-126500, 138701-139100, 180201-180500.
S. B. Jacobs	W. O. Slade	126501-126900, 130101-130500, 134001-134400, 139101-139500, 143501-143900, 148201-148600, 151801-152200, 153401-153800, 160601-161000, 165701-166100, 175601-176000, 182501-182900, 185801-186200, 190001-190300.
J. B. S. Dimitry	W. Nott	125901-127300, 130501-130800, 139501-139900, 143901-144300, 148601-149000, 153001-153400, 157001-157400, 161001-161400, 166101-166500, 168201-168600, 170601-170800.
W. F. Hoge	Tho. J. Miller	127301-127700, 129501-129700, 132401-132800, 136801-137200, 142301-142700, 147501-147800, 152601-153000, 156201-156600, 160201-160600, 165301-165700, 169801-170200.
J. C. Joplin	S. Dutcher	127701-128100, 132001-132400, 135601-136000, 140701-141100, 144301-144700, 150201-150600, 154601-155000, 158601-159000, 161801-162200, 180601-181100.
T. J. Hatch	J. P. Swords	128101-128500, 133201-133600, 134801-135200, 141101-141500, 146701-147100, 151401-151800, 167201-167600.
Do	W. B. Walston	155001-155400, 158201-158600, 163001-163300, 164501-164900, 169401-169800, 172001-172400, 172801-173200, 177601-178000, 181401-181800, 185001-185400, 187301-187700, 191101-191500.
B. H. Berry	J. T. Holt	128501-128900, 131601-132000, 136001-136400, 140301-140700, 144701-145100, 186201-186500, 188101-188400, 190701-191100.
C. Ashford	S. Sinton	128901-129300, 131201-131600, 146301-146700, 150601-151000, 153801-154200, 157401-157800, 162201-162600, 164101-164500, 168601-169000, 171601-172000, 174401-174800, 178401-178800, 179401-179800, 184201-184600, 188401-188800, 190301-190700.
F. C. Weisiger	W. P. Caldwell	129301-129500, 132801-133200, 137201-137500, 141501-141900, 145101-145500, 149801-150200, 155801-156200, 159401-159800, 168001-168200, 170801-171200, 173201-173600, 178801-179100, 179801-180200, 183801-184200, 187701-188100, 191901-192300.
N. A. Bass	A. S. Watkins	129701-130100, 134401-134800, 135201-135600, 145901-146300, 149001-149400, 156601-157000, 159001-159400, 162601-163000, 163301-163700, 166801-167200, 170201-170600, 171201-171600, 174001-174400, 176801-177200, 181101-181400, 181801-181900, 188801-189200, 191501-191900.
Do	W. B. Walston	184601-185000.
T. C. Gale	E. H. Smith	130801-131200, 176401-176800, 181901-182100, 186901-187300.
F. H. Link	L. P. Rogers	136401-136800, 139901-140300, 145501-145900, 149401-149800, 154201-154600, 164901-165300, 166501-166800, 167601-168000, 169001-169400, 174801-175200, 178001-178400.
W. G. Allen	C. S. Taylor	137501-137900, 141901-142300, 172401-172800, 173601-174000, 180501-180600, 182101-182500, 185401-185800, 189201-189600, 192301-192700.
J. E. Henderson	J. T. Dickson	151001-151400, 157801-158200, 161401-161800, 163701-164100.
Do	Tho. J. Miller	175201-175600, 177201-177600, 179101-179400.
A. W. Gray	W. Hancock	183301-183800, 192701-192800.
		$10—A to H.
* * * *	* * * *	* * * * * * *
L. C. Minor	B. M. Abbott	36601-36900, 45001-45300, 58401-58700, 72401-72700, 90501-90800, 99001-99300, 116201-116500, 132601-132900, 147601-147900.

Register of Confederate States Treasury Notes—Continued.

ACT OF MARCH 23, 1863—Continued.

For Treasurer.	For Register.	Numbers of the notes signed.
		MAY ISSUE—Continued.
		$10—A to H—Continued.
V. M. Stanard	S. C. Ellett	36901-37200, 48701-49000, 57401-57700, 68701-69000, 80401-80600, 85301-85600, 97601-97900, 100101-100400, 109601-109900, 114801-115100, 119101-119400, 127801-128100, 137001-137300, 150901-151200, 156101-156400, 160101-160400.
M. B. Christian	M. S. Apperson	37201-37500, 50101-50400, 105601-105900, 133201-133500.
M. C. Irvine	M. Johnson	37501-37800, 47501-47800, 91101-91400, 107001-107300, 118301-118500, 148201-148500, 163801-164100.
M. Godwin	E. A. Adams	37801-38100, 46901-47200, 67501-67800, 80301-80400, 84801-85000, 91701-92000, 98501-98700, 101201-101500, 108101-108400, 114201-114400, 120001-120300, 128501-128800, 153201-153500, 158901-159200.
R. Haynes	B. Dabney	38101-38400, 48101-48400, 56501-56800, 82601-82900, 85601-85900, 97001-97300, 104501-104800, 113101-113300, 115901-116200, 162701-163000.
A. B. Capron	K. Walker	38401-38700, 47801-48100, 60201-60500, 70701-70900, 82901-83000, 86801-87100, 98701-99000, 102101-102400, 111001-111300, 115701-115900, 130301-130600, 138201-138500, 158201-158500, 159701-160000.
S. F. Shaver	M. Dixon	38701-39000, 49501-49800, 56801-57100, 81801-82100, 89701-90000, 104201-104500, 115101-115400, 131801-132100, 148501-148800, 161001-161300.
E. D. Layne	V. C. Watson	39001-39400, 49001-49200, 70901-71200.
S. Lambert	P. Pleasants	39401-39700, 61801-62000, 71501-71800, 80901-81200, 102701-103000, 112901-113100, 116501-116800, 122301-122600, 129401-129700, 137301-137600, 155801-156100, 163001-163200.
A. Harrison	E. C. Winston	39701-40000, 48401-48700, 60501-60800, 82401-82600.
Do	H. Winston	88301-88600, 98201-98500, 104801-105100, 107301-107400, 110801-111000.
Do	M. Wade	114501-114800, 123201-123400, 157301-157600, 160701-161000.
R. F. Ball	L. M. Hunter	40001-40300, 55701-56000, 69901-70200, 86201-86500, 97901-98200, 101801-102100, 111501-111800, 131201-131500, 151501-151800, 154601-154900, 160001-160100.
F. M. Dickins	F. E. Bernard	40301-40600, 41801-42100, 59001-59300, 67801-68100, 94601-94800, 95001-95300, 103001-103300, 129101-129400.
L. Breeden	M. Wade	40601-41000, 58701-59000.
Do	E. C. Winston	87401-87700, 156701-157000, 163201-163500.
M. Jones	E. Garlick	41001-41300, 50401-50600, 59601-59900, 60801-60900, 94301-94600, 99701-99800, 103301-103600, 122001-122300, 131501-131800, 137601-137900, 154101-154400, 160401-160700.
H. Starke	M. Morrison	41301-41600, 43901-44200, 57901-58200, 71201-71500, 81501-81800, 86501-86800, 112301-112600, 130601-130900.
E. Mason	M. C. Lathrop	41601-41800, 49201-49500, 60901-61300, 73201-73600, 88001-88300, 99301-99700, 105901-106200, 113601-113900, 118001-118300, 134401-134700, 157001-157300, 163501-163800.
A. Points	M. Gay	42101-42400, 59301-59600, 83001-83300, 92801-93100, 120601-120900.
V. Bridges	E. W. Pendleton	42401-42700, 54501-54800, 62001-62300, 91401-91700, 95601-95900, 99801-100100, 119701-120000, 126901-127200, 134701-135000, 150601-150900, 165601-165700.
H. M. Douglass	F. C. Jones	42701-43000, 55401-55700, 69001-69300, 90001-90300, 95301-95600, 103601-103900, 112001-112300, 115401-115700, 129701-130000, 152301-152600.
M. V. Tyler	B. M. Payne	43001-43300, 80001-80300, 83301-83600, 92601-92800, 95901-96100, 100401-100600, 107801-108100, 119401-119700, 127501-127800, 135001-135300, 148901-149200, 150301-150600, 152601-152900, 165001-165300.
V. B. Briggs	J. B. Tiffey	43301-43600, 58201-58400, 68401-68700, 80601-80900, 84501-84800, 92301-92600, 97301-97600, 100901-101200, 109901-110200, 121201-121500, 128101-128300, 136401-136700, 154401-154600.

Register of Confederate States Treasury Notes—Continued.

ACT OF MARCH 23, 1863—Continued.

For Treasurer.	For Register.	Numbers of the notes signed.
		MAY ISSUE—Continued.
		$10—A to H—Continued.
M. Allen	B. T. Lyon	43601–43900, 55001–55400, 72101–72400, 79001–79400, 83601–83900, 94801–95000, 96101–96400, 100601–100900, 107401–107800, 114401–114500, 118801–119100, 127201–127500, 135301–135600, 149201–149500, 150001–150300, 152001–152300, 164701–165000.
I. Benton	M. Pace	44201–44500, 70201–70400, 90301–90500, 93901–94100, 105401–105600, 111301–111500, 121801–122000, 128301–128500, 135601–135800, 148801–148900, 151801–152000, 159501–159700.
W. A. Garrett	J. McGarr	44501–44800, 61501-61800, 71801-72100, 103901-104200, 109301–109600, 117701–118000, 118501–118800, 133501–133800, 154901–155200, 165301–165600.
Do	J. Nelson	84201–84500.
F. C. Green	B. McRae	44801–45000, 57101–57400, 72701–72900.
M. E. Dudley	M. E. Norton	45301–45600, 56001–56300, 70401–70700, 85001–85300, 101501–101800, 110201–110500, 128801–129100, 136701–137000, 149801–150000, 153801–154100, 158801–158900.
H. Watkins	M. L. Savage	45601–45900, 57701–57900, 73601–73700, 88601–88800, 94101–94300, 132401–132600, 161901–162200.
S. G. Sanxay	L. Macon	45901–46200, 61301–61500, 68101–68400, 79701–80000, 93401–93600, 96401–96700, 109001–109300, 120301–120600, 149501–149800, 153501–153800.
M. L. Quarles	F. G. Giles	46201–46600, 54801–55000, 62301–62500, 67401–67500, 79401–79700, 83901–84200, 93601–93900, 108701–109000, 120901–121200, 136101–136400, 155201–155500, 159201–159500.
M. S. Nicholas	J. McCarthy	46601–46900, 56301–56500, 69301–69600, 87701–88000, 93101–93400, 106701–107000, 110501–110800, 113901–114200, 122901–123200, 130001–130300, 137901–138200, 151201–151500, 152901–153200, 161601–161800.
V. M. Rind	V. K. Davies	47201–47500, 59901–60200, 69601–69900, 81201–81500, 87101–87400, 96701–97000, 102401–102700, 108401–108700, 121501–121800, 132101–132400, 155501–155800, 161801–161900, 162201–162400.
M. S. Knox	M. W. Bailey	49801-50100, 72901–73200, 90801-91100, 106201–106400, 158501–158800, 162401–162700.
F. C. Weisiger	W. P. Caldwell	50601–51000, 54201–54500, 62501–62600, 73901–74300, 125501–125900, 142501–142700, 147101–147300.
S. B. Jacobs	W. O. Slade	51001–51400, 63001–63400, 64401–64800, 74701–75100, 76701–77100, 123801-124200, 126701-126900, 138501-138700, 144501–144700, 145501–145600, 145701–145800, 147401–147500.
J. B. S. Dimitry	W. Nott	51401–51800, 63401–63800, 64801–65400, 75501–75900, 77101–77400, 78601–79000, 124301–124700, 142101–142500.
W. F. Hoge	Tho. J. Miller	51801–52200, 62601–63000, 65801–66200.
E. C. Goddin	J. M. Kinney	52201–52600, 77401–77800, 141301–141700, 144701–144900, 146101–146200, 147501–147600.
F. H. Link	L. P. Rogers	52601–52700, 66801–67200, 76301–76700, 139501–139900, 143901–144100, 146801–146900, 147001–147100.
J. E. Henderson	J. T. Dickson	52701–53000, 75901–76300, 125101–125500.
Do	Tho. J. Miller	143101–143300, 146701–146800, 146901–147000.
T. J. Hatch	W. B. Walston	53001–53400, 65401–65800, 138701–139100, 143501–143700, 146001–146100, 146201–146300.
N. A. Bass	A. S. Watkins	53401–53800, 66401–66800, 125901–126300, 144301–144500, 146501–146700.
C. Ashford	S. Sinton	53801–54200, 64001–64400, 74301–74700, 126301–126700, 142901–143100, 145901–146000, 147301–147400.
J. C. Joplin	S. Dutcher	63801–64000, 139101–139500, 142701–142900, 145601–145700, 145801–145900.
B. H. Berry	J. T. Holt	66201–66400, 78201–78600, 140301–140500, 143701–143900.
W. G. Allen	C. S. Taylor	67201–67400, 73701–73900, 123401–123800, 140501–140900, 143301–143500, 146301–146500.
T. C. Gale	E. H. Smith	75101–75500, 77801–78200, 124701–125100, 140901–141300, 144901–145100.
A. W. Gray	W. Hancock	124201–124300, 141701–142100, 145101–145500.
M. A. Dewees	S. E. Hughes	82101–82400, 85901–86200, 92001–92300, 111801–112000, 122601–122900, 130901–131200, 135801–136100, 156401–156700, 161301–161600.

Register of Confederate States Treasury Notes—Continued.

ACT OF MARCH 23, 1863—Continued.

For Treasurer.	For Register.	Numbers of the notes signed.
		MAY ISSUE—Continued.
		$10—A to H—Continued.
S. G. Grattan	H. L. Cooke	88801-89100, 105101-105400, 113301-113600, 116801-117100, 132901-133200, 147901-148200, 164101-164400.
E. P. Porter	A. P. Pellet	89101-89400, 117401-117700, 134101-134400, 157901-158200.
H. Bartlett	M. Taylor	89401-89700, 106401-106700, 112601-112900, 117101-117400, 133801-134100, 157601-157900, 164401-164700.
J. W. Jones	J. O. Snyder	139901-140300, 144101-144300.
		$5—A to H.
* * * *	* * * *	* * * * * * *
V. M. Rind	V. K. Davies	150901-151200, 165301-165600, 176901-177200, 183901-184200, 188301-188600, 193601-193900, 202901-203200, 205701-206000.
S. G. Sanxay	L. Macon	151201-151500, 159301-159600, 174601-174900, 185301-185600, 188901-189200, 197101-197400.
L. C. Minor	B. M. Abbott	151501-151800, 161801-162100, 179801-180100, 185101-185300, 185601-185700, 196001-196300.
F. M. Dickins	F. E. Bernard	151801-152100, 162101-162400, 179501-179800, 184501-184800, 188001-188300, 197401-197700.
A. Points	M. Gay	152101-152400, 160101-160400, 168801-169100, 183301-183600, 189501-189800, 194201-194500.
V. M. Stanard	S. C. Ellett	152401-152700, 161501-161800, 171801-172100, 178601-178900, 187501-187800, 195401-195700.
S. F. Shaver	M. Dixon	152701-153000, 189801-190100, 198701-199000.
I. Benton	M. Pace	153001-153200, 162701-163000, 168601-168800, 170701-171000, 192001-192200, 196901-197100, 199001-199200, 201201-201300.
E. D. Layne	V. C. Watson	153201-153500, 162401-162700, 180401-180600, 199601-199800.
M. S. Nicholas	J. McCarthy	153501-153900, 160401-160600, 167701-168000, 174901-175200, 183601-183900, 190401-190700, 196301-196600.
A. B. Capron	K. Walker	153901-154100, 189201-189500, 195701-196000, 200401-200600.
A. Harrison	E. C. Winston	154101-154400, 160601-160900, 175201-175500.
Do	M. Wade	204501-204800.
H. Graham	M. B. Kirby	154401-154700, 169501-169800, 172501-172800.
E. Mason	M. C. Lathrop	154701-155100, 164301-164700, 201601-201900.
M. B. Christian	M. S. Apperson	155101-155400, 160901-161200, 175501-175800, 191701-192000, 204301-204500.
K. Heth	M. E. Gilliam	155401-155700, 163701-164000, 170101-170400.
H. Watkins	M. L. Savage	155701-156000, 164701-165000, 173201-173400, 182701-183000, 203701-204000.
M. S. Knox	M. W. Bailey	156001-156300, 199301-199600.
M. C. Irvine	M. Johnson	156301-156600, 192201-192400, 200101-200300.
H. Starke	M. Morrison	156601-156900, 172801-173200, 180601-180700, 182401-182500, 202601-202900, 205101-205400.
W. A. Garrett	J. McGarr	156901-157200, 159601-159900, 169101-169400, 174001-174300, 179201-179500, 183001-183300, 188801-188900, 197701-197900, 201301-201600.
S. G. Grattan	H. L. Cooke	157201-157500, 165001-165300, 175801-175900, 177801-178100, 186301-186400, 191401-191700, 200301-200400, 204801-205100.
E. P. Porter	A. P. Pellet	157501-157600, 165601-165900, 202201-202500, 204001-204300.
H. Bartlett	M. Taylor	157601-157800, 165901-166200, 199801-200100, 201901-202200, 203401-203700.
V. Bridges	E. W. Pendleton	157801-158100, 166201-166500, 170401-170700, 176601-176900, 181201-181500, 187001-187300, 193001-193300.
M. V. Tyler	B. M. Payne	158101-158400, 166801-167100, 193301-193600.
H. M. Douglass	F. C. Jones	158401-158700, 166501-166800, 171001-171300, 178101-178400, 181801-182100, 186401-186700, 193901-194200, 200901-201200, 205401-205700.
V. B. Briggs	J. B. Tiffey	158701-159000, 168001-168300, 173701-174000, 178901-179200, 182101-182400, 194501-194800.
M. L. Quarles	F. G. Giles	159001-159300, 168301-168600, 171501-171600, 175901-176200, 180901-181200, 187801-188000, 192701-193000.
M. E. Dudley	M. E. Norton	159901-160100, 167401-167700, 173401-173700, 178401-178600, 185701-186000, 188601-188800, 196601-196900.

Register of Confederate States Treasury Notes—Continued.

ACT OF MARCH 23, 1863—Continued.

For Treasurer.	For Register.	Numbers of the notes signed.
		MAY ISSUE—Continued.
		$5—A to H—Continued.
E. C. Green	B. McRae	161201–161500, 167101–167400, 171601–171800.
L. Breeden	M. Wade	163001–163400, 169801–170100, 191001–191300.
M. Jones	E. Garlick	163401–163700, 169401–169500, 177201–177500, 184201-184500, 190701–191000, 191301–191400, 198201–198700.
R. Haynes	B. Dabney	164001–164300, 180101–180400, 182501–182700, 195001–195200.
M. Godwin	E. A. Adams	171301–171500, 177501–177800, 180701–180900, 187301–187500, 194801–195000.
M. Allen	B. T. Lyon	172101-172500, 176201–176600, 181501–181800, 186701-187000, 192401–192700.
R. F. Ball	L. M. Hunter	174301–174600, 186001–186300, 197901–198200, 200601-200900, 202501–202600, 203201–203400, 206001–206400.
S. Lambert	P. Pleasants	184801–185100, 190101–190400, 195201–195400, 199201-199300.
		JUNE ISSUE.
		$100—A to D.
A. W. Gray	W. Hancock	1–800, 3301–4100, 5001–6000, 6801–7600, 10001–10800, 12401-13300, 16101–16700.
T. C. Gale	E. H. Smith	801–1600.
Do	M. Winston	13301–13700, 23701–24100, 26501–27300, 29001–29800, 33701-34100, 37301–38100.
W. G. Allen	C. S. Taylor	1601–2500, 9201-10000, 21301–22100, 27301-28200, 31301-32100, 32901–33700, 35701–36500, 38101–39700, 41001–42400.
F. C. Weisiger	W. P. Caldwell	2501–3300, 22901–23700, 24901–25700, 28201–29000, 29801-30500, 32101–32900, 34101–34900, 43201–44000, 44601-45400, 47001–47800, 48901–49700, 50501–52100.
J. C. Joplin	S. Dutcher	4101–5000, 13701–14500, 16701–18500, 18901–19300, 20101-20500, 22101–22900, 24101–24900, 30501–31300, 34901-35700, 36501–37300, 40201–41000, 42401–43200, 44001-44600, 45401-47000, 47901–48900, 49701–50500, 52101–52900.
W. R. Todd	J. H. Cooke	6001–6800, 7601–8400, 10801–11600, 15301–16100, 18501-18900, 20501–21300, 25701–26300.
T. J. Hatch	W. B. Walston	8401–9200, 11601–12400, 14501–15300.
Do	H. Smith	19301–20100.
J. B. S. Dimitry	W. Nott	26301–26500.
E. C. Goddin	W. G. Harvey	39701–40200, 52901–53200.
A. Patton	W. Hancock	47801–47900.
		$50—wA to zA.
J. C. Joplin	S. Dutcher	1–900, 2701–3600, 7601–8500, 8701–11200, 12801–13600, 20701-20900.
T. J. Hatch	W. B. Walston	901–1700, 1901–2700, 4401–5200, 6801–7600.
Do	H. Smith	15701–16500, 16701–17500.
S. B. Jacobs	W. O. Slade	1701–1900, 12001–12800, 18301–19100, 19901–20700, 21701-22500, 23301–24100, 25601–26400, 27601–28400.
J. B. S. Dimitry	W. Nott	3601–4400.
W. G. Allen	C. S. Taylor	5201–6000, 8501–8700, 16501–16700.
T. C. Gale	M. Winston	6001–6800, 13601–14000, 17501–18300, 19101–19900, 20901-21700, 22501–23300, 24101–24900, 27201–27600, 28401-29200.
A. Patton	W. Hancock	11201–12000, 14001–15600, 24901–25600, 26401–27200, 29201-30000.
E. C. Goddin	W. G. Harvey	15601–15700, 30001–30300.
		$20—A to H.
S. B. Jacobs	W. O. Slade	1–400, 3101–3400, 10101–10400, 11601-12000, 16501–16900, 19301–19700, 23401–23800, 27001–27400, 30201-30600, 32501-32700, 35501–35900, 39501–39900, 44801–45200, 48001-48400, 51601–52000, 55501–55900, 58301–58700.
E. C. Goddin	J. M. Kinney	401–800, 52301–52400.
Do	W. G. Harvey	52001–52300.
T. C. Gale	E. H. Smith	801–1200, 12401–12800.
Do	M. Winston	5001–5400, 9701-10100, 15901-16100, 26601-27000, 47601-48000, 55101–55500, 70501–70700.

Register of Confederate States Treasury Notes—Continued.

ACT OF MARCH 23, 1863—Continued.

For Treasurer.	For Register.	Numbers of the notes signed.
		JUNE ISSUE—Continued.
		$20—A to H—Continued.
N. A. Bass	A. S. Watkins	1201-1600, 4601-5000, 6601-7000, 8601-9000, 12001-12400, 15501-15900, 17601-17800, 21501-21900, 26201-26600, 29801-30200, 31601-31800, 34701-35100, 37901-38400, 41501-42000.
Do	W. P. Caldwell	57501-57900.
C. Ashford	S. Sinton	1601-2000, 3801-4200, 7001-7400, 8201-8600, 10801-11200, 13201-13600, 17801-18200, 20701-21100, 24601-25000, 31001-31400, 32701-33100, 37101-37500, 42001-42400, 44401-44800, 47201-47600, 50001-50400, 52401-52800, 61101-61500.
B. H. Berry	J. T. Holt	2001-2400, 3401-3800, 5401-5800, 9001-9400, 11201-11600, 14701-15100, 18501-18900, 21201-21500, 22301-22400, 25401-25800, 29001-29400, 31801-32000, 33501-33900, 36701-37100, 39901-40300, 42801-43200, 45601-46000, 50801-51200, 53901-54300, 55901-56300, 59101-59500, 61501-61900, 64501-64900, 66101-66500, 69301-69700, 71501-71700.
F. C. Weisiger	W. P. Caldwell	2401-2800, 5801-6200, 48801-49200, 53601-53900, 56701-57100, 58701-59100.
W. G. Allen	C. S. Taylor	2801-3100, 9401-9700, 15101-15500, 18901-19300, 61901-62300, 64901-65300, 67701-68100, 69701-70100.
F. H. Link	L. P. Rogers	4201-4600, 6201-6600, 7801-8200, 10401-10800, 13901-14300, 16901-17300, 20301-20700, 24201-24600, 29401-29800, 33901-34300, 37501-37900, 40301-40700, 43201-43600, 46401-46800, 49201-49600, 53201-53600, 57101-57500, 59501-59900, 62301-62700, 63701-64100, 66501-66900, 68501-68900, 71101-71500.
J. B. S. Dimitry	W. Nott	7401-7800, 16101-16500, 19701-20100, 23101-23400, 27801-28200, 30601-31000, 35901-36300, 39201-39500, 42401-42800, 45201-45600, 48401-48800, 63501-63700, 65701-66100, 68101-68500, 70701-71100.
W. J. Doyle	G. N. Warren	12801-13200, 13601-13900, 17301-17600, 21101-21200, 22401-22700, 25801-26200, 28201-28600, 32301-32500, 33101-33500, 38401-38800, 41101-41500, 44001-44400, 46801-47200, 50401-50800, 54301-54700, 59901-60300, 67301-67700, 70101-70500.
J. E. Henderson	Tho. J. Miller	14301-14700, 18201-18500, 20201-20300, 25001-25400, 28601-29000, 31401-31600, 34301-34700, 36301-36700, 40701-41100, 43601-44000, 46001-46400, 49601-50000, 52801-53200, 56301-56700, 60301-60700, 62701-63100, 64101-64500, 66901-67300, 68901-69300.
A. W. Gray	W. Hancock	20101-20200, 23801-24200, 27501-27800.
T. J. Hatch	H. Smith	21901-22300.
W. R. Todd	J. H. Cooke	22701-23100.
A. Patton	W. Hancock	27401-27500, 32001-32300, 35101-35500, 38801-39200, 51201-51600, 54701-55100, 57901-58300, 60701-61100, 63101-63500, 65301-65700.
		$10—A to H.
M. A. Dewees	S. E. Hughes	1-300, 13401-13700, 20401-20700, 29701-30000, 33101-33300, 41401-41700, 55701-56000, 101601-101800.
M. S. Knox	M. W. Bailey	301-600, 13701-14000, 21601-21900, 57201-57500, 61501-61800, 69901-70000, 75001-75200, 84401-84600, 96501-96800.
M. C. Irvine	M. Johnson	601-900, 17501-17700, 23501-23600, 45301-45400, 48601-48900, 57901-58200, 63901-64200, 70401-70700, 95001-95300, 105101-105400.
R. Haynes	B. Dabney	901-1000, 7201-7400, 16101-16400, 20201-20400, 33001-33100, 34801-35100, 40501-40800, 56601-56900, 62401-62700, 92201-92500.
M. V. Tyler	B. M. Payne	1001-1300, 10201-10500, 17801-18100, 24601-24900, 30501-30800, 38101-38400, 46301-46600, 58201-58500, 85001-85300, 90301-90500, 98801-99000.
M. Godwin	E. A. Adams	1301-1600, 10501-10700, 39701-39900, 46901-47200, 51701-52000, 59701-60000, 77301-77600.
W. A. Garrett	J. McGarr	1601-1900, 9601-9900, 19001-19300, 25501-25800, 36901-37200, 39401-39700, 49201-49500, 52001-52300, 58501-58800, 65701-66000, 70101-70400, 78801-79100, 92901-93200, 98501-98800.
V. Bridges	E. W. Pendleton	1901-2200, 9301-9600, 37801-38100, 45701-46000, 73501-73800.

Register of Confederate States Treasury Notes—Continued.

ACT OF MARCH 23, 1863—Continued.

For Treasurer.	For Register.	Numbers of the notes signed.
		JUNE ISSUE—Continued.
		$10—A to H—Continued.
S. G. Sanxay	L. Macon	2201–2500, 10701–11000, 18701–19000, 30001–30200, 31001-31400, 38401–38700, 52301–52600, 58801–59100, 65401-65700, 78201–78500, 85301–85600, 90001–90300, 100801–101100.
V. M. Rind	V. K. Davies	2501–2800, 11601–11900, 23201–23500, 28801–29100, 36001-36300, 44701–45000, 45401–45700, 51401–51700, 63601-63900, 72201–72500, 74701–75000, 81701–82000, 95601–95900.
H. M. Douglass	F. C. Jones	2801–3100, 12401–12700, 13301–13400, 18101–18400, 28601-28800, 33601–33900, 42901–43200, 47501–47800, 54701-55000, 62101–62400, 71001–71300, 75201–75500, 82001-82300, 93801-94100, 102501–102800.
M. E. Dudley	M. E. Norton	3101–3400, 11001–11300, 19301–19600, 25201–25500, 31701-32000, 40201–40500, 50801–51000, 53101–53400, 59101-59400, 66301-66600, 77601-77900, 86501-86800, 89401-89700, 100501-100800.
H. Watkins	M. L. Savage	3401–3700, 14001–14300, 22801–22900, 35701–36000, 44101-44300, 49801–50000, 57501–57600, 61201–61500, 74201-74400, 87901–88200, 89701–90000, 102101–102200.
A. B. Capron	K. Walker	3701–4000, 11901–12200, 22501–22800, 27101–27400, 32701-33000, 41701–42000, 48901–49200, 55001–55200, 60601-60900, 71301-71600, 75501-75800, 83801-84000, 94401-94700, 104601-104800.
M. Allen	B. T. Lyon	4001–4300, 9901–10200, 18401-18700, 24301-24600, 30201-30500, 37501–37800.
Do	H. L. Cooke	46001–46300, 65001–65400, 76701–77100, 84601–85000, 89001-89400, 98101–98500.
M. L. Quarles	F. G. Giles	4301–4600, 24901–25200, 39001–39400, 46601–46900, 53401-53800.
E. D. Layne	V. C. Watson	4601–4900, 12701–13000, 20701–21000, 28001–28300, 31401-31700, 39901–40200, 47201–47500, 53801–54100, 60001-60300, 66001-66300, 83201-83500, 86301-86500, 91101-91400, 101101-101300.
H. Starke	M. Morrison	4901–5200, 14301–14600, 35401–35700, 42301–42600, 55201-55500, 60301–60600, 67601–67900, 80501–80800, 96201-96500, 104001–104300.
V. M. Stanard	S. C. Ellett	5201–5500, 11301–11600, 23901–24100, 52601–52900, 60901-61200, 67901–68200, 80301–80500, 86001–86300, 90801-91100, 100201–100500.
S. Lambert	P. Pleasants	5501–5800, 17301–17500, 17701–17800, 19601–19900, 26501-26800, 35101–35400, 43801–44100, 50301–50500, 51301-51400, 56001–56300, 63301–63600, 76401–76700, 83501-83800, 87301-87600, 93201–93500.
A. Harrison	M. Wade	5801–6100, 12201–12400, 27701–27949.
Do	J. Douglas	27950–28000, 36301–36600, 43201–43500, 68501–68700, 70001-70100, 79401–79700, 88801-89000, 91401-91700, 99901-100200.
S. F. Shaver	M. Dixon	6101–6400, 15201–15500, 32001–32300, 42001–42300, 54401-54700, 62701–63000, 67201–67600, 79101–79400, 85601-86000, 92501–92900, 99201–99600.
M. B. Christian	M. S. Apperson	6401–6700, 14901–15200, 21301–21600, 28301–28600, 33901-34200, 75801–76100, 77101–77300, 88201–88500, 94101-94400, 101801–102100.
M. S. Nicholas	J. McCarthy	6701–7000, 15501–15800, 21901–22200.
M. Jones	E. Garlick	7001–7200, 7701–7800, 13001–13300, 24101–24300, 25801-26100, 34501–34800, 40801–41100, 47801–48100, 56301-56600, 61801-62100, 70701–71000, 76101–76400, 80801–81100, 95301-95600, 103201–103500.
H. Bartlett	M. Taylor	7401–7700, 15801–16100, 19901–20200, 27401–27700, 33301-33600, 42601–42900, 48301–48600, 54101–54400, 64201-64500, 68701–69000, 71601-71900, 81101-81400, 97101-97400, 103801-104000.
L. C. Minor	B. M. Abbott	7801–8100, 41101–41400, 50001–50300, 69001–69300, 72501-72800, 82901–83200, 93501–93800, 102201–102500.
K. Heth	M. E. Gilliam	8101–8400, 16701–17000, 23601–23900, 50501–50800, 64501-64800, 78501–78800, 97801–98100, 104301–104600.

Register of Confederate States Treasury Notes—Continued.

ACT OF MARCH 23, 1863—Continued.

For Treasurer.	For Register.	Numbers of the notes signed.
		JUNE ISSUE—Continued.
		$10—A to H—Continued.
E. Mason	M. C. Lathrop	8401-8700, 16401-16700, 22901-23200, 29401-29700, 36601-36900, 45001-45300, 49501-49800, 56901-57200, 63001-63300, 72801-73200, 73801-74200, 84001-84400, 97401-97800, 102801-103200.
L. Breeden	E. C. Winston	8701-9000, 14601-14900, 21001-21300, 26801-27100, 34201-34500, 43501-43800, 48101-48300, 55501-55700, 68201-68500, 82601-82900, 88501-88800.
S. G. Grattan	H. L. Cooke	9001-9300, 17001-17300, 22201-22500, 26101-26500, 32301-32700, 44301-44700, 51001-51300.
H. Graham	M. B. Kirby	29101-29400, 37201-37500.
V. B. Briggs	J. B. Tiffey	30801-31000, 38701-39000, 52901-53100, 59401-59700, 66601-66900, 77901-78200, 87601-87900, 91901-92200.
F. M. Dickins	F. E. Bernard	57601-57900, 69301-69600, 73201-73500, 81401-81700; 96801-97100, 104801-105100, 105401-105600.
E. P. Porter	A. P. Pellet	64801-65000, 71901-72200, 74401-74700, 82301-82600, 95901-96200, 103501-103800.
M. Sommers	M. B. Kirby	66901-67200, 80001-80300, 86801-87000, 90501-90800, 99601-99900.
R. F. Ball	L. M. Hunter	69601-69900, 79701-80000, 87001-87300, 94701-95000, 101301-101600.
I. Benton	M. Pace	91701-91900, 99001-99200.
B. H. Berry	J. T. Holt	105601-105800, 108101-108500.
J. E. Henderson	Tho. J. Miller	105801-106200, 112601-113000.
C. Ashford	S. Sinton	106201-106600, 108901-109300, 113001-113400.
W. J. Doyle	G. N. Warren	106601-107000, 109301-109700, 112201-112600.
W. G. Allen	C. S. Taylor	107001-107400, 110201-110600, 115001-115400.
E. C. Goddin	J. M. Kinney	107401-107700.
Do	W. G. Harvey	109701-109800, 114601-115000.
J. B. S. Dimitry	W. Nott	107701-108100, 111401-111800, 116201-116500.
F. H. Link	L. P. Rogers	108501-108900, 113801-114600.
T. C. Gale	M. Winston	109801-110200.
S. B. Jacobs	W. O. Slade	110601-111000, 115401-115800.
A. Patton	W. Hancock	111001-111400, 115801-116200.
T. J. Hatch	H. Smith	111801-112200.
J. C. Joplin	S. Dutcher	113401-113800.
		$5—A to H.
V. Bridges	E. W. Pendleton	1-200, 30601-30900, 37501-37800, 44101-44400.
M. Godwin	E. A. Adams	201-400, 19201-19500, 24001-24300, 45501-45800.
S. G. Sanxay	L. Macon	401-700, 8601-8900, 18101-18400, 25201-25500, 33001-33300, 38101-38400, 46101-46400.
M. L. Quarles	F. G. Giles	701-1000.
M. E. Dudley	M. E. Norton	1001-1300, 8401-8600, 17101-17400, 27001-27200.
I. Benton	M. Pace	1301-1500.
V. M. Stanard	S. C. Ellett	1501-1800, 10501-10800, 17401-17700, 26701-27000, 32801-33000, 37801-38100, 45801-46100.
R. F. Ball	L. M. Hunter	1801-2100, 11101-11400, 18401-18700, 24601-24900, 33901-34200, 41601-41900.
A. B. Capron	K. Walker	2101-2400, 14201-14500, 21801-22100, 28101-28400, 35301-35500.
V. M. Rind	V. K. Davies	2401-2700, 11401-11700, 20201-20500.
M. S. Nicholas	J. McCarthy	2701-3000.
L. Breeden	E. C. Winston	3001-3300, 12801-13200, 20501-20900, 34801-35000, 43301-43600.
M. S. Knox	M. W. Bailey	3301-3600, 14501-14800, 22601-22900, 29101-29400, 34201-34500, 42401-42700.
A. Harrison	M. Wade	3601-3900.
Do	J. Douglas	12401-12500, 22301-22600, 26101-26400, 31801-32100.
M. A. Dewees	S. E. Hughes	3901-4200, 25801-26100, 34501-34800, 39801-40100.
M. Jones	E. Garlick	4201-4500, 11701-12000, 27201-27500, 30001-30100, 35501-35800, 40401-40700.
H. Bartlett	M. Taylor	4501-4800, 9701-9900, 13201-13300, 21501-21800, 41301-41600.
E. Mason	M. C. Lathrop	4801-5100, 13301-13700, 19501-19900, 28401-28800, 40701-41000.

Register of Confederate States Treasury Notes—Continued.

ACT OF MARCH 23, 1863—Continued.

For Treasurer.	For Register.	Numbers of the notes signed.
		JUNE ISSUE—Continued.
		$5—A to H—Continued.
H. Watkins	M. L. Savage	5101–5300, 13901–14200, 22101–22300, 33301–33600, 38701–38900.
M. C. Irvine	M. Johnson	5301–5600, 7001–7200, 30101–30300, 36501–36700, 43601–43900.
M. B. Christian	M. S. Apperson	5601–5900, 14801–14900, 27501–27800.
K. Heth	M. E. Gilliam	5901–6100, 7201–7500, 15001–15300, 29401–29700, 42701–43000.
S. Lambert	P. Pleasants	6101–6300, 9001–9300, 15301–15400, 23101–23300, 32401–32800, 43901–44100, 45101–45500.
S. F. Shaver	M. Dixon	6301–6600, 12001–12400, 17701–18100, 24301–24600, 39201–39500, 46401–46700.
S. G. Grattan	H. L. Cooke	6601–7000.
H. Graham	M. B. Kirby	7501–7800.
M. V. Tyler	B. M. Payne	7801–8000, 15401–15700, 23701–24000, 37001–37100.
M. Allen	H. L. Cooke	8001–8400, 15701–16100, 23301–23700, 30901–31300, 37101–37500, 44401–44800.
E. P. Porter	A. P. Pellet	8901–9000, 9901–10200, 21201-21500, 30301-30600, 36101-36400, 41001–41300.
W. A. Garrett	J. McGarr	9301–9700, 16101–16500, 25501–25800, 31501–31800, 39501–39800.
E. D. Layne	V. C. Watson	10201–10500, 16801–17100, 26401–26700, 31301–31500, 38901–39200.
H. Starke	M. Morrison	10801–11100, 20901–21200, 33601–33900.
H. M. Douglass	F. C. Jones	12501–12800, 19901–20200, 27801–28100, 35001–35300, 42101–42400.
F. M. Dickins	F. E. Bernard	13701–13900, 22901–23100, 29701–30000, 36401–36500, 43001–43300.
L. C. Minor	B. M. Abbott	14901–15000, 18701–19000, 36701–37000, 40101–40400.
V. B. Briggs	J. B. Tiffey	16501–16800.
M. Sommers	M. B. Kirby	19001–19200, 24901–25200, 32101–32400, 38401–38700, 44801–45100.
R. Haynes	B. Dabney	28801–29100, 35801–36100, 41901–42100.
		JULY ISSUE.
		$100—A to D.
J. C. Joplin	S. Dutcher	1–1600, 2801–3600, 8001–8800, 9601–10500, 15601-16400, 22401–22700.
T. C. Gale	M. Winston	1601–2000, 17701–17800, 21201–21600.
W. G. Allen	C. S. Taylor	2001–2800, 19501–20400.
J. W. Jones	W. O. Slade	3601–4400, 5601–6400, 7201–8000, 10501–11400, 13401–14200, 16801–17700, 18601–19500, 21601–22400, 22701-23500, 23901–24000.
E. C. Goddin	W. G. Harvey	4401–5200, 6401–7200, 8801–9600, 11801–13400, 17801–18600, 20401–21200, 23501–23900.
J. B. S. Dimitry	W. Nott	5201–5600.
C. Ashford	S. Sinton	11401–11800, 14201–15000, 16401–16800.
S. B. Jacobs	W. O. Slade	15001–15600.
		$50—wA to zA.
T. C. Gale	E. H. Smith	1–800.
Do	M. Winston	10601–11400, 13001–13800, 16601–16800, 26001–26800, 34801–35600, 39301–40000, 43601–43800, 47101–47900, 50301-51100, 53101–53500, 54301–54500, 56101–56500, 62901-63100, 69301–70000.
T. J. Hatch	H. Smith	801–1600, 3401–5000, 7301–8100, 12201–13000, 14601–15400, 19201–20000, 20801–21600, 24401–25200, 26801-27600, 30401–31200, 33801–34800, 37601–38500, 40601–41200, 45101-46300, 48701–49500, 53501–54300, 58901–59700, 65301–66100.
S. B. Jacobs	W. O. Slade	1601–2400, 7001–7300, 8101–8600, 36601–36800.
Do	J. H. Cooke.	25201–26000, 27601–28400, 32001–32800, 40001–40600, 42001–42800, 51101–51500, 52301–53100, 62101–62900, 66901-67700.
E. C. Goddin	W. G. Harvey	2401–3200, 5001–5400, 9401–10200, 16201–16600, 17601–18400, 44301–45100, 49501–50300, 51501–52300, 55301-56100, 60501–61300, 64701–65300, 66101–66900, 70001–70300, 71901-72400.

Register of Confederate States Treasury Notes—Continued.

ACT OF MARCH 23, 1863—Continued.

For Treasurer.	For Register.	Numbers of the notes signed.
		JULY ISSUE—Continued.
		$50—wA to zA—Continued.
W. G. Allen	C. S. Taylor	3201-3400, 6201-7000, 15401-16200, 20001-20800, 21601-22400, 23601-24400, 28401-29200, 46301-47100, 61301-62100, 67701-69300.
J. C. Joplin	S. Dutcher	5401-6200, 11401-12200, 13801-14600, 18401-19200, 30001-30200, 43801-44300, 71101-71900.
A. Patton	W. Hancock	8601-9400, 22401-23200, 29201-30000, 31201-32000, 36401-36600, 38501-39300, 42801-43600.
N. A. Bass	W. P. Caldwell	10201-10600, 59701-60500.
J. W. Jones	W. O. Slade	16801-17600, 30201-30400, 47901-48700, 54501-55300, 63101-64700.
J. B. S. Dimitry	W. Nott	23201-23600.
W. J. Doyle	G. N. Warren	32801-33400, 35601-36400, 36801-37600, 41201-42000, 57301-58100.
B. H. Berry	J. T. Holt	33401-33800.
J. E. Henderson	Tho. J. Miller	56501-57300.
C. Ashford	S. Sinton	58101-58900.
F. C. Weisiger	W. P. Caldwell	70301-71100.
		$20—A to H.
N. A. Bass	W. P. Caldwell	1-400, 5101-5500, 11101-11500, 14301-14500, 16901-17300, 20901-21300, 27301-27700, 30401-30800, 47801-48200, 51501-51900, 54801-55100, 57701-58100, 58201-58400, 60801-61000, 62201-62600, 66901-67300, 70401-70800, 74001-74300, 79101-79500, 82801-83200, 86401-86800.
B. H. Berry	J. T. Holt	401-800, 4301-4700, 8101-8500, 12701-13100, 15301-15700, 19201-19600, 23801-24100, 26101-26500, 28501-28900, 30901-31300, 33701-34100, 35201-35600, 36501-36800, 37901-38300, 41001-41300, 43501-43900, 45701-46100, 50001-50400, 52701-53100, 55401-55800, 58101-58200.
J. E. Henderson	Tho. J. Miller	801-1200, 5901-6300, 9301-9700, 13901-14300, 16501-16900, 20101-20500, 22901-23200, 26501-26900, 28901-29300, 31701-32100, 32901-33300, 34101-34500, 34801-35200, 37201-37900, 41701-42100, 44301-44700, 47001-47400, 49601-50000, 53101-53500, 56101-56500, 63001-63400, 64101-64500, 71601-72000, 75201-75500, 78301-78700, 81201-81600, 85201-85600.
F. H. Link	L. P. Rogers	1201-1600, 3901-4300, 8501-8900, 13501-13900, 16101-16500, 20001-20100, 23201-23500, 26901-27300, 35601-36000, 36801-37200, 38301-38700, 56901-57200, 61001-61800, 65701-66100, 71201-71600.
W. J. Doyle	G. N. Warren	1601-2000, 5501-5900, 8901-9300, 12301-12700, 14901-15300, 20501-20900, 24101-24500, 27701-28100, 29701-30100, 32101-32700, 33501-33700, 38701-38800, 41301-41700, 44701-45100, 46101-46500, 50801-51100, 53901-54100, 54201-54400, 57201-57600, 60001-60400, 62601-63000, 64501-64900, 69201-69600, 75501-75800, 77101-77500, 85101-85200.
C. Ashford	S. Sinton	2001-2400, 4701-5100, 9701-10100, 13101-13500, 15701-16100, 19601-20000, 23501-23800, 25701-26100, 29301-29700, 31301-31700, 32701-32900, 33301-33500, 36101-36500, 39801-40200, 42101-42500, 43901-44300, 46601-47000, 50401-50800, 53501-53600, 53701-53900, 54701-54800, 56501-56900, 60401-60800, 61801-62200, 65301-65700, 70801-71200, 74601-74900, 77901-78300, 81601-82000, 86801-87200.
A. Patton	W. Hancock	2401-2800, 6901-7300, 10501-10900, 17701-18000, 24501-24900, 30101-30400, 30801-30900, 34501-34800, 39401-39800, 42501-42900, 45101-45500, 68101-68500, 73201-73600, 74901-75200, 80101-80500, 83601-84000, 88401-88800.
W. G. Allen	C. S. Taylor	2801-3100, 18001-18400, 38801-39200, 46501-46600, 48201-48500, 51901-52300, 54101-54200, 55101-55400, 59201-59600, 67701-68100, 72001-72400, 76201-76500, 79701-80100, 84001-84400, 87201-87600.
J. B. S. Dimitry	W. Nott	3101-3500, 7701-8100, 11501-11900, 14501-14900, 18801-19200, 22601-22900, 25301-25700, 63701-64000, 68801-69200, 73601-74000, 80901-81200, 84801-85100.

Register of Confederate States Treasury Notes—Continued.

ACT OF MARCH 23, 1863—Continued.

For Treasurer.	For Register.	Numbers of the notes signed.
		JULY ISSUE—Continued.
		$20—A to H—Continued.
T. C. Gale	M. Winston	3501–3900, 6701–6900, 22301–22600, 40601–41000, 49301-49600, 52301–52700, 55801–56100, 59601–60000, 68501–68800, 72401-72800, 76501–76800, 80501–80900, 84401–84800, 87801–88200.
Do	E. H. Smith	11901–12300.
S. B. Jacobs	W. O. Slade	6301–6700, 10101–10500, 17301–17700.
Do	J. H. Cooke	21301–21700, 24901–25300, 28101–28500, 36001–36100, 40201-40600, 42901–43300, 45501–45700, 47401–47800, 51101-51500, 58801–59200, 63401–63700, 64001–64100, 66501-66900, 72801-73200, 79501–79700, 83201–83600, 88201–88400.
E. C. Goddin	W. G. Harvey	7301–7700, 10901–11100, 18401–18800, 22101–22300, 43301-43500, 48901–49300, 57601–57700, 67301–67700, 76801-77100, 88801–89200.
J. W. Jones	W. O. Slade	21701–22100, 48501–48900, 53601–53700, 54401–54700.
T. J. Hatch	H. Smith	39201–39400, 58401–58800, 87601–87800.
J. C. Joplin	S. Dutcher	64901–65300, 70001–70400, 75801–76200, 77501–77900, 82001-82400, 86001–86400.
F. C. Weisiger	W. O. Slade	66101–66500, 69601–70000, 74301–74600, 78701–79100, 85601-86000.
		$10—A to H.
V. Bridges	E. W. Pendleton	1–300, 8101–8400, 66801–67100, 70801–71100, 76201–76500, 82701–83000, 89901–90200.
M. Allen	H. L. Cooke	301–700, 9301–9700, 17001–17400, 25401–25800, 49701–50100, 62701–63100, 68901–69300, 75801–76200, 82101-82500, 89501-89900, 95901–96300.
V. M. Stanard	S. C. Ellett	701–1000, 11801–12100, 17401-17700, 33401–33700, 40601–40900, 44101–44500, 53301–53600, 57301–57600.
Do	L. Devine	63101–63400, 69301–69600, 75501–75800, 82501–82700, 94201-94500, 96601–96900.
M. Sommers	M. B. Kirby	1001–1300, 10801–11100, 18801–19100, 27501–27800, 33701-34000, 44901–45200, 50901–51200, 56501–56800, 64701–65000, 70501–70800, 77801–78100, 84401–84700, 92001–92300.
W. A. Garrett	J. McGarr	1301–1600, 9001–9300, 17701–18000, 24801–25100, 57901–58200, 64101–64400, 70201–70500, 78101–78400.
S. Lambert	P. Pleasants	1601–2000, 10201-10500, 26401–26800, 35801–36100, 45201-45600, 66201–66500, 72101–72400, 78701–79000.
S. G. Sanxay	L. Macon	2001–2300, 8401–8700, 18001–18300, 26801–27100, 32501–32800, 57601–57900, 63801–64100, 69901–70200, 76801-77100, 83001-83300, 89301–89500, 96301–96600.
M. Godwin	E. A. Adams	2301–2600, 9701–9900, 19401–19700, 27101–27400, 39801–40000, 49201–49400, 55501–55700, 59601–59900, 65301–65600, 69601-69900.
M. E. Dudley	M. E. Norton	2601–2900, 8701–9000, 34701–35000, 44601–44900, 51201–51500, 56801–57100, 72401–72700, 77101–77300, 86701–86900.
M. A. Dewees	S. E. Hughes	2901–3200, 9901–10200, 19701–20000, 25801-26100, 34201-34500, 52401–52700, 61201–61500, 64401–67700, 73001-73300, 80201-80500, 83601–83900, 90201–90500.
H. Watkins	M. L. Savage	3201–3400, 14801–15000.
A. Harrison	J. Douglas	3401–3600, 12101–12400, 27401–27500, 37301–37600, 40301-40600, 47401–47600, 53601–53800, 60201–60500, 66001–66200, 73301–73600, 86201–86500, 92301–92600.
H. M. Douglass	F. C. Jones	3601–3900, 11101–11400, 24401–24600, 29501–29800, 37601-37900, 40001–40300, 46201–46500, 52701–53000, 58901–59200, 79301–79600, 83901–84200, 91301–91600.
R. Haynes	B. Dabney	3901–4200, 13801–14100, 18501–18800, 26101–26400, 39401-39500, 54901–55200, 61501–61700, 86901–87200, 91001–91300.
L. C. Minor	B. M. Abbott	4201–4500, 11401–11500, 13601–13800, 23501–23800, 31601-31900, 38101–38400, 55701–56000, 80801–81100, 87501–87800, 92801–93100.
H. Bartlett	M. Taylor	4501–4800, 12401–12700, 20901–21200, 28401–28700, 36701-37000, 39101–39400, 46801–47100, 60501–60800, 67101–67400, 73901–74200, 79901–80200, 85401–85700, 93101–93400.
E. P. Porter	A. P. Pellet	4801–5100, 12701–13000, 21201–21500, 29201–29500, 36401-36700, 46501–46800, 60801–61000, 66501–66800, 73601–73900, 79601–79900, 85701–85900, 93401–93600.

Register of Confederate States Treasury Notes—Continued.

ACT OF MARCH 23, 1863—Continued.

For Treasurer.	For Register.	Numbers of the notes signed.
		JULY ISSUE—Continued.
		$10—A to H—Continued.
L. Breeden	E. C. Winston	5101-5400, 14101-14400, 20601-20900, 28101-28400, 78401-78700, 84701-85000, 92601-92800.
M. B. Christian	M. S. Apperson	5401-5700, 13301-13600, 23801-24100, 30701-31000, 38701-39000, 42401-42700, 47901-48200, 74601-74900, 88401-88700.
E. Mason	M. C. Lathrop	5701-6100, 14401-14800, 21801-22300.
H. Starke	M. Morrison	6101-6400, 15001-15300.
M. Jones	E. Garlick	6401-6700, 15601-15900, 20001-20300, 24701-24800, 28701-28900, 35301-35600, 42901-43200, 49401-49700, 54201-54500, 56401-56500.
K. Heth	M. E. Gilliam	6701-7000, 16201-16400, 23201-23500, 30301-30700, 36101-36400, 41201-41500, 61701-61900, 67701-68000, 72701-73000.
R. F. Ball	L. M. Hunter	7001-7300, 16701-17000, 21501-21800, 31901-32200.
Do	M. L. Savage	41801-42100, 45901-46200, 53801-54200, 59201-59600, 81801-82100, 85101-85200, 87801-88100, 95001-95300.
A. B. Capron	K. Walker	7301-7500, 15901-16200, 31001-31300, 35601-35800, 39001-39100, 40901-41200, 49001-49200, 56101-56400, 62101-62400, 67401-67700, 74901-75200, 80501-80800, 85001-85100, 85201-85400, 94801-95000.
F. M. Dickins	F. E. Bernard	7501-7600, 22901-23200, 31301-31600, 56001-56100, 62401-62700, 68601-68900, 71101-71400, 76501-76800, 87201-87500, 93601-93900.
M. S. Knox	M. W. Bailey	7601-7800, 13001-13300, 22601-22900, 37901-38100, 42701-42900, 48701-49000.
M. C. Irvine	M. Johnson	7801-8100, 15301-15600, 24101-24400, 32201-32500, 38401-38700, 42101-42400, 47601-47900, 55201-55500, 61901-62100, 68301-68600, 75201-75500, 88701-89000, 95301-95500.
M. L. Quarles	F. G. Giles	10501-10800, 22301-22400, 30001-30300, 43201-43500, 48201-48400, 53001-53300, 61001-61200, 68001-68300, 74301-74600.
E. D. Layne	V. C. Watson	11501-11800, 28901-29200, 51901-52200, 58701-58900, 71801-72100, 86501-86700.
S. F. Shaver	M. Dixon	16401-16700, 20301-20600, 35001-35300, 39501-39800, 47101-47400, 54501-54900, 59901-60200, 65601-66000, 81101-81500.
V. B. Briggs	J. B. Tiffey	18301-18500, 24601-24700, 25101-25400, 33101-33400, 50401-50700, 57101-57300, 83301-83600, 90701-91000.
M. S. Nicholas	J. McCarthy	19101-19400, 27801-28100, 32801-33100, 43501-43800, 52201-52400, 65001-65300, 74201-74300, 81501-81800, 88101-88400, 93901-94200.
E. A. Dennison	J. L. Johnston	22401-22600, 29801-30000, 37001-37300, 41501-41800, 45601-45900.
M. V. Tyler	B. M. Payne	34001-34200, 43801-44100, 50101-50400.
I. Benton	M. Pace	34501-34700, 44401-44600, 50701-50900, 58501-58700, 77601-77800, 84201-84400, 90501-90700.
A. Points	M. Gay	48401-48700, 51501-51900, 58201-58500, 63401-63800, 71401-71800, 77301-77600, 85901-86200, 91601-92000, 95501-95900.
V. M. Rind	V. K. Davies	79001-79300, 89001-89300, 94501-94800.
		$5—A to H.
V. Bridges	E. W. Pendleton	1-300, 8301-8600, 25101-25300, 33701-34000, 64701-65000, 71501-71800, 79801-80100, 90901-91200.
M. Allen	H. L. Cooke	301-700, 7901-8300, 15301-15700, 49501-49800, 71101-71500, 78301-78700, 90501-90900.
M. Godwin	E. A. Adams	701-900, 22101-22300, 29801-30100, 35201-35500, 46701-47000, 52201-52500, 59801-60000, 68801-69100, 92801-93100.
S. G. Sanxay	L. Macon	901-1100, 25901-26200, 32201-32500, 57601-57900, 65301-65600, 72101-72400, 80101-80400, 91601-91900.
S. Lambert	P. Pleasants	1101-1500, 9801-10100, 18401-18700, 25301-25600, 34001-34300, 40601-40900, 44201-44500, 55201-55400, 66201-66500.
M. Sommers	M. B. Kirby	1501-1800, 10401-10700, 17201-17500, 23901-24200, 31301-31600, 37201-37500, 43401-43700, 50601-50900, 58401-58700, 66501-66800, 73801-74100, 81001-81300, 85201-85500, 92201-92500, 96601-96900.
A. Harrison	J. Douglas	1801-2100, 27201-27500, 37801-38100, 48401-48700, 50901-51200, 53001-53300, 59001-59300, 67401-67700, 79001-79300, 85501-85800, 93701-94000.

Register of Confederate States Treasury Notes—Continued.

ACT OF MARCH 23, 1863—Continued.

For Treasurer.	For Register.	Numbers of the notes signed.
		JULY ISSUE—Continued.
		$5—A to H—Continued.
M. E. Dudley	M. E. Norton	2101–2300, 9301–9500, 38401–38700, 45101–45300, 58101–58400, 66801–67100, 74101–74300.
V. M. Stanard	S. C. Ellett	2301–2600, 8601–8900, 16001–16300, 26501–26800, 30701-31000, 39701–40000, 42901–43100, 51201–51500, 61201-61500, 65001-65300.
Do	L. Devine	71801–72100, 78701–79000.
L. Breeden	E. C. Winston	2601–2900, 11001–11300, 19101–19400, 29501–29800, 35801-36000, 77401–77700, 82401–82700, 86901–87200, 93101–93400.
W. A. Garrett	J. McGarr	2901–3200, 9001–9300, 15701–16000, 28101–28300, 31601–31900, 57901–58100, 64401–64700, 73201–73500.
H. M. Douglass	F. C. Jones	3201–3500, 10701–11000, 16301–16700, 26901–27200, 32801-33100, 44501–44800, 51901–52200, 59301–59600, 65601–65900, 73501–73800, 80701–81000, 89301–89500, 92501–92800, 96901-97200.
M. A. Dewees	S. E. Hughes	3501–3800, 14501–14700, 17501–17800, 24201–24500, 31001-31300, 38101–38400, 45601–45800, 50101–50400, 58701–59000, 68501–68800, 78101–78300, 82101–82400.
H. Starke	M. Morrison	3801–4100, 88101–88400, 93401–93700, 97301–97400.
M. S. Knox	M. W. Bailey	4101–4400, 14701–15000, 41701–42000, 48701–49000.
H. Bartlett	M. Taylor	4401–4700, 12401–12700, 19401–19700, 24801–25100, 33101-33400, 38701–39000, 49201–49500, 53301–53600, 63801–64100, 69101–69400, 74901–75200, 81301–81600, 94001–94300.
E. P. Porter	A. P. Pellet	4701–5000, 12701–13000, 19701–19900, 24501–24800, 33401-33700, 36901–37200, 53601–53900, 64101–64400, 69401–69700, 75201–75500, 81601–81900, 85801–86100, 94601–94900.
M. C. Irvine	M. Johnson	5001–5300, 15001–15300, 22601–22900, 26201–26500, 30101-30400, 42001–42300, 45301–45600, 54901–55200, 63501–63800, 70401–70700, 76801–77100, 95701–96000.
M. Jones	E. Garlick	5301–5600, 20801–21100, 42301–42600, 56001–56400, 62701-63000.
R. F. Ball	L. M. Hunter	5601–5900, 13301–13600, 19901–20200.
Do	M. L. Savage	47301–47700, 51501–51900, 60001–60400, 69701–70100, 76401-76800, 83001–83400, 89501–89900, 94901–95100.
L. C. Minor	B. M. Abbott	5901–6200, 13601–13900, 22301–22600, 36601–36900, 41201-41500, 44801–45100, 55701–56000, 60901–61200, 68001–68300, 77101–77400, 84601–84900, 87801–88100, 96001–96300.
H. Watkins	M. L. Savage	6201–6500, 11301–11500.
K. Heth	M. E. Gilliam	6501–6800, 14201–14500, 21501–21800, 28301–28700, 36001-36400, 63001–63300.
E. Mason	M. C. Lathrop	6801–7100, 11501–11800, 18801–19100.
A. B. Capron	K. Walker	7101–7400, 13001–13300, 20201–20500, 28901–29200, 36401-36600, 41501–41700, 46101–46400, 55401–55700, 62101–62400, 70101–70400, 74601–74900, 83401–83700, 89001–89300, 95101-95400.
F. M. Dickins	F. E. Bernard	7401–7700, 21801–22100, 29201–29500, 34901–35200, 56401-56600, 63301–63500, 65901–66200, 84901–85200, 89901-90200, 95401–95700.
R. Haynes	B. Dabney	7701–7900, 13901–14200, 20501–20800, 25601–25900, 32501-32800, 56901–57000, 61801–62100, 74301–74600, 84001–84300, 88401–88700.
V. B. Briggs	J. B. Tiffey	8901–9000, 16701–16900, 23001–23300, 30401–30700, 39001-39300, 43901–44200, 50401–50600, 60601–60900, 72401–72700, 79301–79600, 86401–86700, 91901–92200.
E. D. Layne	V. C. Watson	9501–9800, 18701–18800, 23301–23600, 61501–61800, 67101-67400, 72701–73000, 81901–82100, 87501–87800, 97201-97300.
M. L. Quarles	F. G. Giles	10101–10400, 21301–21500, 27501–27800, 34301–34600, 47701-48000, 54601–54900, 62401–62700, 70901–71100.
M. B. Christian	M. S. Apperson	11801–12100, 18101–18400, 27801–28100, 35501–35800, 40301-40600, 45801–46100, 56601–56900, 82701–83000.
S. F. Shaver	M. Dixon	12101–12400, 17801–18100, 22901–23000, 26801–26900, 40001-40300, 46401–46700, 54301–54600, 59601–59800, 75501–75800, 87201–87500.
M. S. Nicholas	J. McCarthy	16901–17200, 23601–23900, 31901–32200, 37501–37800, 43101-43400, 52501–52800, 67701–68000, 76101–76400, 80401–80700 88701–89000, 94301–94600.

Register of Confederate States Treasury Notes—Continued.

ACT OF MARCH 23, 1863—Continued.

For Treasurer.	For Register.	Numbers of the notes signed.
		JULY ISSUE—Continued.
		$5—A to H—Continued.
E. A. Dennison	J. L. Johnston	21101-21300, 28701-28900, 34601-34900, 40901-41200, 47001-47300.
I. Benton	M. Pace	39301-39500, 43701-43900, 52801-53000, 60401-60600, 68301-68500, 73001-73200, 79601-79800, 86701-86900.
M. V. Tyler	B. M. Payne	39501-39700, 42601-42900, 49801-50100, 57001-57300, 86101-86400.
A. Points	M. Gay	48001-48400, 53901-54300, 57301-57600, 77701-78100, 84301-84600, 91201-91600.
M. Jones	E. Garlick	49001-49200.
V. M. Rind	V. K. Davies	70701-70900, 75801-76100, 83701-84000, 90201-90500, 96301-96600.
		AUGUST ISSUE.
		$100—A to D.
J. C. Joplin	G. W. Garrett	1-800, 2001-2800, 4601-5400, 8601-9400, 10201-11000, 11801-12600, 17501-18800, 20001-20800, 22001-22800, 23601-24400, 25201-26000, 26401-27200, 28001-28800, 29601-30400, 31201-32000, 34401-35200, 36501-37300.
T. J. Hatch	H. Smith	801-1200, 2801-3200, 5401-6200, 14701-15500, 15901-16700, 18801-19600, 20801-21600, 22801-23600, 24401-25200, 26001-26400, 27201-28000, 28801-29600, 30401-31200, 32001-32800, 35201-36000, 37301-38100.
E. C. Goddin	W. G. Harvey	1201-2000, 3201-4000, 6201-7000, 9401-10200, 11001-11800, 12701-13500, 13901-14700, 16701-17500, 19601-20000.
Do	W. A. Cocke	21601-22000, 33601-34400.
T. C. Gale	M. Winston	4001-4600, 7801-8600.
S. B. Jacobs	J. H. Cooke.	7001-7800, 15501-15900.
A. West	S. Dutcher	12601-12700.
W. G. Allen	C. S. Taylor	13501-13900.
Do	J. O. Sale	32801-33600, 36001-36500, 38101-38900.
		$50—wA to zA.
F. C. Weisiger	W. O. Slade	1-800, 4801-5600, 6401-7200, 9601-10400, 13601-14400, 17601-18400, 19901-20700, 24301-25100, 27501-28300, 30701-31500, 32301-33100, 45601-46400, 50201-51000, 51801-52600, 55801-56600, 60601-61400.
A. West	S. Dutcher	801-1400, 3801-4800, 7201-8000, 8801-9600, 15201-16000, 19201-19900, 21501-22700, 23501-24300, 29101-29900, 33901-34700, 35501-36300, 39101-39900, 42301-43100, 46401-47200, 51001-51800, 53401-54200, 56601-57400, 63001-63800, 67001-67800, 68301-69100.
A. Patton	W. Hancock	1401-2200, 5601-6400, 8001-8800, 12801-13600, 29901-30700, 39901-40700, 44701-45300, 59001-59800, 65401-66200.
S. B. Jacobs	J. H. Cooke	2201-3000, 16601-17400, 37901-38300, 43901-44700, 48001-48800, 58201-59000, 63801-64600.
T. C. Gale	M. Winston	3001-3800.
Do	W. P. Caldwell	69901-70700.
N. A. Bass	do	10401-11200, 14401-15200, 25101-25900, 33101-33900, 38301-39100, 43101-43900, 47201-48000, 49401-50200, 52601-53400.
W. J. Doyle	G. N. Warren	11201-12000, 20701-21500.
T. J. Hatch	H. Smith	12001-12800, 16001-16600, 17401-17600, 18401-19200, 34701-35100, 55001-55800, 61401-62200, 67801-68300.
W. G. Allen	C. S. Taylor	22701-23500, 25901-26700, 36301-37100, 69101-69900.
Do	J. O. Sale	45301-45600, 49001-49400, 57401-58200, 64601-65400.
T. W. Brown	W. Nott	26701-27500, 28301-29100, 40701-41500, 48801-49000.
E. C. Goddin	W. A. Cocke	31501-32300, 35101-35500, 37101-37900, 41501-42300, 54201-55000, 59801-60600, 66201-67000, 70701-71000.
J. C. Joplin	G. W. Garrett	62201-63000.
		$20—A to H.
J. E. Henderson	Tho. J. Miller	1-400, 2001-2400, 3601-4000, 5201-5600, 8801-9200, 12901-13300, 16001-16400, 20501-20800, 21101-21500, 24501-24900, 27901-28300, 31801-32200, 36601-37000, 38001-38400, 42501-42900.

Register of Confederate States Treasury Notes—Continued.

ACT OF MARCH 23, 1863—Continued.

For Treasurer.	For Register.	Numbers of the notes signed.
		AUGUST ISSUE—Continued.
		$20—A to H—Continued.
J. E. Henderson	G. N. Warren	43901–44300, 47801–48200, 50601–51000, 53001–53400, 56101–56500, 60001–60400.
Do	S. Dutcher	64801–65200, 68401–68800.
W. J. Doyle	G. N. Warren	401–800, 1601–2000, 2401–2800, 4801–5200, 6201–6600, 11101–11500, 18701–19100, 22301–22700, 24901–25300, 28701–29100, 31401–31800, 36201–36600, 38401–38800.
C. Ashford	S. Sinton	801–1600, 2801–3600, 4401–4800, 6601–7000, 9201–9600, 13301–13700, 17401–17700, 21501–21900, 23701–24100, 27101–27500, 32601–33000, 35001–35400, 39201–39600, 42001–42400, 44301–44700, 46601–47000, 50201–50600, 54201–54500, 55701–56100, 57701–58100, 65201–65600.
S. B. Jacobs	J. H. Cooke	4001–4400, 11501–11700, 15601–16000, 19501–19900, 22701–23100, 25901–26300, 31001–31400, 33401–33800, 37401–37600, 40401–40800, 48201–48600, 52201–52600, 61801–62200, 66801–67200.
Do	W. O. Slade	8201–8600.
A. Patton	W. Hancock	5601–6000, 7801–8200, 12501–12900, 16401–16800, 19901–20300, 23101–23500, 30601–31000, 33801–34200, 37001–37400, 42401–42500, 45801–46200, 48601–49000, 51801–52200, 62201–62600, 67601–68000.
T. W. Brown	W. Nott	6001–6200, 7001–7400, 11701–12100, 14101–14500, 19101–19500, 29501–29900, 34201–34600, 37601–38000, 42901–43300, 45501–45800, 49001–49400, 52601–53000, 54901–55300, 57301–57700, 61401–61800, 66401–66800.
N. A. Bass	W. P. Caldwell	7401–7800, 10401–10700, 14701–15200, 18301–18700, 26301–26700, 27501–27900.
W. G. Allen	C. S. Taylor	8601–8800, 15201–15600, 26701–27100, 30201–30600, 34601–35000, 40001–40400.
Do	J. O. Sale	43301–43500, 61001–61400, 66001–66400.
F. H. Link	L. P. Rogers	9601–10000, 13701–14100, 17901–18300, 21901–22300, 24101–24500, 28301–28700, 33001–33400, 35401–35800, 39601–40000, 41601–42000, 44701–45100, 47001–47400, 51001–51400, 54501–54900, 56501–56900, 58401–58800, 64001–64400, 69201–69600.
A. West	S. Dutcher	10001–10400, 14501–14700, 29101–29500, 63201–63600.
F. C. Weisiger	W. O. Slade	10701–11100, 17001–17400, 40801–41200, 59201–59600, 64401–64800, 70001–70100.
J. C. Joplin	G. W. Garrett	12101–12500, 16801–17000, 59601–60000, 62801–63200, 69601–70000.
B. H. Berry	J. T. Holt	17701–17900, 20801–21100, 25301–25500, 29901–30200, 32201–32600, 35801–36200, 38801–39200, 41201–41600, 43501–43900, 46201–46600, 49801–50200, 53401–53800, 55301–55700, 58101–58400, 63601–64000, 68801–69200.
E. C. Goddin	W. G. Harvey	20301–20500.
Do	W. A. Cocke	23501–23700, 25501–25900, 49401–49800, 60801–61000, 68001–68400.
J. Nethers	M. Winston	45101–45500, 47401–47800, 51401–51800, 53801–54200, 56901–57300, 60401–60800, 65601–66000.
T. J. Hatch	H. Smith	58801–59200, 62601–62800.
T. C. Gale.	W. P. Caldwell	67201–67600.
		$10—A to H.
M. Allen	H. L. Cooke	1–400, 5801–6200, 12301–12800, 13401–13800, 20301–20700, 28001–28400, 35101–35400, 42801–43200, 58601–59000, 67301–67700, 73901–74300.
S. G. Sanxay	L. Macon	401–700, 7401–7700, 13101–13400, 14401–14700, 21001–21300, 34601–34800, 35701–36000, 43501–43800, 51301–51600, 59501–59800, 68001–68300, 74301–74600.
V. Bridges	E. W. Pendleton	701–1000, 6801–7100, 12801–13100, 14101–14400, 20701–21000, 28401–28700, 34801–35100, 42501–42800, 58301–58600, 67701–68000, 74601–74900.
A. Points	M. Gay	1001–1400, 15801–16200, 21501–21900, 34201–34600, 36001–36200, 43801–44200, 51001–51300, 58101–58300, 68901–69100.
V. B. Briggs	J. B. Tiffey	1401–1700, 14701–14900, 20201–20300.
F. M. Dickins	F. E. Bernard	1701–2000, 11101–11400, 15201–15500, 25101–25400, 31601–31900, 38301–38600, 54401–54500, 72501–72700.

Register of Confederate States Treasury Notes—Continued.

ACT OF MARCH 23, 1863—Continued.

For Treasurer.	For Register.	Numbers of the notes signed.
		AUGUST ISSUE—Continued.
		$10—A to H—Continued.
H. Starke	M. Morrison	2001–2200, 9601–9900, 18801–19100, 24901–25100, 40301–40600, 47701–48000, 53801–54100, 61301–61600, 67001-67300, 78001–78300.
L. Breeden	E. C. Winston	2201–2500, 8901–9300, 19701–19900, 26201–26400, 30401–30700, 41401–41700, 49001–49300.
W. A. Garrett	J. McGarr	2501–2800, 6201–6600, 23601–23900, 28701–29000, 36501–36800, 45401–45700, 52201–52500, 59001–59300, 68601–68900.
M. S. Nicholas	J. McCarthy	2801–3100, 10501–10800, 17401–17700, 25901–26200, 33901–34200, 37401–37700, 49601–49800, 55401–55700, 62601–62900.
R. Haynes	B. Dabney	3101–3400, 11701–12000, 18501–18800, 21901–22200, 38001–38300, 50401–50700, 56001–56300, 60101–60400, 73301–73600, 78301–78600.
A. B. Capron	K. Walker	3401–3700, 32601–32800, 41701–42000, 48301–48600, 56801–57100, 63401–63700, 65201–65500, 72201–72500, 78901-79200.
M. C. Irvine	M. Johnson	3701–3900, 66101–66400, 71301–71600.
S. F. Shaver	M. Dixon	3901–4300, 7701–8100, 14901–15200.
Do	J. Douglas	49301–49600, 52901–53200.
E. P. Porter	A. P. Pellet	4301–4600, 25701–25900.
H. Bartlett	M. Taylor	4601–4900, 10801–11100, 19901–20200, 25401–25700, 30101–30400, 37101–37400, 46001–46300, 57701–58000, 62001-62300, 66401–66700, 71901–72200, 77701–78000.
R. F. Ball	M. L. Savage	4901–5200, 9701-10200, 17001-17200, 26401-26800, 33601-33900, 40601–41000, 49801–50100, 52501–52900, 63701-34000, 72701–73000, 76101–76500.
V. M. Rind	V. K. Davies	5201–5400, 5701–5800, 11401–11700, 19101–19400, 26801-27100, 31001–31300, 42001–42300, 47201–47500, 57101-57400, 65501–65800, 73601–73900, 79201–79500.
A. Harrison	J. Douglas	5401–5700, 9301–9600, 16701–17000.
M. V. Tyler	B. M. Payne	6601–6800, 13801–14100, 21301–21500, 35401–35700, 43201–43500, 59301–59500.
M. A. Dewees	S. E. Hughes	7101–7400, 15501–15800, 22501–22800, 33401–33600, 36801–37100, 45101–45400, 54801–55100, 61601–62000, 68301-68600, 74901–75200.
I. Benton	M. Pace	8101–8300, 17701–17900, 23101–23300, 32801–33000, 47501–47700, 56301–56500, 62901–63100, 69101–69300, 77501-77700.
M. Sommers	M. B. Kirby	8301–8600, 17901–18200, 24601–24900, 31301–31600, 38901–39200, 46601–46900, 54101–54400, 61001–61300, 71001-71300, 75201–75500.
H. M. Douglass	F. C. Jones	8601–8900, 16201–16400, 23301–23600, 36201–36500, 44201–44500, 51601–51900, 60401–60700.
E. D. Layne	V. C. Watson	10201–10500, 18201–18500, 24301–24600, 29301–29600, 44801–45100.
M. B. Christian	M. S. Apperson	12001–12300, 19401–19700, 29601–29900, 50101–50400, 55101–55400, 62301–62600, 70801–71000, 76901–77200.
M. Godwin	E. A. Adams	16401–16700.
M. L. Quarles	F. G. Giles	17201–17400, 22201–22500, 30701–31000, 40001–40300, 44501–44800, 53501–53800, 60701–61000, 69301–69600.
V. M. Stanard	L. Devine	22801–23100, 29901–30100, 38601–38900, 46301–46600, 69901–70200.
E. O. Beall	E. A. Adams	23901–24300, 33001–33400, 39601–40000, 48601–49000, 54501–54800, 64601–64900, 65801–66100, 70201–70500, 76501-76900.
E. Mason	M. C. Lathrop	27101–27500, 41001–41400, 57401–57700, 64301–64600, 71601–71900.
E. A. Dennison	M. E. Gilliam	27501–27800, 32201–32600, 46901–47200, 53201–53500, 64001–64300, 77201–77500.
M. Jones	E. Garlick	27801–28000, 42301–42500, 50701–51000, 56501–56800, 64901–65200, 66701–67000, 73001–73300, 78601–78900.
M. E. Dudley	M. E. Norton	29001–29300, 37701–38000, 45701–46000, 51901–52200, 59801–60100, 69601–69900, 75801–76100.
S. Lambert	P. Pleasants	31901–32200, 39201–39600, 48001–48300, 55701–56000, 63101–63400, 70501–70800, 75501–75800.
		$5—A to H.
M. Allen	H. L. Cooke	1–400, 6501–6900, 13501–13900, 19901–20300, 35601–36000, 43801–44200, 50901–52300, 60201–60600, 61601–62000.

Register of Confederate States Treasury Notes—Continued.

ACT OF MARCH 23, 1863—Continued.

For Treasurer.	For Register.	Numbers of the notes signed.
		AUGUST ISSUE—Continued.
		$5—A to H—Continued.
V. Bridges	E. W. Pendleton	401–700, 12901–13200, 28201–28500, 36001–36300, 44201–44500, 53001–53300, 60601–60900, 62301–62600.
S. G. Sanxay	L. Macon	701–1000, 7801–8000, 13901–14200, 21001–21300, 28501–28800, 36301–36600, 44701–45000, 53601–53900, 62001–62300.
W. A. Garrett	J. McGarr	1001–1400, 7101–7500, 14601–14900, 22501–22800, 29101–29400, 36601–36900, 45001–45300, 54801–55100, 63001–63300.
M. S. Nicholas	J. McCarthy	1401–1700, 10601–10900, 19601–19800, 23901–24200, 35301–35600, 41001–41300, 47101–47400, 58501–58800.
M. A. Dewees	S. E. Hughes	1701–2000, 10301–10600, 16601–16900, 20701–21000, 27901–28200, 37301–37600, 45901–46200, 54201–54500, 62601–63000.
S. F. Shaver	M. Dixon	2001–2500, 8401–8800, 15701–16000, 24901–25200, 29401–29700, 51001–51300.
Do	J. Douglas	56901–57200.
E. D. Layne	V. C. Watson	2501–2800, 9601–9900, 23401–23700, 38101–38400, 44501–44700.
H. M. Douglass	F. C. Jones	2801–3100, 8801–9100, 14901–15200, 31701–32000, 38401–38700, 45601–45900, 55701–56000, 66001–66300.
M. Sommers	M. B. Kirby	3101–3400, 9301–9600, 15201–15500, 24201–24500, 31101–31400, 40401–40700, 47801–48100, 55401–55700, 64401–64700.
H. Starke	M. Morrison	3401–3700, 16901–17200, 31401–31700, 37801–38100, 48101–48400, 58001–58300.
H. Bartlett	M. Taylor	3701–4000, 11801–12100, 19301–19600, 25901–26200, 30601–30900, 40101–40400, 46801–47100, 57401–57700.
L. Breeden	E. C. Winston	4001–4300, 9901–10300, 17201–17500, 25601–25900, 32001–32300, 41901–42200, 49401–49700, 57201–57400.
F. M. Dickins	F. E. Bernard	4301–4600, 11501–11800, 21801–22200, 33101–33400, 42601–42900, 48601–48800, 64701–64900.
V. M. Rind	V. K. Davies	4601–4900, 12101–12400, 18701–19000, 26201–26500, 34301–34600, 43501–43800, 51301–51600, 59701–60000.
L. C. Minor	B. M. Abbott	4901–5200, 12401–12700.
A. Harrison	J. Douglas	5201–5500, 10901–11200.
Do	M. C. Lathrop	16001–16300.
R. F. Ball	M. L. Savage	5501–5900, 8001–8400, 19001–19300, 25201–25600, 34601–35000, 39001–39400, 50601–51000, 59401–59700, 65601–66000.
R. Haynes	B. Dabney	5901–6200, 11201–11500, 17501–17800, 21501–21800, 34001–34300, 41301–41600, 48801–49100, 53901–54200, 66301–66600.
M. B. Christian	M. S. Apperson	6201–6500, 12701–12900, 18001–18200, 22201–22500, 33401–33700, 42901–43200, 49701–50000, 60001–60200, 65201–65600.
M. V. Tyler	B. M. Payne	6901–7100, 13201–13500, 21301–21500, 28801–29100, 52701–53000, 60901–61200.
V. B. Briggs	J. B. Tiffey	7501–7800, 15501–15700, 19801–19900.
I. Benton	M. Pace	9101–9300, 18201–18400, 23701–23900, 30901–31100, 37601–37800, 48401–48600, 56701–56900, 64201–64400.
A. Points	M. Gay	14201–14600, 20301–20700, 36901–37300, 52301–52700, 61201–61600.
S. Lambert	P. Pleasants	16301–16600, 26501–26800, 32301–32700, 42201–42600, 49101–49400, 57701–58000.
M. L. Quarles	F. G. Giles	17801–18000, 23101–23400, 30001–30300, 45301–45600, 55101–55400, 63301–63600.
E. Beall	E. A. Adams	18401–18700, 24501–24900, 32701–33100, 39701–40100, 47401–47800, 56301–56700.
M. E. Dudley	M. E. Norton	22801–23100, 29701–30000, 38701–39000, 46201–46500, 53301–53600, 63901–64200.
E. A. Dennison	M. E. Gilliam	26801–27100, 33701–34000, 40701–41000, 50001–50300, 59101–59400.
E. Mason	M. C. Lathrop	27101–27500, 56001–56300, 64901–65200.
A. B. Capron	K. Walker	27501–27800, 39401–39700, 51601–51900, 58301–58500.
V. M. Stanard	L. Devine	27801–27900, 30301–30600, 41601–41900, 46501–46800, 54501–54800, 63601–63900.
M. Jones	E. Garlick	35001–35300, 43201–43500, 50301–50600, 58801–59100.
		SEPTEMBER ISSUE.
		$100—A to D.
T. J. Hatch	H. Smith	1–800, 3001–3800, 8201–9800, 10601–11400, 13001–14600.
Do	W. T. French	16201–17800, 26601–28000, 28201–29000.

Register of Confederate States Treasury Notes—Continued.

ACT OF MARCH 23, 1863—Continued.

For Treasurer.	For Register.	Numbers of the notes signed.
		SEPTEMBER ISSUE—Continued.
		$100—A to D—Continued.
W. G. Allen	C. S. Taylor	801–1600, 4601–5400, 6201–7000, 7401–8200, 9801-10600, 18601-19400, 22401–23000, 23401–24200, 25801–26600, 29001-29800.
S. B. Jacobs	J. H. Cooke	1601–2200, 23001–23400.
J. C. Joplin	G. W. Garrett	2201–3000, 3801–4600, 5401–6200, 11401–13000, 14601–16200, 17801–18600, 19401–21000, 21801–22400, 25001-25800, 28001-28200.
E. C. Goddin	W. A. Cocke	7001–7400, 21001–21800, 24201–25000.
		$50—wA to zA.
T. J. Hatch	H. Smith	1–800, 1601–2400, 4001–4800, 6001–6800, 8401–9200, 11301-12100, 13301–14100, 20101–20900, 21701–22500, 26901-27700, 49101–49900.
W. G. Allen	C. S. Taylor	801–1600.
E. C. Goddin	W. A. Cocke	2401–3200, 6801–7600, 9201–10000, 12101–12900, 14101–14900, 22501–23300, 24101–24900, 25701–26100, 27701–27900, 28701-30300, 31901–32700, 33901–34700, 41501–41900, 44501-45300, 47501–48300, 50701–51500.
F. C. Weisiger	W. O. Slade	3201–4000, 5201–6000, 7601–8400, 10501–11300, 16101–16900, 19301–20100, 24901–25700, 27901–28700, 35301–36100, 38501-39300, 40901–41500, 43701–44500, 45301–45900, 46701-47500, 48301–49100.
N. A. Bass	Tho. J. Miller	4801–5200.
Do	J. J. Matthews	17701–18500.
S. B. Jacobs	J. H. Cooke	10001–10500, 12901–13300, 15701–16100, 18501–19300, 20901-21700, 23301–24100, 30301–31100, 36901–37700, 43101–43700, 45901–46700.
T. C. Gale	W. P. Caldwell	14901–15700, 16901–17700.
Do	G. N. Warren	32701–33100, 34701–35300, 36101–36900, 40101–40900, 41901-42500, 49901–50700.
J. C. Joplin	G. W. Garrett	26101–26900.
A. Patton	W. Hancock	31101–31900, 42501–43100.
F. H. Link	L. P. Rogers	33101–33900.
T. W. Brown	W. Nott	37701–38500.
A. West	S. Dutcher	39301–40100.
		$20—A to H.
F. C. Weisiger	W. O. Slade	1–300, 2701–3000, 7201–7600, 26401–26800, 31701-32100, 39401-39800, 43501–43900, 47401–47800, 56001–56400, 63701-64100, 67301–67700, 70701–71100, 81901–82200.
T. J. Hatch	H. Smith	301–700.
Do	W. T. French	87901–88200.
J. Nethers	M. Winston	701–1100, 5201–5600, 9301–9700, 13101–13500, 18701–19100, 20901–21300, 24001–24400, 28001–28400, 30501–30900, 33301-33700, 37401–37800, 71101–71500, 74701–75100, 77401–77800, 80301–80600, 83301–83900, 87101–87500, 89601–90000, 93601-94000, 97201–97600.
S. B. Jacobs	J. H. Cooke	1101–1500, 6001–6400, 10301–10700, 15501–15900, 19101–19500, 21901–22000, 28801–28900, 38601–39000, 49801–50200, 53401-53800, 58001–58400, 61801–62200, 67701–68100, 72701–73100, 77801–78200, 84101–84200, 87501–87900, 94001–94400, 98001-98400.
T. W. Brown	W. Nott	1501–1900, 10701–11100, 15901–16300, 19501–19900, 22001-22400, 25601–26000, 28901–29300, 30901–31300, 34501–34900, 42401–42800, 46601–47000, 50601–51000, 54201–54600, 59001-59400, 62601–63000, 66901–67300, 73301–73500, 80901–81100, 84501–84900, 94801–95200.
A. Patton	W. Hancock	1901–2100, 5001–5200, 10101–10300, 15101–15500, 21501-21900, 24401–24800, 28401–28800, 31301–31700, 33701–34100, 38201-38600, 42001–42400, 45501–45900, 48601–49000, 53801-54200, 58401–58800, 62201–62600, 65701–66100, 73101–73300, 78901-79300, 84201–84500, 88201–88400, 91201–91600, 92801–93200.
E. C. Goddin	W. A. Cocke	2101–2300, 5601–6000, 14701–15100, 34101–34500, 41001-41200, 54601–54800, 58801–59000, 75801–76200, 90801–91200.

Register of Confederate States Treasury Notes—Continued.

ACT OF MARCH 23, 1863—Continued.

For Treasurer.	For Register.	Numbers of the notes signed.
		SEPTEMBER ISSUE—Continued.
		$20—A to H—Continued.
J. C. Joplin	G. W. Garrett	2301-2700, 8001-8400, 11501-11900, 17901-18300, 22401-22800, 23601-24000, 27201-27600, 44301-44700, 48201-48600, 82601-83000, 96401-96800.
F. H. Link	L. P. Rogers	3001-3400, 9101-9300, 12301-12700, 18301-18700, 20501-20900, 23201-23600, 27601-28000, 29301-29700, 32501-32900, 35801-36200, 39801-40200, 44701-45100, 47801-48200, 51401-51800, 55601-56000, 60201-60600, 64101-64500, 69301-69700, 73901-74300, 77001-77400, 80001-80300, 82201-82600, 85901-86300, 89201-89600, 92401-92800, 96001-96400.
J. E. Henderson	S. Dutcher	3401-3800, 7601-8000.
Do	Tho. J. Miller	13501-13900, 16701-17100.
B. H. Berry	J. T. Holt	3801-4200, 6801-7200, 12701-13100, 17501-17900, 20101-20500, 22801-23200, 26001-26400, 29701-30100, 32901-33300, 36201-36600, 41201-41600, 45901-46200, 49001-49400, 51801-52200, 54801-55200, 59401-59800, 63301-63700, 68501-68900, 71901-72300, 75501-75800, 76201-76600, 79301-79500, 81101-81500.
Do	W. T. French	85101-85500, 88801-89200.
C. Ashford	S. Sinton	4201-4600, 9701-10100, 11901-12300, 17101-17500, 24801-25200, 32101-32500, 37001-37400, 40201-40600, 43101-43500, 47001-47400, 51001-51400, 55201-55600, 59801-60200, 64501-64900, 68901-69300, 70301-70700, 73501-73900, 76601-77000, 79501-79700, 81501-81900, 85501-85900, 90001-90400, 92001-92400, 95201-95600.
A. West	S. Dutcher	4601-5000, 8401-8800, 16301-16700, 34901-35300, 36601-37000, 41601-42000, 45101-45500, 50201-50600, 52601-53000, 56401-56800, 61401-61800, 65301-65700, 68101-68500, 71501-71900, 74301-74700, 80601-80900, 83701-84100, 86301-86700, 90401-90800, 94401-94800, 97601-98000.
T. C. Gale	W. P. Caldwell	6401-6800, 11101-11500, 14301-14700, 35301-35700, 39001-39400, 42801-43100, 46201-46600.
Do	G. N. Warren	49401-49800, 57601-58000, 63001-63300, 66501-66900, 70101-70300, 84901-85100.
Do	M. Winston	53001-53400.
W. G. Allen	C. S. Taylor	8801-9100, 13901-14300, 19901-20100, 35701-35800, 52201-52600, 57201-57600, 60601-61000, 66101-66500, 69701-70100, 72301-72700, 78501-78900, 91601-92000, 96801-97200.
N. A. Bass	Tho. J. Miller	21301-21500, 25201-25600, 26801-27200, 30101-30500.
Do	J. J. Matthews	37801-38200, 40601-41000, 43901-44300, 56801-57200, 61001-61400, 64901-65300, 75101-75500, 78201-78500, 79701-80000, 83001-83300, 86701-87100, 88401-88800, 93201-93600, 95601-96000.
		$10—A to H.
M. Allen	H. L. Cooke	1-400, 6401-6800, 14501-14900, 22901-23200, 39901-40300, 48401-48800, 57701-58100, 68301-68700, 76201-76600, 86701-87000, 96601-96800, 101401-101800.
Do	J. L. Johnston	87001-87100.
V. Bridges	E. W. Pendleton	401-700, 7701-8000, 15801-16100, 23301-23600, 32801-33100, 40601-40900, 49401-49700, 78701-79000, 87701-87800, 98801-99000, 102101-102400.
S. G. Sanxay	L. Macon	701-1000, 7101-7400, 15501-15800, 25601-25900, 37401-37700, 49101-49400, 58701-59000, 69901-70200, 77201-77500, 87401-87700, 97101-97300.
I. Benton	M. Pace	1001-1200, 8901-9100, 17501-17700, 34901-35100.
Do	M. Stevens	44101-44300.
Do	L. Forde	55701-55900, 61901-62100, 88101-88300, 98201-98300.
Do	M. L. Savage	72901-73100.
Do	E. W. Pendleton	86301-86500.
H. M. Douglass	F. C. Jones	1201-1500, 8301-8600, 16301-16600, 24701-25000.
Do	E. A. Adams	34001-34300.
Do	M. Pace	43801-44100, 50001-50200, 59001-59300, 69601-69900, 78401-78700.
M. Sommers	J. B. Tiffey	1501-1800.
Do	E. Garlick	27101-27400, 35101-35400.
Do	E. A. Adams	43201-43500, 80401-80700.

Register of Confederate States Treasury Notes—Continued.

ACT OF MARCH 23, 1863—Continued.

For Treasurer.	For Register.	Numbers of the notes signed.
		SEPTEMBER ISSUE—Continued.
		$10—A to H—Continued.
M. Sommers	S. E. Hughes	54801-55100.
Do	M. Pace	90101-90400.
Do	M. B. Kirby	97701-97800, 101301-101400.
S. Lambert	P. Pleasants	1801-2100, 14301-14500, 21701-22000, 25001-25300, 32201-32300, 36801-37100, 41701-42000, 48201-48400, 55101-55400, 82201-82500, 88801-89100.
M. C. Waller	H. Clarke	2101-2300, 7401-7700, 16101-16300, 28301-28500, 36601-36800.
Do	L. Forde	41501-41700.
Do	S. E. Hughes	53801-53900.
Do	A. P. Pellet	53901-54000.
Do	M. L. Savage	79901-80100.
Do	M. Pace	99101-99200.
L. Breeden	E. C. Winston	2301-2600, 12001-12300, 18301-18600, 29101-29400, 36301-36600, 45101-45400, 54501-54800, 63001-63300, 80101-80400, 90401-90700, 98001-98200.
Do	C. Sessions	75301-75600.
E. A. Dennison	M. E. Gilliam	2601-2900, 12501-12800, 28801-29100, 38001-38300, 46601-46900, 52601-52900, 64201-64400, 73401-73700, 80701-81000, 93301-93500, 93601-93700, 99501-99700.
Do	L. Forde	64401-64500.
Do	M. Johnson	93501-93600.
E. Beall	E. A. Adams	2901-3300, 9401-9800, 19501-19900, 74001-74400, 94701-95000, 100401-100600.
Do	M. L. Savage	64501-64800.
Do	M. Gay	65801-66100.
V. M. Rind	V. K. Davies	3301-3600, 12801-13100, 21401-21700, 30001-30300, 38901-39200, 43501-43800, 57401-57700, 65401-65700, 66601-66900, 72601-72900, 81901-82200, 95801-96100, 100801-100900.
L. C. Minor	B. M. Abbott	3601-3900, 13401-13700, 18601-18900, 27401-27700, 42001-42300, 51301-51600, 62401-62600, 66901-67200, 73101-73400, 84601-84900, 92001-92300, 99201-99400.
Do	S. E. Hughes	62601-62700.
A. B. Capron	K. Walker	3901-4200, 10401-10700, 19901-20200, 31401-31700, 37701-38000, 46001-46300, 63901-64200, 73701-74000, 83701-84000, 92301-92600, 99701-99800.
M. C. Irvine	M. Johnson	4201-4500, 14001-14300, 20801-21100, 29701-30000, 35401-35700, 52301-52600, 65101-65400, 81601-81900, 96101-96300.
Do	E. Garlick	98701-98800.
R. F. Ball	M. L. Savage	4501-4900, 11601-11900, 20201-20600, 31101-31400, 38301-38600, 46901-47200, 56801-57100, 100201-100400.
Do	M. Johnson	67201-67400.
H. Bartlett	M. Taylor	4901-5200, 11301-11600, 22301-22600, 30601-30900, 39401-39700, 48001-48200, 56201-56500, 61101-61400, 75001-75300, 82801-83100, 92901-93200, 101101-101200.
R. Haynes	B. Dabney	5201-5500, 30301-30600, 36001-36300, 46301-46600, 53201-53500, 63601-63900, 66101-66400, 71401-71700, 91401-91700, 100601-100700.
Do	M. L. Savage	82501-82800.
E. P. Porter	A. P. Pellet	5501-5800, 10101-10400, 22001-22300, 30901-31100, 47801-48000, 56501-56800, 61401-61600, 74701-75000, 83401-83700, 92601-92900, 101201-101300.
M. A. Dewees	S. E. Hughes	5801-6100, 11001-11300, 17701-17800, 39701-39900, 78301-78400, 95301-95500, 97301-97500.
Do	P. Pleasants	78101-78200.
Do	M. W. Bailey	78201-78300.
H. Starke	M. Morrison	6101-6400, 10701-11000, 18001-18300.
Do	F. E. Bernard	28501-28800.
Do	S. E. Hughes	55401-55700.
Do	C. Sessions	85201-85500, 94001-94200, 98301-98500.
W. A. Garrett	J. McGarr	6801-7100, 14901-15200, 23801-24100, 32301-32600, 40901-41200, 49701-50000, 58401-58700, 69001-69300, 76901-77200, 89101-89200, 96501-96600.
Do	M. S. Apperson	89201-89400.
V. M. Stanard	L. Devine	8001-8300, 18901-19200, 25901-26200, 34301-34600, 47501-47800, 53501-53800, 59901-60200, 71701-72000, 84901-85200, 91701-92000, 99001-99100.

Register of Confederate States Treasury Notes—Continued.

ACT OF MARCH 23, 1863—Continued.

For Treasurer.	For Register.	Numbers of the notes signed.
		SEPTEMBER ISSUE—Continued.
		$10—A to H—Continued.
M. E. Dudley	M. E. Norton	8601-8900, 17201-17500, 26501-26800, 33701-34000, 42601-42900, 51001-51300, 59301-59600, 70501-70800, 77801-78100, 90701-91000, 99401-99500.
N. Semple	M. W. Bailey	9101-9400, 19201-19500, 29401-29700, 35701-36000, 41201-41500, 50501-50800, 60501-60800, 74401-74700, 79601-79900.
Do	F. E. Bernard	93201-93300, 96301-96400.
Do	B. J. Clarke	97501-97700.
S. F. Shaver	J. Douglas	9801-10100.
Do	M. Dixon	20601-20800, 28001-28300, 51901-52300, 81001-81300, 94201-94500.
L. Carter	P. C. Bagby	12301-12500, 21101-21400, 27701-28000.
Do	J. McCarthy	37101-37300.
Do	M. Gay	37301-37400, 45001-45100.
Do	M. Dixon	44801-45000.
Do	M. F. Stevens	52901-53200, 63301-63600, 70201-70500, 79301-79600, 88301-88600, 96901-97100.
E. Mason	M. C. Lathrop	13101-13400, 22601-22900, 31701-32000, 38601-38900, 47201-47500, 57101-57400, 64801-65100, 68001-68300, 75601-75900, 86001-86300, 95001-95300, 100901-101100.
F. M. Dickins	F. E. Bernard	13701-14000, 15201-15500.
V. B. Briggs	J. B. Tiffey	16601-16900, 24401-24700, 34601-34900, 44501-44800, 50201-50500, 59601-59900, 69301-69600, 79001-79300, 87801-88100.
Do	M. S. Apperson	98501-98600.
E. D. Layne	B. M. Payne	16901-17200.
Do	M. Dixon	26801-27100, 33401-33700.
Do	F. E. Bernard	44301-44500, 50801-51000, 62101-62400, 67801-68000, 71101-71400.
Do	V. C. Watson	77501-77800, 89401-89500, 89601-89700, 97901-98000.
Do	M. L. Savage	89501-89600.
V. M. Tyler	B. M. Payne	22601-22800, 32601-32800, 40301-40600, 48801-49100, 58101-58400, 68701-69000, 76601-76900, 87101-87400, 96801-96900, 101801-102100.
A. Points	M. Gay	24101-24400, 84301-84600, 95501-95800, 99801-100000.
M. Godwin	J. L. Johnston	25301-25600, 33101-33400, 45701-46000, 54301-54500, 60201-60500, 72001-72100, 83101-83400, 88601-88800.
Do	L. Forde	72101-72200.
Do	M. L. Savage	72201-72300.
Do	M. Pace	102401-102500.
Do	K. Walker	102501-102600.
M. L. Quarles	S. E. Hughes	26201-26500, 72301-72500.
Do	M. Johnson	42301-42600, 62801-63000.
Do	M. S. Apperson	54001-54100, 90001-90100.
Do	E. Garlick	54101-54300.
Do	C. Sessions	62701-62800.
Do	H. M. Douglass	72501-72600.
Do	B. J. Clarke	85501-85800, 89701-90000.
M. S. Nicholas	E. A. Adams	32001-32200.
Do	J. McCarthy	39201-39400, 42901-43200, 51601-51900, 61601-61900, 70801-71100, 84001-84300, 91001-91300, 98601-98700.
M. Jones	E. Garlick	45401-45700, 55901-56200, 65701-65800, 67401-67800, 75901-76100, 81301-81600, 93701-94000, 100701-100800.
A. Harrison	M. Dixon	60801-61100.
Do	H. M. Douglass	86501-86700, 100001-100100.
M. Gwynn	M. S. Apperson	66401-66600, 76101-76200, 85801-86000, 91301-91400, 96401-96500, 97801-97900.
M. S. Knox	M. W. Bailey	94501-94700, 100101-100200.
		$5—A to H.
M. C. Waller	B. J. Clarke	1-300, 9401-9600, 19801-20000, 28601-28800, 33601-33800.
Do	S. E. Hughes	39701-39900, 63401-63600.
Do	M. L. Savage	70901-71100.
Do	M. Pace	89401-89600.
V. Bridges	E. W. Pendleton	301-600, 8501-8800, 16501-16800, 33301-33600, 39401-39700, 61601-61900, 78001-78300.

Register of Confederate States Treasury Notes—Continued.

ACT OF MARCH 23, 1863—Continued.

For Treasurer.	For Register.	Numbers of the notes signed.
		SEPTEMBER ISSUE—Continued.
		$5—A to H—Continued.
S. G. Sanxay	L. Macon	601-900, 17701-18000, 26201-26500, 33001-33300, 39101-39400, 47601-47900, 57901-58000, 61301-61600, 78701-79000, 88501-88800.
W. A. Garrett	J. McGarr	901-1200, 9101-9400, 17401-17700, 34101-34400, 40601-40900, 48301-48600, 55201-55500, 57501-57600, 61001-61300, 74101-74400, 88201-88500.
Do	M. Taylor	88101-88200.
A. Points	M. Gay	1201-1500, 16801-17100, 25901-26200, 37601-37900, 64501-64600, 82601-82900, 95001-95300.
Do	M. Dixon	64601-64800.
M. E. Dudley	M. E. Norton	1501-1800, 9901-10200, 18001-18300, 26501-26800, 38201-38400, 40901-41200, 50301-50600, 59801-59900, 65601-65900, 73501-73800, 81101-81400, 93401-93700.
A. B. Capron	K. Walker	1801-2000, 12101-12400, 20301-20600, 30301-30500, 36701-37000, 43201-43500, 53701-54000, 59301-59400, 68401-68700, 70101-70400, 82001-82300, 91701-92000.
V. M. Stanard	L. Devine	2001-2200, 9601-9900, 19501-19800, 28001-28300, 35001-35300, 42101-42400, 50001-50300, 59701-59800, 65301-65600, 73201-73500, 85201-85500, 95301-95700.
F. M. Dickins	F. E. Bernard	2201-2500, 14001-14300.
H. M. Douglass	F. C. Jones	2501-2800, 10401-10600, 19201-19500.
Do	M. Pace	39901-40300, 48601-48900, 57601-57700, 61901-62200, 71701-72000.
M. Sommers	J. B. Tiffey	2801-3100 (A and B).
Do	M. B. Kirby	2801-3100 (C to H), 89901-90100.
Do	E. Garlick	29701-30000, 34701-35000.
Do	S. E. Hughes	41801-42100.
Do	M. L. Savage	62201-62500.
Do	J. McGarr	71401-71700.
Do	P. Pleasants	79901-80100.
Do	M. Dixon	80101-80200.
Do	M. Taylor	90101-90200.
I. Benton	M. Pace	3101-3300, 10201-10400, 22101-22300, 29301-29500, 35601-35800, 42401-42500.
Do	L. Forde	42501-42600, 49801-50000, 86401-86600, 92001-92200.
Do	C. Sessions	59001-59100.
Do	B. J. Clarke	65101-65300.
H. Starke	M. Morrison	3301-3600, 13001-13300, 20901-21200.
Do	E. C. Winston	37901-38200.
Do	C. Sessions	66601-66900, 85801-86100, 92201-92500.
E. O. Beall	E. A. Adams	3601-4000, 12601-13000, 68701-69000, 74701-75000, 86601-86900, 93701-94000.
M. A. Dewees	S. E. Hughes	4001-4300, 23601-23900, 79001-79300, 88801-89100.
L. Breeden	E. C. Winston	4301-4600, 12401-12600, 20601-20900, 28801-29100, 44901-45200, 51101-51400, 59101-59300, 63101-63400, 71101-71400, 82901-83200, 91101-91400.
V. M. Rind	V. K. Davies	4601-4900, 14301-14600, 30001-30300, 36101-36400, 52301-52600, 55801-56100, 58401-58600, 69001-69300, 77301-77600, 87801-88100.
Do	M. A. Dewees	25101-25300.
M. L. Quarles	E. A. Adams	4901-5200.
Do	F. E. Bernard	18601-18900.
Do	C. Sessions	50601-50800.
Do	M. Johnson	55501-55600.
Do	M. S. Apperson	55601-55800.
Do	S. E. Hughes	58801-58900.
Do	B. J. Clarke	75801-76100, 84901-85200, 92801-93100.
E. A. Dennison	M. E. Gilliam	5201-5500, 13701-14000, 22901-23200, 41201-41500, 52901-53200, 59601-59700, 86101-86400, 94301-94400.
Do	L. Forde	56101-56300.
Do	J. McCarthy	74401-74700.
N. Semple	M. W. Bailey	5501-5700, 10601-10900, 20001-20300, 31401-31700, 44201-44500, 52601-52900, 58901-59000, 66401-66600, 72301-72600.
Do	F. E. Bernard	84201-84400, 89601-89900.
Do	J. L. Johnston	84401-84500.
L. Carter	P. C. Bagby	5701-5900, 11201-11500, 21801-22100, 28301-28450.

Register of Confederate States Treasury Notes—Continued.

ACT OF MARCH 23, 1863—Continued.

For Treasurer.	For Register.	Numbers of the notes signed.
		SEPTEMBER ISSUE—Continued.
		$5—A to H—Continued.
L. Carter	E. Garlick	28451–28500.
Do	J. McCarthy	28501–28600.
Do	M. Gay	43901–44200.
Do	M. Stevens	50801–51100, 58001–58100, 62801–63100, 80501–80800.
Do	H. M. Douglass	73801–74100.
Do	M. Dixon	90201–90400.
Do	L. Forde	90401–90500.
S. F. Shaver	J. Douglas	5901–6200, 11501–11700.
Do	M. Dixon	11701–11800, 18301–18600, 44501–44900, 66901–67200, 85501–85800.
R. F. Ball	M. L. Savage	6201–6600, 13301–13700, 23201–23600, 30801–31100, 37301–37600, 45201–45500, 54001–54300, 56301–56600, 81701–82000.
L. C. Minor	B. M. Abbott	6601–6900, 10901–11200, 18901–19200, 27401–27700, 45501–45800, 54601–54900, 58201–58400, 64801–65100, 81401–81700.
Do	L. Macon	75001–75300.
Do	J. B. Tiffey	94401–94700.
R. Haynes	B. Dabney	6901–7100, 23901–24200, 30501–30800, 37001–37300, 43501–43800, 51401–51700, 58101–58200, 66101–66400, 75501–75800, 80201–80500, 90801–91100.
S. Lambert	P. Pleasants	7101–7400, 14601–14900, 21501–21800, 29501–29700, 35301–35600, 43801–43900, 84001–84200, 92501–92800.
Do	C. Sessions	76101–76400.
H. Bartlett	M. Taylor	7401–7700, 15501–15800, 22601–22900, 32001–32300, 36401–36700, 46401–46700, 53201–53500, 57101–57200, 60201–60300, 63901–64200, 72901–73200, 84501–84800.
E. P. Porter	A. P. Pellet	7701–8000, 15201–15500, 22301–22600, 31701–32000, 46701–47000, 53501–53700, 60101–60200, 63601–63900, 69801–70100, 83501–83800.
M. C. Irvine	M. Johnson	8001–8100, 14901–15200, 24501–24800, 32301–32600, 46101–46400, 51701–52000, 59401–59500, 67801–68100, 77001–77300, 86901–87200.
M. Allen	H. L. Cooke	8101–8500, 16101–16500, 25301–25700, 32601–33000, 38401–38800, 47901–48300, 57201–57400, 60301–60700, 69701–69800, 78301–78700.
Do	E. W. Pendleton	69401–69700.
E. D. Layne	B. M. Payne	8801–9100, 34401–34700.
Do	S. E. Hughes	26801–27100.
Do	F. E. Bernard	41501–41800, 49201–49300, 58601–58700.
Do	C. Sessions	49301–49500.
Do	V. C. Watson	70601–70900, 79601–79800, 89101–89400.
Do	J. L. Johnston	79801–79900.
M. Godwin	do	11801–12100, 21201–21500, 45801–46100, 52001–52300, 56901–57100, 65901–66100, 75301–75500, 83801–84000.
Do	E. W. Pendleton	57801–57900.
E. Mason	M. C. Lathrop	15801–16100, 24801–25100, 31101–31400, 35801–36100, 47001–47300, 54301–54600, 56601–56900, 60001–60100, 67201–67500, 76701–77000, 87201–87500, 94701–95000.
V. B. Briggs	J. B. Tiffey	17101–17400, 27701–28000, 33801–34100, 40301–40600, 48901–49200, 62501–62800, 72601–72900, 80801–81100, 93101–93400.
Do	B. J. Clarke	57701–57800.
M. Jones	E. Garlick	24201–24500, 42901–43200, 54901–55200, 59901–60000, 68101–68400, 76401–76700, 87501–87800.
M. V. Tyler	B. M. Payne	25701–25900, 38801–39100, 47301–47600, 57401–57500, 60701–61000, 70401–70600, 77701–78000.
J. Douglas	E. A. Adams	27101–27400.
M. S. Nicholas	do	29101–29300.
Do	J. McCarthy	42601–42900, 49501–49800, 58701–58800, 64201–64500, 79301–79600, 90501–90800.
M. Gwynn	M. S. Apperson	59501–59600, 69301–69400, 77601–77700, 84801–84900.
A. Harrison	H. M. Douglass	67501–67800, 72001–72300, 82301–82600, 94001–94300.
M. S. Knox	M. W. Bailey	83201–83500, 91401–91700.

Register of Confederate States Treasury Notes—Continued.

ACT OF MARCH 23, 1863—Continued.

For Treasurer.	For Register.	Numbers of the notes signed.
		OCTOBER ISSUE.
		$100—A to D.
T. J. Hatch	W. T. French	1–800, 2001–2800.
Do	J. J. Matthews	6001–6800, 10501–10900, 13501–14700, 16501–17300, 19301–20100, 20501–21300, 21801–22200, 25501–25900, 29501–30300, 33901–34700, 34901–35700, 38101–38400.
W. G. Allen	C. S. Taylor	801–1200, 2801–3600, 4401–5200, 6801–7600, 7901–8700, 12101–12500, 12701–13500, 14701–15500, 15701–16500, 20101–20500, 22201–22800, 24301–25500, 31101–31600.
J. C. Joplin	G. W. Garrett	1201–2000, 3601–4400, 7601–7900, 8701–9500, 10901–11300.
Do	J. Gibson	30301–31100, 33101–33900, 35701–36500.
E. C. Goddin	W. A. Cocke	5201–6000, 10101–10500.
Do	W. O. Slade	17301–18100, 18501–19300, 22801–23200.
T. C. Gale	G. W. Garrett	9501–10100, 11301–11700, 18101–18500.
S. B. Jacobs	J. H. Cooke	11701–12100, 15601–15700, 21301–21400, 23201–23900, 28101–28700, 31601–32300, 34701–34900.
T. W. Brown	W. Nott	12501–12700, 23901–24300, 27301–28100, 38901–39200.
J. Nethers	M. Winston	15501–15600, 38501–38900, 44301–44900.
Do	W. Hancock	45501–46300, 47101–47600.
F. C. Weisiger	W. O. Slade	21401–21800.
Do	G. N. Warren	28701–29500, 32301–33100, 36501–38100, 38401–38500, 39201–39700, 40101–40500, 41701–42500, 43001–43800, 44901–45500, 46301–47100.
C. Ashford	J. Gibson	25901–26500.
A. Patton	W. Hancock	26501–27300.
Do	W. O. Slade	40501–41300.
F. H. Link	W. Miller	39701–40100.
R. H. Berry	W. T. French	41301–41700, 43801–44300.
J. S. Dix	J. Sands	42501–43000.
		$50—wA to zA.
F. C. Weisiger	W. O. Slade	1–400, 4401–5200.
Do	G. N. Warren	46001–46800, 71001–71800, 76601–77000.
T. J. Hatch	W. T. French	401–800.
Do	J. J. Matthews	14501–14900, 31701–32500, 34901–35300.
N. A. Bass	do	801–1200, 6401–7200.
Do	L. P. Rogers	74001–74800.
E. C. Goddin	W. A. Cocke	1201–1600, 5601–6400, 8001–8800, 12301–13100, 14901–15700, 16901–17200.
Do	W. O. Slade	17201–18000.
A. West	S. Dutcher	1601–2000, 13901–14300, 15701–16900, 19201–20000, 24401–25200, 27801–28600, 31101–31500, 34101–34900, 39901–40100.
J. Nethers	M. Winston	2001–2400, 9601–10400, 13501–13900, 18001–18400, 20001–21400, 25201–26000, 29101–29500, 32501–33300, 35301–36100, 37501–38300, 41901–42700, 47601–48400, 50601–50800, 53001–53800, 54001–54800, 57601–58400, 59401–59800, 62001–62600, 64401–65000.
Do	W. Hancock	69301–69600, 71801–72600, 76501–76600.
A. Patton	do	2401–2800, 13101–13500, 18401–19200, 21401–22200, 26001–26800, 29901–30300, 39001–39900, 41401–41900, 46801–47600, 51801–52200, 54801–54900.
Do	W. O. Slade	54901–55600, 56801–57600, 64001–64400, 65001–65800, 68001–68800, 69601–70400, 74801–75600.
T. W. Brown	W. Nott	2801–3200, 14301–14500, 23601–24400, 30301–30700, 45201–46000, 50801–51000.
T. C. Gale	G. N. Warren	3201–3600, 7201–8000, 40101–40700.
Do	G. W. Garrett	8801–9600, 31501–31700.
S. B. Jacobs	J. H. Cooke	3601–4000, 10401–11000, 22201–23000, 28601–29100, 30701–31100, 33301–34100, 40701–40900, 43501–44300, 53801–54000, 55601–56400, 59201–59400.
W. G. Allen	C. S. Taylor	4001–4400, 5201–5600, 23001–23600, 26801–27800, 44901–45200, 49201–49800, 51001–51400, 60001–60200.
J. C. Joplin	G. W. Garrett	11001–12300.
Do	J. Gibson	48401–49200, 50201–50600.
Do	S. Dutcher	75601–76000.
C. Ashford	J. Gibson	29501–29900, 36901–37500, 38301–39000.
Do	G. W. Garrett	49801–50200.

Register of Confederate States Treasury Notes—Continued.

ACT OF MARCH 23, 1863—Continued.

For Treasurer.	For Register.	Numbers of the notes signed.
		OCTOBER ISSUE—Continued.
		$50—wA to zA—Continued.
F. H. Link	W. Miller	36101-36900, 59801-60000, 60201-60400, 61201-62000, 63401-64000, 65801-66600, 72601-73400.
Do	Tho. J. Miller	42701-43500, 51401-51800, 52201-53000.
B. H. Berry	W. T. French	40901-41400, 44301-44900, 56401-56800, 60401-60800, 68801-69300, 70401-70900, 76001-76500.
J. S. Dix	J. Sands	58401-59200, 60801-61200, 62601-63400, 66601-68000, 70901-71000, 73401-74000.
		$20—A to H.
T. W. Brown	W. Nott	1-400, 3701-4100, 6901-7300, 9401-9800, 13101-13400, 16101-16500, 20701-21100, 22501-22800, 30901-31300.
A. Patton	W. Hancock	401-800, 2101-2500, 5301-5700, 8901-9300, 11901-12300, 15701-16100, 19301-19700, 23501-23800, 29701-30100.
C. Ashford	J. Gibson	801-1000, 1301 1700, 4501-4900, 7301-7700, 11101-11500, 13401-13800, 16901-17100, 18301-18700, 21901-22200, 24201-24600, 26101-26500, 26801-27200.
Do	S. Sinton	28801-29100.
F. H. Link	L. P. Rogers	1001-1200, 1701-2100, 4101-4500, 7701-8100, 9901-10300, 15401-15700, 17101-17300, 17901-18300, 21101-21500, 23801-24200.
Do	W. Miller	28601-28800, 29101-29400.
J. C. Joplin	G. W. Garrett	1201-1300.
J. Nethers	M. Winston	2501-2900, 6501-6900, 12301-12700, 14601-15000, 20301-20700, 25201-25300.
T. C. Gale	G. N. Warren	2901-3300, 18901-19300, 22801-23200, 28001-28400, 30501-30900.
S. B. Jacobs	J. H. Cooke	3301-3700, 5701-6100, 12701-13100, 16501-16900, 19701-20100, 23201-23500, 25301-25700, 27901-28000.
F. C. Weisiger	W. O. Slade	4901-5300, 8101-8500, 10301-10700, 13801-14200, 17301-17900, 21501-21900, 24601-24900, 25701-26100, 27501-27900.
A. West	S. Dutcher	6101-6500, 8501-8900, 11501-11900, 14201-14600, 18701-18900.
N. A. Bass	J. J. Matthews	9301-9400, 9801-9900, 10701-11000.
E. C. Goddin	W. A. Cocke	15001-15400.
Do	W. O. Slade	30101-30500.
B. H. Berry	W. T. French	20101-20300, 22201-22500, 24901-25200, 26501-26800, 27201-27500, 28401-28600.
W. G. Allen	C. S. Taylor	29401-29700.
		$10—A to H.
M. Allen	H. L. Cooke	1-400.
Do	M. Pace	9401-9600, 9701-9800.
Do	B. Dabney	9601-9700, 14801-15100, 24701-25000, 34201-34500, 67301-67600, 83701-84000
M. V. Tyler	B. M. Payne	401-700, 9801-9900, 15101-15400, 25001-25300, 34501-34800, 60301-60600, 73801-74000, 77601-77800, 85501-85700.
S. G. Sanxay	L. Macon	701-1000, 10001-10200, 16001-16300, 25601-25900, 35701-36000, 61801-62100, 77801-78100, 86001-86300.
W. A. Garrett	J. McGarr	1001-1300, 9901-10000, 74501-74700, 75701-76000, 85201-85500.
Do	J. B. Tiffey	15701-15900.
Do	M. S. Apperson	15901-16000, 25901-26100.
Do	B. J. Clarke	35101-35400.
M. A. Dewees	S. E. Hughes	1301-1600, 12501-12700, 15401-15700, 25301-25600, 35401-35700, 60901-61200, 76001-76300, 84601-84900.
M. C. Waller	M. Pace	1601-1800.
Do	M. C. Lathrop	19701-19900.
Do	L. Forde	27601-27700, 36001-36200, 45101-45300, 67101-67300, 70301-70500, 80401-80600, 82101-82300.
Do	B. J. Clarke	27701-27800.
Do	M. S. Apperson	86301-86500.
M. Sommers	M. B. Kirby	1801-2100, 10401-10600, 17101-17400, 26401-26700, 41501-41800, 61501-61800, 69101-69400, 77201-77500, 86501-86800.
L. Carter	M. Stevens	2101-2400, 10601-10800, 16501-16800, 30801-31100, 36201-36500, 42701-43000, 77501-77600, 83601-83700, 87101-87400.
Do	J. McGarr	63601-63900.
Do	J. B. Tiffey	70801-71100.

Register of Confederate States Treasury Notes—Continued.

ACT OF MARCH 23, 1863—Continued.

For Treasurer.	For Register.	Numbers of the notes signed.
		OCTOBER ISSUE—Continued.
		$10—A to H—Continued.
M. C. Irvine	M. Johnson	2401-2700, 13101-13200, 23801-24100, 31701-32000, 37401-37700, 64201-64500, 71901-72200, 80601-80900.
Do	E. Garlick	13201-13300.
C. Hix	M. Gay	2701-3000, 13601-13800, 17901-18200, 31401-31500, 43301-43600, 63901-64200, 69401-69700, 82601-82900.
Do	E. W. Pendleton	31501-31700.
A. Harrison	H. M. Douglass	3001-3300, 10301-10400, 28101-28400, 43901-44200, 66601-66800.
Do	L. Forde	19401-19700.
Do	J. Douglas	80101-80400.
Do	B. Dabney	88601-88900.
N. Semple	F. E. Bernard	3301-3600, 9301-9400, 16801-17100, 26101-26400, 61201-61500, 67601-67900.
Do	C. Sessions	79601-79900.
M. L. Quarles	B. J. Clarke	3601-3900, 20201-20500, 33201-33400, 64801-65100, 69701-70000, 79001-79300, 88301-88600.
L. C. Minor	B. M. Abbott	3901-4200, 10901-11100, 22601-22900, 42401-42700, 75101-75200, 82901-83200.
Do	M. Dixon	29601-29900, 40001-40300.
Do	E. A. Adams	71301-71600.
Do	M. S. Apperson	74901-75100.
M. E. Dudley	M. E. Norton	4201-4500, 11501-11600, 17601-17900, 27301-27600, 36501-36800, 63301-63600, 70001-70300, 76301-76600, 84901-85200.
A. B. Capron	K. Walker	4501-4800, 11401-11500, 14501-14800, 33101-33200, 45601-45900, 64501-64800, 83301-83600, 89601-89900.
Do	J. L. Johnston	32901-33100.
M. Godwin	M. Dixon	4801-5100.
Do	L. Forde	11101-11200.
Do	J. L. Johnston	16301-16500, 34801-35100, 60601-60900, 74301-75500, 84001-84300.
E. A. Dennison	M. E. Gilliam	5101-5400, 12701-12900, 18201-18500, 29001-29300, 39701-40000, 76601-76900, 86901-87100.
Do	M. Taylor	65101-65300.
Do	J. McCarthy	65301-65400.
Do	J. B. Tiffey	71601-71900, 86801-86900.
M. S. Nicholas	J. McCarthy	5401-5700, 12201-12400, 17401-17600, 27001-27300, 37101-37400, 42101-42400, 65701-66000, 68701-68800, 76901-77200, 87401-87700.
E. O. Beall	E. A. Adams	5701-6000, 11601-11800, 18501-18800, 30501-30800, 38701-39000, 65401-65700.
V. M. Stanard	L. Devine	6001-6300, 12401-12500, 20501-20800, 28401-28700, 38001-38300.
Do	M. Dixon	44201-44500.
Do	J. B. Tiffey	62101-62400, 80901-81200.
E. D. Layne	V. C. Watson	6301-6600, 10201-10300, 19101-19300, 31101-31400, 37701-38000, 45901-46200, 66001-66300, 67901-68200, 71101-71300, 78701-79000.
Do	E. W. Pendleton	19301-19400.
Do	M. Johnson	87701-88000.
M. S. Knox	M. W. Bailey	6601-6900, 13501-13600, 21401-21700, 32601-32900, 39001-39300, 41801-42100, 66801-67100, 72201-72500, 79301-79600, 88001-88300.
V. M. Rind	J. L. Johnston	6901-7100.
Do	E. Garlick	7101-7200.
Do	L. Forde	12901-13100.
Do	E. W. Pendleton	23201-23400.
Do	M. C. Lathrop	23401-23500.
Do	V. K. Davies	32001-32300, 43601-43900, 62701-63000, 68501-68700, 68801-69100, 78401-78700.
S. Lambert	P. Pleasants	7201-7500, 11801-12000, 22001-22300, 29301-29500, 43001-43300-66301-66600, 70501-70800.
Do	J. B. Tiffey	29501-29600.
R. F. Ball	M. L. Savage	7501-7800, 12001-12200, 22901-23200, 24301-24600, 33701-34000, 40901-41200, 72901-73200, 75401-75700, 82301-82600.
R. Haynes	B. Dabney	7801-8100, 10801-10900, 22301-22600, 44801-45100, 73501-73800.

Register of Confederate States Treasury Notes—Continued.

ACT OF MARCH 23, 1863—Continued.

For Treasurer.	For Register.	Numbers of the notes signed.
		OCTOBER ISSUE—Continued.
		$10—A to H—Continued.
R. Haynes	J. B. Tiffey	32301-32600, 40601-40900.
H. Bartlett	M. Taylor	8101-8400, 14101-14200, 20801-21100, 29901-30200, 44501-44800, 68201-68500, 75201-75400, 85701-86000.
Do	M. B. Kirby	38501-38700.
Do	J. L. Johnston	78101-78400.
E. P. Porter	A. P. Pellet	8401-8700, 14201-14300, 21101-21400, 24201-24300, 30201-30500, 38301-38500.
M. Gwynn	M. S. Apperson	8701-8800, 14301-14500, 24101-24200, 24601-24700, 34001-34200, 39601-39700, 46201-46300, 72801-72900, 89201-89300.
Do	L. Forde	83201-83300.
E. Mason	M. C. Lathrop	8801-9100, 13901-14100, 33401-33700, 40301-40600, 72501-72800, 81501-81800.
L. Breeden	E. C. Winston	9101-9300, 11201-11400, 21701-22000, 26701-27000, 36801-37100, 79901-80100.
H. Starke	C. Sessions	13301-13500, 18801-19100, 28701-29000, 39301-39600, 46301-46500, 74701-74900.
Do	M. Winston	89301-89600.
S. F. Shaver	M. Dixon	13801-13900, 19901-20200, 81801-82100, 88901-89200.
Do	M. E. Gilliam	62401-62700.
M. Jones	E. Garlick	23501-23800, 27801-28100, 41201-41500, 45301-45600, 73201-73500, 81201-81500.
E. C. Goddin	W. O. Slade	46501-46800.
C. Ashford	W. A. Garrett	46801-47100, 49101-49300, 54601-54800, 59201-59400, 59601-60000.
Do	J. Gibson	47101-47200, 48901-49100, 51201-51600, 52801-54600, 54801-55300.
T. J. Hatch	J. J. Matthews	47201-47400, 57101-57300.
F. H. Link	Tho. J. Miller	47401-47800, 56101-56500, 59401-59600.
B. H. Berry	W. T. French	47801-48100, 49301-49500, 57701-57900.
S. B. Jacobs	J. H. Cooke	48101-48500, 49501-49700, 56501-56900.
T. W. Brown	W. Nott	48501-48800, 50401-50800, 52401-52800, 58901-59200.
W. G. Allen	C. S. Taylor	48801-48900, 49701-50100, 52001-52400, 57901-58300.
Do	A. P. Pellet*	60001-60200.
Do	L. Forde*	60201-60300.
J. S. Dix	J. Sands	50101-50400, 51601-52000, 58301-58600.
A. Patton	W. Hancock	50801-51200.
Do	W. O. Slade	55301-55700.
J. C. Joplin	S. Dutcher	55701-56100.
F. C. Weisiger	G. N. Warren	56901-57100.
N. A. Bass	L. P. Rogers	57301-57700.
J. Nethers	W. Hancock	58601-58900.
V. Bridges	E. W. Pendleton	63001-63300, 74001-74300, 84301-84600.
		$5—A to H.
M. C. Waller	M. Pace	1-200.
Do	B. J. Clarke	10701-10900.
Do	L. Forde	26801-27000, 34301-34400, 42101-42200, 48401-48600, 56101-56200, 62101-62300, 76101-76300.
M. Sommers	M. B. Kirby	201-500, 9801-10100, 17701-18000, 25601-25900, 34401-34600, 55701-55900, 60901-61200, 75801-76100, 83601-83900.
N. Semple	F. E. Bernard	501-800, 9201-9500, 21601-21900, 27301-27600, 56701-56900, 61501-61800, 76301-76600.
L. Breeden	E. C. Winston	801-1100, 11201-11500, 19801-20100, 28201-28500, 34601-34800, 38501-38800, 70801-71100, 77501-77800.
L. Carter	M. F. Stevens	1101-1400, 8001-8300, 18601-18900, 27001-27200, 34901-35100, 50601-50900, 74901-75200.
Do	V. C. Watson	27201-27300.
Do	J. B. Tiffey	58101-58300, 66201-66500.
M. S. Nicholas	J. McCarthy	1401-1700, 10901-11200, 17401-17700, 28501-28800, 35101-35200, 42501-42800, 50001-50300, 57301-57500, 65301-65600.
A. Harrison	H. M. Douglass	1701-2000, 10101-10400, 20101-20400, 30901-31200, 35701-35800, 53601-53900, 58301-58400, 62901-63200.
Do	J. Douglas	77801-78100.

* These two entries are according to "record," but, if correct, are the first and only instances of male and female signers as partners.—R. P. T.

Register of Confederate States Treasury Notes—Continued.

ACT OF MARCH 23, 1863—Continued.

For Treasurer.	For Register.	Numbers of the notes signed.
		OCTOBER ISSUE—Continued.
		$5—A to H—Continued.
M. C. Irvine	M. Johnson	2001-2200, 8901-9200, 26201-26500, 37101-37300, 40601-40900, 45601-45900, 47501-47800, 67701-68000.
R. Haynes	B. Dabney	2201-2500, 14501-14800, 18001-18300, 53001-53100, 79001-79300.
Do	J. B. Tiffey	28801-29100, 36201-36300, 42201-42500.
Do	M. S. Apperson	53101-53200, 68501-68800.
Do	L. Forde	53201-53300.
Do	E. C. Winston	58401-58500.
Do	M. Dixon	66801-67100.
S. Lambert	P. Pleasants	2501-2800, 15401-15700, 24301-24600, 31201-31500, 35501-35700, 39101-39400, 51201-51500, 57701-57900, 63801-64100.
V. M. Stanard	L. Devine	2801-3100, 8601-8900, 20701-21000, 29101-29400, 35801-35900.
Do	E. C. Winston	52401-52700, 64501-64700.
Do	A. P. Pellet	57901-58000, 64401-64500, 76601-76800.
Do	E. A. Adams	72001-72300.
Do	J. McCarthy	76801-76900.
V. M. Rind	V. K. Davies	3101-3400, 32101-32400, 36301-36400, 38201-38500, 43401-43700, 49401-49700, 58701-58900, 63501-63800, 77201-77500.
Do	E. Garlick	12401-12600.
Do	J. B. Tiffey	12601-12700, 22801-23100.
C. Hix	do	3401-3700, 21001-21100.
Do	M. Gay	14801-15100, 21101-21300, 29701-30000, 35901-36100, 51501-51800, 56001-56100, 61201-61500, 78701-79000.
Do	M. S. Apperson	55901-56000.
R. F. Ball	M. L. Savage	3701-4000, 16001-16300, 25201-25500, 37501-37700, 39701-40000, 44001-44300, 45301-45600, 54301-54600, 59401-59500, 68001-68300, 70001-70300, 80901-81100.
A. B. Capron	K. Walker	4001-4200, 15101-15400, 22201-22500, 29401-29700, 38801-39100, 42801-43100, 48601-48800, 56601-56700, 67101-67400, 71101-71400, 79301-79600.
Do	J L. Johnston	36601-36700.
L. C. Minor	J. B. Tiffey	4201-4500, 41801-42100.
Do	B. M. Abbott	6401-6700, 22501-22800, 30401-30600, 52701-53000, 56201-56400, 67401-67700, 68801-68900, 80601-80900.
Do	J. L. Johnston	30301-30400.
Do	P. Pleasants	36401-36600.
I. Benton	L. Forde	4501-4700.
E. A. Dennison	M. E. Gilliam	4701-5000, 11501-11800, 23801-24000, 27901-28200, 36701-36900, 40901-41200, 44701-45000, 57101-57300, 65001-65300, 75201-75500.
Do	J. B. Tiffey	50301-50600.
E. O. Beall	E. A. Adams	5001-5300, 13601-13900, 21301-21600, 31801-32100, 35301-35500, 49701-50000, 58901-59100, 66501-66800.
Do	K. Walker	44401-44500.
Do	A. P. Pellet	44501-44700.
H. Starke	C. Sessions	5301-5600, 13001-13300, 20401-20700, 31501-31800, 37301-37500, 44301-44400, 51801-52100, 58501-58700, 65601-65900, 71701-72000, 79901-80000.
Do	H. M. Douglass	68401-68500.
E. P. Porter	A. P. Pellet	5601-5900, 13301-13600, 23401-23700, 33301-33500, 37701-37900, 39401-39700.
M. Gwynn	M. S. Apperson	5901-6000, 6301-6400, 16301-16500, 45901-46000, 54601-54700, 68301-68700.
Do	M. Dixon	53901-54000.
E. Mason	M. C. Lathrop	6001-6300, 15701-16000, 32401-32700, 36901-37100, 41201-41500, 43101-43400, 45001-45300, 53301-53600, 59101-59300, 64701-65000, 69101-69400, 79601-79900.
M. Allen	M. Pace	6701-7000, 16501-16700, 33501-33700, 54701-54900, 59501-59800, 72301-72600, 80301-80600, 81301-81600.
Do	M. S. Apperson	7001-7100, 16701-16800.
Do	M. B. Kirby	46301-46600.
V. M. Tyler	B. M. Payne	7101-7400, 16801-17100, 46001-46300, 54901-55000, 59801-60100, 73201-73400, 82201-82400.
Do	M. S. Apperson	33701-33800.
S. G. Sanxay	L. Macon	7401-7700, 18301-18600, 34101-34300, 47801-48100, 55401-55500, 60601-60900, 70701-70800, 74001-74300, 82701-83000.

Register of Confederate States Treasury Notes—Continued.

ACT OF MARCH 23, 1863—Continued.

For Treasurer.	For Register.	Numbers of the notes signed.
		OCTOBER ISSUE—Continued.
		$5—A to H—Continued.
W. A. Garrett	J. McGarr	7701–8000, 17101–17400, 70301–70400, 73401–73700.
Do	B. J. Clarke	33801–33900.
Do	E. C. Winston	83901–84000.
M. A. Dewees	S. E. Hughes	8301–8600, 24601–24900, 25901–26200, 33901–34100, 55001–55200, 70401–70700, 73701–74000, 81601–81900.
Do	M. Dixon	47201–47500.
E. D. Layne	V. C. Watson	9501–9800, 19201–19500, 35201–35300, 48101–48400, 56501–56600, 62601–62900, 74601–74900.
Do	E. W. Pendleton	30001–30100.
Do	M. S. Apperson	30101–30200.
Do	M. L. Savage	30201–30300.
M. E. Dudley	M. E. Norton	10401–10700, 19501–19800, 26501–26800, 34801–34900, 48801–49100, 56401–56500, 62301–62600, 74301–74600.
Do	P. Pleasants	83301–83600.
S. F. Shaver	M. Dixon	11801–12100, 21901–22200, 25501–25600, 71401–71700, 78101–78400.
M. Godwin	B. J. Clarke	12101–12200.
Do	L. Forde	12201–12300.
Do	J. B. Tiffey	12301–12400.
Do	M. C. Lathrop	18901–19100.
Do	J. L. Johnston	19101–19200, 55201–55400, 60101–60300, 72901–73100, 82401–82700.
Do	E. W. Pendleton	46601–46900.
Do	E. C. Winston	73101–73200.
H. Bartlett	M. Taylor	12701–13000, 23101–23400, 33001–33300, 37901–38100, 40001–40300, 54001–54300, 57501–57700, 61801–61900, 83001–83300.
Do	A. P. Pellet	61901–62000.
Do	E. C. Winston	62001 62100.
Do	C. Sessions	69701–70000.
M. S. Knox	M. W. Bailey	13901–14200, 24901–25200, 30601–30900, 36101–36200, 41501–41800, 49101–49400, 59301–59400, 75501–75800.
Do	B. J. Clarke	65901–66200.
M. L. Quarles	do	14201–14500, 23701–23800, 27601–27900, 50901–51200, 56901–57100, 76901–77200.
Do	M. W. Bailey	63201–63500.
M. Jones	E. Garlick	24001–24300, 32701–33000, 38101–38200, 40301–40600, 43701–44000, 52101–52400, 58001–58100, 64101–64400, 69401–69700, 78401–78700, 81101–81300.
V. Bridges	J. L. Johnston	46901–47200.
Do	E. W. Pendleton	55501–55700, 60301–60600, 80001–80300, 81901–82200.
Do	M. Johnson	72601–72900.
		NOVEMBER ISSUE.
		$100—A to D.
J. C. Joplin	S. Dutcher	1–400, 2801–3200, 8801–9600, 12701–13100, 18201–19000, 22401–23000, 26001–26800, 32301–32900, * * * .
Do	J. Gibson	59701–60100, 61501–62100, * * * .
F. C. Weisiger	G. N. Warren	401–800, 16601–17000, 25601–26000, 30701–31100, * * * , 60901–61500, * * * .
J. Nethers	W. Hancock	801–1200, 8001–8800, 13101–13500, 21201–21800, * * * , 62101–62700, * * * .
T. J. Hatch	J. J. Matthews	1201–1600, 4801–5200, 7201–8000, 12301–12700, 19001–19800, 23001–23600, 28201–29000, 31101–31700, * * * .
A. Patton	W. O. Slade	1601–2000, 4001–4400, 6801–7200, 13501–13900, 24201–24800, 26801–27400, 31701–32300, 58901–59300, * * * .
S. B. Jacobs	J. H. Cooke	2001–2400, 3201–3600, 15101–15500, 28001–28200, 29601–29800, 30401–30500, 30601–30700, * * * .
J. S. Dix	J. Sands	2401–2800, 9601–10000, 15501–15800, 19801–20400, 24801–25200, 30501–30600, * * * , 60101–60500, 63301–63700, * * * .
N. A. Bass	L. P. Rogers	3601–4000, 6001–6400, 10001–10800, 13901–14300, 17001–17800, 21801–22400, 29801–30400, * * * , 58101–58500, * * * .
F. H. Link	W. Miller	4401–4800, 11901–12300, * * * .

Register of Confederate States Treasury Notes—Continued.

ACT OF MARCH 23, 1863—Continued.

For Treasurer.	For Register.	Numbers of the notes signed.
		NOVEMBER ISSUE—Continued.
		$100—A to D—Continued.
C. Ashford	G. W. Garrett	5201-5600, 6401-6800, 10801-11600, 14701-15100, 15801-16600, 25201-25600, 27401-28000, * * *, 58501-58900, * * *.
W. G. Allen	C. S. Taylor	5601-6000, 14301-14700, 29001-29600, * * *, 59301-59700, 62701-63300, * * *.
B. H. Berry	W. T. French	11601-11900, 17801-18200, * * *.
T. W. Brown	H. Smith	20401-21200, 23601-24200, * * *, 60501-60900, * * *.
* * * *	* * * *	* * * * * * *
		$50—wA to zA.
B. H. Berry	W. T. French	1-200, 7201-7600, 12801-13100, 19801-20200.
N. A. Bass	L. P. Rogers	201-600, 2901-3700, 12301-12800, 43501-44100, 51301-51700, 57301-57500.
F. H. Link	W. Miller	601-1400, 7601-8400, 15301-15700, 17401-18200, 21801-22600, 25801-26400, 28401-29000, 29901-30500, 31101-31700, 33701-34300, 36101-36700, 37701-38500, 40501-40900, 41701-42300, 44901-45700, 50101-50700, 55701-56500.
F. C. Weisiger	G. N. Warren	1401-2100, 10801-11200, 14101-14500, 16501-16900.
T. J. Hatch	J. J. Matthews	2101-2900, 9201-10000, 16101-16500.
Do	H. Smith	42301-42900, 56501-57300.
J. C. Joplin	S. Dutcher	3701-4500, 11201-11800, 14501-14900.
Do	J. Gibson	46501-47300.
A. Patton	W. O. Slade	4501-5300, 11801-12300, 18201-19000, 22601-23400, 36701-37300, 39101-39900, 48101-48900, 50701-51300.
S. B. Jacobs	J. H. Cooke	5301-6100, 13101-13700, 15701-16100, 20201-21000, 24201-25000, 26401-27000, 32301-33300, 34901-35500, 37301-37700, 38501-39100, 41301-41700, 42901-43500, 47301-48100, 51701-52300, 54901-55700.
J. S. Dix	J. Sands	6101-6500, 10401-10800, 13701-14100, 16901-17400, 29401-29900, 49701-50100, 52901-53500.
W. G. Allen	C. S. Taylor	6501-7200, 8401-9200, 14901-15300, 19001-19800, 25001-25800, 27001-27600, 35501-35700, 45701-46500, 52301-52900.
C. Ashford	G. W. Garrett	10001-10400, 44101-44900.
T. W. Brown	H. Smith	21001-21800, 29001-29400, 33301-33700, 35701-36100.
Do	G. W. Garrett	53501-54100.
J. Nethers	W. Hancock	23401-24200, 27601-28400, 30501-31100, 31701-32300, 34301-34900, 39901-40500, 40901-41300, 48901-49700, 54101-54900.
* * * *	* * * *	* * * * * * *
		$20—A to H.
		None issued.
		$10—A to H.
W. A. Garrett	E. C. Winston	1-200.
Do	J. McGarr	5801-6000, 11701-12000, 29801-30100, 41801-42100, 55401-55700, 60901-61000, 72101-72200, 77601-77900.
Do	F. E. Bernard	48801-48900.
Do	S. E. Hughes	48901-49100.
Do	V. K. Davies	64001-64200.
Do	V. C. Watson	64201-64300.
M. S. Nicholas	J. McCarthy	201-500, 8001-8200, 15101-15400, 23201-23500, 28901-29200, 47401-47600.
Do	J. B. Tiffey	51501-51600.
Do	M. L. Savage	51601-51700.
Do	K. Walker	59201-59400.
Do	B. M. Payne	63201-63300.
V. M. Rind	J. B. Tiffey	501-800, 15701-16000.
Do	V. K. Davies	18301-18600, 27201-27500, 37601-37900, 44801-45100, 53701-53900, 58601-58900, 62701-62800, 67201-67500, 72701-72900.
Do	K. Walker	80401-80700.
L. Carter	M. Stevens	801-1100, 8201-8400, 13601-13900, 30601-30800, 43101-43400, 50401-50600, 54901-55100, 61401-61500, 71101-71300, 77301-77600.
Do	J. B. Tiffey	21401-21700.
Do	M. Pace	30801-30900.

Register of Confederate States Treasury Notes—Continued.

ACT OF MARCH 23, 1863—Continued.

For Treasurer.	For Register.	Numbers of the notes signed.
		NOVEMBER ISSUE—Continued.
		$10—A to H—Continued.
L. Carter	B. M. Payne	50601-50700, 64301-64600.
Do	C. Sessions	54801-54900.
M. L. Quarles	B. J. Clarke	1101-1300, 9401-9600, 13301-13600, 21701-22000, 28601-28900, 52301-52500, 68101-68400, 72401-72500, 78601-78900.
Do	H. M. Douglass	62601-62700.
A. B. Capron	K. Walker	1301-1600, 8601-8800, 74301-74400.
M. S. Knox	M. W. Bailey	1601-1900, 7001-7200, 16001-16300, 33401-33700, 38801-39100, 47901-48200, 51901-52100, 57401-57700, 67501-67800, 73201-73300, 79501-79800.
Do	M. Johnson	62801-62900.
M. C. Waller	L. Forde	1901-2100, 7601-7800, 13101-13300, 28101-28300, 35101-35300, 44001-44200, 56901-57100, 70501-70600.
Do	M. S. Apperson	20101-20300, 75601-75800.
Do	C. Sessions	61201-61300.
Do	A. P. Pellet	64601-64800.
V. M. Stanard	L. Devine	2101-2400, 10001-10200, 12201-12500, 22901-23200, 29501-29800, 38501-38800, 42501-42800, 51101-51300, 68801-69000, 71801-71900.
Do	H. M. Douglass	77001-77300.
E. D. Layne	V. C. Watson	2401-2700, 6901-7000, 12801-13100, 36901-37000, 43401-43700, 53301-53500, 62301-62400, 67801-68100, 73301-73400, 75001-75300.
Do	E. Garlick	19801-20100.
Do	K. Walker	26401-26700.
Do	J. McCarthy	36701-36900.
N. Semple	J. Douglas	2701-3000.
Do	F. E. Bernard	7801-8000, 12501-12800, 19201-19500, 31901-32200, 35901-36100, 45101-45400, 57701-58000, 66001-66300, 72201-72400.
Do	H. M. Douglass	62201-62300.
Do	K. Walker	75801-76100.
M. Jones	E. Garlick	3001-3300, 8801-9000, 17801-18000, 34201-34400, 47601-47900, 54301-54500, 62501-62600, 69001-69300.
H. Starke	C. Sessions	3301-3600, 8401-8600, 18001-18300, 22001-22300, 31601-31900, 46301-46600, 53901-54100, 61901-62000, 68401-68700.
E. A. Dennison	M. E. Gilliam	3601-3900, 6601-6900, 36601-36700, 43001-43100, 46001-46200, 52101-52300.
C. Hix	M. Gay	3901-4200, 9001-9200, 22601-22900, 28301-28600, 37301-37600, 45601-45900, 53501-53700, 58301-58600, 62001-62100, 73701-73900.
Do	M. Johnson	13901-14200.
S. F. Shaver	M. Dixon	4201-4500, 9201-9400, 11401-11700, 25001-25300, 33701-34000, 46601-46900, 52501-52700, 71901-72100, 76401-76700.
R. Haynes	B. Dabney	4501-4800, 10401-10500, 24401-24700, 34401-34600, 39801-40100, 62401-62500, 70701-70800, 77901-78200.
M. Gwynn	M. S. Apperson	4801-5000, 34701-34800, 39401-39500, 40401-40600, 45901-46000, 54501-54600, 68701-68800, 70201-70300, 78501-78600.
Do	B. M. Payne	61601-61700.
M. Allen	M. Pace	5001-5200.
Do	H. L. Cooke	21101-21300, 25501-25800, 40901-41200, 49501-49800, 70901-71100, 75301-75600.
Do	M. S. Apperson	21301-21400.
V. M. Tyler	B. M. Payne	5201-5400, 27001-27200, 36101-36300, 42301-42500.
V. Bridges	E. W. Pendleton	5401-5600, 11101-11400, 26101-26400, 40601-40900, 49801-50100, 55101-55400.
Do	M. Pace	18601-18900.
Do	E. Garlick	34801-34900, 74401-74700.
Do	A. P. Pellet	34901-35100.
Do	J. L. Johnston	61001-61100.
Do	M. Dixon	63401-63700.
Do	H. M. Douglass	70301-70500.
M. A. Dewees	S. E. Hughes	5601-5800, 20901-21100, 44501-44800, 58001-58300, 61101-61200.
Do	K. Walker	38201-38500.
Do	E. Garlick	70601-70700.
S. G. Sanxay	L. Macon	6001-6200, 12001-12200, 19501-19800, 27801-28100, 45401-45600, 50101-50200, 50301-50400.

Register of Confederate States Treasury Notes—Continued.

ACT OF MARCH 23, 1863—Continued.

For Treasurer.	For Register.	Numbers of the notes signed.
		NOVEMBER ISSUE—Continued.
		$10—A to H—Continued.
S. G. Sanxay	H. M. Douglass	50201-50300.
Do	K. Walker	60701-60800.
Do	M. Taylor	65701-65900.
Do	C. Sessions	65901-66000.
L. C. Minor	B. M. Abbott	6201-6400, 14801-15100, 37901-38200, 43701-44000, 54101-54200.
Do	B. M. Payne	24701-25000.
Do	M. E. Gilliam	32201-32500.
Do	M. C. Lathrop	54201-54300.
M. Godwin	J. L. Johnston	6401-6600, 10801-11100, 18901-19200, 25801-26100, 71301-71400, 74701-75000.
Do	M. Johnson	42101-42300.
Do	S. E. Hughes	49301-49400.
Do	K. Walker	49401-49500.
M. Sommers	M. B. Kirby	7201-7400, 14201-14500, 20601-20900, 29201-29500, 35301-35600, 41201-41500, 51301-51500, 56601-56900, 61301-61400, 71401-71600, 78201-78500.
L. Breeden	E. C. Winston	7401-7600, 15401-15700, 31301-31600, 44201-44500, 51701-51900, 61801-61900, 65101-65300, 71601-71800, 79201-79500.
Do	M. S. Apperson	65301-65400.
M. C. Irvine	M. Johnson	9601-9800, 34001-34200, 63101-63200, 70001-70200, 73101-73200, 78901-79200.
Do	E. C. Winston	59801-60000, 60401-60700.
E. Mason	M. C. Lathrop	9801-10000, 16601-16900, 32801-33100, 40101-40400, 48501-48800, 59401-59700, 60101-60400, 63001-63100, 66601-66800, 72501-72700, 81001-81200.
Do	L. Forde	24101-24400.
Do	J. L. Johnston	66801-66900.
R. F. Ball	J. B. Tiffey	10201-10400.
Do	M. L. Savage	17501-17800, 23801-24100, 39501-39800, 63301-63400, 66301-66500, 69601-69800.
Do	M. S. Apperson	59701-59800.
Do	B. Dabney	66501-66600.
Do	B. M. Payne	73501-73700.
E. P. Porter	A. P. Pellet	10501-10600, 17201-17500, 25301-25500, 30901-31100, 52901-53100, 62901-63000.
Do	B. M. Payne	60001-60100.
Do	C. Sessions	74201-74500, 80101-80400.
H. Bartlett	M. Taylor	10601-10800, 16901-17200, 20301-20600, 26701-27000, 35601-35900, 53101-53300, 57101-57400, 69901-70000, 74101-74200, 79801-80100.
S. Lambert	P. Pleasants	14501-14800, 22301-22600, 27501-27800, 46901-47200, 50701-50900, 58901-59200, 62101-62200, 65401-65600, 72901-73100, 76101-76400.
Do	V. C. Watson	65601-65700.
A. Harrison	J. Douglas	16301-16600, 23501-23800, 32501-32800.
Do	H. M. Douglass	39101-39400.
M. E. Dudley	M. E. Norton	30101-30400, 36301-36600, 42801-43000, 46201-46300, 50901-51100, 64801-65000, 73401-73500, 80701-81000.
Do	M. L. Savage	56301-56600.
Do	K. Walker	61701-61800, 65001-65100.
J. Wilson	M. Pace	30401-30600.
Do	B. J. Clarke	41501-41800.
Do	K. Walker	49101-49200.
Do	S. E. Hughes	49201-49300, 63701-64000.
Do	J. B. Tiffey	55701-56000, 60801-60900, 70801-70900, 76701-77000.
B. J. Clarke	do	31101-31300, 34601-34700.
Do	E. A. Adams	37001-37300, 48201-48500, 54601-54700, 56001-56300, 66901-67000, 67101-67200, 69301-69600, 73901-74100.
Do	F. E. Bernard	54701-54800.
Do	H. L. Cooke	61501-61600.
Do	L. Devine	67001-67100.
E. O. Beall	M. L. Savage	33101-33300.
Do	C. Sessions	33301-33400.
F. G. Giles	K. Walker	47201-47400.
Do	M. S. Apperson	69801-69900.

Register of Confederate States Treasury Notes—Continued.

ACT OF MARCH 23, 1863—Continued.

For Treasurer.	For Register.	Numbers of the notes signed.
		NOVEMBER ISSUE—Continued.
		$10—A to H—Continued.
K. Walker	L. Forde	52701–52800.
Do	B. Dabney	52801–52900.
		$5—A to H.
L. C. Minor	B. M. Abbott	1–300, 6701–7000, 22001–22200, 37101–37400, 46801–46900, 51701–51800.
Do	K. Walker	14801–15100, 46701–46800.
Do	M. E. Gilliam	21901–22000.
Do	M. Johnson	28501–28700.
Do	C. Sessions	46601–46700.
Do	H. M. Douglass	58301–58500.
E. Mason	M. C. Lathrop	301–600, 7901–8200, 15501–15800, 23101–23400, 38001–38300, 49701–50000, 53301–53400, 56701–56900, 77001–77300.
Do	J. B. Tiffey	30301–30500.
R. F. Ball	M. L. Savage	601–900, 8701–8900, 16401–16700, 24101–24400, 39801–40100, 58701–58900, 64101–64400, 76401–76500.
Do	C. Sessions	28101–28200.
Do	J. B. Tiffey	76501–76600.
Do	B. M. Abbott	76601–76700.
M. C. Irvine	M. Johnson	901–1200, 7301–7600, 18101–18400, 30601–30700, 38701–38900, 40601–40900, 49401–49700, 50901–51000, 78501–78800.
Do	B. M. Payne	58901–59100.
M. Allen	M. Pace	1201–1500.
Do	H. L. Cooke	16701–17000, 25401–25600, 30701–31000, 40901–41200, 66101–66400, 72301–72600, 78901–79200.
V. M. Tyler	B. M. Payne	1501–1700, 27801–27900, 31601–31800, 41801–42000.
V. Bridges	E. W. Pendleton	1701–2000, 31001–31300, 41501–41800, 59101–59400, 67301–67600, 71101–71400.
Do	M. E. Gilliam	9101–9400.
Do	K. Walker	17301–17600.
Do	J. McGarr	26401–26600.
Do	M. Johnson	51001–51100, 53701–53900.
Do	E. Garlick	79201–79500.
S. G. Sanxay	L. Macon	2001–2300, 9401–9700, 19901–20200, 25601–25800, 41201–41500, 52001–52100, 67001–67200.
Do	B. Dabney	55701–55900.
Do	B. M. Abbott	59701–60000, 67201–67300.
W. A. Garrett	J. McGarr	20301–20600, 10001–10300, 20501–20800, 28701–28800, 32701–32900, 42601–42900, 53901–54100, 62601–62900, 66401–66700, 71701–72000, 81801–82100.
Do	M. S. Apperson	32901–33000, 53401–53500.
M. A. Dewees	S. E. Hughes	2601–2900, 10301–10500, 20801–21100, 44301–44600, 65601–65900.
Do	B. J. Clarke	26201–26400.
Do	J. B. Tiffey	34101–34400.
Do	J. L. Johnston	68801–69100.
Do	E. Garlick	73701–74000.
M. Godwin	J. L. Johnston	2901–3100, 11101–11400, 17601–17800, 26801–26900, 35801–36000, 43201–43400, 54301–54500, 70801–71100.
Do	S. E. Hughes	51101–51200.
Do	M. S. Apperson	53601–53700.
A. B. Capron	K. Walker	3101–3300.
M. S. Nicholas	J. McCarthy	3301–3600, 17001–17300, 27301–27500, 31801–32100, 81201–81500.
Do	B. M. Payne	47701–47800.
Do	M. S. Apperson	47801–48000.
Do	K. Walker	60001–60300.
Do	M. C. Lathrop	70001–70300.
V. M. Rind	J. Douglas	3601–3900.
Do	J. B. Tiffey	9701–10000.
Do	V. K. Davies	18401–18700, 27501–27700, 32301–32400, 44901–45200, 52201–52300, 55901–56100, 63201–63500, 73201–73500.
Do	B. J. Clarke	32101–32300.
E. A. Dennison	M. E. Gilliam	3901–4200, 38301–38500, 47201–47500, 51501–51600.

Register of Confederate States Treasury Notes—Continued.

ACT OF MARCH 23, 1863—Continued.

For Treasurer.	For Register.	Numbers of the notes signed.
		NOVEMBER ISSUE—Continued.
		$5—A to H—Continued.
L. Carter	M. Stevens	4201–4500, 13201–13500, 20201–20500, 27101–27300, 33801-34000, 42901–43200, 51401–51500, 61401–61700, 74001–74100, 74201–74300.
Do	M. Taylor	34001–34100.
Do	B. M. Payne	54901–55100, 82401–82700.
Do	M. Johnson	67901–68200.
Do	M. S. Apperson	74101–74200.
M. Sommers	M. B. Kirby	4501–4800, 12001–12300, 19001–19300, 32401–32700, 44601-44900, 51801–51900, 54701–54900, 61701–62000, 69701–70000, 74301–74600.
Do	E. C. Winston	26001–26200.
M. L. Quarles	B. J. Clarke	4801–5100, 12301–12600, 21301–21600, 26901–27100, 46301-46600, 53101–53200, 78201–78500.
Do	H. L. Cooke	62301–62600.
S. Lambert	P. Pleasants	5101–5300, 13701–13900, 23701–24000, 28901–29100, 45501-45800, 51301–51400, 55501–55700, 62901–63200, 74601–74900, 82701–83000.
Do	K. Walker	67601–67900.
E. D. Layne	E. C. Winston	5301–5500.
Do	B. M. Payne	5501–5600.
Do	M. Johnson	11401–11700.
Do	M. Pace	19601–19900.
Do	J. McCarthy	26601–26700.
Do	V. C. Watson	34401–34600, 45201–45500, 59401–59700, 71401–71700.
Do	J. B. Tiffey	52701–52800.
M. C. Waller	L. Forde	5601–5800, 13501–13700, 27701–27800, 36001–36200, 47501-47700, 61201–61400, 70301–70500, 73501–73700.
Do	B. M. Abbott	80701–80900.
N. Semple	F. E. Bernard	5801–6100, 11801–12000, 18701–19000, 33501–33800, 44001-44300, 55101–55300, 64701–65000, 68201–68500, 72001–72300.
Do	B. M. Payne	11701–11800.
Do	M. Johnson	29401–29600.
Do	M. S. Apperson	81501–81800.
C. Hix	M. Gay	6101–6400, 14201–14500, 22201–22500, 25801–26000, 38501-38700, 43701–44000, 51601–51700, 55301–55500, 60901–61200, 72601–72900.
V. M. Stanard	L. Devine	6401–6700, 13901–14200, 17801–18100, 34601–34900, 46401-46700, 52601–52700, 75201–75500.
Do	J. L. Johnston	26701–26800.
Do	E. Garlick	56901–57100.
M. S. Knox	M. Dixon	7001–7300, 65001–65300.
Do	M. W. Bailey	12601–12900, 21601–21900, 29301–29400, 36501–36800, 43401-43700, 53001–53100, 57901–58100, 76101–76400, 82101–82400.
R. Haynes	B. Dabney	7601–7900, 15801–16100, 24401–24700, 30501–30600, 37401-37700, 40101–40400, 50001–50300, 50801–50900, 53501–53600, 65301–65600, 69101–69400, 74901–75200.
H. Bartlett	M. Taylor	8201–8500, 10501–10800, 24701–25000, 30101–30200, 35601-35800, 39601–39700, 49101–49400, 57701–57900, 63501–63800, 77901–78200, 79501–79800.
Do	K. Walker	35501–35600.
Do	J. B. Tiffey	39701–39800.
E. P. Porter	A. P. Pellet	8501–8700, 15101–15400, 25201–25300, 38901–39100, 48801-49100, 52801–52900, 65901–66100.
Do	B. M. Payne	25001–25200, 39301–39400, 77601–77900.
Do	H. M. Douglass	39201–39300.
Do	K. Walker	39401–39500.
Do	M. Taylor	39501–39600.
Do	J. L. Johnston	57501–57700.
H. Starke	C. Sessions	8901–9100, 10801–11100, 22501–22800, 29101–29300, 35201-35500, 50301–50500, 52401–52500, 56101–56300, 60301–60600, 77301–77600.
S. F. Shaver	M. Dixon	12901–13200, 22801–23100, 28301–28500, 33201–33500, 48001-48300, 53201–53300, 56501–56700, 75801–76100, 80101–80400.
M. Jones	E. Garlick	14501–14800, 30201–30300, 36201–36500, 48601–48800, 52901-53000, 57301–57500, 64401–64700.
M. Gwynn	B. M. Payne	15401–15500.

Register of Confederate States Treasury Notes—Continued.

ACT OF MARCH 23, 1863—Continued.

For Treasurer.	For Register.	Numbers of the notes signed.
		NOVEMBER ISSUE—Continued.
		$5—A to H—Continued.
M. Gwynn	M. S. Apperson	24001–24100, 39101–39200, 50701–50800, 78801–78900.
Do	B. Dabney	25301–25400.
Do	J. L. Johnston	79801–80100.
A. Harrison	J. McGarr	16101–16400.
Do	J. Douglas	23401–23700, 40401–40600.
Do	E. Garlick	28201–28300.
Do	H. M. Douglass	36801–37100, 50501–50700, 51901–52000, 58101–58300.
M. E. Dudley	M. E. Norton	19301–19600, 29601–29700, 31301–31600, 42001–42300, 54501–54700, 60601–60900, 68501–68800, 72901–73200, 80401–80700.
L. Breeden	E. C. Winston	21101–21300, 27901–28100, 34901–35200, 46001–46300, 52101–52200, 56301–56500, 69401–69700, 75501–75800.
J. Wilson	H. L. Cooke	28801–28900.
Do	E. Mason	33001–33200.
Do	M. L. Savage	42301–42600.
Do	J. B. Tiffey	51201–51300, 62001–62300, 70501–70800, 80901–81200.
Do	V. C. Watson	54101–54300.
Do	H. M. Douglass	66701–67000.
F. G. Giles	J. B. Tiffey	29701–29900.
Do	K. Walker	45801–46000, 52301–52400, 57101–57300.
Do	L. Macon	83001–83100.
B. J. Clarke	E. A. Adams	29901–30100, 37701–38000, 48301–48600, 63801–64100, 76701–77000.
Do	F. E. Bernard	52501–52600.
Do	H. L. Cooke	58501–58700.
		DECEMBER ISSUE.
		$100—A to D.
N. A. Bass	L. P. Rogers	1–600, 6401–6800, 11001–11800, 18201–19000, 20801–21400, 24401–25000, 27401–27600, 28401–29200, 32201–33000, 35801–36600, 38601–39400, 43401–44200.
J. C. Joplin	J. Gibson	601–1400, 8001–8400, 9401–10200, 15801–16600, 20201–20800, 22201–22400, 23201–23800, 25001–25800, 29201–30000.
Do	J. J. Matthews	34601–35400, 37801–38600, 46601–47400, 51201–52000, 55601–56400, 59801–60600.
Do	J. H. Cooke	65601–66400.
C. Ashford	G. W. Garrett	1401–2200.
Do	J. Gibson	39401–40200, 44201–45000, 48201–48800, 49601–50400, 54001–54800, 58201–59000, 63801–64400.
T. W. Brown	G. W. Garrett	2201–3000, 6801–7200, 11801–12600.
Do	W. Hancock	52801–53400, 57201–57800, 62001–62600, 68801–69400.
A. Patton	W. O. Slade	3001–3400, 7601–8000, 17401–18200, 21401–21600, 35401–35800, 68201–68800.
W. G. Allen	C. S. Taylor	3401–4200, 7201–7600, 12601–13400, 16601–17400, 48801–49600, 57801–58200, 69401–69600.
J. S. Dix	J. Sands	4201–4800, 8401–8600, 19001–19600, 21601–22200, 33801–34600, 41001–41800, 53401–54000, 61401–62000, 67001–67600.
J. Nethers	W. Hancock	4801–5200, 14201–15000, 30601–31400, 36601–37000, 40201–41000, 45001–45800.
F. C. Weisiger	G. N. Warren	5201–5600, 8601–9400, 13401–14200, 19601–20200, 22601–23200, 26601–27400.
Do	S. Dutcher	27601–28400, 37001–37800, 41801–42600, 45801–46600, 50401–51200, 54801–55600, 59001–59800, 65001–65600.
T. J. Hatch	H. Smith	5601–6000, 10201–11000, 15001–15800, 22401–22600, 23801–24400, 25801–26600, 30001–30600, 31401–32200, 33001–33800.
Do	G. N. Warren	42601–43400, 47401–48200, 52001–52800, 56401–57200, 60601–61400, 64401–65000.
S. B. Jacobs	J. H. Cooke	6001–6400, 63001–63800, 67601–68200.
J. A. Jones	L. P. Rogers	62601–63000.
F. H. Link	W. Miller	66401–67000.
		$50—wA to zA.
J. S. Dix	J. Sands	1–200, 2201–3000, 12001–12600, 16201–17000, 20201–20600, 23801–24200, 28601–29400, 31001–31800, 43201–44000, 46601–47400, 52001–52800, 68201–68800.

Register of Confederate States Treasury Notes—Continued.

ACT OF MARCH 23, 1863—Continued.

For Treasurer.	For Register.	Numbers of the notes signed.
		DECEMBER ISSUE—Continued.
		$50—wA to zA—Continued.
F. H. Link	W. Miller	201-600, 3001-3800, 5401-6200, 6801-7400, 10201-10800, 13201-14000, 26201-27000, 35001-35600, 39201-40000, 45001-45800, 49201-50000, 53601-54400, 57001-57800, 61001-61800, 64201-65000, 67401-68200, 70801-71600.
J. Nethers	W. Hancock	601-1400, 7401-8000, 12601-13200, 17801-18600, 21401-21800, 23001-23400, 29401-30200, 36401-37200, 40001-40800, 45801-46600, 56001-56400.
S. B. Jacobs	J. H. Cooke	1401-2200, 4601-5400, 6201-6800, 9601-10200, 14601-15400, 19401-19800, 25001-25400, 33201-33800, 38401-39200, 47401-48200, 50401-51200, 55201-56000, 58601-59400, 62601-64200, 65801-66600, 69601-70400.
A. Patton	W. O. Slade	3801-4600, 9201-9600, 10801-11400, 15401-16200, 19801-20200, 23401-23800, 30201-31000, 35601-36400, 44001-44800, 48201-49000, 52801-53600, 60201-61000, 66601-67400, 68801-69600, 72401-73000.
T. J. Hatch	H. Smith	8001-8600, 18601-19000, 22601-23000, 27001-27800, 33801-34200, 44801-45000.
Do	G. N. Warren	57801-58600.
W. G. Allen	C. S. Taylor	8601-9200, 11401-12000, 17001-17800, 20601-21000, 24201-24600, 37201-37800, 42401-43200, 49001-49200, 50001-50400, 54401-55200, 59401-60200, 61801-62600, 65001-65800, 70401-70800, 71601-72400.
N. A. Bass	L. P. Rogers	14001-14600, 21001-21400, 22201-22600, 27801-28600, 34201-35000, 41601-42400.
J. C. Joplin	J. Gibson	19001-19400, 21801-22200, 25401-26200, 32401-33200, 40801-41600, 51201-52000.
F. C. Weisiger	G. N. Warren	24601-25000, 31801-32400, 37801-38400.
Do	S. Dutcher	56401-57000.
		$20—A to H.
		None issued.
		$10—A to H.
E. D. Layne	V. C. Watson	1-300, 6201-6500, 14901-15000, 21501-21800, 31001-31300, 40201-40500, 51301-51600, 57101-57300, 59101-59300, 61801-62000.
Do	M. Gay	42701-42800.
E. P. Porter	C. Sessions	301-600.
Do	B. M. Payne	8901-9200, 14001-14100.
Do	J. McGarr	23601-23700.
Do	A. P. Pellet	32401-32700, 43801-43900, 54601-54900, 62501-62800.
V. M. Rind	B. J. Clarke	601-900.
Do	V. K. Davies	10401-10700, 14201-14300, 23001-23100, 23201-23300, 30701-30900, 39001-39300, 44601-44700, 46101-46400, 53901-54200, 58101-58300.
Do	M. S. Apperson	23101-23200.
Do	E. Garlick	30901-31000.
M. Sommers	M. B. Kirby	901-1200, 5901-6200, 12701-12900, 21201-21500, 30101-30400, 35701-36000, 43201-43300, 50401-50700, 56201-56500, 63401-63700.
L. Breeden	E. C. Winston	1201-1500, 9201-9500, 14501-14700, 22401-22700, 32101-32400, 41101-41400, 44201-44300, 47301-47400, 53301-53600, 57801-58100.
R. Haynes	B. Dabney	1501-1800, 7101-7400, 14401-14500, 19101-19400, 44301-44400, 46701-47000, 53601-53900, 56801-57100, 58301-58500, 62301-62500.
V. M. Stanard	L. Devine	1801-2100, 8301-8600, 14101-14200, 18301-18600, 28301-28600, 37701-38000, 44401-44500, 47401-47700, 50101-50400, 56501-56800, 61601-61800.
R. F. Ball	M. L. Savage	2101-2300, 16101-16300, 23301-23600, 31301-31600, 39901-40200, 43701-43800, 52101-52400, 62001-62300.
Do	B. M. Abbott	2301-2400.
Do	L. Forde	10701-11000.
B. J. Clarke	E. A. Adams	2401-2700, 6801-7100, 15001-15200, 20901-21200, 43301-43400.
Do	M. C. Lathrop	33001-33300.

Register of Confederate States Treasury Notes—Continued.

ACT OF MARCH 23, 1863—Continued.

For Treasurer.	For Register.	Numbers of the notes signed.
		DECEMBER ISSUE—Continued.
		$10—A to H—Continued.
M. C. Irvine	M. Johnson	2701–3000, 9801–10100, 15201-15300, 25101-25400, 40801-41100, 45001-45100, 54201-54300, 59301-59600.
Do	B. Dabney	34401-34700.
M. A. Dewees	J. Douglas	3001-3300.
Do	S. E. Hughes	9501-9800, 14301-14400, 22701-23000, 33301-33600, 38801-39000, 43601-43700.
E. Mason	M. C. Lathrop	3301-3600, 11301-11600, 15901-16100, 25401-25700, 41701-42000, 44501-44600, 46401-46700.
F. G. Giles	L. Macon	3601-3700.
Do	B. J. Clarke	16401-16600.
M. Gwynn	M. S. Apperson	3701-3800, 11601-11700, 12001-12100, 16701-16800, 26501-26600, 34701-34800, 38601-38800, 45101-45200, 48001-48100.
S. G. Sanxay	L. Macon	3801-4100, 12301-12500, 26601-26900, 35401-35700, 42401-42500, 48901-49200, 60901-61200.
Do	B. J. Clarke	17701-18000.
V. Bridges	do	4101-4400.
Do	E. Garlick	12101-12300.
Do	B. M. Payne	16801-17100.
Do	J. McCarthy	27501-27800.
Do	M. E. Gilliam	37201-37500.
L. Carter	M. F. Stevens	4401-4700, 12901-13100, 18001-18300, 54301-54600, 60601-60900.
Do	B. M. Payne	28901-29200.
Do	J. B. Tiffey	35101-35200.
Do	H. L. Cooke	35201-35300.
Do	J. Douglas	35301-35400.
Do	M. E. Gilliam	42801-42900.
Do	S. E. Hughes	49201-49500.
J. Wilson	J. B. Tiffey	4701-5000, 13801-13900, 20601-20900, 29501-29800, 38301-38600, 45201-45300, 58701-58900, 64001-64200.
W. A. Garrett	J. McGarr	5001-5300, 30401-30700, 38001-38300, 43101-43200, 55201-55300.
Do	M. S. Apperson	55301-55500, 58501-58600.
Do	B. M. Payne	58601-58700.
N. Semple	K. Walker	5301-5600.
Do	F. E. Bernard	16601-16700, 18801-19100, 29201-29500, 36301-36600, 43501-43600, 51801-52100, 55801-56100.
Do	B. J. Clarke	63101-63400.
M. Allen	H. L. Cooke	5601-5900, 13301-13500, 17401-17700, 28001-28300, 36001-36300, 42301-42400, 48101-48400, 60301-60600.
S. F. Shaver	M. Dixon	6501-6800, 13501-13700, 22101-22400, 27201-27500, 37501-37700, 43401-43500, 59601-59800.
M. S. Nicholas	J. McCarthy	7401-7700, 15601-15700.
M. E. Dudley	M. E. Norton	7701-8000, 14701-14800, 20001-20300, 31801-32100, 39601-39900, 43901-44000, 49501-49800, 52701-53000, 64201-64400.
S. Lambert	P. Pleasants	8001-8300, 13101-13300, 19701-20000, 55501-55800.
Do	B. M. Payne	28601-28900, 42501-42600, 50701-51000.
Do	B. J. Clarke	36901-37200.
H. Bartlett	M. Taylor	8601-8900, 13901-14000, 23901-24200, 32701-33000, 44701-44800, 49801-50100, 54901-55200, 62801-63100.
M. S. Knox	M. W. Bailey	10101-10400, 14801-14900, 19401-19700, 41401-41700, 44001-44100.
C. Hix	M. Gay	11001-11300, 15701-15900, 24801-25100, 33601-33700, 44901-45000, 60201-60300.
Do	E. Garlick	33701-33900.
M. Jones	do	11701-12000, 20301-20600, 25901-26200, 60001-60200.
M. Godwin	J. L. Johnston	12501-12700, 17101-17400, 26901-27200, 34801-35100, 42601-42700, 45301-45500, 48601-48900.
M. C. Waller	L. Forde	13701-13800, 18601-18800.
Do	M. E. Gilliam	27801-28000.
Do	B. J. Clarke	36601-36700, 43001-43100, 48401-48600.
Do	M. S. Apperson	36701-36900.
Do	M. W. Bailey	51601-51800.
L. C. Minor	B. M. Abbott	15301-15500, 24201-24500, 42901-43000, 45801-46100, 61201-61500.
Do	M. W. Bailey	31601-31800.

Register of Confederate States Treasury Notes—Continued.

ACT OF MARCH 23, 1863—Continued.

For Treasurer.	For Register.	Numbers of the notes signed.
		DECEMBER ISSUE—Continued.
		$10—A to H—Continued.
L. C. Minor	J. Douglas	40501–40800.
H. Starke	C. Sessions	15501–15600, 24501–24800, 25701–25900.
Do	B. J. Clarke	33901–34200.
Do	J. McCarthy	39301–39600, 44801–44900.
Do	H. L. Cooke	47701–48000.
Do	E. W. Pendleton	51001–51300.
Do	S. E. Hughes	58901–59100.
A. B. Capron	K. Walker	16301–16400, 26201–26500, 34201–34400, 44101–44200, 47001–47300, 59801–60000.
E. A. Dennison	M. E. Gilliam	21801–22100, 53001–53300, 57501–57800, 63701–64000.
Do	E. Garlick	45501–45800.
V. M. Tyler	B. M. Payne	23701–23900, 56101–56200, 61501–61600.
A. Harrison	J. Douglas	29801–30100, 42001–42300.
S. Clark	E. A. Adams	52401–52700, 57301–57500.
		$5—A to H.
M. Allen	H. L. Cooke	1–300, 8601–8900, 24401–24700, 49301–49600, 56701–57000.
M. Godwin	J. L. Johnston	301–600, 8301–8600, 23901–24100, 35501–35700, 56401–56500.
Do	B. M. Payne	48701–48900, 49001–49100.
Do	B. J. Clarke	52501–52800.
S. F. Shaver	M. Dixon	601–900, 9501–9800, 27401–27700, 36501–36700, 40201–40500, 46101–46400, 50901–51200.
V. Bridges	E. Garlick	901–1200, 10301–10600.
Do	B. J. Clarke	23601–23900.
V. M. Stanard	L. Devine	1201–1500, 12101–12200, 20301–20600, 28301–28600, 35701–35900, 48401–48700, 59301–59500.
S. G. Sanxay	L. Macon	1501–1800, 8901–9200, 24101–24400, 33701–33900, 39301–39600, 48101–48400, 56101–56400.
L. Carter	M. F. Stevens	1801–2100, 9201–9500, 24701–25000, 33901–34100, 39601–39900, 48901–49000, 49101–49300, 57901–58200.
W. A. Garrett	J. McGarr	2101–2400, 10901–11200, 20601–20800, 42201–42400.
Do	M. Johnson	34101–34200.
Do	J. Douglas	34201–34300.
Do	K. Walker	51501–51800.
J. Wilson	J. B. Tiffey	2401–2700, 11801–12100, 19401–19700, 27101–27400, 34301–34500, 43901–44100, 44401–44700, 51201–51500.
N. Semple	B. M. Payne	2701–3000.
Do	B. J. Clarke	10601–10900.
Do	F. E. Bernard	25001–25300, 35101–35300, 41701–42000, 47301–47600, 58401–58600.
Do	M. Gay	58301–58400.
M. Sommers	M. B. Kirby	3001–3300, 11501–11800, 25601–25900, 36301–36500, 40801–41100, 50201–50500, 57601–57900.
M. C. Waller	L. Forde	3301–3500, 9801–10000.
Do	M. E. Gilliam	26201–26300.
Do	E. Garlick	26301–26500.
Do	B. J. Clarke	35901–36100.
Do	E. C. Winston	42001–42200.
S. Lambert	P. Pleasants	3501–3800, 12501–12800, 19101–19400, 49901–50200, 59501–59800.
Do	B. M. Payne	25901–26200, 34901–35100, 39901–40200.
E. D. Layne	V. C. Watson	3801–4100, 11201–11500, 17901–18200, 28901–29200, 37101–37300, 43301–43600, 45301–45600, 52101–52200.
M. S. Knox	M. W. Bailey	4101–4400, 13101–13400, 21401–21700, 30001–30300, 41401–41700.
M. E. Dudley	M. E. Norton	4401–4700, 10001–10300, 20001–20300, 29201–29400, 37501–37700, 42401–42700, 52201–52500, 58601–58800.
B. J. Clarke	E. A. Adams	4701–5000, 12201–12500, 18501–18800, 29701–30000, 33301–33600, 39101–39300.
R. Haynes	B. Dabney	5001–5300, 13401–13700, 17301–17600, 25301–25600, 32201–32500, 38301–38500, 48001–48100.
L. Breeden	E. C. Winston	5301–5600, 13701–14000, 22301–22600, 27701–28000, 38501–38700, 45601–45900, 55201–55500.
V. M. Rind	V. K. Davies	5601–5900, 14001–14300, 17601–17900, 36901–37100, 46701–47000.

Register of Confederate States Treasury Notes—Continued.

ACT OF MARCH 23, 1863—Continued.

For Treasurer.	For Register.	Numbers of the notes signed.
		DECEMBER ISSUE—Continued.
		$5—A to H—Continued.
V. M. Rind	J. McCarthy	29401–29700.
Do	B. J. Clarke	54901–55200.
R. F. Ball	M. L. Savage	5901–6200, 15501–15800, 21701–22000, 35301–35500, 44701–45000, 54301–54600, 59801–60100.
Do	J. Douglas	43601–43900.
H. Bartlett	M. Taylor	6201–6500, 14601–14900, 20801–21100, 26801–27100, 31901–32200, 34501–34700, 41101–41400, 51801–52100, 57301–57600.
E. P. Porter	B. J. Clarke	6501–6800.
Do	K. Walker	14301–14600.
Do	B. M. Payne	21101–21400.
Do	J. Douglas	26501–26800.
Do	A. P. Pellet	31601–31900, 34701–34900, 40501–40800, 44101–44400, 50501–50800, 57001–57300.
M. A. Dewees	J. Douglas	6801–7100.
Do	S. E. Hughes	12801–13100, 18201–18500, 28601–28900, 36101–36300, 43001–43300.
M. C. Irvine	M. Johnson	7101–7400, 14901–15200, 22001–22300, 30901–31200, 45001–45300.
Do	J. Douglas	56001–56100.
M. S. Nicholas	J. McCarthy	7401–7700, 16101–16400, 22901–23200, 59101–59300.
E. Mason	M. C. Lathrop	7701–8000, 16401–16700, 23201–23500, 30601–30900, 38701–38900, 47001–47300, 54001–54300, 56501–56700.
C. Hix	M. Gay	8001–8300, 15801–16100, 22601–22900, 31201–31500, 33001–33300, 37901–38100, 47601–47900, 55701–56000.
Do	M. Johnson	42701–43000.
L. C. Minor	B. M. Abbott	15201–15500, 19701–20000, 28001–28300, 36701–36900, 58801–59100.
Do	B. J. Clarke	49601–49900.
Do	S. E. Hughes	53401–53700.
H. Starke	C. Sessions	16701–17000, 31501–31600.
Do	H. L. Cooke	38101–38300.
Do	M. S. Apperson	53701–54000.
F. G. Giles	B. M. Payne	17001–17200.
M. Gwynn	M. S. Apperson	17201–17300, 23501–23600, 33601–33700.
Do	B. J. Clarke	47901–48000.
E. A. Dennison	M. E. Gilliam	18801–19100, 30301–30600, 37301–37500, 46401–46700, 52801–53100.
M. Jones	E. Garlick	32501–32700, 37801–37900.
Do	J. McCarthy	37701–37800, 55501–55700.
A. B. Capron	K. Walker	32701–33000, 38901–39100, 45901–46100, 54601–54900.
V. M. Tyler	B. M. Payne	50801–50900, 58201–58300.
S. Clark	E. A. Adams	53101–53400, 60101–60200.
		JANUARY (1864) ISSUE.
		$100—A to D.
W. G. Allen	C. S. Taylor	1–400, 2801–3400, 7801–8400, 10001–10800, 29801–30600, 77401–78200, 86201–87000.
J. C. Joplin	J. H. Cooke	401–1000, 5601–6200, 13401–14200, 15001–15800, 18001–18800, 22001–22800, 25801–26600, 49401–50400.
Do	J. J. Matthews	32801–33600.
Do	W. Hancock	35801–36800, 43001–44000, 53801–54000, 54801–55600, 64601–65600, 70401–71000, 74401–75200, 80001–80800, 87601–88400.
C. Ashford	J. Gibson	1001–1600, 4601–5200, 10801–11600.
Do	J. H. Cooke	42201–43000, 50401–51200, 55601–56400, 61201–62000, 69201–69800, 76801–77400, 79201–80000, 87001–87600.
T. J. Hatch	G. N. Warren	1601–2200, 6201–6800, 11601–12400, 14201–15000, 17201–18000, 22801–23600, 27401–28200, 33601–34400, 37601–38600, 47601–47800, 51201–52200, 58001–58800, 63601–64600, 71001–71600, 73601–74400, 81601–82400, 88401–89000.
J. S. Dix	J. Sands	2201–2800, 6801–7400, 40201–40600, 46401–46800.
Do	W. O. Slade	66401–67200, 72701–73000, 83201–83800, 89601–90200.
J. A. Jones	L. P. Rogers	3401–4000, 7401–7800, 9401–10000, 16401–17200, 19601–20000, 23601–24400, 28201–29000, 32001–32800, 38601–39400, 44801–45600, 47801–48600, 57201–58000, 60401–60600, 62001–62800, 69801–70400, 75201–76000, 82401–83200.

Register of Confederate States Treasury Notes—Continued.

ACT OF MARCH 23, 1863—Continued.

For Treasurer.	For Register.	Numbers of the notes signed.
		JANUARY (1864) ISSUE—Continued.
		$100—A to D—Continued.
T. W. Brown	W. Hancock	4001-4600, 8401-8800, 12401-12600, 20801-21400, 25201-25800, 30601-31400, 34401-35000.
Do	J. J. Matthews	40601-41400, 46801-47600, 53001-53800, 60601-60800, 67601-68400, 79001-79200, 84601-85400.
Do	G. N. Warren	60801-61000.
Do	C. S. Taylor	61001-61200.
Do	W. Miller	72401-72700.
F. C. Weisiger	S. Dutcher	5201-5600, 8801-9400, 15801-16400, 18801-19600, 21401-22000, 26601-27400, 31401-32000, 36801-37600, 41401-42200, 48601-49400, 56401-57200, 62801-63600, 68401-69200, 73001-73600, 89001-89600.
A. Patton	W. O. Slade	12601-13400, 20001-20800, 24401-25200, 29001-29800.
Do	J. Gibson	35001-35800, 39401-40200, 45601-46400, 54001-54800, 59601-60400, 67201-67600, 78201-79000, 83801-84600, 90801 91300.
N. A. Bass	J. Sands	44001-44800, 52201-53000, 58801-59600, 65601-66400, 71601-72400, 76001-76800, 85401-86200, 90201-90800.
F. H. Link	W. Miller	80801-81600.
		$50—wA to zA.
F. H. Link	W. Miller	1-600, 1201-1800, 2401-3200, 4001-4800, 7001-7800, 9001-9800, 11001-11800, 12601-13400, 15001-15800, 17001-17800, 19001-19800, 21401-22200, 23801-24600, 25801-26400, 28801-29600.
A. Patton	W. O. Slade	601-1200, 1801-2400, 5401-6200.
Do	J. Gibson	25401-25800, 27001-27600.
J. S. Dix	J. Sands	3201-4000, 4801-5400, 9801-10600, 11801-12600, 14201-15000, 16601-17000, 18601-19000.
Do	J. Gibson	7801-8600.
Do	W. O. Slade	20601-21400, 23001-23800, 26401-27000, 28501-28800.
W. G. Allen	C. S. Taylor	6201-7000, 8601-9000, 10601-11000, 13401-14200, 15801-16600, 17801-18600, 19801-20600, 22201-23000, 24601-25400, 27601-28200.
T. W. Brown	W. Hancock	28201-28500.
Do	J. J. Matthews	29601-30100.
		$20—A to H.
		None issued.
		$10—A to H.
S. G. Sanxay	L. Macon	1-200, 6901-7100, 10201-10500, 18901-19200, 24701-25000, 39301-39600, 48201-48500, 56701-57000.
M. Allen	H. L. Cooke	201-400, 7101-7300, 11301-11600, 19501-19800, 25001-25300, 41101-41400, 52801-53100.
Do	M. Taylor	33201-33500.
Do	B. M. Payne	33501-33600.
L. Carter	M. F. Stevens	401-600, 7501-7700, 10501-10800, 20901-21200, 28301-28600, 31901-32200, 39801-40100, 54001-54300, 58001-58200.
Do	B. M. Payne	58201-58300.
M. A. Dewees	S. E. Hughes	601-800, 9201-9400, 12201-12500, 34201-34500, 55201-55500.
Do	M. L. Savage	22001-22300.
Do	E. A. Adams	26101-26400.
Do	M. W. Bailey	42601-42900.
V. M. Tyler	B. M. Payne	801-900, 7801-7900, 11101-11300, 20401-20600, 27501-27700, 32201-32400, 40101-40300, 49401-49600, 57501-57700.
M. S. Nicholas	J. McCarthy	901-1100.
Do	M. Johnson	5001-5200.
Do	E. W. Pendleton	9801-9900.
Do	E. C. Winston	16301-16600, 30701-31000.
Do	V. C. Watson	38301-38600.
Do	B. J. Clarke	43501-43800, 56101-56400.
Do	M. Taylor	60401-60700.
M. Godwin	J. L. Johnston	1101-1300, 6201-6400, 19201-19500, 37501-37700, 46001-46300, 51901-52200.
M. Sommers	M. B. Kirby	1301-1500, 7901-8100.
E. A. Dennison	M. E. Gilliam	1501-1700, 9001-9200, 13901-14200, 16701-16800, 23201-23500, 35401-35700, 45301-45600, 52201-52500.

Register of Confederate States Treasury Notes—Continued.

ACT OF MARCH 23, 1863—Continued.

For Treasurer.	For Register.	Numbers of the notes signed.
		JANUARY (1864) ISSUE—Continued.
		$10—A to H—Continued.
E. A. Dennison	B. M. Payne	4001–4100.
Do	M. S. Apperson	4101–4200.
Do	M. B. Kirby	26701–26900.
Do	M. Taylor	45601–45700.
E. D. Layne	V. C. Watson	1701–1900, 4201–4300.
S. F. Shaver	M. Dixon	1901–2100, 5601–5800, 42001–42300, 48801–49100, 58301-58600.
Do	V. C. Watson	12501–12700.
Do	B. J. Clarke	12701–12800.
Do	E. C. Winston	22901–23200.
Do	J. Douglas	28901–29200, 36001–36300.
J. Wilson	J. B. Tiffey	2101–2300, 8101–8300, 11601–11900, 20101–20400, 26901-27200, 33601–33900, 41401–41700, 49101–49400.
Do	B. McRae	57701–58000.
W. A. Garrett	J. McGarr	2301–2500, 11901–12200, 20601–20900, 27201–27500, 32601-32900, 44401–44500, 60101–60400.
Do	B. J. Clarke	8301–8500, 44501–44600.
Do	H. L. Cooke	44601–44700.
Do	E. C. Winston	50101–50200.
Do	J. B. Tiffey	50201–50300.
Do	E. A. Adams	50301–50400.
M. C. Waller	B. J. Clarke	2501–2700, 50001–50100.
Do	A. P. Pellet	8501–8600, 13101–13300, 21801–22000, 25601–25800, 32401-32600.
Do	M. C. Lathrop	39601–39700.
Do	E. C. Winston	39701–39800.
Do	H. L Cooke	49901–50000.
Do	M. S. Apperson	57301–57500.
H. Bartlett	M. Taylor	2701–2900.
L. C. Minor	B. M. Payne	2901–3100.
Do	B. J. Clarke	4401–4600.
Do	B. M. Abbott	26401–26700, 34801–35100, 43201–43500, 51001–51300, 58601-58900.
M. Gwynn	M. S. Apperson	3101–3200, 6401–6500, 7701–7800, 18801–18900, 31301–31400, 38901–39000, 48101–48200, 61601–61700.
E. P. Porter	A. P. Pellet	3201–3300.
R. F. Ball	M. L. Savage	3301–3500, 4601–4800, 9401–9600, 14801–15100, 31001–31300.
Do	J. L. Johnston	17401–17600.
Do	M. S. Apperson	17601–17700.
Do	E. C. Winston	36301–36600, 46901–47200, 51601–51900.
M. E. Dudley	M. E. Norton	3501–3700, 4301–4400, 8601–8700, 9901–10000, 21501–21800, 43801–44100, 50701–51000, 59801–60100.
Do	M. B. Kirby	10001–10200, 32901–33200.
S. Clark	E. A. Adams	3701–3800.
V. M. Rind	M. Taylor	3801–3900.
Do	J. B. Tiffey	3901–4000.
Do	V. K. Davies	9601–9800, 15101–15400, 17101–17400, 21201–21500, 25301-25600, 36901–37200, 45701–46000, 53701–54000.
C. Hix	M. Gay	4801–5000, 16601–16700, 18201–18500, 23501–23800, 29201-29500, 37701–38000, 42901–43200, 54901–55100.
Do	B. M. Payne	55101–55200.
A. B. Capron	K. Walker	5201–5400, 16001–16200, 17701–17900, 24401–24700, 30101-30400, 31601–31900, 38001–38300.
Do	B. J. Clarke	16201–16300.
Do	M. B. Kirby	47201–47500, 52501–52800, 61001–61300.
R. Haynes	B. Dabney	5401–5600, 14501–14800, 28001–28300, 34501–34800, 42301-42600, 55501–55800.
L. Breeden	E. C. Winston	5801–6000.
E. Mason	M. C. Lathrop	6001–6200, 15701–16000, 16801–17100, 24101–24400, 29801-30100, 39001–39300, 46601–46900, 56401–56700, 61301-61600.
M. Jones	E. Garlick	6501–6700, 13301–13600, 31401–31600, 35701–36000, 41701-42000, 54301–54600, 60701–61000.
M. C. Irvine	M. Johnson	6701–6900, 15401–15600, 17901–18200, 30401–30700, 37201-37500.
Do	F. E. Bernard	15601–15700.
Do	M. Taylor	47501–47800, 53101–53400.

Register of Confederate States Treasury Notes—Continued.

ACT OF MARCH 23, 1863—Continued.

For Treasurer.	For Register.	Numbers of the notes signed.
		JANUARY (1864) ISSUE—Continued.
		$10—A to H—Continued.
N. Semple	F. E. Bernard	7301-7500, 10801-11000, 19801-20100, 29501-29800, 35101-35400, 40801-41100, 49601-49900, 58901-59200.
Do	B. J. Clarke	11001-11100.
S. Lambert	P. Pleasants	8701-8900, 14201-14500, 28601-28900, 59201-59300.
Do	E. A. Adams	22301-22600, 50401-50700.
Do	B. J. Clarke	36601-36900.
Do	M. S. Apperson	44101-44400.
Do	B. J. Clarke	59301-59500.
V. M. Stanard	L. Devine	8901-9000, 12801-13100, 22601-22900, 25801-26100, 44701-45000, 54601-54900.
Do	E. A. Adams	33901-34200.
A. Harrison	J. Douglas	13601-13900, 46301-46600, 53401-53700.
H. Starke	E. W. Pendleton	18501-18800, 23801-24100, 27701-28000, 38601-38900, 40301-40600, 51301-51600, 59501-59800.
W. L. Smalley	B. M. Payne	40601-40700.
Do	M. Gay	40701-40800.
Do	A. P. Pellet	48501-48800, 57001-57300.
E. S. Read	do	45001-45300.
—— Morris	B. McRae	47801-48100.
F. G. Giles	M. W. Bailey	55801-56100.
		$5—A to H.
W. A. Garrett	J. McGarr	1-200, 6101-6300, 13001-13200, 18701-19000, 31601-31900, 38501-38800, 45001-45300, 52201-52500, 62601-62900.
Do	M. E. Gilliam	23301-23600.
S. Lambert	P. Pleasants	201-500, 2201-2400, 5801-6000, 10401-10700, 30101-30400.
Do	B. J. Clarke	19001-19300, 45801-46100, 53101-53400.
Do	M. L. Savage	22301-22500.
Do	M. Johnson	22501-22600.
Do	K. Walker	37001-37300.
M. Gwynn	M. S. Apperson	501-600, 8801-8900, 9501-9600, 15801-15900, 21301-21400, 27801-27900, 30901-31000, 34901-35100, 47001-47100, 50201-50300, 50601-50700, 58501-58600.
Do	B. M. Payne	43201-43300.
M. C. Waller	K. Walker	601-800.
Do	A. P. Pellet	6301-6400, 10901-11100, 17401-17600, 22901-23100, 30701-30900, 62901-63100.
Do	M. S. Apperson	35701-35900, 54601-54800.
M. S. Nicholas	J. McCarthy	801-1000.
Do	M. C. Lathrop	1001-1100.
Do	E. W. Pendleton	7001-7100.
Do	E. C. Winston	14901-15200, 20201-20500, 34301-34600.
Do	K. Walker	26601-26900.
Do	B. J. Clarke	40001-40300.
Do	M. B. Kirby	47101-47400.
V. M. Rind	V. K. Davies	1101-1300, 3201-3400, 14301-14600, 26001-26300, 30401-30700, 47401-47700, 56701-57000, 58601-58800.
Do	E. Garlick	1301-1400.
Do	V. C. Watson	39401-39700.
S. F. Shaver	M. Dixon	1401-1600, 25101-25300, 37901-38200, 51301-51600.
Do	M. Taylor	14801-14900, 18101-18300, 25301-25400.
Do	M. B. Kirby	18301-18400.
Do	E. A. Adams	31001-31300.
B. J. Clarke	do	1601-1900, 2101-2200.
Do	V. C. Watson	23701-23900.
E. Mason	M. C. Lathrop	1901-2100, 8201-8400, 15201-15500, 27201-27500, 33101-33400, 42101-42400, 49001-49300, 57001-57300.
V. M. Stanard	L. Devine	2401-2600, 6001-6100, 10701-10900, 19901-20200, 23901-24200, 32501-32800, 49601-49900, 55501-55800, 60301-60600.
Do	A. P. Pellet	38201-38500.
H. Starke	E. W. Pendleton	2601-2800, 5601-5800, 8901-9200, 13201-13500, 27501-27800, 28401-28700, 41201-41500, 44401-44700, 57301-57600.
N. Semple	F. E. Bernard	2801-3000, 4501-4700, 16201-16500, 24201-24500, 28701-29000, 38801-39100, 43301-43400, 50701-51000, 61801-62100.
Do	K. Walker	6901-7000.
L. Breeden	E. C. Winston	3001-3200.

Register of Confederate States Treasury Notes—Continued.

ACT OF MARCH 23, 1863—Continued.

For Treasurer.	For Register.	Numbers of the notes signed.
		JANUARY (1864) ISSUE—Continued.
		$5—A to H—Continued.
R. Haynes	B. Dabney	3401–3600, 8001–8200, 14001–14300, 19301–19600, 21001-21300, 25401–25700, 29801–30100, 37601–37900, 43401-43700, 54001-54100, 55001–55200, 59401–59700.
A. Harrison	J. Douglas	3601–3700, 4901–5100, 48001–48300, 55801–56100, 62101-62400.
M. C. Irvine	M. Johnson	3701–3900, 7401–7600, 15201–15700, 32801–33100, 40901-41200.
Do	M. B. Kirby	15701–15800.
Do	M. Taylor	48601–48800, 57901–58200.
C. Hix	do	3901–4000.
Do	M. Gay	4001–4100, 7801–8000, 8601–8800, 13701–14000, 26901–27200, 34601–34900, 41801–42100, 48801–49000, 55401-55500, 60001-60300.
Do	M. E. Gilliam	55201–55400.
A. B. Capron	K. Walker	4101–4300, 7201–7400, 14601–14800, 33401–33700.
Do	M. B. Kirby	58201–58500.
S. G. Sanxay	L. Macon	4301–4500, 9601–9900, 15901–16200, 21401–21700, 27901-28200, 35101–35400, 54101–54400, 61201–61500.
M. Allen	H. L. Cooke	4701–4900, 10101–10400, 17101–17400, 21701–22000, 35901-36200, 53401–53700, 59101–59400.
M. Sommers	M. B. Kirby	5101–5300, 12301–12400.
L. Carter	M. F. Stevens	5301–5500, 11101–11400, 16501–16800, 24801–25100, 29001-29300, 46101–46400.
Do	M. B. Kirby	35401–35700.
Do	B. McRae	51601–51800.
Do	M. E. Gilliam	51801–51900.
V. M. Tyler	B. M. Payne	5501–5600, 9901-10100, 17901-18100, 23101-23300, 28201-28400, 36501–36700, 45601–45800, 62401–62600.
S. Clark	E. A. Adams	6401–6600, 7101–7200.
Do	E. Garlick	23601–23700.
M. A. Dewees	S. E. Hughes	6601–6800, 11601–11900, 16801–17100, 36701–37000, 44101-44400, 53701–54000, 59701–60000.
Do	B. J. Clarke	25701–26000.
Do	M. Taylor	29601–29800.
J. Wilson	J. B. Tiffey	6801–6900, 11401–11600, 17601–17900, 22601–22900, 29301-29600, 36201–36500, 51901–52200, 61501–61800.
M. Jones	E. Garlick	7601–7800, 34001–34300, 37301–37600, 49301–49600, 56401-56700.
L. C. Minor	B. M. Abbott	8401–8600, 9201–9500, 12701–13000, 20701–21000, 26301-26600, 32201–32500, 40301–40600, 46401–46700, 52801–53100.
M. E. Dudley	M. E. Norton	11901–12100, 19601–19900, 22001–22300, 31301–31600, 39701-39900, 44701–45000, 51001–51300.
Do	B. M. Payne	39901–40000.
R. F. Ball	M. L. Savage	12101–12300, 13601–13700, 33701–34000.
Do	E. C. Winston	40601–40900, 45301–45600, 52501–52800, 58801–59100.
E. A. Dennison	M. E. Gilliam	12401–12700, 20501–20700, 31901–32200, 39101–39400, 43701-44000.
Do	J. McGarr	44001–44100.
E. D. Layne	V. C. Watson	13501–13600.
M. Godwin	J. L. Johnston	24501–24800, 42401–42700, 47701–47900, 54801–54900.
Do	H. L. Cooke	47901–48000.
Do	M. E. Gilliam	54901–55000.
F. G. Giles	M. W. Bailey	41501–41800, 48301–48600, 56101–56400, 60601–60900.
—— Morris	M. Taylor	42701–42900.
Do	R. McRae	49901–50200, 50301–50600.
Do	E. A. Adams	57601–57900.
E. S. Read	do	42901–43200, 46701–47000, 60901–61200.
W. L. Smalley	A. P. Pellet	54401–54600.
		FEBRUARY (1864) ISSUE.
		$100—A to D.
		None issued.
		$50—wA to zA.
F. H. Link	W. Miller	1–600, 2601–3200, 3801–4600, 8001–8600.
T. W. Brown	J. J. Matthews	601–1200.
W. G. Allen	C. S. Taylor	1201–1800.

Register of Confederate States Treasury Notes—Continued.

ACT OF MARCH 23, 1863—Continued.

For Treasurer.	For Register.	Numbers of the notes signed.
		FEBRUARY (1864) ISSUE—Continued.
		$50—wA to zA—Continued.
A. Patton	J. Gibson	1801–2000, 9401–9600.
N. A. Bass	J. Sands	2001–2600, 6801–7600.
Do	W. Hancock	8601–9400.
C. Ashford	L. P. Rogers	3201–3800.
F. C. Weisiger	J. Gibson	4601–5400, 6001–6800.
T. J. Hatch	W. Hancock	5401–5600.
Do	W. Miller	5601–5800.
Do	J. Sands	5801–6000.
J. S. Dix	W. O. Slade	7601–8000.
		$20—A to H.
		None issued.
		$10—A to H.
M. Jones	E. Garlick	1–300, 35701–35800, 55801–56000.
Do	M. C. Lathrop	35501–35700, 68201–68500.
E. A. Dennison	M. E. Gilliam	301–600, 55501–55800, 66201–66500.
Do	M. B. Kirby	34001–34300.
Do	L. Macon	43301–43600.
M. E. Dudley	M. E. Norton	601–900, 31901–32200, 43001–43300, 48401–48700, 64001–64300.
A. Harrison	J. Douglas	901–1200, 34601–34900, 54901–55200, 65201–65500.
M. S. Nicholas	J. L. Johnston	1201–1500.
Do	H. L. Cooke	34901–35200, 67901–68200.
Do	M. W. Bailey	54601–54900.
S. Lambert	N. Palmer	1501–1700.
Do	P. Pleasants	1701–1800, 33201–33400, 42401–42600, 53901–54100, 64901–65100.
Do	B. M. Payne	33401–33500, 53801–53900.
Do	M. S. Apperson	42601–42700.
Do	M. W. Bailey	65101–65200.
V. M. Rind	V. K. Davies	1801–2100, 34301–34600, 44201–44500, 56001–56300, 66501–66800.
Do	E. A. Adams	3301–3600.
C. Hix	M. Gay	2101–2400.
Do	M. Taylor	35201–35300.
Do	B. J. Clarke	35301–35400.
Do	J. Douglas	35401–35500.
Do	M. E. Gilliam	44801–45000.
Do	B. M. Payne	45001–45100.
Do	M. B. Kirby	56301–56600.
R. Haynes	B. Dabney	2401–2700, 30701–31000, 49401–49600, 53001–53100, 64601–64900.
Do	M. W. Bailey	43601–43900.
M. A. Dewees	S. E. Hughes	2701–3000, 29301–29600, 48701–49000, 64301–64600.
M. C. Irvine	M. Taylor	3001–3200, 44501–44800, 56601–56900, 66801–67100.
Do	M. S. Apperson	3201–3300.
Do	M. W. Bailey	36501–36700.
N. Giles	do	3601–3900.
R. F. Ball	E. C. Winston	3901–4200, 32901–33200, 55201–55500, 65901–66200.
E. Mason	M. C. Lathrop	4201–4500, 41601–42000, 53401–53800, 60601–60900.
Do	N. Palmer	60901–61000.
A. B. Capron	M. B. Kirby	4501–4800, 67401–67600.
Do	B. M. Abbott	57501–57700.
H. Starke	E. W. Pendleton	4801–5100, 47201–47500, 60301–60600.
Do	M. S. Apperson	33701–33800.
Do	E. C. Winston	33801–33900.
Do	H. L. Cooke	33901–34000.
—— Morris	R. McRae	5101–5400.
S. G. Sanxay	L. Macon	5401–5700, 28701–29000, 45801–46100, 59201–59500.
M. Allen	H. L. Cooke	5701–6000.
J. C. Joplin	W. Hancock	6001–6400, 10101–10500, 12901–13300, 15101–15500.
Do	C. S. Taylor	25801–26200, 28401–28700, 38701–38800.
Do	H. Smith	50701–51100, 61901–62300.
F. H. Link	Tho. J. Miller	6401–6800, 13701–14100, 15901–16000, 17801–18200, 20201–20600, 22501–22900, 26901–27200, 38801–39200, 50301–50700, 61401–61600.

Register of Confederate States Treasury Notes—Continued.

ACT OF MARCH 23, 1863—Continued.

For Treasurer.	For Register.	Numbers of the notes signed.
		FEBRUARY (1864) ISSUE—Continued.
		$10—A to H—Continued.
F. C. Weisiger	J. Gibson	6801-7200.
T. J. Hatch	G. N. Warren	7201-7600.
Do	J. Gibson	10001-10100.
Do	C. S. Taylor	17601-17800.
Do	J. Sands	21001-21400, 22901-23300, 26201-26600, 39201-39600, 51101-51500, 62601-63000.
J. A. Jones	L. P. Rogers	7601-8000, 10501-10900, 13301-13700, 16001-16400, 18601-19000.
Do	H. Smith	49601-49800.
N. A. Bass	J. Sands	8001-8400, 11701-12100.
Do	W. Hancock	19401-19800, 24701-25100, 27601-28000, 41001-41400, 52601-53000, 61001-61400.
Do	W. O. Slade	41401-41600.
C. Ashford	J. H. Cooke	8401-8700, 9601-10000, 12501-12900, 15501-15900, 18201-18600, 21801-22200, 23301-23700, 25501-25800, 39601-39900, 50001-50300, 61601-61900.
J. S. Dix	W. O. Slade	8701-9000, 11301-11700, 14101-14300, 17201-17600, 19801-20200, 20601-21000, 23901-24300, 26601-26900.
Do	J. Gibson	40301-40600, 51501-51800, 62301-62600.
W. G. Allen	C. S. Taylor	9001-9300, 10901-11300, 14301-14700, 16801-17200, 21401-21800.
Do	H. Smith	24301-24700, 52201-52600.
T. W. Brown	J. J. Matthews	9301-9600, 40601-41000.
Do	J. Sands	12101-12500, 14701-15100, 28101-28200.
Do	J. Gibson	25101-25500.
Do	W. Hancock	28001-28100.
Do	H. Smith	28201-28400.
A. Patton	J. Gibson	16401-16800, 19001-19400, 22201-22500.
Do	L. P. Rogers	23701-23900, 27201-27600, 39901-40300, 51801-52200, 63001-63400. *
Do	H. Smith	49801-50000.
V. M. Stanard	L. Devine	29001-29300, 54101-54400.
Do	E. Garlick	43901-44200.
Do	B. McRae	63701-64000.
V. M. Tyler	B. M. Payne	29601-29800, 37101-37300, 47001-47200, 57801-58000, 68901-69100.
N. Semple	F. E. Bernard	29801-30100, 36801-37100, 46101-46400, 58901-59200, 68601-68900.
S. F. Shaver	M. Dixon	30101-30400, 37601-37900, 48101-48400, 59501-59800.
L. Carter	M. F. Stevens	30401-30700, 38201-38500, 46401-46700, 58601-58900.
J. Wilson	J. B. Tiffey	31001-31300, 37301-37600, 46701-47000, 58001-58300.
W. A. Garrett	J. McGarr	31301-31600, 53101-53400, 58301-58600.
Do	E. C. Winston	37901-38200.
M. Godwin	J. L. Johnston	31601-31900, 45401-45700, 47501-47800.
W. L. Smalley	B. J. Clarke	32201-32500, 47801-48100, 59801-60100.
Do	E. W. Pendleton	42701-43000.
L. C. Minor	N. Palmer	32501-32800.
Do	M. C. Lathrop	32801-32900.
Do	H. L. Cooke	42001-42400.
Do	B. J. Clarke	49001-49400.
Do	B. M. Abbott	65501-65800.
Do	M. W. Bailey	65801-65900.
M. C. Waller	A. P. Pellet	33501-33700, 38501-38700, 54401-54600, 60101-60300.
E. S. Read	E. A. Adams	35801-36100, 57201-57500, 67601-67900.
Do	M. B. Kirby	45101-45400.
S. Clark	B. McRae	36101-36400, 56901-57200.
Do	M. Johnson	67101-67400.
M. Gwynn	M. S. Apperson	36401-36500, 36701-36800, 45701-45800, 57701-57800, 68501-68600, 69101-69200.

* Nos. 63401-63700 missing; not signed and never issued.

Register of Confederate States Treasury Notes—Continued.

ACT OF MARCH 23, 1863—Continued.

For Treasurer.	For Register.	Numbers of the notes signed.
		FEBRUARY (1864) ISSUE—Continued.
		$5—A to H.
L. C. Minor	B. Dabney	1-300.
Do	B. M. Abbott	6701-7000, 18501-18800, 30101-30400, 34801-35100, 44801-45100, 57701-58000, 66201-66500, 73401-73700, 89201-89500, 99001-99200, 108401-108700, 119901-120200, 130801-131100, 147501-147700.
Do	M. Taylor	51501-51800.
Do	M. B. Kirby	66501-66600.
Do	N. Palmer	73701-73800, 99201-99300.
Do	A. P. Pellet	120201-120300.
Do	M. S. Apperson	131101-131200.
Do	M. Gay	147701-147800.
Do	B. McRae	149201-149300.
Do	F. E. Bernard	161201-161500.
M. A. Dewees	S. E. Hughes	301-600, 9301-9600, 52101-52400, 65901-66200, 71601-71900, 84401-84700, 99901-100200, 110301-110600, 121401-121700, 134901-135200, 146901-147200, 163501-163800.
Do	M. Gay	19101-19300.
Do	H. L. Cooke	19301-19400.
Do	L. Devine	25701-26000.
Do	N. Palmer	34201-34500, 45101-45400.
W. L. Smalley	B. J. Clarke	601-900, 7001-7300, 17001-17300, 23301-23600, 37401-37600, 51201-51500, 57101-57400, 63701-64000, 69901-70200, 83501-83800, 90301-90600, 101501-101800, 117501-117900, 129701-130100, 149301-149700, 156001-156200.
M. E. Dudley	M. E. Norton	901-1200, 9901-10200, 15301-15600, 26001-26200, 31801-32100, 42101-42400, 50601-50900, 58601-58900, 64601-64900, 74701-75000, 87301-87400, 145201-145500, 156201-156300, 156401-156500.
Do	M. Taylor	26201-26300.
Do	N. Palmer	87101-87300.
Do	B. McRae	87601-87700.
Do	M. S. Apperson	156301-156400.
E. A. Dennison	M. E. Gilliam	1201-1500, 7601-7900, 17601-17900, 24501-24800, 62901-63200, 73101-73400, 86801-87100, 96001-96300, 111201-111500, 122701-123000, 133001-133300, 146601-146800.
Do	B. M. Payne	33301-33400.
Do	B. J. Clarke	33401-33500.
Do	L. Devine	33501-33600, 48501-48700.
Do	E. C. Winston	41601-41700.
Do	H. L. Cooke	41701-41800.
Do	E. A. Adams	41801-41900.
Do	M. S. Apperson	48401-48500.
Do	A. P. Pellet	146801-146900.
Do	N. Palmer	160601-160900.
L. Carter	M. F. Stevens	1501-1800, 5601-5800, 17301-17500, 23601-23900, 40001-40200, 62001-62300, 94801-95000, 105501-105800, 118501-118800, 146201-146500, 156801-157100.
Do	B. M. Payne	5801-5900, 17501-17600, 40201-40300.
Do	M. Dixon	35901-36200.
Do	M. B. Kirby	48101-48400.
Do	S. E. Hughes	57401-57700.
Do	B. McRae	70501-70800, 84001-84100, 95001-95100, 146501-146600.
Do	M. Gay	83801-84000.
Do	N. Palmer	105801-105900.
Do	E. C. Winston	118401-118500.
Do	J. L. Johnston	133901-134200.
Do	M. S. Apperson	134201-134300.
M. Allen	H. L. Cooke	1801-2100, 14001-14300, 22501-22800, 32101-32400, 40601-40900, 47801-48100, 104801-105200, 113401-113700, 117401-117500, 129301-129700, 144801-145200, 155001-155300.
Do	A. P. Pellet	155301-155400.
M. Godwin	J. L. Johnston	2101-2300, 35401-35600, 46001-46300, 53901-54200, 64001-64300, 75301-75500, 83201-83500, 90001-90200, 105201-105500, 118101-118400, 144501-144800, 157101-157200, 159801-159900.
Do	J. Douglas	90201-90300.

Register of Confederate States Treasury Notes—Continued.

ACT OF MARCH 23, 1863—Continued.

For Treasurer.	For Register.	Numbers of the notes signed.
		FEBRUARY (1864) ISSUE—Continued.
		$5—A to H—Continued.
S. F. Shaver	M. Dixon	2301-2600, 7301-7600, 16701-17000, 59201-59500, 62301-62600, 69601-69900, 78401-78600, 82801-82900, 95701-96000, 105901-106200, 120301-120700, 130401-130800, 145501-145800, 154601-154900.
Do	N. Palmer	106201-106300.
Do	A. P. Pellet	145801-145900, 154901-155000.
M. S. Nicholas	M. B. Kirby	2601-2900, 150301-150600.
Do	J. L. Johnston	10801-11100, 27901-28200.
Do	N. Palmer	19701-20000.
Do	M. Dixon	43901-44200.
Do	E. Garlick	54201-54500.
Do	H. L. Cooke	60401-60700, 65601-65900, 72501-72800, 85501-85800, 98701-99000.
Do	B. McRae	110901-111200, 122401-122700.
Do	M. E. Norton	135201-135500.
E. S. Read	E. A. Adams	2901-3200, 43301-43600, 52701-53000, 60701-61000, 68701-69000, 77001-77300, 88901-89200, 101101-101400, 121001-121300, 143401-143800, 162901-163200.
Do	M. S. Apperson	101401-101500.
Do	A. P. Pellet	121301-121400.
M. C. Irvine	M. Taylor	3201-3500, 20901-21200, 27701-27900, 36501-36800, 45401-45700, 54801-55100, 69001-69300, 77601-77900, 89501-89700, 100801-101100, 112401-112700, 125901-126100, 142801-143100, 153601-153900, 164401-164700.
Do	F. E. Bernard	11101-11200.
S. Lambert	P. Pleasants	3501-3600, 10501-10700, 18201-18300, 27101-27200, 49201-49300, 58301-58500, 66901-67200, 74401-74500, 88301-88500, 98401-98600, 109101-109300, 123201-123500, 133601-133900, 151201-151500, 160901-161200.
Do	E. W. Pendleton	3601-3800, 98601-98700.
Do	N. Palmer	10701-10800, 27201-27400.
Do	J. L. Johnston	18301-18500.
Do	M. Dixon	32701-33000.
Do	B. J. Clarke	41301-41600.
Do	E. Garlick	49301-49500.
Do	B. M. Payne	58501-58600.
Do	M. S. Apperson	74501-74700, 109301-109400.
Do	J. Douglas	88501-88600.
V. M. Rind	V. K. Davies	3801-4100, 11901-12200, 20001-20300, 28201-28500, 37101-37400, 43601-43900, 53001-53300, 59501-59800, 68101-68400, 76701-77000, 88601-88800, 99601-99900, 110601-110900, 118001-118100, 123601-123700, 143101-143300, 151901-152200, 164901-165000.
Do	E. A. Adams	12701-13000, 18801-19100, 38501-38800, 107001-107300, 152501-152800.
Do	M. Dixon	28501-28800.
Do	M. W. Bailey	88801-88900.
Do	M. S. Apperson	107301-107400.
Do	L. Devine	123701-123800.
Do	M. Taylor	123801-123900.
Do	L. Forde	143301-144400.
Do	N. Palmer	152801-152900.
C. Hix	B. M. Abbott	4101-4300.
Do	B. McRae	4301-4400, 64301-64600, 149901-150000.
Do	M. Gay	11401-11700, 21201-21500, 28801-29100, 31501-31800, 44201-44400, 102501-102800, 104701-104800, 131501-131900, 160301-160600.
Do	M. S. Apperson	44401-44500.
Do	N. Palmer	53301-53600.
Do	M. W. Bailey	61001-61300.
Do	M. Taylor	72801-72900.
Do	B. M. Payne	72901-73000.
Do	J. L. Johnston	73001-73100.
Do	F. E. Bernard	125501-125800, 149701-149900, 150001-150100.
Do	L. Forde	125801-125900.

Register of Confederate States Treasury Notes—Continued.

ACT OF MARCH 23, 1863—Continued.

For Treasurer.	For Register.	Numbers of the notes signed.
		FEBRUARY (1864) ISSUE—Continued.
		$5—A to H—Continued.
M. Jones	E. Garlick	4401-4700, 8201-8500, 15601-15900, 27401-27700, 35101-35400, 42401-42700, 53601-53900, 67201-67500, 75801-76100, 82901-83200, 98101-98400, 109701-110000, 119601-119900, 130101-130400.
Do	J. B. Tiffey	150901-151200.
Do	B. McRae	159901-160000, 162301-162600.
F. G. Giles	M. W. Bailey	4701-5000.
R. F. Ball	E. C. Winston	5001-5300, 20601-20900, 26801-27100, 37901-38200, 45701-46000, 54501-54800, 59801-60100, 75501-75800, 87701-88000, 97901-98100, 108701-109000, 124801-125100, 135501-135900, 152901-153200, 162601-162900.
Do	M. L. Savage	67501-67800.
Do	A. P. Pellet	109001-109100.
Do	M. S. Apperson	125101-125200.
Do	N. Palmer	153201-153300.
—— Morris	M. C. Lathrop	5301-5600.
Do	B. McRae	13301-13600, 22101-22400, 30401-30700, 37601-37800.
Do	L. Devine	37801-37900.
V. M. Stanard	do	5901-6200, 15001-15300, 58001-58300, 71301-71600, 87401-87600, 96301-96600, 109401-109700, 122101-122400, 133301-133600, 150601-150900, 164701-164900.
Do	N. Palmer	61401-61700.
V. M. Tyler	B. M. Payne	6201-6400, 14501-14700, 23101-23300, 31301-31500, 39801-40000, 49001-49200, 56401-56600, 71101-71300, 77901-78100, 89801-90000, 102201-102500, 113101-113400, 129001-129300, 144201-144500, 154301-154600.
J. Wilson	J. B. Tiffey	6401-6700, 14701-15000, 23901-24200, 31001-31300, 55501-55800, 62601-62900, 70801-71100, 84101-84400, 97601-97900, 108101-108400, 119201-119500, 131201-131500, 156501-156800.
Do	P. Pleasants	39501-39600.
Do	H. L. Cooke	39601-39700.
Do	L. Devine	39701-39800.
Do	J. L. Johnston	49801-50100.
Do	M. S. Apperson	119501-119600.
A. Harrison	J. Douglas	7901-8200, 15901-16200, 24801-25100, 38201-38500, 43001-43300, 77301-77600, 111801-112100, 123901-124200, 132701-133000, 152201-152500, 163201-163500.
Do	M. Taylor	50901-51200.
N. Semple	F. E. Bernard	8501-8800, 14301-14500, 24201-24500, 32401-32700, 39201-39500, 56101-56400, 69301-69600, 100501-100800, 106601-107000, 117901-118000.
Do	J. Douglas	48701-49000.
M. C. Waller	A. P. Pellet	8801-9000, 16201-16400, 26601-26800, 33001-33200, 41901-42100, 50401-50600, 56601-56800, 63201-63400, 74201-74400, 85001-85200, 120701-121000.
Do	L. Forde	90601-90800, 107401-107700, 134301-134400, 150101-150300, 161801-162000.
Do	N. Palmer	134401-134600.
W. A. Garrett	J. McGarr	9001-9300, 16401-16700, 25101-25400, 40301-40600, 55801-56100, 63401-63700, 72201-72500, 85801-86100, 106301-106600, 118801-119200, 131901-132300, 145901-146200, 155701-156000.
Do	M. S. Apperson	33601-33700.
Do	B. Dabney	33701-33900.
Do	M. C. Lathrop	49501-49800.
Do	M. Gay	95101-95400.
R. Haynes	B. Dabney	9601-9900, 19401-19700, 25401-25700, 33901-34200, 46901-47000, 56801-57100, 71901-72200, 84701-85000, 100201-100500, 124501-124800, 135901-136200, 147201-147500, 163801-164100.
Do	M. Dixon	52401-52700.
Do	J. Douglas	66601-66900.
Do	M. E. Norton	110001-110300.

Register of Confederate States Treasury Notes—Continued.

ACT OF MARCH 23, 1863—Continued.

For Treasurer.	For Register.	Numbers of the notes signed.
		FEBRUARY (1864) ISSUE—Continued.
		$5—A to H—Continued.
H. Starke	E. W. Pendleton	10201–10500, 17901–18200, 26301–26600, 34501–34800, 42701–43000, 50101–50400, 58901–59200, 65301–65600, 76401–76700, 85201–85500, 97001–97200, 124201–124400, 153901–154200, 161501–161800.
Do	N. Palmer	97201–97300.
Do	M. E. Norton	124401–124500.
Do	P. Pleasants	136201–136500.
M. Jones	M. S. Apperson	11201–11300.
M. Gwynn	do	11301–11400, 13601–13700, 22401–22500, 30001–30100, 33201–33300, 38801–38900, 47001–47100, 55101–55200, 61301–61400, 89701–89800, 123501–123600, 126101–126200, 143801–143900, 154201–154300.
N. Giles	M. W. Bailey	11701–11900, 20301–20600, 29701–30000, 35601–35900, 46601–46900.
E. Mason	M. C. Lathrop	12201–12500, 13001–13300, 21801–22100, 29401–29700, 36801–37100, 40901–41300, 47401–47800, 64901–65200, 73801–74100, 86401–86700, 96601–96900, 107701–108000, 121701–122100, 132301–132700, 151501–151800, 160001–160300.
Do	M. B. Kirby	65201–65300.
Do	N. Palmer	74101–74200, 151801–151900.
Do	J. Douglas	86701–86800.
Do	B. McRae	96901–97000.
Do	A. P. Pellet	108001–108100.
A. B. Capron	M. B. Kirby	12501–12700, 21501–21800, 29101–29400, 36201–36500, 46301–46600, 76101–76400, 88001–88300, 99301–99600, 111501–111800, 123001–123200, 134601–134900, 162001–162200.
Do	B. Dabney	68401–68700.
Do	L. Forde	162201–162300.
S. G. Sanxay	L. Macon	13701–14000, 22801–23100, 30701–31000, 38901–39200, 47101–47400, 55201–55500, 61701–62200, 70201–70500, 78101–78400, 95401–95700, 101801–102100, 112701–113000, 126201–126400, 128801–128900, 143901–144200, 155401–155700.
Do	M. Taylor	102101–102200, 128901–129000.
Do	F. E. Bernard	113001–113100.
S. Clark	B. McRae	44501–44800, 51801–52100, 60101–60400.
Do	M. W. Bailey	67801–68100, 75001–75300, 97301–97500, 112101–112400, 125201–125500, 136501–136800, 153301–153600, 164101–164400.
Do	F. E. Bernard	86101–86400.
Do	A. P. Pellet	97501–97600.
J. A. Jones	J. Gibson	78601–79000, 82601–82800, 90801–91000.
Do	L. P. Rogers	158301–158600.
C. Ashford	J. H. Cooke	79001–79300, 91001–91400, 94401–94800, 113701–114100, 117301–117400, 126401–126700, 137101–137500, 140601–141000, 157501–157700.
Do	J. Gibson	148001–148400.
J. C. Joplin	W. Hancock	79301–79800, 91801–92200, 115301–115700, 128701–128800, 136801–137100, 140201–140600, 157201–157500.
F. H. Link	Tho. J. Miller	79801–80200, 94201–94400, 102801–103200, 114901–115300, 126701–127100, 139001–139400, 141001–141400, 142601–142800, 147801–148000, 157701–158000.
T. J. Hatch	J. Sands	80201–80700, 91401–91800, 114501–114900, 137501–137900, 141401–141800, 158001–158300.
N. A. Bass	Tho. J. Miller	80701–81100.
Do	H. Smith	92601–93000, 115701–116100, 127101–127500, 138201–138600, 141801–142200, 148801–149200, 158601–158900.
Do	J. J. Matthews	104301–104700.
A. Patton	L. P. Rogers	81101–81500, 93801–94200, 103501–103900, 116501–116900, 142201–142600.
Do	J. J. Matthews	128301–128700.
Do	J. Gibson	139801–140200, 159501–159800.
Do	J. Sands	148401–148800.
J. S. Dix	W. O. Slade	81501–81800, 93001–93400.
Do	J. Gibson	103201–103500, 114101–114500, 127501–127900, 137901–138200.
T. W. Brown	J. J. Matthews	81801–82200, 93401–93800, 139401–139800, 158901–159200.
Do	W. O. Slade	116101–116500.
W. G. Allen	C. S. Taylor	82201–82600, 92201–92600, 103901–104300, 116901–117300, 127901–128300.
Do	W. O. Slade	138601–139000, 159201–159500.

Register of Confederate States Treasury Notes—Continued.

ACT OF MARCH 23, 1863—Continued.

For Treasurer.	For Register.	Numbers of the notes signed.
		$2—A to H (1st series).
H. Graham	M. B. Kirby	1-300.
L. C. Minor	B. M. Abbott	301-600, 12701-13000, 18001-18300.
F. M. Dickins	F. E. Bernard	601-900, 21101-21400.
V. M. Rind	V. K. Davies	901-1200, 6201-6500, 8501-8700, 10401-10700, 16601-16900, 21901-22200.
M. S. Knox	M. W. Bailey	1201-1500, 13501-13600, 19401-19700.
S. F. Shaver	M. Dixon	1501-1800, 6101-6200, 14101-14400, 18301-18600.
L. Breeden	L. C. Royster	1801-2100, 19701-20000.
M. S. Nicholas	J. McCarthy	2101-2400, 8201-8500.
H. Starke	M. Morrison	2401-2700.
K. Heth	M. E. Gilliam	2701-3000, 5301-5500.
R. F. Ball	L. M. Hunter	3001-3300, 5501-5800, 13201-13500.
M. Godwin	E. A. Adams	3301-3500, 9301-9500, 23601-23900.
E. A. Dennison	J. L. Johnston	3501-3700.
S. G. Grattan	H. L. Cooke	3701-4000, 7101-7400, 9801-9900, 11801-12100.
A. B. Capron	K. Walker	4001-4200, 7501-7700, 14701-15000, 18601-18700.
R. Haynes	B. Dabney	4201-4400, 15001-15200, 25801-25900.
A. Harrison	E. C. Winston	4401-4600.
Do	M. Wade	13901-14100, 19001-19100.
H. Watkins	M. L. Savage	4601-4700.
H. Bartlett	M. Taylor	4701-5000, 7801-8000, 9501-9800, 15501-15800.
E. P. Porter	A. P. Pellet	5001-5300, 15201-15500.
P. C. Bagby	J. Douglas	5801-6100, 6501-6700, 6901-7000, 7701-7800.
E. Mason	M. C. Lathrop	6701-6900, 7001-7100, 8701-9000, 14401-14700.
E. D. Layne	V. C. Watson	7401-7500, 20801-21100.
M. B. Christian	M. S. Apperson	8001-8200, 13001-13200, 17801-18000.
M. A. Dewees	S. E. Hughes	9001-9300, 12101-12400, 17501-17800, 24501-24800.
V. B. Briggs	J. B. Tiffey	9901-10100, 16901-17200, 21401-21600.
M. Allen	B. T. Lyon	10101-10400.
Do	H. L. Cooke	23201-23600.
M. E. Dudley	M. E. Norton	10701-11000, 16401-16600, 21601-21900.
V. M. Stanard	S. C. Ellett	11001-11300, 22501-22800, 24801-25100.
I. Benton	M. Pace	11301-11500.
M. L. Quarles	F. G. Giles	11501-11800, 16201-16400.
M. Jones	E. Garlick	12401-12700, 18701-19000.
H. M. Douglass	F. C. Jones	13601-13900, 17201-17500, 20001-20300, 24201-24500.
M. C. Irvine	M. Johnson	15801-16100.
S. Lambert	P. Pleasants	16101-16200, 19101-19400, 20301-20500, 22801-22900, 25701-25800.
V. M. Tyler	B. M. Payne	20501-20800.
W. A. Garrett	J. McGarr	22201-22500, 25401-25700.
V. Bridges	E. W. Pendleton	22901-23200.
S. G. Sanxay	L. Macon	23901-24200.
M. Sommers	M. B. Kirby	25101-25400.
		$2—A to H (2d series).
M. Godwin	E. A. Adams	1-300, 7701-8000, 11601-11800.
Do	J. L. Johnston	40201-40500, 42401-42600, 47201-47500.
M. Sommers	M. B. Kirby	301-600, 5801-6100, 14801-15100, 26501-26800.
V. M. Tyler	B. M. Payne	601-800, 11801-12000, 19801-20000, 24201-24500, 38101-38400, 39901-40200, 53201-53400.
S. Lambert	P. Pleasants	801-1100, 3101-3200, 15101-15200, 17501-17800, 29401-29700.
V. B. Briggs	J. B. Tiffey	1101-1400, 12601-12900, 22001-22300.
I. Benton	M. Pace	1401-1600, 13501-13700, 22301-22500.
Do	L. Forde	29701-29900.
M. A. Dewees	S. E. Hughes	1601-1900, 6501-6800, 13201-13500, 26201-26500, 40501-40800.
Do	B. J. Clarke	52901-53200.
H. M. Douglass	F. C. Jones	1901-2200, 2501-2800, 8701-8900, 12901-13200.
Do	F. E. Bernard	21101-21400.
E. D. Layne	V. C. Watson	2201-2500, 7401-7700, 13701-14000, 26801-27100.
Do	E. A. Adams	20301-20500.
A. Harrison	J. Douglas	2801-3100, 9901-10200, 28001-28300.
S. F. Shaver	M. Dixon	3201-3500, 14401-14800, 37101-37400, 39401-39600, 48901-49200.
A. B. Capron	K. Walker	3501-3800, 16301-16600, 18401-18600, 30501-30800, 37401-37600.

Register of Confederate States Treasury Notes—Continued.

ACT OF MARCH 23, 1863—Continued.

For Treasurer.	For Register.	Numbers of the notes signed.
		$2—A to H (2d series)—Continued.
H. Bartlett	M. Taylor	3801–4100, 9301–9600, 15601–15900, 18101–18400, 23401-23700, 35901–36200, 43901–44200.
E. P. Porter	A. P. Pellet	4101–4400, 9601–9900, 17801–18100, 23701–24000, 33501-33800, 36401–36700, 44201–44400.
R. F. Ball	M. L. Savage	4401–4700, 8901–9300, 14001–14400, 23101–23400, 32301-32600, 37801–38000, 45201–45500.
F. M. Dickins	F. E. Bernard	4701–5000, 11001–11300, 12301–12600.
S. G. Sanxay	L. Macon	5001–5200, 20001–20300, 20501–20600, 24501–24800, 38401-38700, 40801–41100, 46101–46400, 51001–51300.
Do	J. Douglas	49501–49800.
V. M. Stanard	L. Devine	5201–5500, 21701–22000, 31401–31700, 42601–42900.
M. C. Irvine	M. Johnson	5501–5800, 8601–8700, 11301–11600, 22601–22800, 33201-33500, 50901–51000.
A. Points	M. Gay	6101–6500, 33801–34100.
M. S. Nicholas	J. McCarthy	6801–7100, 12001–12300, 20801–21100, 27701–27800, 35001-35300, 42301–42400.
W. A. Garrett	J. McGarr	7101–7400, 16601–16900, 24901–25200.
Do	M. L. Savage	24801–24900.
Do	H. M. Douglass	39001–39100.
Do	E. W. Pendleton	39101–39300.
Do	P. Pleasants	39301–39400.
Do	E. C. Winston	41401–41700.
M. L. Quarles	F. G. Giles	8001–8300.
Do	S. Clark	21401–21505.
Do	M. S. Apperson	21506–21700.
Do	L. Forde	29901–30000.
Do	B. J. Clarke	30001–30200, 34401–34700, 42001–42300, 44401–44700.
K. Heth	M. E. Gilliam	8301–8600.
V. M. Rind	V. K. Davies	10201–10500, 16901–17200, 18901–19200, 22801–23100, 32001-32300, 36201–36400, 45501–45800.
R. Haynes	B. Dabney	10501–10700, 28601–28900, 43501–43800, 47501–47700.
Do	J. B. Tiffey	35301–35600.
L. C. Minor	B. M. Abbott	10701–11000, 31701–32000, 36701–37000, 48001–48300.
E. A. Dennison	M. E. Gilliam	15201–15600, 30801–31100.
E. Mason	M. C. Lathrop	15901–16300, 19201–19500, 32901–33200, 37601–37800, 44901-45200, 49801–49900.
M. B. Christian	M. S. Apperson	17201–17500.
M. Jones	E. Garlick	18601–18900, 32601–32900, 34701–35000, 43201–43500, 50501-50700, 52601–52900.
M. Allen	H. L. Cooke	19501–19800, 46701–47000, 48601–48900, 51601–52000.
Do	M. W. Bailey	25201–25500.
Do	M. S. Apperson	25501–25600.
Do	M. Pace	38701–39000.
Do	J. B. Tiffey	39601–39900.
M. C. Waller	S. Clark	20601–20800.
Do	M. Pace	28901–29100.
Do	L. Forde	47001–47200.
Do	M. W. Bailey	48301–48600.
L. Breeden	E. C. Winston	22501–22600, 27101–27400, 50201–50500.
M. Gwynn	M. S. Apperson	24001–24200, 34101–34200, 37001–37100, 38001–38100, 43801-43900.
V. Bridges	E. W. Pendleton	25601–25900, 41101–41400.
Do	E. Garlick	45801–46100.
N. Semple	F. E. Bernard	25901–26200, 46401–46700.
L. Carter	M. Taylor	27401–27700.
Do	M. F. Stevens	52301–52600.
M. S. Knox	M. W. Bailey	28301–28600, 34201–34400, 47701–48000.
M. E. Dudley	M. E. Norton	29101–29400, 41701–42000.
E. O. Beall	E. A. Adams	30201–30500.
H. Starke	C. Sessions	31101–31400.
Do	E. W. Pendleton	49901–50200, 52001–52300.
C. Hix	M. Gay	35601–35900.
Do	S. E. Hughes	50701–50900.
B. J. Clarke	M. Gay	42901–43200.
F. G. Giles	B. M. Payne	44701–44900.
J. Wilson	J. B. Tiffey	49201–49500, 51301–51600.

Register of Confederate States Treasury Notes—Continued.

ACT OF MARCH 23, 1863—Continued.

For Treasurer.	For Register.	Numbers of the notes signed.
		$2—A to H (3d series).
M. C. Waller	A. P. Pellet	1-300.
R. F. Ball	E. C. Winston	301-600.
M. E. Dudley	M. E. Norton	601-700.
Do	M. W. Bailey	701-900.
N. Semple	F. E. Bernard	901-1200.
Do	E. C. Winston	4201-4300.
Do	B. J. Clarke	4301-4400.
Do	M. Taylor	4401-4500.
W. A. Garrett	J. McGarr	1201-1500.
Do	M. S. Apperson	3901-4000.
Do	H. L. Cooke	4001-4100.
Do	B. M. Payne	4101-4200.
S. F. Shaver	M. Dixon	1501-1800, 4801-5100.
M. Godwin	J. L. Johnston	1801-2000.
Do	M. B. Kirby	2001-2100.
E. A. Dennison	M. E. Gilliam	2101-2400.
R. Haynes	B. Dabney	2401-2700.
S. Lambert	E. A. Adams	2701-3000.
L. C. Minor	B. M. Abbott	3001-3300.
V. M. Stanard	M. Taylor	3301-3500.
M. Gwynn	M. S. Apperson	3501-3600.
S. G. Sanxay	L. Macon	3601-3900.
J. Wilson	J. B. Tiffey	4501-4800.
		$1—A to H (1st series).
F. Wray	E. Garlick	1-200, 2401-2700, 6301-6500, 32501-32700.
V. B. Briggs	J. B. Tiffey	201-400, 2901-3200, 6101-6300, 26501-26700, 32301-32500, 35701-35900, 53701-53900, 106901-107200, 112001-112200, 128101-128400.
I. Benton	C. F. Windle	401-600, 7001-7200, 17801-18000, 24801-25000, 28901-29100, 34301-34500.
Do	M. Pace	69801-70000, 89201-89400, 105101-105300, 133701-133900.
A. B. Capron	K. Walker	601-800, 2701-2900, 21701-21900, 30701-30900, 49401-49500, 78401-78700, 83501-83800, 88101-88400, 96901-97200, 105601-105900, 111901-112000, 113901-114000, 118301-118600, 124401-124600, 132101-132400.
M. C. Irvine	M. Upshur	801-1000, 5601-5800, 21201-21400.
Do	M. Johnson	58301-58600, 62901-63100, 66901-67100, 72001-72300, 82301-82600, 87501-87800, 90701-91000, 91601-91700, 93301-93600, 108901-109100, 110801-111000, 120001-120300, 126601-126700, 133001-133300.
S. G. Grattan	H. L. Cooke	1001-1200, 6001-6100, 16901-17200, 21401-21700, 36501-36700, 38301-38400, 39201-39400, 39701-40000, 40601-40900, 49101-49300, 50901-51200, 60501-60800, 69001-69300, 74101-74400, 75601-75900, 76301-76500, 88401-88600, 95501-96000, 98101-98400, 108601-108900, 111301-111600.
M. S. Knox	M. W. Bailey	1201-1400, 7201-7400, 13601-13900, 18801-19100, 27901-28100, 33901-34100, 38401-38500, 45101-45300, 50101-50400, 53401-53700, 60201-60500, 64401-64500, 70601-70900, 79601-79900, 84401-84700, 90001-90300, 91301-91600, 94901-95200, 106301-106600, 114901-115200, 119401-119600, 126401-126600.
H. Watkins	M. L. Savage	1401-1600, 21901-22100, 31101-31300, 32101-32300, 35901-36100, 49001-49100, 59101-59400, 64501-64800, 70901-71100, 73201-73500, 84101-84400, 86801-86900, 91901-92100, 93201-93300, 113301-113600, 117201-117400, 122701-123000.
H. Graham	M. B. Kirby	1601-1700, 9701-10000, 12901-13200, 22901-23200, 30101-30300, 37401-37700, 40301-40600, 45801-46100, 53901-54200, 62001-62300, 63501-63800, 65701-66000, 71401-71700, 83801-84100, 86401-86700.
M. Godwin	E. A. Adams	1701-1900, 20001-20300, 23901-24200, 29701-29900, 127301-127500.
H. Starke	M. Morrison	1901-2100, 11201-11500, 22401-22700, 45301-45600, 54201-54500, 56101-56400, 67201-67500, 81501-81600, 96601-96900, 104501-104800, 113601-113900, 119101-119400.
V. M. Rind	V. K. Davies	2101-2300, 9501-9700, 14501-14800, 19101-19400, 31901-32000, 45601-45800, 49801-50100, 51601-51900, 55501-55800, 61101-61400, 68701-69000, 78701-79000, 104201-104500.

Register of Confederate States Treasury Notes—Continued.

ACT OF MARCH 23, 1863—Continued.

For Treasurer.	For Register.	Numbers of the notes signed.
		$1—A to H (1st series)—Continued.
R. F. Ball	L. M. Hunter	2301-2400, 10601-10900, 11501-11800, 15501-15800, 31701-31900, 38201-38300, 40001-40300, 47201-47400, 49501-49800, 51901-52200, 60801-61100, 75901-76200, 81201-81500, 92101-92400, 96301-96600, 105901-106300, 112201-112500, 121201-121500, 126701-127000.
V. M. Tyler	B. M. Payne	3201-3500, 17201-17500, 26301-26500, 33701-33900, 47801-48000, 101201-101500, 109401-109600, 133401-133700.
E. D. Layne	V. C. Watson	3501-3800, 19701-20000, 23301-23600, 29101-29300, 33501-33700, 42901-43100, 49301-49400, 51401-51600, 68101-68400, 79001-79300, 116101-116400, 123001-123300, 130101-130300.
R. Haynes	B. Dabney	3801-4100, 13901-14200, 22101-22400, 30901-31100, 33301-33500, 44501-44800, 50601-50900, 53101-53400, 59901-60200, 76801-77100, 87801-88100, 97801-97900, 108401-108600, 110501-110800, 116601-116900, 128701-129000.
S. G. Sanxay	L. Macon	4101-4400, 33101-33300, 43701-44000, 52501-52800, 56401-56700, 62601-62700, 83201-83500, 128401-128700.
M. E. Dudley	M. E. Norton	4401-4700, 18001-18300, 28501-28700, 34901-35100, 67801-68100, 102101-102400, 116401-116600, 121801-122000.
V. M. Stanard	S. C. Ellett	4701-5000, 18501-18800, 28701-28900, 34701-34900, 48201-48400, 68401-68700, 101801-102100, 127801-128100.
A. Harrison	E. C. Winston	5001-5300, 11801-12000, 13201-13600, 19401-19700, 23601-23900, 30301-30500, 32901-33100, 48601-48800, 55801-56100, 70001-70300, 81601-81900.
Do	J. Douglas	66861-66900, 112501-112800, 117701-118000, 130601-130800.
Do	M. Wade	96201-96300, 103901-104200.
E. C. Green	B. McRae	5301-5600, 12001-12300, 27501-27700, 35101-35300, 44801-45100, 57001-57300.
M. B. Christian	M. S. Apperson	5801-6000, 18301-18500, 35501-35700, 42701-42900, 51201-51400, 58901-59100, 62701-62900, 71101-71400, 84701-85000, 88901-89200, 93901-94200, 102701-103000, 113101-113300, 122401-122700, 130301-130600.
A. Points	M. Gay	6501-6800, 43401-43700, 52201-52500.
H. M. Douglass	F. C. Jones	6801-7000, 58601-58900, 97501-97800, 102401-102700, 116901-117200, 131101-131400.
M. S. Nicholas	J. McCarthy	7401-7700, 14201-14500, 22701-22900, 25001-25300, 29901-30100, 36101-36300, 48001-48200, 67501-67800, 80901-81200, 96001-96200, 103601-103900, 129001-129300, 133901-134200.
K. Heth	M. E. Gilliam	7701-8000, 15801-16100, 31301-31500, 36901-37100, 38001-38200, 39401-39700, 41801-42100, 42401-42700, 46401-46600, 50401-50600, 55101-55200, 62301-62600, 64101-64400, 65401-65700, 69301-69600, 74401-74700, 100001-100300, 103301-103600, 115201-115500, 120901-121200, 123301-123600.
L. C. Minor	B. M. Abbott	8001-8300, 23201-23300, 27301-27500, 34501-34700, 47601-47800, 59401-59600, 69601-69800, 79301-79600, 91701-91900, 97201-97500, 99701-100000, 105301-105600, 120301-120600, 126101-126400, 132401-132700.
L. Breeden	L. C. Royster	8301-8600, 16701-16900, 20901-21200, 25901-26100, 30501-30700, 38501-38800.
Do	M. Wade	57701-58000, 80601-80900, 88601-88900, 93601-93900.
Do	E. C. Winston	112801-113100, 118001-118300, 125801-126100.
E. Mason	M. C. Lathrop	8601-8900, 15101-15500, 29501-29700, 36701-36900, 46101-46400, 61401-61700, 63101-63500, 71701-72000, 73001-73200, 77701-78100, 81901-82300, 89401-89700, 91001-91300, 94501-94900, 98401-98700, 100301-100600, 106601-106900, 111001-111300, 115501-115800, 119601-120000, 124901-125200.
F. M. Dickins	F. E. Bernard	8901-9200, 12301-12600, 27101-27300, 34101-34300, 48801-49000, 52801-53100, 57301-57700, 78101-78400, 97901-98100, 99601-99700, 121501-121800, 132701-133000.
P. C. Bagby	J. Douglas	9201-9500, 12601-12900, 28301-28500, 38801-39100, 42101-42400, 47401-47600, 55201-55500, 61701-62000, 66701-66860.
E. P. Porter	A. P. Pellet	10001-10300, 16101-16400, 25601-25900, 32001-32100, 37701-38000, 41501-41800, 46901-47200, 54501-54800, 66001-66300, 72601-73000, 73801-74100, 74801-75100, 80201-80500, 85301-85600, 86101-86400, 92701-93000, 99301-99600, 108101-108400, 109901-110200, 114301-114600, 118901-119100, 125201-125500, 129601-129900, 135101-135400.

Register of Confederate States Treasury Notes—Continued.

ACT OF MARCH 23, 1863—Continued.

For Treasurer.	For Register.	Numbers of the notes signed.
		$1—A to H (1st series)—Continued.
H. Bartlett	M. Taylor	10301-10600, 11101-11200, 16401-16700, 25301-25600, 35301-35500, 41201-41500, 46601-46900, 54801-55100, 66301-66700, 72301-72600, 73501-73800, 75101-75400, 79901-80200, 85001-85300, 85801-86100, 86901-87200, 90301-90600, 92401-92700, 95201-95500, 99001-99300, 107801-108100, 109601-109900, 114601-114900, 118601-118900, 125501-125800, 129301-129600.
S. F. Shaver	M. Dixon	10901-11100, 28101-28300, 39101-39200, 59601-59900, 64801-65100, 70301-70600, 76501-76800, 82601-82900, 86701-86800, 87201-87500, 89701-90000, 94201-94500, 98701-99000, 107501-107800, 114001-114300, 123601-123900, 131401-131600, 133301-133400.
E. A. Dennison	J. L. Johnston	14801-15100, 20301-20600, 24201-24500, 27701-27900, 37101-37400, 40901-41200, 124201-124400, 131901-132100.
M. A. Dewees	S. E. Hughes	17501-17800, 26901-27100, 103001-103300, 117401-117700, 127501-127800, 134501-134800.
M. L. Quarles	F. G. Giles	20601-20900, 24501-24800, 44001-44200, 58001-58300, 76201-76300, 90601-90700, 101501-101800, 123901-124200, 131601-131900.
V. Bridges	E. W. Pendleton	26101-26300, 32701-32900, 43101-43400, 100901-101200, 109101-109400.
M. Allen	B. T. Lyon	26701-26900, 36301-36500, 44201-44500, 100601-100900.
W. A. Garrett	J. McGarr	29301-29500, 48401-48600, 110201-110500, 115801-116100, 129901-130100.
S. Lambert	P. Pleasants	56701-57000, 74701-74800, 75401-75600, 77101-77400, 82901-83200, 85701-85800, 107201-107500, 122001-122400, 130801-131100, 134801-135100.
M. Jones	E. Garlick	63801-64100, 65101-65400, 67101-67200, 77401-77700, 80501-80600, 85601-85700, 93001-93200, 104801-105100, 111601-111900, 120601-120900, 124601-124900.
M. Sommers	M. B. Kirby	127001-127300, 134201-134500.
		$1—A to H (2d series).
M. E. Dudley	M. E. Norton	1-300, 4201-4500, 12201-12500, 16401-16700, 18101-18400, 26201-26500, 28401-28700, 33601-33900, 36301-36600, 42001-42300, 45101-45400.
V. M. Stanard	S. C. Ellett	301-600.
Do	L. Devine	4901-5200, 11401-11700, 39201-39500, 42601-42900, 48601-48900.
Do	C. Sessions	25301-25600.
Do	M. Taylor	51001-51100.
S. F. Shaver	M. Dixon	601-900, 7601-8000, 19501-19800, 53701-54000.
M. B. Christian	M. S. Apperson	901-1200, 9101-9400, 16701-17000.
A. Harrison	J. Douglas	1201-1500, 8801-9100, 37701-38000.
E. P. Porter	A. P. Pellet	1501-1800, 29001-29300, 46601-46900.
H. Bartlett	M. Taylor	1801-2100, 10301-10500, 20901-21200, 23301-23600, 28701-29000, 46901-47200.
E. A. Dennison	J. L. Johnston	2101-2300.
Do	M. E. Gilliam	20301-20600, 30401-30700, 38001-38300, 47201-47500, 49601-49700.
M. L. Quarles	F. G. Giles	2301-2600, 11901-12200.
Do	C. Sessions	30101-30400.
Do	B. J. Clarke	34501-34800.
A. Points	M. Gay	2601-3000, 5201-5600.
M. Jones	E. Garlick	3001-3300.
L. C. Minor	B. M. Abbott	3301-3600, 9701-10000, 45401-45700.
Do	S. E. Hughes	24801-25000.
A. B. Capron	K. Walker	3601-3900, 8201-8500, 19801-20000, 31001-31300, 51701-52000.
M. S. Knox	M. W. Bailey	3901-4200, 39801-39900, 48301-48600.
M. Allen	H. L. Cooke	4501-4900, 10501-10900, 14801-15200, 26501-26900, 31701-32100, 52901-53200.
Do	M. Gay	22401-22800.
Do	M. Pace	34801-35100, 44001-44300.
Do	B. J. Clarke	39901-40200.
V. Bridges	E. W. Pendleton	5601-5900, 10901-11200, 15601-15900, 33001-33300.
I. Benton	M. Pace	5901-6100, 11701-11900, 16101-16300.
Do	L. Forde	29901-30100.

Register of Confederate States Treasury Notes—Continued.

ACT OF MARCH 23, 1863—Continued.

For Treasurer.	For Register.	Numbers of the notes signed.
		$1—A to H (2d series)—Continued.
S. G. Sanxay	L. Macon	6101–6400, 15901–16100, 27201–27500, 32401–32700, 35701–36000, 41101–41400, 44801–45100, 53401–53700.
V. B. Briggs	J. B. Tiffey	6401–6700, 23001–23300, 27501–27800.
M. Sommers	M. B. Kirby	6701–7000, 17001–17300, 36601–36900, 41401–41700, 45701–46000.
Do	E. Garlick	18901–19200.
H. Starke	M. Morrison	7001–7300, 8501–8800.
Do	C. Sessions	41701–42000, 47701–48000.
L. Breeden	E. C. Winston	7301–7600, 13301–13600, 18401–18600, 24501–24600, 30701–31000, 36901–37200, 47501–47700.
Do	L. Macon	24601–24800.
E. D. Layne	V. C. Watson	8001–8200, 14001–14300, 34201–34500, 42301–42600, 48101–48300.
Do	F. E. Bernard	23901–24200.
Do	E. W. Pendleton	38901–39000, 48001–48100.
Do	M. Johnson	39001–39200.
R. Haynes	B. Dabney	9401–9700, 12701–13000, 25901–26200.
V. M. Rind	V. K. Davies	10001–10300, 21201–21500, 43701–44000, 51101–51300.
Do	M. B. Kirby	51301–51400.
V. M. Tyler	B. M. Payne	11201–11400, 22801–23000, 26901–27200, 32101–32400, 35101–35400, 40201–40500, 44301–44500.
F. M. Dickins	F. E. Bernard	12501–12700.
H. M. Douglass	F. C. Jones	13001–13300, 16301–16400.
Do	M. Pace	23601–23900, 28101–28400.
E. O. Beall	E. A. Adams	13601–14000, 17701–18100, 38601–38900, 43401–43700, 48901–49200.
S. Lambert	P. Pleasants	14301–14500, 18601–18900, 39501–39800, 49201–49500.
E. Mason	M. C. Lathrop	14501–14800, 22101–22400, 50001–50300, 52401–52700.
M. A. Dewees	S. E. Hughes	15201–15300, 33901–34200, 36001–36300, 40801–41100, 46301–46600.
W. A. Garrett	J. McGarr	15301–15600, 20001–20300, 27801–28100.
Do	M. Dixon	32701–33000.
Do	C. Sessions	38301–38600.
R. F. Ball	M. L. Savage	17301–17700, 21801–22100.
L. Carter	M. Gay	19201–19400.
Do	M. Dixon	19401–19500.
Do	M. F. Stevens	25001–25300, 29601–29900, 37401–37700, 42901–43200, 46001–46300.
M. C. Irvine	M. Johnson	20601–20900, 49701–50000, 52701–52900.
M. Godwin	do	21501–21800, 29301–29600, 40501–40800.
Do	L. Forde	33301–33400.
Do	M. Pace	33401–33500.
Do	B. J. Clarke	33501–33600.
Do	J. L. Johnston	35401–35700, 44501–44800, 50301–50600.
M. S. Nicholas	J. McCarthy	24201–24500.
Do	M. B. Kirby	50601–50900.
Do	J. Douglas	51401–51700.
N. Semple	M. W. Bailey	25601–25900, 31301–31700.
Do	F. E. Bernard	54601–54800.
M. C. Waller	L. Forde	37201–37400, 43201–43400, 49501–49600.
Do	M. S. Apperson	53201–53400.
M. Gwynn	do	50901–51000, 52301–52400.
C. Hix	M. Gay	52001–52300.
W. L. Smalley	A. P. Pellet	54001–54300.
J. Wilson	J. B. Tiffey	54301–54600.
		$1—A to H (3d series).
J. Wilson	L. Forde	1–300.
Do	J. B. Tiffey	10401–10700.
V. Bridges	E. W. Pendleton	301–600.
L. Carter	M. F. Stevens	601–900, 7701–7800.
Do	B. J. Clarke	9401–9600.
Do	M. Taylor	9601–9700.
M. Allen	H. L. Cooke	901–1200, 9701–10100.
N. Semple	F. E. Bernard	1201–1500, 10101–10400.
W. A. Garrett	J. McGarr	1501–1800, 10901–11200.
M. Sommers	M. B. Kirby	1801–2100, 7401–7700.
M. A. Dewees	L. Macon	2101–2400, 5401–5700.

Register of Confederate States Treasury Notes—Continued.

ACT OF MARCH 23, 1863—Continued.

For Treasurer.	For Register.	Numbers of the notes signed.
		$1—A to H (3d series)—Continued.
M. A. Dewees	M. Gay	12601–12900.
L. Breeden	E. C. Winston	2401–2700.
M. C. Waller	L. Macon	2701–2900.
Do	A. P. Pellet	10701–10900.
M. E. Dudley	M. E. Norton	2901–3200, 14101–14400.
M. S. Knox	J. Douglas	3201–3500.
S. G. Sanxay	L. Macon	3501–3800, 9101–9400.
S. Lambert	P. Pleasants	3801–4100, 13501–13800.
H. Starke	C. Sessions	4101–4400.
Do	E. W. Pendleton	8501–8800, 11701–12000.
A. B. Capron	K. Walker	4401–4600, 6001–6300.
E. D. Layne	V. C. Watson	4601–4800.
S. F. Shaver	M. Dixon	4801–5100, 7101–7400.
Do	E. A. Adams	13201–13500.
M. S. Nicholas	M. S. Apperson	5101–5300.
Do	J. McCarthy	6801–7000.
E. Mason	M. C. Lathrop	5301–5400, 8201–8500.
B. J. Clarke	E. A. Adams	5701–6000.
R. F. Ball	L. Forde	6301–6600.
Do	E. C. Winston	12001–12300.
F. G. Giles	B. M. Payne	6601–6800.
M. Gwynn	M. S. Apperson	7001–7100.
M. C. Irvine	M. Johnson	8001–8200.
C. Hix	M. Gay	8801–9100.
V. M. Rind	V. K. Davies	11201–11500.
V. M. Tyler	B. M. Payne	11501–11700.
L. C. Minor	B. M. Abbott	12301–12600.
R. Haynes	B. Dabney	12901–13200.
V. M. Stanard	V. C. Watson	13801–14100.
M. Jones	E. Garlick	14401–14600.
E. A. Dennison	M. E. Gilliam	14601–14800.

ACT OF FEBRUARY 17, 1864.

For Treasurer.	For Register.	Numbers of the notes signed.
		$500—A to D.
J. C. Joplin	W. Miller	1–20000.
R. Haynes	L. W. Elliott	20001–28100, 30401–31500.
Do	V. Penrifoy	31501–31900.
A. S. Stuart	do	28101–30400, 31901–32900.
* * * *	* * * *	* * * * * * *
		$100—A to D.
T. W. Brown	J. Sands	1–300.
Do	J. H. Cooke	35501–35600.
Do	G. N. Warren	35601–36000.
A. Patton	L. P. Rogers	301–600, 6201–7000, 9401–10200, 11001–11800, 14601–15400, 16201–16400, 17201–18000, 19201–20000, 22201–23000, 24601–25400, 26201–27000, 32401–33200, 34001–34800.
F. C. Weisiger	J. H. Cooke	601–1700, 2201–3000, 4601–5400, 7001–7800, 11801–12600, 13401–13800, 18001–18400, 20801–21400, 27801–28400, 30801–31600, 34801–35500.
T. J. Hatch	W. Hancock	1701–2200, 3001–4600, 7801–8600, 12601–13400, 16401–17200.
C. Ashford	C. S. Taylor	5401–6200, 8601–9400, 10201–11000.
N. A. Bass	do	13801–14600.
J. A. Jones	G. N. Warren	15401–16200, 18401–19200, 20001–20800, 23001–23800, 25401–26200, 28401–29200, 30001–30800, 33201–34000.
W. G. Allen	C. S. Taylor	21401–22200, 23801–24600, 27001–27800, 29201–30000, 31601–32400.
N. Semple	M. E. Norton	36001–36500, 39301–39800.
Do	S. E. Hughes	46401–47000.
R. Macmurdo	B. W. Tyler	36501–36800.
Do	F. Rhett	41401–41800, 43001–43400, 44001–44400, 45001–45400, 46001–46400.

Register of Confederate States Treasury Notes—Continued.

ACT OF FEBRUARY 17, 1864—Continued.

For Treasurer.	For Register.	Numbers of the notes signed.
		$100—A to D—Continued.
N. Goodwin	L. Henry	36801-37200.
Do	E. Coffin	38801-39300, 41801-42400, 45401-46000.
M. Allen	H. L. Cooke	37201-38000, 40401-41400, 49001-49800.
A. Points	F. C. Jones	38001-38800, 59501-59600.
Do	E. S. Read	59401-59500, 59601-60000.
E. A. Dennison	M. E. Gilliam	39801-40400, 97401-98000.
Do	H. L. Cooke	85701-86300.
M. Selden	A. Zealy	42401-43000, 43401-44000, 44401-45000.
Do	A. P. Pellet	49801-50400.
Do	B. Dabney	83801-84400.
V. M. Rind	L. A. Norris	47001-47400.
Do	F. E. Bernard	78801-79400.
S. Scott	L. A. Norris	47401-48300, 54401-55000, 74701-75300, 89501-89900.
Do	J. McGarr	48301-48400.
Do	E. Davis	74501-74700.
J. Wilson	J. McGarr	48401-48800, 58001-59100, 65701-66300.
Do	E. Coffin	48801-49000.
N. Giles	E. S. Read	50401-51200.
A. Gray	M. Taylor	51201-51800.
M. Wade	E. Matthews	51801-52200.
Do	F. Rhett	52201-52400.
E. M. Bell	M. F. Jarvis	52401-52800, 55001-55700, 59101-59300, 88201-88900, 91401-91900.
Do	S. A. Doar	59301-59400.
M. S. Gist	M. J. Black	52801-53300.
Do	L. Pelot	90201-90400.
M. Godwin	B. W. Tyler	53301-53900.
J. Gill	L. Pelot	53901-54400.
L. Holmes	E. Davis	55701-56200.
Do	L. Michel	65101-65600, 67101-67700, 68401-68700, 73901-74500.
Do	E. S. Read	65601-65700.
J. Logan	N. Brisbane	56201-56400.
S. McCants	M. J. Black	56601-56900.
Do	C. Percival	67701-68400, 80801-81400.
A. Harrison	L. Macon	56901-57400.
M. Darby	H. E. Bryan	57401-57500.
Do	B. W. Tyler	57501-58000.
E. Kelly	J. De Leon	60001-60400.
J. Jacobs	M. E. Brady	60401-61000.
M. Dargan	L. W. Elliott	61001-61400, 66301-66700, 69401-69700.
Do	L. Arthur	83001-83300.
M. Kingman	L. Michel	61401-62000.
Do	K. P. Howell	69701-70100, 76101-76500, 81801-82300, 85001-85400, 96201-96300.
Do	M. A. Yates	76501-77100.
Do	E. Laurens	95801-96200, 96301-96400.
M. Reeves	C. Huger	62001-62400, 77901-78500.
J. Gott	M. E. Cullen	62401-63000, 80001-80800, 84401-85000.
J. H. Angel	M. A. Mobley	63001-63400.
E. Willis	J. M. Connor	63401-64000, 70101-70700.
S. R. Simons	S. Johnson	64001-64300.
Do	J. A. Acosta	64301-64400, 68701-69300, 86701-86800, 91901-92500, 92901-93500.
Do	H. L. Cooke	69301-69400.
C. White	M. J. Black	64401-65000.
Do	H. L. Cooke	65001-65100.
Do	M. E. Hamilton	90401-90600.
C. Morris	S. Johnson	66701-67100.
K. Korff	H. Heriot	70701-71200, 72701-73200.
Do	M. J. Black	88901-89500.
E. C. Trescot	V. Penrifoy	71201-71700, 83301-83800, 93801-94400.
A. Miller	S. E. Laval	71701-72400, 75501-76100, 81401-81800, 92501-92900, 95201-95400.
M. Cooper	C. C. Veal	72401-72700, 73201-73900, 82301-83000, 86801-87600.
Do	B. J. Clarke	94401-95200, 95401-95800.
M. Carrington	M. E. Hamilton	75301-75500.
H. Moise	S. Johnson	77101-77500.
S. Neill	B. Dabney	77501-77900.

Register of Confederate States Treasury Notes—Continued.

ACT OF FEBRUARY 17, 1864—Continued.

For Treasurer.	For Register.	Numbers of the notes signed.
		$100—A to D—Continued.
E. Baker	S. Johnson	78501–78600.
Do	J. M. Connor	78601–78800.
Do	H. Heriot	90601–91400.
K. Nelson	A. M. Foran	79401–80000.
J. Ambler	A. Zealy	85401–85700, 97001–97400.
R. Haynes	M. E. Harper	86301–86600.
Do	M. Gaither	86601–86700.
P. Savage	M. Dixon	87601–88200.
M. A. Dewees	H. E. Bryan	89901–90200.
H. Moore	E. Davis	93501–93800.
F. Waties	H. Barnwell	96401–97000.
		$100—A to D (1st series).
M. Kingman	K. P. Howell	1–600, 1501–2100, 4101–4300, 5101–5900, 9501–10100, 13501–14100, 17501–18100, 28901–29200.
Do	F. Rhett	19201–19500.
Do	M. F. Jarvis	49701–50000.
Do	N. E. Wingate	50001–50100.
Do	M. E. Hamilton	64501–65000.
Do	B. Dabney	88501–88900.
Do	F. E. Bernard	90801–91300.
M. Wade	E. Matthews	601–1200, 9301–9500, 18101–18500.
Do	M. A. Yates	52901–53400.
J. Jacobs	M. E. Brady	1201–1500, 22601–22800, 27301–27600.
J. Gott	M. E. Cullen	2101–2500, 10501–11100, 20501–21000.
E. M. Bell	E. Coffin	2501–3300.
Do	M. F. Jarvis	5901–7100, 34101–34600, 38401–38800, 43601–44200.
Do	M. Taylor	25401–25600.
S. McCants	C. Percival	3301–3500, 62301–62500, 74601–75200.
Do	J. D. Treadwell	79901–80500.
M. Cooper	C. C. Veal	3501–4100, 16101–16500.
Do	M. F. Jarvis	4501–5100.
Do	H. Heriot	42601–43300.
C. Morris	L. W. Elliott	4301–4500.
Do	L. Courtney	14101–14500.
Do	F. Rhett	16501–16700.
Do	M. Taylor	20201–20500.
L. Sims	H. Barnwell	7101–7300, 37601–38400.
Do	C. Percival	7301–7500.
Do	R. King	36601–37300.
Do	M. E. Cullen	46901–47100.
E. Baker	H. Heriot	7501–7700, 26601–27300, 29201–29700.
Do	B. W. Tyler	31401–31600.
Do	C. C. Veal	40001–40600, 57401–58200, 73201–74000, 75501–76300, 83501–84300.
S. R. Simons	B. J. Clarke	7701–8200.
Do	J. A. Acosta	12101–12500.
Do	E. C. Winston	82001–82600, 91301–91900.
K. Korff	M. J. Black	8201–8500.
Do	M. E. Hamilton	12501–13100.
Do	L. Michel	34601–34800.
C. White	M. E. Hamilton	8501–8800, 21501–22000, 30301–30600, 46601–46900.
Do	E. S. Read	75201–75500, 79201–79300.
S. Neill	F. E. Bernard	8801–9300, 14501–15100.
Do	E. S. Proctor	44201–44500.
S. G. Sanxay	M. Dixon	10101–10500, 42001–42600.
Do	B. Dabney	23701–23900.
Do	S. Johnson	23901–24100.
O. McGowan	L. Arthur	11101–11500, 17001–17500, 23601–23700.
M. Allen	F. C. Jones	11501–11900.
Do	S. Johnson	11901–12100.
E. A. Dennison	M. E. Gilliam	13101–13500.
Do	L. Michel	87901–88500.
H. Moore	E. Davis	15101–15500.
L. Holmes	F. Rhett	15501–16100.
Do	S. Huard	44501–44600.
J. Ambler	A. Zealy	16701–17000, 85201–85400.

Register of Confederate States Treasury Notes—Continued.

ACT OF FEBRUARY 17, 1864—Continued.

For Treasurer.	For Register.	Numbers of the notes signed.
		$100—A to D (1st series)—Continued.
J. Ambler	M. Pleasants	23101–23400.
Do	M. E. Brady	35601–36000.
Do	J. De Leon	38801–39300.
Do	L. Michel	48701–49000.
Do	H. E. Bryan	66301–66800.
Do	C. Huger	84901–85200.
A. Miller	S. E. Laval	18501–19200, 19501–20200, 22001–22600, 28601–28900, 31001–31400, 33601–34100, 54601–55200, 77601–78300, 81101–81400.
S. J. Adams	H. C. Thomas	21001–21500, 35301–35600, 56801–57400, 60301–60600, 63501–64000.
Do	E. S. Read	61701–62300.
Do	M. Kirk	66101–66300, 67001–67600, 79301–79900, 84301–84900.
Do	M. E. Harper	69301–69900.
F. Waties	H. Barnwell	22801–23100, 46101–46600, 47701–48200, 62501–62900.
N. Goodwin	E. Coffin	23401–23600, 41601–42000, 50601–50900, 54301–54600, 58201–58400, 60601–61100.
Do	E. Davis	67601–68200.
Do	L. Macon	68701–69200.
Do	M. Dixon	69201–69300, 70501–71100, 89301–89500, 90401–90800.
Do	E. S. Read	82901–83500.
Do	L. A. Norris	86701–87300.
Do	M. B. Kirby	88901–89300.
J. H. Angel	C. Huger	24101–24400, 62901–63500.
J. Gill	B. J. Clarke	24401–24600, 32601–33100.
M. A. Dewees	H. E. Bryan	24601–25000, 25801–26300, 29701–30000, 31901–32200, 36001–36600, 48201–48700, 50101–50600, 58401–59000, 80501–80600, 89501–90100, 90301–90400.
R. Haynes	M. Gaither	25001–25200, 25601–25800, 30001–30300, 85401–85900, 92301–92600.
Do	M. Taylor	25201–25400.
Do	S. K. Wells	31601–31900.
Do	E. Davis	34801–35300.
Do	L. W. Elliott	56601–56800, 72001–72600.
Do	M. Pleasants	77001–77500.
M. Selden	B. Dabney	26301–26600, 27601–27900, 71101–71500, 77501–77600, 86201–86700.
Do	L. Devine	47101–47700, 49001–49600.
Do	A. Zealy	59001–59400.
M. Boyd	S. A. Doar	27901–28300, 33101–33500.
Do	F. Rhett	51201–51600.
H. Balaguer	S. Huard	28301–28600, 53801–54300.
S. Scott	M. F. Stevens	30601–31000.
Do	L. A. Norris	39301–39600, 53601–53800.
E. Kelly	J. A. Acosta	32201–32600.
Do	B. W. Tyler	64001–64500.
F. Stocker	N. E. Wingate	33501–33600.
Do	M. F. Stevens	76301–76900.
P. Savage	L. Macon	37301–37600.
M. Dargan	L. W. Elliott	39601–40000, 44601–45100.
Do	L. Arthur	56101–56600, 65301–65500.
Do	R. King	61101–61700.
Do	J. M. Connor	69901–70500.
M. S. Gist	F. C. Jones	40601–41400.
Do	B. Dabney	82601–82900.
Do	C. Huger	91901–92100.
A. Caldwell	J. D. Treadwell	41401–41600, 78901–79200.
Do	F. Rhett	49601–49700.
J. Wilson	N. Brisbane	43301–43600.
Do	E. S. Read	52401–52900.
M. Banks	M. E. Harper	45101–46100, 59701–60300, 65501–66100, 66801–67000, 72601–73200, 87301–87900.
M. Carrington	M. Pleasants	50901–51200, 65001–65300.
M. Reeves	E. S. Proctor	51601–52000, 53401–53600.
E. McCully	L. Arthur	52001–52400.
Do	A. S. Parry	55201–55600.
Do	J. D. Treadwell	85901–86200.
J. Logan	N. Brisbane	55601–56100.
M. Godwin	M. Dixon	59401–59700.

Register of Confederate States Treasury Notes—Continued.

ACT OF FEBRUARY 17, 1864—Continued.

For Treasurer.	For Register.	Numbers of the notes signed.
		$100—A to D (1st series)—Continued.
N. Semple	M. E. Norton	68201–68700, 74001–74600, 76901–77000.
Do	R. King	71501–72000.
Do	M. Taylor	78301–78900.
E. C. Trescot	V. Penrifoy	80601–80900.
Do	S. E. Laval	80901–81100.
A. S. Stuart	M. Taylor	81401–82000.
Do	B. Dabney	92601–93200.
A. Harrison	E. C. Winston	90101–90300.
Do	M. E. Norton	93201–93600.
R. Macmurdo	E. S. Proctor	92101–92300.
		$100—A to D (2d series).
* * * *	* * * *	* * * * * * *
		$50—wA to zA.
N. A. Bass	J. Gibson	1–400, 3801–4600.
Do	C. S. Taylor	18401–19200, 22001–22800, 23901–24300.
Do	J. H. Cooke	35101–35700.
Do	W. O. Slade	38101–38700, 40501–41300.
Do	J. Sands	38701–38900.
J. A. Jones	G. N. Warren	401–800, 1701–2100, 5401–6200, 9001–9800, 11201–12000, 16001–17600, 19601–20400, 21201–22000, 23101–23900.
T. W. Brown	J. Sands	801–900, 2101–2900, 9801–10600, 12801–13600, 14401–15200, 19201–19600.
Do	W. O. Slade	26701–27100, 27901–28500, 30901–31500, 33101–33500, 35701–36500.
Do	J. H. Cooke	33501–33900.
Do	W. Hancock	42101–42300.
C. Ashford	J. J. Matthews	901–1700, 4601–5400.
F. H. Link	W. O. Slade	2901–3800, 8401–9000, 12001–12800, 17601–18400, 20401–20800.
Do	J. Sands	20801–21000, 24301–25100, 27101–27900, 29301–30100, 31501–32300, 34701–35100, 36501–37300, 38901–39700.
Do	J. H. Cooke	21001–21200.
A. Patton	L. P. Rogers	6201–7000, 22801–23100.
Do	J. Sands	7801–8200.
Do	W. O. Slade	8201–8400.
T. J. Hatch	W. Hancock	7001–7800, 25101–25900, 28501–29300, 30101–30900, 32301–33100, 33901–34700, 37301–38100, 39701–40500.
W. G. Allen	J. J. Matthews	10601–11200, 13601–14400.
Do	C. S. Taylor	15201–16000, 25901–26700, 41301–42100.
N. Semple	M. E. Norton	42301–42900, 51501–51900.
A. Harrison	L. Devine	42901–43500.
M. A. Dewees	S. E. Hughes	43501–44100.
E. A. Dennison	M. E. Gilliam	44101–44700.
N. Goodwin	L. Henry	44701–45100.
Do	E. Coffin	51901–52300, 55901–56300, 57901–58400, 64001–64400, 67001–67400.
Do	H. L. Cooke	60001–60400.
Do	M. Kirk	67401–68000.
R. Macmurdo	B. W. Tyler	45101–45500.
N. Giles	E. S. Read	45501–46100, 48901–49700, 55101–55900, 57101–57900, 59201–60000, 80601–81200.
Do	E. Matthews	81201–81400.
L. C. Minor	E. C. Winston	46101–46300, 65801–66400.
M. Selden	A. P. Pellet	46301–46900, 48301–48900, 50301–50900, 52501–52700, 52801–52900, 78201–78800.
Do	M. Kirk	52301–52500.
Do	J. De Leon	52701–52800.
M. Allen	H. L. Cooke	46901–47700, 53501–55100, 56301–57100, 58401–59200, 60401–61100, 61301–61400, 62401–63200, 64401–65200.
Do	F. C. Jones	61101–61300.
Do	A. S. Parry	84601–84800, 85001–85400.
Do	H. Heriot	84801–85000.
A. Points	F. C. Jones	47701–48300, 50901–51500, 52901–53500, 61401–62100, 62301–62400, 63201–64000, 65201–65800, 69201–69900, 73401–74100, 77001–77600, 79401–80000.

Register of Confederate States Treasury Notes—Continued.

ACT OF FEBRUARY 17, 1864—Continued.

For Treasurer.	For Register.	Numbers of the notes signed.
		$50—wA to zA—Continued.
A. Points	H. L. Cooke	62101–62300.
Do	M. A. Yates	93401–94000.
M. Darby	B. W. Tyler	49701–50300, 80401–80600.
Do	K. P. Howell	80001–80200.
Do	C. Huger	80201–80300.
Do	S. K. Wells	80301–80400.
P. Savage	L. Macon	66401–66900.
Do	M. Kirk	66901–67000.
E. M. Bell	M. F. Jarvis	68001–68600, 76201–76400, 81401–82000.
S. McCants	B. J. Clarke	68601–69100.
Do	M. F. Jarvis	69101–69200.
Do	M. J. Black	85401–86000.
Do	C. Percival	95401–96000.
L. Holmes	E. Davis	69901–71000.
S. Scott	L. A. Norris	71001–71600, 90701–91400.
J. Gill	L. Pelot	71601–72200.
Do	B. J. Clarke	92801–93400.
J. Logan	N. Brisbane	72201–72600, 74801–75200, 79201–79400, 87401–87900.
Do	M. Kirk	72601–72800, 75201–75400.
Do	F. Rhett	87901–88000.
M. S. Gist	M. Kirk	72801–73000.
Do	S. Johnson	73001–73400.
J. Wilson	M. Kirk	74101–74300.
Do	S. E. Laval	74301–74500.
Do	K. P. Howell	74501–74700.
Do	S. Southall	74701–74800.
Do	J. McGarr	76401–77000.
Do	J. M. Connor	77601–78200.
Do	A. S. Parry	83201–83400.
M. Reeves	C. Huger	75401–75800, 94001–94500.
Do	E. S. Read	94501–94600.
C. Morris	E. S. Proctor	75801–76200, 78801–79200.
E. Kelly	J. De Leon	82001–82400, 84001–84600, 91501–91800, 94901–95100.
Do	L. Michel	82401–82600.
Do	B. W. Tyler	91401–91500, 95101–95400.
Do	A. S. Parry	91801–92200, 94601–94900.
M. Kingman	L. Michel	82601–83200, 83401–83700, 83901–84000.
Do	H. Heriot	83701–83900.
V. M. Tyler	M. Kirk	86001–86600.
M. Boyd	S. A. Doar	86601–87000.
S. Neill	E. Laurens	87001–87400.
M. Wade	E. Matthews	88001–88400.
J. Gott	M. E. Cullen	88401–88900.
M. Carrington	M. E. Hamilton	89001–89200.
Do	L. Pelot	89201–89300.
Do	S. Southall	89301–89400.
H. Moise	S. Johnson	89401–89900.
M. Cooper	M. S. Apperson	89901–90700.
E. Willis	J. M. Connor	92201–92800.
J. Jacobs	M. E. Brady	96001–96600.
A. Miller	S. E. Laval	96601–97000.
		$50—wA to zA (1st series).
F. Stocker	S. K. Wells	1–600, 58101–58300.
Do	A. Zealy	89301–89400.
S. Neill	M. F. Jarvis	601–700.
Do	M. Dixon	701–1100.
Do	J. M. Connor	1101–1200.
Do	M. A. Yates	10901–11500.
L. Sims	A. S. Parry	1201–1800.
Do	N. E. Wingate	43801–44600.
Do	E. Matthews	81301–81500.
M. Dargan	L. W. Elliott	1801–2000, 58901–59500, 91201–91300.
Do	L. Arthur	33901–34200.
A. Points	E. C. Winston	2001–2600, 9201–9400, 12701–12900.
Do	M. A. Yates	9401–9500.
Do	C. Percival	9501–9600.

Register of Confederate States Treasury Notes—Continued.

ACT OF FEBRUARY 17, 1864—Continued.

For Treasurer.	For Register.	Numbers of the notes signed.
		$50—wA to zA (1st series)—Continued.
A. Points	R. King	9601-9800.
Do	M. Gaither	9801-10000.
J. Gill	B. J. Clarke	2601-3000, 45601-46400.
Do	M. Taylor	3001-3400.
M. Wade	E. Matthews	3401-4000, 16301-16900, 39401-40100, 88101-88700.
M. Godwin	M. B. Kirby	4001-4600, 8801-9200, 12101-12700.
A. Miller	S. E. Laval	4601-5200, 6001-6800, 38001-38200, 54401-55200, 67101-67800, 75401-76200, 83801-84400, 86301-86900, 91301-92000.
Do	H. E. Alexander	5201-5300.
M. Cooper	M. Taylor	5301-5900.
Do	H. E. Alexander	5901-6000.
Do	C. C. Veal	7501-8800, 14901-15700, 36601-37400, 42301-43100, 50501-51300, 55801-56400, 92001-92700.
Do	L. Devine	10601-10700.
Do	J. D. Treadwell	64101-64900.
Do	B. J. Clarke	68401-68800, 70301-71000, 72901-74200, 79301-79900.
Do	M. E. Hamilton	72301-72900.
E. C. Trescot	V. Penrifoy	6801-7500, 10001-10600, 14301-14900, 15701-16300, 35401-35500, 63501-64100, 66001-66500, 67801-68400, 76201-76800.
O. McGowan	L. Arthur	10701-10900, 51301-51900, 64901-65500, 78301-78500, 88701-89300.
Do	J. A. Acosta	80901-81300.
S. R. Simons	do	11501-12100, 30001-30500, 66501-67100.
Do	M. E. Hamilton	30501-30600.
Do	E. Coffin	56401-56900.
H. Moise	M. B. Kirby	12901-13100.
Do	S. Johnson	29201-29400, 65501-66000.
Do	M. Taylor	80501-80900.
K. Korff	H. Heriot	13101-13700, 25901-26200, 34201-34800.
Do	M. Taylor	27701-27900.
Do	M. J. Black	52401-52600.
C. White	do	13701-14300, 17801-18400, 23301-24000, 31701-32400.
Do	M. E. Hamilton	86901-87300.
M. Selden	M. Gaither	16901-17500.
Do	B. Dabney	40101-40900, 44601-45200, 56901-57500.
S. Fuller	R. King	17501-17800, 89601-89800.
V. M. Tyler	M. Kirk	18401-19000.
J. H. Angel	E. Coffin	19001-19100.
Do	M. A. Mobley	19101-19300.
Do	M. E. Brady	37401-37900.
Do	M. B. Kirby	40901-41200, 58301-58900.
J. Gott	M. E. Cullen	19301-20000, 22601-23300, 26201-26900, 27901-28400, 30601-30900, 87301-88100.
Do	S. A. Doar	20001-20100.
E. Kelly	B. W. Tyler	20101-20800, 22001-22500, 28401-29200.
Do	S. Huard	22501-22600.
Do	F. Rhett	71001-71600.
J. Jacobs	M. E. Brady	20801-21300.
Do	J. D. Treadwell	21301-21400.
F. Waties	N. E. Wingate	21401-21900, 33401-33900.
Do	M. A. Yates	21901-22000.
Do	H. Barnwell	49201-49500, 52601-53200, 57501-58100, 81501-82000.
Do	E. Matthews	90801-91000.
E. Baker	A. P. Pellet	24001-24100, 38201-38300.
Do	S. Johnson	24701-25200.
Do	H. Heriot	26901-27700, 30901-31700, 34801-35400, 47301-47600, 84401-84800, 89801-90200.
Do	L. W. Elliott	48201-49000.
C. Morris	M. Taylor	24101-24500.
Do	L. Courtney	24501-24700, 38601-38700, 43101-43400.
Do	H. E. Bryan	51901-52400.
Do	M. E. Norton	61401-61900.
Do	J. De Leon	80301-80500.
M. S. Gist	L. Pelot	25201-25900, 59501-60100, 95001-95400.
Do	A. P. Pellet	37901-38000.
Do	M. E. Brady	94801-95000.
M. Kingman	K. P. Howell	29401-29800, 38301-38400, 38701-39300, 55201-55800, 68801-69400, 77401-77800, 83301-83800, 85801-86300, 93301-93900.

Register of Confederate States Treasury Notes—Continued.

ACT OF FEBRUARY 17, 1864—Continued.

For Treasurer.	For Register.	Numbers of the notes signed.
		$50—wA to zA (1st series)—Continued.
M. Kingman	S. E. Laval	29801–30000.
H. Moore	E. Davis	32401–32800, 41201–41800, 46401–47000.
S. G. Sanxay	M. Dixon	32801–33400, 69901–70300.
L. Armstrong	S. E. Hughes	35501–35900.
Do	H. E. Alexander	41801–42300.
Do	M. S. Apperson	79901–80300.
Do	E. Davis	85301–85800.
Do	J. De Leon	92701–93300.
E. McCully	A. S. Parry	39301–39400.
M. Boyd	S. A. Doar	35901–36300, 84801–85300, 89401–89600.
M. Darby	J. De Leon	36301–36600, 45201–45600.
A. Harrison	L. Devine	38401–38600, 60701–61400, 71601–72300, 82001–82600.
Do	M. E. Harper	49501–49900.
P. Savage	L. Macon	43401–43800, 62901–63400, 74801–75400, 76801–77400, 77801–78300.
Do	E. Matthews	63401–63500.
M. Carrington	M. B. Kirby	47001–47300.
Do	E. S. Proctor	69401–69900.
J. Ambler	A. Zealy	47601–48200, 49901–50500, 53801–54100, 62501–62900, 83001–83300.
Do	E. Matthews	54101–54400.
G. Loyd	H. E. Alexander	49001–49200, 91001–91200.
J. Logan	N. Brisbane	53201–53800, 82601–83000.
E. Willis	J. M. Connor	60101–60700.
R. Haynes	E. Coffin	61901–62500.
S. McCants	C. Percival	74201–74800, 78801–79300.
E. M. Bell	M. F. Jarvis	90201–90600, 93901–94700.
A. Caldwell	J. D. Treadwell	90601–90800.
E. A. Dennison	M. E. Gilliam	94701–94800.
		$50—wA to zA (2d series).
J. Gott	M. E. Cullen	1–800, 6501–7100, 12501–13100, 16301–17200, 18501–18900.
S. J. Adams	H. C. Thomas	801–1400, 23501–23900, 25601–26100, 33001–33300, 65501–65900, 76201–76700, 80001–80500, 94301–94600, 95901–96500.
Do	E. Davis	59501–60100, 62001–62600.
Do	M. Taylor	65901–66100.
Do	F. Rhett	84301–84800.
K. Korff	M. J. Black	1401–2000, 7101–7500, 11401–12000, 14001–14500, 15201–15800.
Do	F. C. Jones	64901–65500.
Do	J. A. Acosta	87301–87900.
E. A. Dennison	M. E. Gilliam	2001–2100.
A. Harrison	L. Devine	2101–2500, 22101–22400, 32501–32700, 34701–34800, 93401–94000.
H. Moore	E. Davis	2501–2700.
A. Miller	S. E. Laval	2701–3500, 8501–9300, 27201–27900, 78801–79500.
S. McCants	C. Percival	3501–4100, 9301–9900, 57501–57900, 77801–78400.
C. Morris	L. Courtney	4101–4500.
Do	F. Rhett	8301–8500, 15801–16300.
Do	S. Huard	12001–12500.
Do	M. Taylor	13101–13400, 48101–48500.
Do	M. E. Norton	48501–48600.
Do	M. Kirk	58901–59200.
M. Kingman	K. P. Howell	4501–5100, 13401–14000, 23901–24400, 50901–51500, 62901–63500, 72501–73000.
Do	F. Rhett	10501–10800.
Do	L. Macon	75301–75700.
Do	L. Pelot	75701–75800.
Do	M. F. Jarvis	80501–80600.
P. Savage	L. Macon	5101–5700, 21801–22100, 26601–26900, 36301–36600, 46701–47200, 78401–78800, 88701–89200.
E. M. Bell	M. F. Jarvis	5701–6500, 18901–19300, 22501–22900, 29001–29400, 40901–41100, 48901–49300, 52301–52900, 55501–56200, 68001–68600.
M. Wade	E. Matthews	7501–7900, 10801–11400, 31901–32200.
Do	A. S. Parry	42601–42800.
Do	R. King	42801–42900.
Do	L. Michel	89201–89700, 94601–95100.

Register of Confederate States Treasury Notes—Continued.

ACT OF FEBRUARY 17, 1864—Continued.

For Treasurer.	For Register.	Numbers of the notes signed.
		$50—wA to zA (2d series)—Continued.
F. Waties	H. Barnwell	7901-8300, 54501-54900, 66101-66600, 71301-71800, 80601-80800, 82901-83400.
Do	M. A. Yates	26101-26600.
Do	M. F. Stevens	39701-40100.
Do	E. Coffin	41101-41300.
Do	A. S. Parry	41301-41600.
Do	E. C. Winston	56601-56900.
M. A. Dewees	H. E. Bryan	9901-10500, 36001-36300, 92401-92800, 96501-96700.
C. White	M. E. Hamilton	14501-15000, 18401-18500, 22901-23500, 32901-33000, 44201-44600.
Do	H. Barnwell	15001-15200.
Do	M. E. Norton	43901-44200.
O. McGowan	F. Rhett	17201-17800.
Do	L. Devine	41601-42000.
Do	A. S. Parry	42001-42100.
Do	E. Davis	81301-81500, 83901-84300.
S. R. Simons	J. A. Acosta	17801-18400.
Do	E. C. Winston	68601-69100, 69401-69600.
J. H. Angel	C. Huger	19301-19700, 82401-82900, 89701-90200.
M. Selden	B. Dabney	19701-20100, 34401-34700.
Do	S. Johnson	25401-25600.
Do	H. E. Alexander	35701-36000.
J. Gill	B. J. Clarke	20101-20500.
H. Balaguer	S. Huard	20501-20900, 28901-29000, 90201-90600.
J. Logan	N. Brisbane	20901-21200, 38601-38900, 91101-91400.
Do	J. A. Acosta	29801-30100.
M. Ringgold	L. Henry	21201-21500.
Do	A. Zealy	92001-92200.
Do	F. C. Jones	92201-92400.
M. Dargan	L. W. Elliott	21501-21800, 30101-30400.
Do	J. D. Treadwell	42101-42600.
Do	M. Kirk	69101-69400.
Do	L. Arthur	81501-81600, 86701-87300.
J. Ambler	M. B. Kirby	22401-22500.
Do	M. A. Yates	30401-30700.
Do	M. Taylor	50601-50900.
Do	L. Michel	58501-58900, 70801-71300, 73001-73600.
N. Goodwin	E. Coffin	24401-24900, 28701-28900, 31301-31600, 43401-43900, 46101-46700, 47601-48100, 50101-50600, 53701-54100, 69601-70000, 85601-86100, 90601-91100, 94001-94300, 95101-95600.
Do	E. S. Proctor	30701-30900.
Do	E. Davis	37201-37500.
M. Boyd	J. D. Treadwell	24901-25200.
Do	M. Kirk	25201-25400.
Do	J. M. Connor	87901-88300.
J. Jacobs	M. E. Brady	26901-27200, 31601-31900, 36601-36900, 37901-38200.
Do	N. Brisbane	74201-74600.
Do	H. Thomas	74601-74800.
E. Kelly	B. W. Tyler	27901-28500, 56201-56600.
Do	L. W. Elliott	28501-28700.
Do	M. E. Cullen	34001-34200.
Do	R. King	34201-34400.
S. Scott	M. E. Cullen	29401-29800.
Do	M. F. Stevens	37501-37900.
Do	L. A. Norris	67201-67400.
E. Baker	H. Heriot	30901-31000.
Do	B. W. Tyler	34901-35100.
Do	R. King	44901-45700.
Do	M. E. Hamilton	49301-50100.
Do	E. Coffin	51501-52300.
Do	C. C. Veal	52901-53100, 56901-57500, 60101-60900, 63501-64300, 86101-86700.
M. Carrington	L. Michel	31001-31300.
Do	M. E. Gilliam	45701-46100.
Do	M. Pleasants	47201-47500.
Do	M. F. Stevens	47501-47600.
Do	E. S. Proctor	54101-54400.
Do	E. Coffin	54401-54500.

Register of Confederate States Treasury Notes—Continued.

ACT OF FEBRUARY 17, 1864—Continued.

For Treasurer.	For Register.	Numbers of the notes signed.
		$50—wA to zA (2d series)—Continued.
R. Haynes	M. Gaither	32201-32500.
Do	B. W. Tyler	64301-64700, 64801-64900.
Do	M. Taylor	64701-64800.
E. McCully	M. E. Cullen	32701-32900.
Do	L. Devine	40501-40900.
Do	A. S. Parry	48601-48700.
Do	J. M. Connor	48701-48900.
M. S. Gist	B. J. Clarke	33301-33700.
Do	M. E. Cullen	38201-38600.
V. M. Tyler	S. Huard	33701-34000.
Do	M. Pleasants	36901-37200.
S. Fuller	R. King	34801-34900, 81101-81300.
S. Neill	F. E. Bernard	35101-35400.
L. Holmes	N. E. Wingate	35401-35700.
Do	S. Huard	60901-61400.
Do	M. A. Yates	66601-67200.
F. Stocker	N. E. Wingate	38901-39200.
Do	M. F. Stevens	83401-83900.
S. G. Sanxay	L. Arthur	39201-39700.
Do	M. Dixon	53101-53700.
M. Banks	M. E. Harper	40101-40500, 42901-43400, 54901-55500, 61401-62000, 79501-80000, 92801-93400.
M. Cooper	A. S. Parry	44601-44900.
Do	H. Heriot	62601-62900, 84801-85400.
A. Caldwell	J. D. Treadwell	57901-58500.
Do	F. Rhett	73601-74100, 76801-77300.
Do	F. H. Marks	74101-74200, 76701-76800.
Do	M. A. Yates	95601-95900.
J. Wilson	N. Brisbane	59201-59500.
L. Sims	M. E. Cullen	67401-68000, 70001-70600, 88301-88700.
Do	B. W. Tyler	70601-70800.
Do	B. J. Clarke	71801-72500.
A. S. Stuart	M. Taylor	74801-75300, 81601-82100, 85401-85600, 91401-92000.
M. Darby	M. B. Kirby	75801-76200.
E. C. Trescot	V. Penrifoy	77301-77800.
L. Armstrong	H. E. Alexander	80801-81100.
M. Reeves	E. S. Proctor	82101-82400.
		$50—wA to zA (3d series).
S. J. Adams	H. C. Thomas	1-500.
Do	M. Kirk	7101-7500, 18601-19200.
M. A. Dewees	H. E. Bryan	501-900, 1801-2400, 25401-25900, 28901-29500.
R. Haynes	L. W. Elliott	901-1100, 2401-2600, 11201-11500.
Do	B. Dabney	24401-24900.
Do	L. A. Norris	26701-26900.
Do	F. C. Jones	26901-27200.
Do	M. Gaither	29501-30000.
Do	E. Davis	35301-35400.
S. Scott	M. Kirk	1101-1600.
F. Waties	H. Barnwell	1601-1800.
Do	J. M. Connor	23701-24100.
J. H. Angel	C. Huger	2601-2700.
S. Neill	F. E. Bernard	2701-2800.
L. Armstrong	M. Kirk	2801-3300.
M. Wade	M. A. Yates	3301-3800.
E. C. Trescot	V. Penrifoy	3801-4800, 7001-7100.
M. Selden	M. F. Jarvis	4801-5400.
Do	B. Dabney	15101-15600.
M. Godwin	E. Davis	5401-5900.
Do	M. Dixon	14501-15100.
M. Kingman	M. E. Hamilton	5901-6100.
Do	F. E. Bernard	33301-33900.
N. Semple	L. Michel	6101-6600.
Do	M. E. Norton	7501-8000, 8901-9400, 16201-16800, 20201-20700.
Do	R. King	12201-12300.
A. S. Stuart	M. Taylor	6601-7000, 8001-8200.
A. Miller	S. E. Laval	8201-8300, 10801-11200, 11501-12200, 21901-22500.

Register of Confederate States Treasury Notes—Continued.

ACT OF FEBRUARY 17, 1864—Continued.

For Treasurer.	For Register.	Numbers of the notes signed.
		$50—wA to zA (3d series)—Continued.
A. Miller	J. M. Connor	22501-22900.
N. Goodwin	L. Arthur	8301-8900.
Do	M. Dixon	30001-30600.
Do	M. B. Kirby	32401-33000.
M. Darby	M. Pleasants	9401-9900.
M. S. Gist	J. D. Treadwell	9901-10500.
Do	H. Heriot	10501-10700.
Do	M. Dixon	13901-14500.
Do	M. E. Harper	27201-27700.
J. Logan	N. Brisbane	10701-10800.
Do	B. W. Tyler	19201-19800, 21301-21900.
E. M. Bell	L. Pelot	12301-13100.
Do	M. F. Jarvis	17201-17800.
E. Baker	C. C. Veal	13101-13900, 28301-28900.
Do	H. E. Bryan	31001-31800.
Do	R. King	33901-34700.
A. Harrison	H. E. Bryan	15601-16200, 16801-17200, 18001-18600.
Do	V. Penrifoy	20701-21300.
C. White	E. S. Read	19801-20200, 25901-26700.
A. Caldwell	J. D. Treadwell	22901-23200.
J. Ambler	M. Pleasants	23201-23700.
Do	A. Zealy	30601-31000.
K. Korff	F. C. Jones	24101-24400.
E. A. Dennison	J. M. Connor	24901-25400.
Do	B. Dabney	34701-35300.
F. Stocker	M. F. Stevens	27701-28300.
M. Banks	M. E. Harper	31801-32400.
L. Sims	M. E. Cullen	33001-33300.
* * * *	* * * *	* * * * * * *
		$50—wA to zA (4th series).
* * * *	* * * *	* * * * * * *
		$20—A to D.
M. Allen	H. L. Cooke	1-500, 19101-19900.
J. Wilson	J. B. Tiffey	501-1000, 4801-4900.
Do	J. McGarr	29201-29600, 61101-61800.
E. A. Dennison	M. E. Gilliam	1001-1100, 2201-2400.
M. E. Dudley	M. E. Norton	1101-1200, 4201-4300.
M. A. Dewees	S. E. Hughes	1201-1300, 2701-2800, 4301-4400, 6501-6700.
C. Hix	M. Gay	1301-1500, 2501-2600, 3401-3500.
Do	E. W. Pendleton	5901-6100.
Do	B. J. Clarke	27801-28400, 39101-39700.
M. S. Nicholas	M. C. Lathrop	1501-1600, 2401-2500.
R. Haynes	B. Dabney	1601-1700, 3201-3300, 36901-37500, 42901-43500.
Do	L. Pelot	24201-24800.
W. L. Smalley	B. J. Clarke	1701-1800, 3501-3600, 3901-4000.
S. F. Shaver	M. Dixon	1801-1900, 3701-3800, 5001-5100, 20301-20700.
Do	B. Dabney	19901-20300.
R. F. Ball	E. C. Winston	1901-2100, 6101-6300.
S. Clark	M. W. Bailey	2101-2200, 2901-3000, 4601-4700, 6301-6500.
S. G. Sanxay	L. Macon	2601-2700, 3001-3100, 7901-8100.
Do	M. Dixon	40701-41300.
V. M. Rind	V. K. Davies	2801-2900, 7101-7500.
Do	do	24801-25400, 33701-34300, 43501-44100.
M. C. Irvine	M. Taylor	3101-3200, 4401-4500.
A. Harrison	J. Douglas	3301-3400, 4901-5000.
L. C. Minor	B. M. Abbott	3601-3700.
Do	M. E. Norton	32701-33300.
Do	E. C. Winston	35701-36300, 48601-49200.
V. M. Stanard	L. Devine	3801-3900, 4001-4100.
L. Carter	M. F. Stevens	4101-4200, 6701-7100.
N. Semple	F. E. Bernard	4501-4600.
V. M. Tyler	B. M. Payne	4701-4800.
Do	M. Pleasants	29601-30000.
Do	M. Taylor	46101-46700.

Register of Confederate States Treasury Notes—Continued.

ACT OF FEBRUARY 17, 1864—Continued.

For Treasurer.	For Register.	Numbers of the notes signed.
		$20—A to D—Continued.
V. M. Tyler	J. A. Acosta	54401-54600.
Do	L. Macon	54601-54900.
Do	B. J. Clarke	57601-58200.
Do	S. E. Laval	61801-62100, 62301-62400.
Do	M. Kirk	62101-62200, 73801-74200.
Do	C. Percival	62201-62300.
Do	S. Huard	76401-76500.
Do	L. Pelot	76501-76600.
E. Mason	M. C. Lathrop	5101-5900.
W. A. Garrett	J. McGarr	7501-7900.
F. H. Link	W. O. Slade	8101-8900, 11701-12500, 14701-15500, 16501-17300, 18201-18600.
Do	J. Sands	18601-18900, 20701-21200.
F. C. Weisiger	J. H. Cooke	8901-9700, 10901-11700, 15701-16500, 17601-18200, 22201-22700.
C. Ashford	J. Sands	9701-10100.
J. A. Jones	G. N. Warren	10101-10900.
Do	W. O. Slade	21201-21700.
T. J. Hatch	W. Hancock	12501-13300, 13901-14700, 22701-23200.
W. G. Allen	J. H. Cooke	13301-13700.
Do	J. Sands	13701-13900.
Do	C. S. Taylor	21701-22200.
T. W. Brown	J. Sands	15501-15700.
Do	G. N. Warren	23701-24200.
A. Patton	L. P. Rogers	17301-17600.
N. A. Bass	do	23201-23700.
A. B. Capron	M. A. Yates	25401-26000, 34901-35100, 38101-38700, 44101-44600.
Do	J. McGarr	44601-44700.
—— Giles	E. S. Read	26001-26800.
S. Wise	V. Penrifoy	26801-27400.
Do	M. B. Kirby	34301-34800.
Do	L. Devine	34801-34900.
M. Reeves	V. Penrifoy	27401-27800.
Do	M. Kirk	44701-44800.
Do	S. E. Hughes	44801-44900.
Do	C. Huger	72101-72500.
Do	S. Johnson	72501-72700.
M. Darby	B. W. Tyler	28401-28800, 31701-32300.
E. C. Trescot	L. Devine	28801-29200, 33301-33700.
Do	V. Penrifoy	45501-46100, 47401-48000, 50801-51300, 79201-79800, 91401-91500.
Do	L. Macon	51301-51400, 55201-55500.
Do	J. A. Acosta	54901-55200.
Do	M. A. Yates	59901-60500.
Do	K. P. Howell	64901-65500.
Do	J. Via	69201-69800.
Do	J. M. Connor	74201-74800.
Do	F. Rhett	90901-91400.
M. Kingman	L. Macon	30001-30100.
Do	S. Southall	44901-45500, 48001-48400.
Do	B. Dabney	48401-48600.
Do	F. Rhett	51401-51600.
Do	L. Michel	51601-51800, 56501-57100, 60501-61100, 76601-77200, 82301-82900, 92101-92700.
Do	S. E. Laval	51801-52000.
S. Scott	S. Southall	30101-30500, 30601-30700.
Do	M. A. Yates	30501-30600.
S. Neill	E. Laurens	30701-31100, 39901-40000, 42501-42900, 53601-54000, 57101-57500, 62401-62800, 62901-63000, 70901-71500, 97101-97500.
Do	S. E. Hughes	39701-39900, 40001-40100.
Do	J. A. Acosta	57501-57600.
Do	K. P. Howell	62801-62900.
Do	S. Johnson	97501-98100.
J. Ambler	L. A. Norris	31101-31700.
L. Holmes	F. C. Jones	32301-32700.
Do	E. Davis	40101-40700, 64701-64900.
E. Kelly	J. De Leon	35101-35500, 59601-59900.
Do	F. Rhett	35501-35700.

Register of Confederate States Treasury Notes—Continued.

ACT OF FEBRUARY 17, 1864—Continued.

For Treasurer.	For Register.	Numbers of the notes signed.
		$20—A to D—Continued.
E. Kelly	B. W. Tyler	79001–79200.
M. Wade	E. Matthews	36301–36800, 41901–42500, 54001–54400, 58201–58800.
Do	L. A. Norris	36801–36900.
E. Willis	J. M. Connor	37501–38100, 50201–50800, 64101–64700, 67501–67700, 67801–68100.
Do	A. S. Parry	67701–67800.
P. Savage	B. Dabney	38701–38800.
Do	L. Macon	38801–39100.
J. Logan	N. Brisbane	41301–41900.
M. Cooper	M. Kirk	46701–47100.
Do	J. McGarr	47101–47300.
Do	F. Rhett	47301–47400, 49601–49800, 75401–75800.
Do	L. Devine	49201–49600.
Do	L. A. Norris	52001–52500.
Do	J. A. Acosta	52501–52600.
Do	M. A. Yates	66501–67100.
Do	A. Zealy	71501–72100.
Do	H. E. Alexander	75801–75900.
Do	M. S. Apperson	75901–76000, 93301–93800.
Do	E. Laurens	84101–84200.
Do	J. M. Connor	93101–93200.
Do	C. C. Veal	93201–93300.
Do	K. P. Howell	93801–93900.
H. Moise	do	49801–50200, 55501–55700.
Do	S. Johnson	55701–55900, 73301–73800, 79801–80300, 90401–90900.
S. McCants	B. J. Clarke	52601–53200.
Do	M. J. Black	65501–66100, 69801–70200, 70301–70400.
Do	E. Laurens	70201–70300.
Do	C. Percival	91501–92100.
O. McGowan	S. Johnson	53201–53600.
Do	M. A. Yates	72701–73100.
Do	E. Matthews	73101–73300.
Do	L. Arthur	82901–83300, 98101–98700.
Do	M. Gaither	83301–83500.
M. Godwin	S. E. Laval	55901–56100.
Do	F. Rhett	56101–56500.
Do	M. Taylor	83501–84100.
Do	M. B. Kirby	85601–86200, 96501–96900.
Do	L. A. Norris	96901–97000.
Do	M. Dixon	97001–97100.
J. Gill	S. E. Laval	58801–59000.
Do	L. Pelot	59001–59600.
Do	B. J. Clarke	63001–63700, 68101–68700.
C. Morris	E. S. Proctor	63701–64100, 88601–88700, 88901–89000.
Do	A. P. Pellet	67101–67400.
Do	M. B. Kirby	67401–67500, 89001–89100.
Do	C. Percival	76001–76200.
Do	L. W. Elliott	76201–76400.
Do	L. A. Norris	88701–88900.
Do	M. E. Hamilton	89101–89200.
C. White	M. Gaither	66101–66500, 70401–70900.
Do	M. J. Black	80301–80700, 80901–81100, 95101–95500.
Do	A. Zealy	80701–80900.
Do	H. E. Bryan	84201–84300, 95501–95800.
Do	B. W. Tyler	84301–84800.
Do	L. Devine	84801–85000.
Do	J. M. Connor	95801–95900.
M. S. Gist	L. Pelot	68701–69000, 81101–81700, 94501–95100.
Do	A. S. Parry	69001–69200.
A. Miller	S. E. Laval	74801–75400, 81701–82300, 86201–86900, 99301–100000.
F. Stocker	S. K. Wells	77201–77800, 88001–88600.
L. Sims	L. Pelot	77801–78000.
Do	F. Rhett	78001–78400.
E. M. Bell	M. F. Jarvis	78401–79000.
H. Balaguer	C. C. Veal	85001–85600, 93901–94500.
M. Boyd	V. Penrifoy	86901–87500.
Do	S. A. Doar	95901–96500.
H. Moore	C. C. Veal	87501–87600.

Register of Confederate States Treasury Notes—Continued.

ACT OF FEBRUARY 17, 1864—Continued.

For Treasurer.	For Register.	Numbers of the notes signed.
		$20—A to D—Continued.
H. Moore	J. De Leon	87601–87900.
Do	M. E. Hamilton	87901–88000.
F. Waties	N. E. Wingate	89201–89800.
S. Fuller	H. E. Bryan	89801–90400.
K. Nelson	M. A. Mobley	92701–93100.
L. Armstrong	M. Taylor	98701–99300.
		$20—A to D (1st series).
K. Korff	H. Heriot	1–600, 5501–6100, 10001–10600, 15001–15600, 20001–20600, 25601–26200, 33801–34300, 62501–63100, 73701–74300.
M. Kingman	L. Michel	601–1200, 14901–15000.
Do	K. P. Howell	6701–7300, 14501–14900, 16401–17000, 20601–21200, 26201-26500, 75101–75300, 93701–94300.
M. Boyd	S. A. Doar	1201–1800, 24501–25000, 45401–45600, 45701–46000, 61101-61500, 75301–75900.
Do	L. Henry	45601–45700.
M. Godwin	M. B. Kirby	1801–2400.
Do	M. F. Jarvis	7301–7900.
Do	H. E. Alexander	17001–17200.
Do	M. Taylor	17201–17400.
F. Stocker	S. K. Wells	2401–3000, 18701–19300, 39801–40300.
Do	L. Henry	40301–40400.
E. C. Trescot	V. Penrifoy	3001–3500, 7901–8500, 12001–12500, 23901–24400, 33201-33800, 65901–66500, 73101–73700.
Do	C. Percival	3501–3600.
Do	L. Arthur	12501–12600.
Do	K. P. Howell	24401–24500.
H. Balaguer	do	3601–4200.
Do	S. Huard	32201–32500.
S. McCants	C. Percival	4201–4800, 12601–13200, 18001–18700, 30301–31000, 35501-36100, 43601–44200, 65301–65900, 79001–79600, 86701-87300, 98701–99300.
Do	A. S. Parry	56701–57300.
S. R. Simons	S. Johnson	4801–5000.
Do	J. A. Acosta	44801–45400, 53801–54400, 66501–67100, 84801–85400, 93101-93700.
H. Moise	S. Johnson	5001–5500, 56101–56500, 67101–67500, 79601–80000.
Do	L. Pelot	56501–56700, 80001–80100.
Do	M. Gaither	67501–67600.
Do	S. Huard	67601–67700.
M. S. Gist	L. Pelot	6101–6700, 13801–14500, 17401–18000, 80801–81400.
M. Cooper	M. E. Hamilton	8501–8800.
Do	V. Penrifoy	8801–8900.
Do	H. L. Cooke	8901–9200.
Do	K. P. Howell	9201–9300.
Do	C. C. Veal	10601–11400, 15601–16300, 43001–43600, 63101–64000, 74301-75100, 82801–83600.
Do	H. E. Alexander	16301–16400.
M. E. Hamilton	H. Moore	9301–9600.
H. Moore	A. M. Foran	9601–10000, 60501–60900.
Do	S. Huard	60901–61000.
Do	H. L. Cooke	61001–61100, 90901–91000.
Do	E. Davis	70501–70900, 75901–76200, 90601–90900.
O. McGowan	L. Arthur	11401–12000, 33301–33900, 42501–43000, 64701–65300, 72501-73100, 91601–92200.
E. Willis	J. M. Connor	13201–13800, 23301–23900, 57301–57900, 78401–79000, 86001-86600.
Do	B. Dabney	47201–47800.
Do	M. E. Hamilton	86601–86700.
J. Wilson	J. McGarr	19301–20000, 21801–22300, 22401–22600, 96601–97200.
Do	M. Kirk	22301–22400.
Do	S. A. Doar	77801–77900.
Do	E. Coffin	77901–78000.
Do	J. D. Treadwell	78001–78100.
Do	H. Heriot	78101–78200.
Do	S. Huard	78201–78300, 89401–89500.
Do	M. E. Harper	78301–78400, 89201–89300.

Register of Confederate States Treasury Notes—Continued.

ACT OF FEBRUARY 17, 1864—Continued.

For Treasurer.	For Register.	Numbers of the notes signed.
		$20—A to D (1st series)—Continued.
J. Wilson	S. E. Laval	88901–89000.
Do	E. Matthews	89001–89100.
Do	S. Johnson	89101–89200.
Do	J. M. Connor	89301–89400.
Do	M. Gaither	89501–89600.
Do	L. Henry	97201–97300.
C. Morris	E. S. Proctor	21201–21800, 34901–35300.
Do	H. Heriot	25001–25100.
Do	M. Gaither	25101–25200.
Do	H. E. Alexander	25201–25400.
Do	S. Johnson	25401–25500.
Do	A. M. Foran	25501–25600.
Do	H. L. Cooke	35301–35400.
Do	L. Michel	35401–35500.
Do	L. Pelot	59001–59100, 62201–62300.
V. M. Tyler	M. Kirk	22601–23100, 46001–46600, 54401–55000, 77201–77800, 87901–88500.
Do	C. C. Veal	23101–23200.
Do	S. E. Laval	23201–23300.
M. Dargan	L. W. Elliott	26501–26800, 36701–37300, 70901–71500, 89601–90200.
J. Jacobs	M. E. Brady	26801–27400, 55501–56100, 68301–68500, 68601–68800, 84201–84500, 95401–96000.
Do	H. L. Cooke	68501–68600, 68801–68900.
Do	A. P. Pellet	84501–84600.
Do	M. Dixon	84601–84800.
S. Neill	M. Taylor	27401–27800, 27901–28000.
Do	M. Kirk	27801–27900, 36101–36600.
Do	M. E. Cullen	36601–36700.
Do	H. L. Cooke	44201–44500.
Do	C. Huger	44501–44800.
Do	J. De Leon	52501–53000.
Do	M. J. Black	53001–53100, 68901–69300.
Do	M. E. Hamilton	69301–69500.
Do	B. Dabney	85401–86000, 92201–92400.
E. Kelly	B. W. Tyler	28001–28500, 82001–82800.
Do	L. Michel	98001–98600.
Do	H. L. Cooke	98601–98700.
C. White	B. W. Tyler	28501–28700.
Do	M. J. Black	28701–29300, 97301–97900.
Do	A. P. Pellet	97901–98000.
M. Wade	E. Matthews	29301–30000, 70101–70500.
M. Carrington	M. E. Hamilton	30001–30300, 90201–90500.
Do	H. L. Cooke	62301–62500.
Do	L. Devine	90501–90600.
L. Armstrong	H. C. Thomas	31001–31300, 31401–31500.
Do	M. E. Cullen	31301–31400.
Do	J. De Leon	80101–80400.
Do	M. E. Hamilton	80401–80500.
Do	H. E. Alexander	88501–88900.
Do	S. A. Doar	94301–94800.
S. G. Sanxay	M. Dixon	31501–32200, 50001–50700, 59901–60300, 69501–70100.
Do	L. Henry	60301–60500.
A. Miller	S. E. Laval	32501–33200, 53101–53800, 64001–64700, 92401–93100.
G. Loyd	L. Michel	37301–37400.
Do	H. E. Alexander	37401–37500, 55001–55500, 76601–77200, 96001–96600.
Do	M. A. Yates	87301–87900.
M. Reeves	C. Huger	37501–37800.
Do	L. Henry	37801–37900.
J. H. Angel	M. A. Mobley	37901–38100, 38301–38400.
Do	M. E. Cullen	38101–38300.
S. Scott	L. A. Norris	38401–39200, 48601–49200, 59101–59700.
Do	L. Macon	49201–49400, 59701–59900.
M. Selden	A. P. Pellet	39201–39800, 52101–52500, 71501–72000.
Do	L. Devine	72001–72100.
A. Harrison	H. E. Alexander	40401–40700.
J. Logan	N. Brisbane	40701–41300.
J. Gott	B. Dabney	41301–41400, 41601–42000.
Do	H. Heriot	41401–41500.

Register of Confederate States Treasury Notes—Continued.

ACT OF FEBRUARY 17, 1864—Continued.

For Treasurer.	For Register.	Numbers of the notes signed.
		$20—A to D (1st series)—Continued.
J. Gott	M. E. Cullen	41501–41600, 51401–52100, 58301–59000, 81401–82000, 91001-91600.
F. Waties	N. E. Wingate	42001–42400.
Do	S. A. Doar	42401–42500.
L. Holmes	L. Michel	46601–47200, 57901–58300.
M. Allen	B. J. Clarke	47801–48500.
Do	M. Gaither	48501–48600.
A. Points	E. C. Winston	49401–50000, 67901–68300, 76201–76500, 83601–84200, 94801-95400.
Do	L. Pelot	67701–67900.
Do	A. P. Pellet	76501–76600.
A. Caldwell	J. D. Treadwell	50701–51400.
E. M. Bell	M. F. Jarvis	61501–62100.
Do	B. Dabney	62101–62200.
L. Sims	H. Barnwell	72101–72500.
M. Ringgold	C. Huger	80501–80700.
Do	H. L. Cooke	80701–80800.
		$20—A to D (2d series).
O. McGowan	L. Arthur	1–500, 10201–10700, 21401–21900, 35401–35500, 46001–46500, 53901–54500, 62401–63000, 70701–71300, 88501–89100.
Do	H. Heriot	21901–22000.
Do	S. Johnson	35001–35400.
Do	L. Pelot	79901–80500.
E. C. Trescot	V. Penrifoy	501–1100, 9601–10200, 23801–24400, 29401–30000, 42101-42700, 51801–52400, 63001–63600, 71301–71900, 80501–81100, 87901-88500, 95301–95900.
K. Korff	H. Heriot	1101–1700, 14001–14600, 44001–44600.
Do	M. E. Harper	32401–33000.
Do	F. Rhett	79301–79900.
G. Loyd	H. E. Alexander	1701–2200, 19501–20100, 34401–35000.
Do	H. L. Cooke	2201–2300.
M. Kingman	K. P. Howell	2301–2900, 12701–13400, 22001–22500, 29001–29400, 55701-56100, 61901–62400, 90201–90700, 98201–98400.
Do	E. Davis	72401–73000.
S. R. Simons	J. A. Acosta	2901–3500, 15101–15700, 25001–25600, 33401–34000, 49401-50000, 55101–55700, 97601–98100.
Do	E. Davis	91301–91400.
Do	C. Percival	91401–91600.
Do	M. E. Hamilton	91601–91800.
Do	E. Coffin	98101–98200.
S. Neill	B. Dabney	3501–4100.
Do	H. C. Thomas	4101–4200, 14601–15100.
Do	L. W. Elliott	20801–21400.
Do	E. Coffin	31101–31700.
Do	H. L. Cooke	47101–47300.
Do	L. Devine	47301–47500.
Do	M. Dixon	47501–47700.
Do	M. E. Norton	56701–57300.
Do	M. B. Kirby	64401–65000, 83301–83900.
Do	J. A. Acosta	73601–74200.
Do	M. A. Yates	93101–93700.
S. McCants	C. Percival	4201–4800, 11301–11900, 28101–28700, 47701–48300, 57701-58300, 65001–65600, 74901–75500.
M. Cooper	C. C. Veal	4801–5600, 11901–12700, 22501–23300, 31701–32400, 45201-46000, 53101–53900, 63601–64400, 81101–81900, 91801-92500, 94501–95300.
H. Moise	S. Johnson	5601–6000, 13401–14000, 26901–27500, 36301–36700, 68201-68700, 76701–77000, 82701–83300, 90701–91300.
Do	L. Macon	6001–6200.
Do	M. E. Hamilton	36101–36300.
Do	F. E. Bernard	95901–96100.
Do	S. K. Wells	96101–96200.
Do	H. L. Cooke	96201–96400.
E. Willis	J. M. Connor	6201–6800, 76101–76700.
Do	M. E. Hamilton	85201–85400.
Do	S. E. Laval	85401–85600.

Register of Confederate States Treasury Notes—Continued.

ACT OF FEBRUARY 17, 1864—Continued.

For Treasurer.	For Register.	Numbers of the notes signed.
		$20—A to D (2d series)—Continued.
E. Willis	C. Percival	85601–85800.
Do	B. J. Clarke	92501–93100.
A. Points	E. C. Winston	6801–7400, 17601–18200, 28701–29000, 36701–37200, 50801–51300.
M. Boyd	S. A. Doar	7401–8000, 15701–16100, 24401–25000, 34001–34400, 44601–45200, 65601–66000.
Do	M. A. Yates	66001–66100.
A. Miller	S. E. Laval	8001–8700, 9001–9600, 25601–26300, 30401–31100, 43301–44000, 52401–53100, 66101–66800, 74201–74900, 83901–84100, 96401–97000, 98401–99100.
V. M. Tyler	M. E. Hamilton	8701–9000.
Do	M. Kirk	26301–26900, 35501–36100.
J. Jacobs	M. E. Brady	10701–11300.
Do	R. King	48301–48500.
Do	M. Dixon	48501–48700.
Do	B. W. Tyler	48701–48900.
J. H. Angel	M. A. Mobley	16101–16300, 30001–30400, 54501–55100.
Do	M. E. Hamilton	16301–16400.
Do	E. C. Winston	46501–46700.
Do	A. M. Foran	46701–47100.
Do	L. Courtney	73001–73200.
Do	S. Huard	73201–73400.
Do	C. Percival	73401–73600.
J. Wilson	J. McGarr	16401–17000.
Do	M. E. Harper	41201–41800.
Do	H. L. Cooke	41801–41900.
S. G. Sanxay	M. Dixon	17001–17600, 37201–37800, 59901–60300.
M. Carrington	S. A. Doar	18201–18300.
Do	M. E. Hamilton	18301–18700, 37801–38200, 58301–58500, 77001–77500, 84101–84400.
E. M. Bell	M. F. Jarvis	18701–19300, 39801–40600, 50001–50800.
Do	A. P. Pellet	19301–19400.
Do	S. Huard	19401–19500.
E. Baker	A. P. Pellet	20101–20200, 39701–39800.
Do	M. Taylor	20201–20400.
Do	M. E. Hamilton	20401–20500, 39001–39200.
Do	H. Heriot	20501–20600, 78501–79300, 84401–85200.
Do	L. W. Elliott	39201–39700.
Do	M. B. Kirby	51301–51700.
Do	E. Davis	51701–51800.
H. Moore	do	20601–20800, 33001–33200, 49301–49400, 57301–57700.
Do	M. E. Norton	33201–33400.
Do	L. Macon	48901–49300.
L. Armstrong	H. Heriot	23301–23500.
Do	F. Rhett	23501–23800.
Do	E. Coffin	42701–42900.
Do	M. E. Norton	42901–43100.
Do	H. Barnwell	43101–43300.
Do	E. Davis	56101–56600.
Do	M. B. Kirby	56601–56700, 71901–72400.
Do	M. E. Brady	89701–90200.
Do	M. E. Harper	97001–97600.
C. Morris	S. Johnson	27501–27700.
Do	L. Courtney	27701–28100.
Do	L. Devine	41001–41200.
Do	H. L. Cooke	41901–42100.
C. White	M. J. Black	38201–38800, 66801–67400, 69901–70500, 81901–82700.
Do	E. Matthews	38801–39000.
Do	L. Courtney	67401–67600.
Do	M. E. Brady	70501–70700.
M. Dargan	L. W. Elliott	40601–41000, 67601–68200, 77501–78000.
Do	A. P. Pellet	78001–78100.
Do	E. Matthews	93701–93900.
J. Gott	M. E. Cullen	58501–59300.
M. Wade	E. Matthews	59301–59900, 75501–76100, 86201–86800, 89101–89700.
A. Caldwell	J. D. Treadwell	60301–60800.
L. Holmes	L. Michel	60801–61300, 85801–86200.
Do	L. Devine	61301–61400.

Register of Confederate States Treasury Notes—Continued.

ACT OF FEBRUARY 17, 1864—Continued.

For Treasurer.	For Register.	Numbers of the notes signed.
		$20—A to D (2d series)—Continued.
M. Selden	A. P. Pellet	61401–61900.
Do	B. Dabney	69301–69900.
M. S. Gist	L. Pelot	68701–68900.
Do	F. Rhett	68901–69300.
M. Darby	J. De Leon	78101–78500.
L. Sims	H. Barnwell	86801–87600.
S. Scott	L. A. Norris	87601–87900.
P. Savage	L. Macon	93901–94500.
		$20—A to D (3d series).
E. C. Trescot	V. Penrifoy	1–600, 5001–5600, 9301–9900, 16501–17100, 25201–25800, 34201–34800, 40401–41000, 56601–57200, 76601–77200, 91601–92000, 95101–95400.
S. Neill	A. Zealy	601–1200.
Do	S. E. Hughes	1201–1300, 6401–6900.
Do	M. A. Yates	10401–11000.
Do	M. Taylor	19101–19700.
Do	C. Percival	26401–27000.
Do	L. A. Norris	45401–46000.
Do	M. E. Norton	50001–50600.
Do	F. E. Bernard	58601–59200, 73001–73600.
M. Kingman	C. Percival	1301–1900.
Do	K. P. Howell	6901–7500, 12201–12800, 20901–21500, 48801–49400, 59201–59800, 71601–72200.
Do	R. King	29501–30100.
Do	H. E. Bryan	34801–35400.
Do	N. E. Wingate	43001–43600.
C. White	M. J. Black	1901–2700.
Do	M. E. Hamilton	31501–32200, 63401–64200.
J. H. Angel	M. B. Kirby	2701–3000, 76001–76600.
Do	C. Percival	20301–20900.
Do	H. C. Thomas	39001–39600.
E. Baker	H. Heriot	3001–3900, 15201–16000, 37001–37800, 46801–47100, 51801–52400, 62601–63400, 77201–78000, 88901–89200.
O. McGowan	L. Arthur	3901–4300, 29401–29500, 35401–35900, 44201–44800, 47701–48300, 79201–79800, 85301–85900.
Do	A. P. Pellet	11001–11100.
Do	M. J. Black	11101–11600.
Do	A. M. Foran	17901–18500.
Do	S. Johnson	28801–29400.
K. Korff	M. E. Hamilton	4301–4900.
Do	M. E. Harper	27601–28200.
Do	S. E. Hughes	35901–36500.
Do	M. J. Black	51201–51800, 78001–78600, 89201–89800.
L. Armstrong	L. A. Norris	4901–5000.
Do	J. McGarr	23501–23900.
Do	M. S. Apperson	43601–43900, 44001–44200.
Do	M. E. Harper	43901–44000, 50601–51200.
Do	L. Macon	78601–79200.
Do	L. Arthur	87301–87900.
Do	J. De Leon	92801–93100.
Do	H. E. Bryan	93701–94200.
M. Cooper	C. C. Veal	5601–6400, 12801–13600, 17101–17900, 30101–30900, 41601–42400, 57801–58600, 72201–73000, 91101–91600, 92001–92400.
H. Moore	E. Davis	7501–8100, 80201–80700, 86801–87300.
S. R. Simons	M. Taylor	8101–8700.
Do	J. A. Acosta	11601–12200, 19701–20300, 30901–31500, 33601–34200, 42901–43000, 48301–48700, 55401–56000, 81301–81900.
Do	E. Coffin	42401–42900.
H. Moise	S. Johnson	8701–9100, 47101–47700, 56001–56600, 74901–75400.
Do	J. D. Treadwell	32201–32500, 32601–32800.
Do	S. K. Wells	32501–32600.
A. Miller	S. E. Laval	9101–9300, 14201–14900, 38201–39000, 46001–46800, 74201–74900, 85901–86300, 94201–94500, 95401–96200.
M. Darby	M. B. Kirby	9901–10400.
P. Savage	L. Macon	13601–14200, 25801–26400, 40001–40400, 92401–92800.
Do	L. Pelot	39801–40000.

Register of Confederate States Treasury Notes—Continued.

ACT OF FEBRUARY 17, 1864—Continued.

For Treasurer.	For Register.	Numbers of the notes signed.
		$20—A to D (3d series)—Continued.
M. Carrington	J. McGarr	14901–15200.
Do	M. B. Kirby	25101–25200.
Do	J. De Leon	37801–38200.
Do	C. Huger	79801–80200.
Do	F. Rhett	87901–88400.
J. Ambler	A. Zealy	16001–16500.
M. Boyd	S. A. Doar	18501–19100, 27001–27600, 44801–45400, 49401–50000.
E. M. Bell	M. F. Jarvis	21501–22100, 32801–33600, 59801–60600, 82501–83200.
Do	E. S. Read	22101–22300.
C. Morris	L. Courtney	22301–22900, 28201–28700, 41001–41600, 53501–54000, 88401–88900.
Do	E. S. Proctor	28701–28800, 36501–36900, 66101–66700.
Do	H. E. Bryan	36901–37000.
Do	L. A. Norris	80701–81300.
M. Wade	H. C. Thomas	22901–23500.
Do	E. Matthews	61401–62000, 81901–82500, 86301–86800, 90501–91100.
J. Gott	M. E. Cullen	23901–24500, 39601–39800, 60601–61400.
F. Stocker	S. K. Wells	24501–25100.
L. Sims	E. Coffin	48701–48800.
Do	N. E. Wingate	68601–69400.
E. Willis	J. M. Connor	52401–52900, 64201–64800.
H. Balaguer	S. Huard	52901–53500.
J. Jacobs	M. E. Brady	54001–54600, 57201–57800, 73601–74200.
S. G. Sanxay	M. Dixon	54601–55200, 62001–62600, 83201–83800.
M. Reeves	L. Henry	55201–55400.
Do	E. Laurens	65601–66100.
E. Kelly	B. W. Tyler	64801–65600.
M. Dargan	L. W. Elliott	66701–67400.
E. A. Dennison	M. E. Gilliam	67401–68000, 84401–85000.
R. Haynes	E. Coffin	68001–68600, 83801–84400.
Do	M. Gaither	93101–93700.
Do	S. Johnson	94501–95100.
M. A. Dewees	H. E. Bryan	69401–70000, 85001–85300.
S. J. Adams	do	70001–70600.
M. Banks	M. E. Harper	70601–71200.
S. Scott	L. A. Norris	71201–71600.
S. McCants	C. Percival	75401–76000, 89801–90500.
		$20—A to D (4th series).
P. Savage	M. E. Brady	1–600.
H. Moise	S. Johnson	601–1100, 38301–38900.
Do	M. Taylor	80801–81300, 83201–83700, 89801–90000.
Do	M. E. Brady	89401–89800.
E. C. Trescot	V. Penrifoy	1101–1700, 39501–40100, 54601–55200, 57201–57800, 84301–84800, 90601–91200, 92501–92900.
M. Wade	E. Matthews	1701–2300, 12101–12700, 26501–27100, 45501–45900, 50101–50700, 60001–60600, 74101–74700, 82901–83200, 84801–85100.
S. R. Simons	J. A. Acosta	2301–2900, 48401–49000, 57801–58300.
M. Cooper	C. C. Veal	2901–3200, 83701–84300, 91201–91600.
Do	E. S. Proctor	3201–3700.
Do	S. E. Hughes	20101–20800.
Do	B. J. Clarke	33501–34300, 78501–79300, 91801–92100.
Do	S. Johnson	91601–91800.
J. Wilson	J. McGarr	3701–4300, 10901–11500, 31301–31900.
Do	M. Kirk	24101–24600.
Do	M. B. Kirby	24601–24700.
L. Armstrong	H. E. Alexander	4301–4800.
Do	B. J. Clarke	25201–25600.
Do	J. A. Acosta	25601–25700, 30101–30700.
Do	J. De Leon	40601–41100, 56701–57200, 70101–70600, 90001–90600.
Do	J. D. Treadwell	76101–76700.
M. Kingman	K. P. Howell	4801–5300, 9301–9900, 18301–18900, 32901–33500, 42901–43400, 56101–56700, 93301–93700.
S. McCants	C. Percival	5301–5900, 19501–20100, 29501–30100, 42301–42900, 47101–47700, 54001–54600, 76701–77100, 88701–89200, 92901–93300.
J. Gott	M. E. Cullen	5901–6400, 27101–27700, 71101–71500, 85601–86200.

Register of Confederate States Treasury Notes—Continued.

ACT OF FEBRUARY 17, 1864—Continued.

For Treasurer.	For Register.	Numbers of the notes signed.
		$20—A to D (4th series)—Continued.
J. Gott	H. Barnwell	79301-80100.
K. Korff	M. J. Black	6401-7000, 12701-13300, 21401-22000, 36601-37200, 44901-45500, 61201-61800, 85101-85600, 94201-94600.
E. A. Dennison	M. E. Gilliam	7001-7600, 64601-65200, 88201-88700.
M. A. Dewees	H. E. Bryan	7601-8200, 46501-47100, 53001-53300, 62401-63000, 64001-64600, 87201-87700.
L. Sims	N. E. Wingate	8201-9000, 63001-63700.
Do	B. J. Clarke	63701-63800.
E. M. Bell	M. F. Jarvis	9001-9300, 14101-14900, 41701-42300.
Do	E. Coffin	68901-69500.
Do	B. J. Clarke	69501-69700.
J. H. Angel	M. B. Kirby	9901-10500, 20801-21400, 55201-55800, 65801-66200.
Do	E. Kelly	28301-28900.
M. Carrington	C. Huger	10501-10900, 24701-25100, 49001-49500.
Do	F. Rhett	25101-25200.
Do	L. Macon	36201-36600.
Do	M. A. Yates	43401-43900.
Do	M. Kirk	59601-60000.
Do	A. S. Parry	81301-81700.
Do	J. De Leon	89201-89400.
Do	L. Michel	94901-95100.
S. J. Adams	H. C. Thomas	11501-12100, 30701-31300, 45901-46500.
Do	M. E. Norton	22001-22600.
E. Kelly	B. W. Tyler	13301-14100, 74701-75500.
Do	L. Henry	63801-64000.
M. Dargan	L. W. Elliott	14901-15400.
K. Nelson	A. M. Foran	15401-16000.
C. Morris	L. Courtney	16001-16500, 18901-19500, 35701-36200, 43901-44400, 51301-51900, 59101-59600, 71701-71800.
Do	L. W. Elliott	71501-71700, 71801-72100.
Do	M. Kirk	77901-78500.
E. Baker	H. Heriot	16501-17300, 25701-26500, 34901-35700, 41101-41300, 58301-59100, 72701-73500.
Do	E. Laurens	41301-41700.
L. Holmes	S. E. Hughes	17301-17800.
R. Haynes	E. Coffin	17801-18300.
Do	J. De Leon	51901-52300.
Do	L. Macon	52301-52500.
Do	M. A. Yates	61801-62400.
Do	E. S. Proctor	67401-67800.
Do	M. Gaither	67801-68000, 88101-88200.
Do	M. B. Kirby	87701-88100.
A. Miller	S. E. Laval	22601-23300, 40101-40600, 47701-48400, 53301-54000, 80101-80800, 81701-82900, 92101-92500.
M. S. Gist	L. Pelot	23301-24100.
E. Willis	J. M. Connor	27701-28300, 69701-70100, 73501-74100.
O. McGowan	L. Arthur	28901-29500, 38901-39500, 49501-50100.
Do	B. J. Clarke	86201-86700.
C. White	M. E. Hamilton	31901-32700, 72101-72700, 93701-94200.
S. Scott	M. Kirk	32701-32900.
Do	J. M. Connor	34301-34500.
Do	L. W. Elliott	34501-34700.
Do	E. Matthews	34701-34900.
Do	L. A. Norris	66801-67400.
H. Moore	E. Davis	37201-37700, 44401-44900, 65201-65800, 94601-94900.
J. Ambler	A. Zealy	37701-38200, 52501-53000, 56001-56100, 68401-68900.
S. Fuller	R. King	38201-38300.
M. Boyd	S. A. Doar	50701-51300.
S. G. Sanxay	M. Dixon	55801-56000, 60601-61200, 66201-66800.
Do	B. J. Clarke	86701-87200.
J. Jacobs	M. E. Brady	68001-68300, 70601-71100.
F. Waties	H. Barnwell	68301-68400, 75501-76100.
M. Allen	F. C. Jones	77101-77900.

Register of Confederate States Treasury Notes—Continued.

ACT OF FEBRUARY 17, 1864—Continued.

For Treasurer.	For Register.	Numbers of the notes signed.
		$20—A to D (5th series).
M. Kingman	K. P. Howell	1-600, 29801-30000, 76101-76800, 85301-85900.
Do	L. Michel	89301-89700.
M. Selden	B. Dabney	601-1200, 3401-4000.
J. Ambler	A. Zealy	1201-1400.
S. McCants	C. Percival	1401-2000, 14801-14900, 17701-17900, 24001-24600, 40401-41000, 47301-47900, 53001-53600, 66601-67200, 75501-76100, 82301-82900.
C. White	M. E. Hamilton	2001-2800, 19201-19800, 52301-53000, 60201-60800.
Do	M. Taylor	19801-20000.
M. A. Dewees	H. E. Bryan	2801-3400, 10601-11000, 25601-26200, 55201-55800, 68401-69000, 72401-73000.
Do	E. Matthews	27301-27500.
J. Gott	M. E. Cullen	4001-4600, 7701-8200, 12601-13000, 16301-17000, 28801-29400, 39101-39800.
E. M. Bell	E. Coffin	4601-5200, 9601-10200.
Do	M. F. Jarvis	22001-22800, 33301-33900, 83401-84000.
O. McGowan	L. Arthur	5201-5800, 31201-31600, 42901-43500, 87601-88000.
Do	J. A. Acosta	66001-66600.
Do	J. M. Connor	71101-71600.
Do	E. S. Proctor	71601-71700, 78301-78500.
C. Morris	L. Henry	5801-6200.
Do	M. Gaither	7201-7700.
Do	J. De Leon	13401-13600.
Do	E. Coffin	53601-54200.
Do	J. D. Treadwell	63101-63700.
Do	F. Rhett	80401-80500.
Do	M. F. Stevens	91001-91300.
K. Korff	M. J. Black	6201-6800, 8201-8600, 13001-13400, 17001-17200, 20001-20600, 30401-30800, 54601-55200, 72301-72400, 89701-90000.
M. Carrington	L. Pelot	6801-7200.
Do	M. Kirk	12201-12400.
Do	J. De Leon	15901-16300.
Do	M. S. Apperson	21601-22000.
Do	M. A. Mobley	32401-32700.
Do	N. E. Wingate	43501-43900.
Do	S. Johnson	57601-57900.
Do	C. C. Veal	93701-94000.
M. Wade	E. Matthews	8601-9000, 17201-17700, 26901-27100, 29401-29800, 55801-56400, 63701-63900, 79101-79700, 84801-85300, 90301-90600.
E. Baker	H. Heriot	9001-9600, 20601-21400, 32701-32800, 42101-42900, 48201-48300, 63901-64700, 76801-77600, 91301-91800.
Do	M. Dixon	32801-33300.
H. Moore	E. Davis	10201-10600, 12401-12600, 30001-30400, 41001-41500, 85901-86200, 90001-90300.
S. Fuller	R. King	11001-11200.
J. Logan	N. Brisbane	11201-11400, 14401-14600.
M. Boyd	C. C. Veal	11401-11600.
Do	S. A. Doar	26201-26300, 36901-37300.
F. Stocker	S. K. Wells	11601-11800, 35901-36300, 91801-92200.
Do	A. Zealy	28101-28200.
N. Giles	L. Michel	11801-12000.
M. S. Gist	L. Pelot	12001-12200.
Do	M. S. Apperson	36301-36500.
Do	B. J. Clarke	36501-36900.
M. Allen	F. C. Jones	13601-14000.
S. R. Simons	L. Arthur	14001-14200.
F. Waties	H. Barnwell	14201-14400.
E. C. Trescot	V. Penrifoy	14601-14800, 28201-28800, 41501-42100, 44601-45200, 48701-49000, 50501-51100, 58301-58700, 61701-62300, 65401-66000, 70001-70600, 74301-74900, 80501-81100, 86601-87000, 92901-93300, 94001-94500.
L. Armstrong	J. A. Acosta	14901-15400.
Do	H. E. Bryan	45201-45800.
Do	J. De Leon	49001-49600, 52201-52300, 60801-61100, 88401-88800.
Do	C. Huger	51701-52200.
Do	M. Taylor	70601-71100.
Do	S. Johnson	82901-83400.
Do	M. E. Cullen	93301-93700.

Register of Confederate States Treasury Notes—Continued.

ACT OF FEBRUARY 17, 1864—Continued.

For Treasurer.	For Register.	Numbers of the notes signed.
		$20—A to D (5th series)—Continued.
P. Savage	M. Taylor	15401-15900.
Do	L. Macon	58701-59200, 61101-61700.
A. Miller	S. E. Laval	17901-18600, 38701-39100, 46601-47300, 59201-59800, 79701-80400, 88801-89300.
E. Willis	H. Barnwell	18601-19200, 26701-26900.
Do	J. M. Connor	74901-75500.
S. G. Sanxay	M. Dixon	21401-21600, 32001-32400.
Do	M. E. Gilliam	27501-27700.
Do	M. Taylor	67801-68400.
Do	E. S. Read	90601-90800.
Do	H. Barnwell	90801-91000.
A. Caldwell	J. D. Treadwell	22801-23400, 30801-31200.
J. H. Angel	E. Coffin	23401-24000, 31601-32000.
Do	C. Huger	73001-73600.
R. Haynes	M. Gaither	24601-25000, 27701-27900, 35101-35500, 44001-44600, 69401-70000, 73701-74300, 81101-81700, 92601-92900.
Do	S. Johnson	49901-50500.
Do	M. E. Harper	57901-58100.
Do	C. Percival	58101-58300.
Do	M. F. Jarvis	64801-65400.
Do	J. D. Treadwell	86201-86600.
E. A. Dennison	M. E. Gilliam	25001-25600, 34701-35100, 56401-57000, 92201-92600.
Do	M. Dixon	27101-27300.
S. Neill	F. E. Bernard	26301-26700, 37901-38300, 39801-40400, 51101-51700, 59801-60200, 71701-72300, 88001-88400.
Do	J. D. Treadwell	81701-82300.
L. Holmes	S. Huard	27901-28100.
Do	M. E. Hamilton	34301-34700.
M. Ringgold	L. Henry	33901-34300.
V. M. Tyler	M. Kirk	35501-35900.
L. Sims	N. E. Wingate	37301-37900.
M. Selden	B. Dabney	38301-38700.
A. Harrison	L. Devine	43901-44000, 64701-64800, 69001-69400, 73601-73700.
M. Cooper	C. C. Veal	45801-46600, 54201-54600, 62301-63100, 87001-87600, 94501-95100.
M. Banks	H. Heriot	47901-48200, 48301-48700.
H. Moise	M. Taylor	49601-49900.
J. Jacobs	M. E. Brady	57001-57600.
J. Gill	B. J. Clarke	67201-67800.
E. Kelly	L. W. Elliott	77601-77800.
Do	B. W. Tyler	77801-78300.
Do	M. A. Yates	84001-84100, 84301-84600.
Do	C. C. Veal	84101-84300.
Do	M. Pleasants	84601-84800.
H. Balaguer	S. Huard	78501-79100.
		$20—A to D (6th series).
S. McCants	C. Percival	1-400, 3601-4100, 17701-18300, 78601-79200, 86701-87300, 91201-91800.
Do	M. E. Gilliam	24601-24900.
Do	H. E. Bryan	30401-30700.
Do	M. Kirk	33501-33800.
S. Neill	F. E. Bernard	401-800, 23201-23600, 29801-30100, 34901-35200.
Do	J. D. Treadwell	5701-6000.
Do	A. Zealy	6001-6200, 9601-9800, 19301-19900.
Do	M. A. Mobley	9801-10100.
Do	M. J. Black	44801-45100.
Do	M. A. Yates	52901-53300.
Do	L. Michel	78101-78600.
Do	E. Davis	88701-89300.
A. Miller	S. E. Laval	801-1300, 6701-7300, 13301-13900, 22701-23200, 32101-32200, 36101-36400, 46101-46500, 61101-61300, 64301-65000, 72701-73400, 79901-80600, 83501-84200, 88001-88700, 95501-96200.
Do	M. E. Cullen	49201-49700.
E. Baker	H. Heriot	1301-1700, 4601-5200, 9001-9600, 20501-20600, 36701-37000, 45101-45500.
Do	J. D. Treadwell	25501-26100.

Register of Confederate States Treasury Notes—Continued.

ACT OF FEBRUARY 17, 1864—Continued.

For Treasurer.	For Register.	Numbers of the notes signed.
		$20—A to D (6th series)—Continued.
E. Baker	C. C. Veal	63501-64100.
Do	L. Devine	64101-64300.
M. Wade	E. Matthews	1701-2100, 4101-4600, 10101-10600, 19901-20500, 24301-24600, 44501-44800, 72101-72700, 91801-92300.
M. Kingman	K. P. Howell	2101-2500, 6201-6700, 18701-19300, 24001-24300, 34301-34600, 41401-41700, 43901-44200, 48801-49200, 62501-63000, 69701-70200, 81601-81900.
Do	E. S. Read	82901-83500.
C. Morris	J. De Leon	2501-2800, 12201-12700, 30101-30400, 33801-34100, 44201-44500, 54201-54600.
Do	M. E. Cullen	7301-7800, 17201-17700.
Do	M. E. Norton	24901-25200.
Do	M. E. Gilliam	40701-41000.
Do	J. D. Treadwell	69101-69600.
Do	M. Taylor	69601-69700.
H. Moore	E. Davis	2801-3100, 10601-11100, 26101-26400, 29501-29800, 34101-34300, 41201-41400, 45801-46100.
F. Stocker	S. K. Wells	3101-3400, 14701-15200.
O. McGowan	L. Arthur	3401-3600, 7801-7900, 11101-11600, 16001-16600, 22301-22700, 28601-28800, 33101-33500, 41701-42000, 46501-46800, 81101-81600.
Do	J. A. Acosta	28801-29000.
Do	L. Macon	48401-48800.
Do	J. D. Treadwell	62001-62500.
K. Korff	M. J. Black	5201-5700, 26401-26800, 31001-31300, 41001-41200, 47501-47800, 77501-78100.
Do	L. W. Elliott	58101-58600.
Do	A. S. Parry	84201-84800.
E. C. Trescot	V. Penrifoy	7901-8400, 15401-16000, 20601-21000, 50501-50900, 70201-70700, 80601-81100, 82401-82900, 89301-89800.
Do	M. A. Yates	26901-27100.
Do	B. Dabney	27101-27300.
Do	L. W. Elliott	32701-33100.
Do	S. K. Wells	39001-39300.
Do	M. B. Kirby	43001-43300.
Do	M. E. Harper	56901-57400.
Do	M. Taylor	67201-67700.
M. Cooper	C. C. Veal	8401-9000, 21001-21500, 27301-27800, 32201-32700, 39301-39700.
Do	B. J. Clarke	68601-69100.
Do	H. Heriot	79201-79900, 84801-85500, 89801-90600.
M. S. Gist	L. Pelot	11601-12200.
Do	M. E. Cullen	74001-74800.
E. M. Bell	M. F. Jarvis	12701-13300, 28201-28600, 36401-36700, 42001-42300.
Do	C. C. Veal	49701-50100.
S. G. Sanxay	M. Dixon	13901-14100, 25201-25500, 31801-32100, 35201-35500, 45501-45800, 56001-56400.
S. Scott	M. F. Stevens	14101-14300.
Do	F. Rhett	14301-14700.
R. Haynes	M. Gaither	15201-15400, 38201-38600.
Do	M. B. Kirby	52501-52900.
Do	L. Michel	71301-71800.
Do	M. F. Stevens	71801-71900.
Do	L. Devine	86101-86700.
L. Armstrong	H. E. Alexander	16601-17200, 21501-21900, 27801-28200.
Do	M. E. Cullen	37801-38200.
Do	L. Arthur	43301-43600.
Do	M. Taylor	50101-50500.
Do	M. E. Brady	61501-62000.
H. Moise	M. Taylor	18301-18700, 21901-22300.
C. White	M. E. Hamilton	23601-24000, 29001-29500, 75401-75800, 94101-94900.
Do	E. C. Winston	39701-39900.
Do	H. Barnwell	39901-40100.
Do	M. E. Harper	46801-47200.
M. Selden	B. Dabney	26801-26900.
Do	M. E. Gilliam	53301-53700.
Do	L. Devine	74801-75400.
M. Ringgold	L. Henry	30701-31000, 40401-40700.

Register of Confederate States Treasury Notes—Continued.

ACT OF FEBRUARY 17, 1864—Continued.

For Treasurer.	For Register.	Numbers of the notes signed.
		$20—A to D (6th series)—Continued.
E. Kelly	B. W. Tyler	31301–31800.
Do	J. A. Acosta	37401–37800.
Do	H. Barnwell	57401–58100.
M. Boyd	S. A. Doar	34601–34900, 40101–40400, 47201–47500, 70701–71300.
M. Carrington	J. M. Connor	35501–35800.
Do	M. E. Norton	42301–42600, 50901–51300.
Do	C. Percival	68201–68600.
Do	M. F. Stevens	87901–88000.
J. Jacobs	M. E. Brady	35801–36100, 76201–76300, 91101–91200.
Do	M. E. Norton	60601–61100.
Do	F. H. Marks	75801–76200.
Do	J. M. Connor	90601–91100.
V. M. Tyler	M. Kirk	37001–37400.
A. Harrison	L. Devine	38601–39000.
A. B. Capron	M. A. Yates	42601–42800.
M. Reeves	E. S. Proctor	42801–43000.
Do	F. Rhett	59601–60100.
Do	M. F. Stevens	66701–67200.
S. R. Simons	E. C. Winston	43601–43800, 66301–66700.
M. Allen	J. M. Connor	43801–43900.
L. Holmes	B. J. Clarke	47801–48100.
Do	S. Huard	55501–55900, 94901–95500.
Do	M. A. Mobley	55901–56000.
J. H. Angel	M. Taylor	48101–48400.
M. A. Dewees	H. E. Bryan	51701–52100, 58601–59100, 63001–63500, 76301–76900, 85501–86100.
H. Balaguer	S. Huard	52101–52500, 67701–68200, 73401–74000.
Do	L. Macon	55001–55500.
J. Wilson	M. A. Yates	53701–53800.
Do	M. B. Kirby	54601–55000.
S. J. Adams	H. C. Thomas	53801–54200, 61301–61500, 92901–93500.
Do	M. Taylor	56401–56900.
M. Banks	E. Coffin	59101–59600.
Do	M. E. Harper	76901–77500, 87301–87900, 92301–92900, 96201–96500.
E. McCully	S. A. Doar	60101–60300.
Do	F. E. Bernard	60301–60600.
L. Sims	M. E. Cullen	65001–65600.
Do	H. E. Alexander	65601–65800.
Do	J. M. Connor	71901–72100.
M. Dargan	L. Arthur	65801–66300.
M. Darby	J. De Leon	81901–82400.
A. Caldwell	M. E. Norton	93501–94100.
		$20—A to D (7th series).
G. Loyd	L. Devine	1–600.
Do	C. Huger	20501–21100.
M. Kingman	K. P. Howell	601–1200, 7201–7800, 10701–11100, 13701–14300, 29301–29900, 33601–33700, 95901–96400.
Do	F. H. Marks	11101–11300.
Do	B. W. Tyler	33101–33600.
Do	M. Kirk	62601–63100.
Do	M. F. Jarvis	66101–66600.
Do	E. S. Read	72001–72500, 75301–75800, 83401–83900, 84701–85300, 89101–89700.
M. Banks	M. E. Harper	1201–1800, 17301–17900, 72501–73000, 86901–87500.
Do	E. C. Winston	78301–78800.
Do	M. J. Black	79601–80100.
S. J. Adams	H. C. Thomas	1801–2400.
Do	M. Taylor	44901–45200.
Do	M. J. Black	93701–94100.
E. C. Trescot	V. Penrifoy	2401–2900, 9101–9600, 24301–24800, 30901–31400, 34401–34900, 38701–39200, 43801–44300, 47201–47700, 59101-59600, 64701-65100, 71501–72000, 76301–76800, 80101–80600, 96901–97200.
Do	M. A. Yates	12001–12600, 21101–21600.
Do	J. M. Connor	85901–86400.
Do	E. S. Proctor	86401–86500.

Register of Confederate States Treasury Notes—Continued.

ACT OF FEBRUARY 17, 1864—Continued.

For Treasurer.	For Register.	Numbers of the notes signed.
		$20—A to D (7th series)—Continued.
M. A. Dewees	H. E. Bryan	2901-3500, 36401-36800, 60101-60600, 77801-78300, 81501-82000.
Do	S. E. Laval	8501-9100.
Do	H. Barnwell	12601-13100.
M. Wade	E. Davis	3501-4000.
Do	E. Matthews	4001-4100.
Do	M. F. Stevens	23701-24300.
Do	F. H. Marks	48701-49200.
Do	L. Michel	74101-74600, 88601-88700.
Do	M. Kirk	88101-88600.
M. Cooper	H. Heriot	4101-4900, 7801-8500, 11301-12000, 26701-27400, 32001-32600, 33701-34400, 40301-40900, 56601-57200, 67601-68200.
Do	B. J. Clarke	49201-49900.
A. Miller	S. E. Laval	4901-5600, 16501-17300, 26001-26700, 51201-51900, 57801-58500.
L. Holmes	S. Huard	5601-6000.
Do	E. Coffin	6001-6100.
Do	M. A. Yates	35901-36400.
M. Selden	M. E. Gilliam	6101-6700.
Do	L. Devine	13101-13700, 22201-22800, 29901-30300, 35301-35900, 41201-41800, 47701-48200, 55501-56100, 65101-65600, 69101-69600, 81001-81500, 88701-89100.
Do	M. Kirk	95001-95600.
J. Wilson	M. E. Gilliam	6701-7200.
Do	L. W. Elliott	9601-10200.
Do	L. Macon	19301-19900.
Do	L. Arthur	28101-28700, 37301-37800.
Do	M. F. Stevens	39701-40300.
M. Boyd	H. Barnwell	10201-10700.
Do	M. J. Black	45201-45800.
Do	F. Rhett	62101-62600.
S. McCants	C. Percival	14301-14900, 21601-22200, 32601-33100, 36801-37300, 38101-38700, 42801-43300, 48201-48700, 54901-55500, 59601-60100.
Do	E. S. Read	67101-67600.
Do	M. Dixon	69601-70100.
Do	M. F. Jarvis	76801-77300, 79101-79600, 87501-88100, 90301-90900, 94101-94400.
A. Caldwell	J. D. Treadwell	14901-15500, 27401-28000, 68701-69100, 74601-75100, 92101-92700.
Do	H. Barnwell	19901-20500.
Do	M. Kirk	28701-29300.
Do	M. F. Jarvis	58501-59100.
Do	A. Zealy	61101-61600.
Do	E. Laurens	75101-75300.
Do	S. Huard	84101-84700.
J. Gill	B. J. Clarke	15501-16100.
J. Ambler	L. Arthur	16101-16500.
Do	L. Michel	52401-52900.
C. Morris	M. Kirk	17901-18700.
Do	E. Davis	96401-96900.
S. G. Sanxay	M. Dixon	18701-19300.
S. Neill	B. W. Tyler	22801-23100, 61601-62100, 68201-68700, 75801-76300, 82901-83400, 91501-92100, 94401-95000.
Do	M. E. Norton	43301-43800.
Do	S. K. Wells	70101-70600.
E. McCully	F. Rhett	23101-23700.
K. Korff	F. C. Jones	24801-25400, 49901-50500.
Do	J. A. Acosta	64101-64700.
L. Armstrong	H. E. Alexander	25401-26000, 41801-42300, 46701-47200, 66601-67100, 77301-77800, 85301-85900.
Do	H. Heriot	80601-81000.
M. Dargan	L. W. Elliott	28001-28100, 31401-32000.
Do	L. Arthur	63701-64100.
P. Savage	L. Macon	30301-30900, 60601-61100, 89701-90300.
M. Godwin	M. E. Norton	34901-35300.
Do	M. Dixon	39201-39700, 45801-46200, 56101-56600, 82001-82400, 95601-95900.
M. Ringgold	L. Henry	37801-38100.

Register of Confederate States Treasury Notes—Continued.

ACT OF FEBRUARY 17, 1864—Continued.

For Treasurer.	For Register.	Numbers of the notes signed.
		$20—A to D (7th series)—Continued.
S. R. Simons	E. C. Winston	40901–41200, 42301–42800, 51901–52400, 57201–57800.
Do	L. Pelot	46201–46700.
S. Scott	M. F. Jarvis	44301–44900.
C. White	M. E. Hamilton	50501–51200.
F. Stocker	M. F. Stevens	52901–53400.
H. Balaguer	S. Huard	53401–53900.
N. Giles	E. S. Read	53901–54500.
J. Jacobs	M. A. Yates	54501–54900.
L. Sims	M. E. Cullen	63101–63700, 73001–73600, 83901–84100.
A. S. Stuart	M. Taylor	65601–66100.
O. McGowan	M. F. Jarvis	70601–71100.
Do	M. Kirk	90901–91500.
M. Carrington	M. Pleasants	71101–71500, 78801–79100, 86501–86900.
S. Fuller	R. King	73601–74100.
F. Waties	H. Barnwell	82401–82900.
E. Willis	J. M. Connor	92701–93300.
R. Haynes	L. W. Elliott	93301–93700.
		$20—A to D (8th series).
M. S. Gist	L. Pelot	1–600.
Do	M. Dixon	82401–82600.
J. Jacobs	H. E. Bryan	601–1100.
Do	A. Zealy	1101–1200.
Do	M. B. Kirby	11701–11900.
Do	E. C. Winston	51001–51500, 66301–66700, 75501–75900.
E. C. Trescot	V. Penrifoy	1201–1700, 5001–5500, 8201–8400, 11901–12400, 16901–17400, 22901–23400, 27901–28400, 42301–42900, 59601–60100, 67901-68400, 77101–77600, 92101–92600.
Do	M. F. Jarvis	64601–65100.
Do	E. Davis	78501–79000.
L. Armstrong	H. E. Alexander	1701–2200, 5501–5800, 9001–9500.
Do	E. Matthews	27401–27900.
A. Miller	S. E. Laval	2201–2900, 40901–41500, 47901–48600, 82601–83200, 86501-87300, 93401–94100.
S. McCants	M. F. Jarvis	2901–3200.
Do	C. Percival	5801–6300, 9501–10100, 23401–23900, 29401–29900, 32401–33000, 38801–39500, 49201–49800, 60101–60700, 64001–64600, 68401-69000, 81201–81800.
Do	M. E. Cullen	95301–95900.
M. Godwin	M. J. Black	3201–3800.
Do	E. S. Proctor	10501–10700.
Do	M. F. Stevens	10701–11100.
Do	E. Davis	43501–44100, 47301–47900.
Do	L. Macon	52301–52900, 57901–58500.
Do	M. Dixon	63501–64000.
M. Selden	E. S. Read	3801–4400.
Do	M. Kirk	15001–15600.
Do	C. Percival	18301–18900.
Do	M. F. Jarvis	24401–25000, 30901–31500, 44701–45300, 50401–51000.
Do	L. Michel	33001–33300, 79001–79600.
Do	J. A. Acosta	55501–56100.
Do	B. Dabney	58501–59100, 71001–71600, 74601–74900, 79601–79700, 89701-90300, 91501–92100.
M. Kingman	K. P. Howell	4401–5000.
Do	H. Heriot	13901–14500.
Do	M. E. Hamilton	18901–19500, 21901–22400, 28901–29400, 36901–37200, 42901-43500, 48601–49200, 52901–53500, 59101–59600, 62901–63500, 70401–71000, 72901–73200, 77601–77900, 85301–85900.
M. Banks	M. F. Jarvis	6301–6900.
Do	M. Kirk	8401–9000.
Do	E. C. Winston	15601–16200.
Do	M. E. Harper	20701–21300, 23901–24400, 30401–30900, 34201–34700, 39501-40100, 45301–45900, 49801–50400, 62501–62900, 77901–78500, 83201–84500, 90901–91500, 94101–94700.
M. A. Dewees	H. E. Bryan	6901–7500, 11101–11700, 25501–26100, 40701–40900, 94701-95300.
O. McGowan	F. E. Bernard	7501–8000.

Register of Confederate States Treasury Notes—Continued.

ACT OF FEBRUARY 17, 1864—Continued.

For Treasurer.	For Register.	Numbers of the notes signed.
		$20—A to D (8th series)—Continued.
O. McGowan	A. Zealy	17801-18300.
M. Carrington	M. Pleasants	8001-8200, 10101-10500, 12901-13300, 17401-17800.
A. Harrison	L. Devine	12401-12900, 41501-42100, 47001-47300, 51501-52100, 61301-61900, 66701-67300, 75901-76500.
Do	H. E. Bryan	88101-88300.
A. Caldwell	J. D. Treadwell	13301-13900, 69001-69600, 81801-82400.
C. Morris	L. Macon	14501-15000, 26901-27400.
Do	E. Davis	22401-22900.
Do	L. Courtney	31901-32400.
E. Baker	C. C. Veal	16201-16900, 26101-26900, 34701-35300, 53501-54100, 73801-74600.
E. Willis	J. M. Connor	19501-20000, 28401-28900.
C. White	E. S. Read	20001-20700, 35301-36100, 37201-37800, 65701-66300, 69601-70400, 84501-85300.
Do	M. Pleasants	37801-38000.
K. Korff	J. A. Acosta	21301-21900.
Do	L. Arthur	44101-44700.
Do	E. Davis	56901-57500.
Do	E. S. Read	61901-62300.
Do	M. F. Jarvis	62301-62500.
Do	H. Barnwell	73201-73800.
Do	L. Devine	79701-79900.
Do	S. Huard	79901-80300.
Do	C. Percival	88301-88900.
M. Wade	M. A. Yates	25001-25500.
M. Allen	S. K. Wells	29901-30400.
J. Ambler	A. Zealy	31501-31900.
Do	L. Michel	67601-67900.
S. Neill	K. P. Howell	33601-34200, 42101-42300, 54101-54700.
Do	E. Davis	60701-61300, 71601-72200, 74901-75500, 85901-86500.
J. H. Angel	C. Huger	36101-36600.
R. Haynes	L. W. Elliott	36601-36900.
Do	L. Macon	80301-80600.
Do	J. D. Treadwell	95901-96300.
E. Kelly	B. W. Tyler	38001-38400, 54701-55300.
Do	M. Kirk	38401-38800.
Do	M. Dixon	55301-55500.
A. S. Stuart	M. Taylor	40101-40700, 45901-46500, 52101-52300.
M. Darby	M. Pleasants	46501-46900.
Do	J. M. Connor	46901-47000.
L. Sims	J. D. Treadwell	56101-56500.
Do	M. E. Cullen	56501-56900.
M. Dargan	L. Arthur	57501-57900, 65101-65700.
J. Logan	N. Brisbane	67301-67600.
Do	B. W. Tyler	90301-90900.
M. Cooper	H. Heriot	72201-72900, 92601-93300.
N. Semple	M. E. Norton	76501-77100.
S. J. Adams	L. Courtney	80601-81200.
J. Gill	M. Dixon	87301-88100.
E. M. Bell	M. F. Jarvis	88901-89700.
Do	B. Dabney	96301-96600.
		$20—A to D (9th series).
S. Neill	E. Davis	1-600, 3001-3600, 8001-8600, 14901-15500, 32901-33500.
E. A. Dennison	M. F. Stevens	601-1200.
J. Gill	M. Dixon	1201-1800, 5001-5700.
M. Banks	M. E. Harper	1801-2400, 6801-7400.
Do	L. Courtney	11801-12400, 16801-17400, 22601-23200, 26801-27400, 28501-29100, 35301-35900, 41101-41700.
M. Kingman	M. E. Hamilton	2401-3000.
Do	L. A. Norris	10001-10600.
Do	K. P. Howell	18601-19200.
Do	F. E. Bernard	23201-23800, 31301-31700, 36501-37100.
C. White	E. S. Read	3601-4200, 11101-11800, 16101-16800, 23801-24600, 25801-26600, 29701-30500, 37701-38500.
E. M. Bell	M. F. Jarvis	4201-5000, 9201-10000, 13601-14400, 19401-20000.
Do	L. W. Elliott	19201-19400.

Register of Confederate States Treasury Notes—Continued.

ACT OF FEBRUARY 17, 1864—Continued.

For Treasurer.	For Register.	Numbers of the notes signed.
		$20—A to D (9th series)—Continued.
S. R. Simons	E. C. Winston	5701–6300, 13001–13600, 26601–26800.
S. McCants	C. Percival	6301–6800, 7401–8000.
Do	L. Pelot	20001–20600, 35901–36500.
Do	B. Dabney	24601–25200, 31701–32300.
M. A. Dewees	H. E. Bryan	8601–9200, 21201–21800, 28001–28500, 40301–40500, 42301–42400.
M. Selden	B. Dabney	10601–11100, 12401–13000.
J. Jacobs	L. Michel	14401–14700.
Do	L. A. Norris	14701–14900.
Do	L. Courtney	21801–22600.
F. Stocker	M. F. Stevens	15501–16100.
Do	M. Gaither	39101–39700.
A. Caldwell	B. Dabney	17401–18000.
Do	J. D. Treadwell	25201–25800, 37101–37700.
S. Scott	L. A. Norris	18001–18600.
J. Logan	E. Davis	20601–21200, 39701–40300.
S. J. Adams	M. Kirk	27401–28000, 29101–29700, 38501–38900, 41701–42300.
Do	R. King	38901–39100.
E. Baker	F. C. Jones	30501–31300.
Do	M. Dixon	34501–35300.
A. Harrison	J. D. Treadwell	32301–32900.
E. Kelly	A. Zealy	33501–34100.
M. Darby	S. Johnson	34101–34500.
Do	M. Pleasants	40501–40700, 40901–41100.
Do	L. Courtney	40701–40900.
* * * *	* * * *	* * * * * * *
		$20—A to D (10th series).
* * * *	* * * *	* * * * * * *
		$20—A to D (11th series).
* * * *	* * * *	* * * * * * *
		$10—A to H.
V. M. Stanard	L. Devine	1–100, 4701–4800, 6401–6600, 12801–13100, 18401–18500, 21301–21600, 27501–27700, 37901–38100, 50901–51200, 57001–57300, 61801–62000, 85401–85700, 92301–92600, 100301–100600, 107601–107900, 115901–116200, 123901–124200, 131001–131300.
M. Allen	H. L. Cooke	101–200, 7901–8200, 11101–11400, 17401–17600, 18701–19000, 25101–25300, 25901–26200, 35701–35900, 40601–40700, 41201–41400, 47201–47400, 52401–52800, 60801–61100, 69801–70200, 75901–76200, 82901–83300, 91601–92000, 99601–100000, 106901–107300, 114401–114800, 131301–131700, 140501–140900.
Do	B. J. Clarke	48601–48900.
Do	S. E. Hughes	48901–49000.
Do	A. P. Pellet	61101–61200.
S. G. Sanxay	L. Macon	201–300, 4301–4500, 5601–5800, 11401–11700, 17901–18000, 25501–25700, 26601–26900, 36901–37100, 40501–40600, 41601–41800, 48301–48400, 53701–54000, 72301–72600, 77901–78100, 83601–83900, 93801–94100, 100001–100300, 118401–118700, 127401–127700, 133101–133400.
Do	A. P. Pellet	35601–35700.
Do	P. Pleasants	48401–48500.
Do	M. S. Apperson	78101–78200.
J. Wilson	J. B. Tiffey	301–400, 6001–6200, 12001–12300, 18001–18100, 20101–20400, 28901–29100, 35201–35300, 36501–36700, 49401–49700, 55801–56100, 60501–60800, 70201–70500, 79801–80100, 86601–86900, 93501–93800, 102901–103200, 112801–113100, 116801–117100, 122401–122700, 132801–133100.
Do	M. B. Kirby	141501–141800.

Register of Confederate States Treasury Notes—Continued.

ACT OF FEBRUARY 17, 1864—Continued.

For Treasurer.	For Register.	Numbers of the notes signed.
		$10—A to H—Continued.
W. A. Garrett	J. McGarr	401-500, 1901-2200, 18101-18200, 28301-28600, 39201-39300, 40701-40800, 42301-42500, 56401-56700, 70801-71100, 76701-76900, 88401-88700, 93201-93500, 103201-103500.
Do	P. Pleasants	6201-6400, 110601-110700, 119201-119300.
Do	E. C. Winston	13701-14000.
Do	N. Palmer	61201-61500.
Do	B. McRae	76901-77000, 136401-136700.
Do	J. Douglas	110401-110600.
Do	E. W. Pendleton	119001-119200.
Do	A. P. Pellet	123301-123600.
Do	M. C. Morton	129701-129900.
Do	M. F. Cary	129901-130000.
Do	B. M. Abbott	142901-143100.
Do	M. Gay	143101-143200.
C. Hix	do	501-600, 5401-5500, 115501-115900, 124901-125300, 135601-136000.
Do	B. J. Clarke	7201-7500, 13301-13500.
Do	E. W. Pendleton	22701-22900, 79101-79200, 97801-97900, 109901-110100.
Do	A. P. Pellet	22901-23100, 36701-36900, 66401-66700.
Do	M. E. Gilliam	30101-30200, 31001-31100.
Do	H. L. Cooke	30201-30300.
Do	M. Taylor	42701-42900, 48101-48200.
Do	P. Pleasants	48201-48300, 84301-84500, 98001-98200.
Do	M. S. Apperson	57301-57500, 84501-84700, 101401-101600.
Do	M. Dixon	57501-57600.
Do	F. E. Bernard	57601-57700.
Do	B. McRae	73801-74100, 97901-98000.
Do	N. Palmer	79201-79400.
Do	B. M. Abbott	101201-101400.
Do	L. Macon	109701-109900.
L. C. Minor	B. M. Abbott	601-700, 3701-4000, 8601-8800, 21901-22200, 29301-29500, 35401-35500, 38101-38300, 40901-41000, 50601-50900, 74601-74900, 82401-82600, 89701-90000, 94101-94400, 111901-112200, 119601-119900, 126801-127100, 137101-137400.
Do	B. McRae	22201-22300, 90001-90100, 94401-94500, 104401-104500.
Do	M. W. Bailey	42501-42700.
Do	P. Pleasants	57701-57900.
Do	A. P. Pellet	57901-58100.
Do	J. L. Johnston	63001-63300, 104201-104400.
Do	M. S. Apperson	82601-82700.
M. E. Dudley	M. E. Norton	701-800, 5301-5400, 7001-7200, 14001-14300, 18201-18300, 19901-20100, 25401-25500, 26401-26600, 31601-31700, 38501-38700, 46701-46800, 51901-52100, 54301-54600, 62301-62600, 71701-72000, 78201-78500, 85701-86000, 92901-93200, 102601-102900, 108601-108900, 118701-119000, 123001-123300, 138001-138300, 142601-142900.
L. Carter	M. F. Stevens	801-900, 2501-2800, 13501-13700, 17801-17900, 25801-25900, 26901-27200, 37501-37600, 40801-40900, 44401-44600, 54001-54300, 69201-69300, 74101-74400, 77601-77800, 83901-84200, 92001-92300, 101601-101900, 109301-109500, 116201-116400, 124201-124500, 130601-130900.
Do	M. S. Apperson	6801-7000, 64301-64600, 74901-75000.
Do	A. P. Pellet	34701-34800.
Do	B. J. Clarke	37601-37700.
Do	B. McRae	77801-77900, 84201-84300, 116401-116500, 143201-143300.
Do	N. Palmer	101901-102000, 109501-109700.
Do	P. Pleasants	124501-124600, 130901-131000.
Do	A. Newman	143301-143400.
E. A. Dennison	M. E. Gilliam	901-1000, 7701-7900, 15401-15700, 20701-21000, 38401-38500, 44001-44200, 141801-142100.
Do	M. S. Apperson	25701-25800, 96601-96800.
Do	M. Taylor	38301-38400, 41001-41100, 80501-80600.
Do	M. C. Lathrop	59301-59700.
Do	E. W. Pendleton	66101-66400.
Do	N. Palmer	72601-72900, 86901-87200.
Do	L. Devine	80401-80500.
Do	J. L. Johnston	80601-80700.
Do	B. Dabney	96801-96900.

Register of Confederate States Treasury Notes—Continued.

ACT OF FEBRUARY 17, 1864—Continued.

For Treasurer.	For Register.	Numbers of the notes signed.
		$10—A to H—Continued.
E. A. Dennison	L. Forde	105401–105700, 110701–111000.
Do	E. A. Adams	119301–119600, 124601–124900, 134701–135000.
V. K. Davies	S. E. Hughes	1001–1100.
R. Haynes	B. Dabney	1101–1200, 3401–3700, 9601–9800, 14601–14900, 23901–24200, 39401–39500, 39901–40000, 58301–58600, 64601–64900, 98801–99000, 101001–101200, 111001–111300, 117101–117400.
E. Mason	M. C. Lathrop	1201–1300, 9001–9200, 15101–15400, 28601–28900, 38701–38900, 40201–40300, 41801–42100, 47901–48100, 51201–51600, 62601–63000, 71101–71300, 81601–81700, 82701–82900, 87801–88100, 97501–97800, 103801–104100, 107901–108200, 114801–115100, 126401–126700, 133701–134100.
Do	M. S. Apperson	71301–71400.
Do	A. P. Pellet	88101–88200, 108201–108300, 115101–115200.
Do	P. Pleasants	97401–97500, 126701–126800.
Do	N. Palmer	104101–104200.
W. L. Smalley	B. J. Clarke	1301–1400, 2801–3100, 10901–11100, 17701–17800, 20401–20700, 27201–27500, 37301–37500, 55501–55800, 64001–64300, 72001–72300, 78801–79100, 86301–86600, 102001–102300, 110101–110400, 117801–118100, 123601–123900, 131701–132100.
Do	S. E. Hughes	55201–55300.
Do	M. Taylor	55301–55400.
Do	E. A. Adams	92601–92900.
V. M. Rind	V. K. Davies	1401–1500, 5101–5200, 10701–10900, 16001–16300, 39801–39900, 40401–40500, 63301–63600, 81701–81900, 88701–89000, 96001–96300, 105701–106000, 112201–112500, 120501 120800, 125301–125600, 140101–140200.
Do	A. P. Pellet	10501–10700, 43501–43700.
Do	E. A. Adams	29901–30100, 34801–34900, 50301–50600.
Do	S. E. Hughes	58901–59300, 75601–75900.
Do	B. McRae	69401–69500.
Do	P. Pleasants	81901–82000.
H. Starke	E. W. Pendleton	1501–1600, 4001–4300, 10301–10500, 16501–16800, 44601–44700, 47001–47200, 135001–135100.
Do	N. Palmer	29701–29900.
Do	M. S. Apperson	39301–39400.
Do	E. A. Adams	54901–55200.
M. C. Waller	L. Forde	1601–1700, 4901–5000, 8401–8600, 13101–13300, 21001–21300, 29101–29300, 35101–35200, 37701–37900, 44201–44400, 49701–50000, 54601–54900, 62001–62300, 71401–71700, 78501–78800, 88201–88400.
Do	M. S. Apperson	126201–126400, 134101–134400, 142301–142600.
S. Clark	M. W. Bailey	1701–1800, 18601–18700, 23401–23600, 31301–31500, 39601–39800, 41101–41200, 58601–58900, 75101–75300, 79401–79600, 90401–90700, 97101–97400, 104501–104800, 111301–111600, 119901–120200, 128801–129100, 138601–138900.
Do	P. Pleasants	23601–23700, 79601–79700.
Do	B. McRae	46801–46900.
Do	S. E. Hughes	65501–65800.
M. C. Irvine	M. Taylor	1801–1900, 4801–4900, 9801–9900, 16301–16500, 24801–25100, 31101–31300, 73501–73800, 80701–81000, 89001–89300, 96901–97100, 104801–105100, 112501–112800, 120801–121000.
Do	L. Forde	121001–121100, 128301–128500, 138301–138600.
S. F. Shaver	M. Dixon	2201–2500, 6601–6800, 12301–12600, 17601–17700, 19601–19900, 25301–25400, 27701–28000, 37101–37200, 42201–42300, 47601–47800, 49001–49200, 53101–53400, 61501–61800, 75301–75600, 77301–77500, 84701–85000, 94801–95100, 100601–100900, 108901–109200, 117401–117700, 132101–132400.
Do	B. McRae	37201–37300, 39501–39600, 40101–40200, 85001–85100.
Do	P. Pleasants	42101–42200, 95201–95300, 109201–109301, 117701–117800.
Do	E. C. Winston	49201–49400.
Do	L. Devine	77501–77600.
Do	A. P. Pellet	95101–95200, 100901–101000.
Do	B. Dabney	132401–132500.
M. A. Dewees	S. E. Hughes	3101–3400, 9201–9400, 14301–14600, 23701–23900, 30901–31000, 140201–140300.

Register of Confederate States Treasury Notes—Continued.

ACT OF FEBRUARY 17, 1864—Continued.

For Treasurer.	For Register.	Numbers of the notes signed.
		$10—A to H—Continued.
N. Semple	F. E. Bernard	4501–4700, 7501–7700, 11701–12000, 18501–18600, 19301-19600, 28001–28300, 36101–36300, 47801–47900, 56101-56400, 60201-60500, 69501–69800, 77001–77300, 87201–87500, 91001-91300, 102301–102600, 108301–108600, 115201–115900, 125601-125900, 132501–132800, 141201–141500.
M. S. Nicholas	M. W. Bailey	5001–5100, 10101–10300.
Do	N. Palmer	14901–15100, 24201–24500.
Do	S. E. Hughes	30701–30900, 35001–35100, 43301–43500, 81001-81300, 87501-87800, 98201–98500, 106601–106900, 111601–111900, 121101-121400, 128501–128800.
Do	M. C. Lathrop	52101–52400.
Do	M. Taylor	56701–57000, 65201–65500.
Do	M. B. Kirby	139501–139800.
M. Jones	B. McRae	5201–5300, 8801–9000.
Do	E. A. Adams	15701–16000, 22301–22700, 105101–105400, 113501–113800.
Do	M. C. Lathrop	18301–18400.
Do	M. B. Kirby	30301–30500, 35301–35400.
Do	P. Pleasants	46901–47000.
Do	A. P. Pellet	79701–79800.
Do	B. Dabney	90101–90400.
Do	L. Forde	96301–96600, 120201–120500.
Do	E. W. Pendleton	127701–128000, 139201–139500.
A. Harrison	J. Douglas	5501–5600, 9401–9600, 16801–17000, 21601–21900, 29501–29700, 34901–35000, 39101–39200, 40001–40100, 43101–43300, 55401-55500, 65101–65200, 73201–73500, 80101–80400, 86001-86300, 94501–94800, 103501–103800, 116501–116800, 125901-126000, 133501–133700.
Do	B. Dabney	64901–65100, 126101–126200.
Do	M. C. Lathrop	126001–126100.
Do	N. Palmer	133401–133500.
V. M. Tyler	B. M. Payne	5801–6000, 12601–12800, 17301–17400, 19001–19300, 26201-26400, 36301–36500, 50001–50300, 52801–53100, 59901-60200, 70501–70800, 76201–76400, 83301–83600, 91301-91600, 99301-96600, 107301-107600, 114101-114400, 122701-123000, 130301-130600, 135101–135300, 140901–141200.
Do	A. P. Pellet	43701–43800, 48501–48600.
R. F. Ball	E. C. Winston	8201–8400, 23101–23400, 30501–30700, 35501–35600, 38901-39100, 40301–40400, 42901–43100, 47401–47600, 58001-58300, 63601–64000, 75001–75100, 82001–82300, 89301-89600, 95301-95600, 106201-106500, 113101-113400, 121701-122000, 130001-130300, 139801–140100.
Do	P. Pleasants	31501–31600.
Do	M. Dixon	69301–69400.
Do	A. P. Pellet	82301-82400, 89601-89700, 95601-95700, 106501-106600, 113401-113500, 122001–122100.
A. B. Capron	M. W. Bailey	9901–10100.
Do	M. B. Kirby	17001–17300, 24501–24800, 43801–44000, 59501–59600, 59701-59900, 81301-81600, 90701-91000, 98501-98800, 106001-106200, 113801–114100, 121401–121600, 129401–129700.
Do	B. McRae	65801–66000, 121601–121700.
Do	B. Dabney	66001–66100.
Do	P. Pleasants	74401–74600.
F. C. Weisiger	J. H. Cooke	31701–32000, 34501–34600, 66701–67100.
F. H. Link	W. O. Slade	32001–32300, 34201–34300, 44701–45000, 68301–68700.
T. J. Hatch	W. Hancock	32301–32600, 34101–34200.
J. A. Jones	G. N. Warren	32601–32900, 34401–34500, 67101–67500.
C. Ashford	J. Sands	32901–33200, 45001–45300.
T. W. Brown	......do	33201–33500, 34301–34400, 67501–67900.
N. A. Bass	C. S. Taylor	33501–33600, 33801–34100, 45301–45600, 45901–46300, 67901-68300.
A. Patton	L. P. Rogers	33601–33800, 34601–34700, 45601–45900, 46301–46700.
Do	J. Sands	69101–69200.
W. G. Allen	J. J. Matthews	68701–69100.
M. Godwin	S. E. Hughes	35901–36100.
Do	M. E. Norton	41401–41500.
Do	B. McRae	41501–41600.

Register of Confederate States Treasury Notes—Continued.

ACT OF FEBRUARY 17, 1864—Continued.

For Treasurer.	For Register.	Numbers of the notes signed.
		$10—A to H—Continued.
M. Godwin	J. L. Johnston	51601-51800, 53401-53700, 72901-73200, 76401-76500, 76601-76700, 85101-85400, 95701-96000, 99101-99300, 118101-118400, 122101-122300.
Do	J. McGarr	51801-51900.
Do	E. W. Pendleton	76501-76600.
Do	N. Palmer	99001-99100.
Do	M. F. Cary	122301-122400.
Do	M. Gay	135301-135500.
Do	M. E. Gilliam	135501-135600, 142101-142200.
Do	V. K. Davies	142201-142300.
H. B. Cone	M. Taylor	127101-127400, 138901-139200.
H. Fort	B. McRae	128001-128300.
Do	M. C. Morton	134401-134700.
E. S. Read	N. Palmer	129101-129400, 136001-136300.
Do	P. Pleasants	136301-136400.
N. Giles	M. F. Cary	136701-137100.
R. Macmurdo	B. W. Tyler	137401-137700.
M. J. Morris	A. Newman	137701-138000.
L. Archer	A. P. Pellet	140301-140500.
		$10—A to H (1st series).
L. Carter	J. L. Johnston	1-100.
Do	M. F. Stevens	8501-8700, 15501-15600, 18601-18700.
Do	S. E. Hughes	8701-8800.
Do	N. Palmer	15601-15700, 18701-18800.
Do	L. C. Royster	15701-15800.
Do	A. Newman	18801-18900.
V. M. Stanard	L. Devine	101-400, 6601-6800, 8801-9000, 15001-15200, 22401-22600.
Do	M. S. Apperson	9001-9100.
S. F. Shaver	M. Dixon	401-700, 11501-11600, 16401-16600, 18901-19100.
Do	A. P. Pellet	701-900, 19101-19200.
Do	M. E. Gilliam	11301-11500.
Do	S. E. Hughes	16601-16700.
E. Mason	M. C. Lathrop	901-1200, 5901-6200, 9101-9300, 13801-14000, 19501-19800.
Do	J. B. Tiffey	6201-6300.
Do	A. P. Pellet	9301-9500.
Do	M. Gay	14001-14200.
Do	E. W. Pendleton	19801-19900.
V. M. Rind	N. Palmer	1201-1500.
Do	B. Dabney	1501-1600, 68801-68900.
Do	V. K. Davies	3601-4000, 23901-24000, 32801-33100, 39601-39900, 46801-47100, 55001-55300, 68601-68800, 76901-77200, 86201-86500.
Do	A. P. Pellet	4001-4100.
Do	S. A. Doar	88501-88600.
Do	K. P. Howell	88601-88800.
Do	E. S. Proctor	97101-97400.
W. L. Smalley	B. J. Clarke	1601-2000, 14301-14500.
Do	B. Dabney	6301-6600.
Do	J. L. Johnston	11001-11100.
Do	B. W. Tyler	11101-11200.
Do	V. K. Davies.	11201-11300.
Do	S. E. Hughes	14201-14300.
Do	A. P. Pellet	18301-18400.
Do	M. S. Apperson	18401-18600.
R. Macmurdo	B. W. Tyler	2001-2200, 22801-22900, 29501-29800.
Do	F. Rhett	96901-97100.
M. A. Dewees	S. E. Hughes	2201-2400, 31301-31600, 48201-48500, 54201-54400.
Do	A. P. Pellet	24001-24200.
Do	M. A. Yates	54401-54500.
Do	B. J. Clarke	54501-54800.
Do	M. Dixon	61301-61600.
Do	A. S. Parry	84501-84700.
Do	M. C. Morton	84701-84800.
S. Clark	L. C. Royster	2401-2700.
Do	M. W. Bailey	6801-7000, 11601-11800, 17001-17200, 21001-21200.
Do	M. E. Norton	7001-7100.
Do	E. A. Adams	11801-11900.

Register of Confederate States Treasury Notes—Continued.

ACT OF FEBRUARY 17, 1864—Continued.

For Treasurer.	For Register.	Numbers of the notes signed.
		$10—A to H (1st series)—Continued.
S. Clark	E. C. Winston	17201–17300.
Do	H. L. Cooke	21201–21300.
H. B. Cone	M. Taylor	2701–3000, 7601–7700.
Do	J. B. Tiffey	7401–7500, 21501–21700.
Do	A. Newman	7501–7600, 21701–21800.
Do	B. McRae	12901–13100.
Do	E. C. Winston	13101–13200.
Do	M. E. Gilliam	17301–17500.
Do	S. E. Hughes	17501–17600.
M. Jones	E. A. Adams	3001–3300.
Do	V. M. Tyler	22001–22200.
H. Fort	B. McRae	3301–3600.
Do	A. P. Pellet	10401–10600.
Do	S. E. Hughes	10601–10700.
M. J. Morris	M. Gay	4101–4400.
L. C. Minor	B. M. Abbott	4401–4700.
Do	E. A. Adams	11901–12000.
Do	M. C. Morton	12001–12200.
Do	L. C. Royster	16701–16900.
Do	M. B. Kirby	16901–17000.
Do	M. Gay	21801–22000.
Do	E. C. Winston	24701–24900, 35701–36000, 41701–41900, 46201–46500, 52301–52600, 72001–72300, 82201–82500, 88001–88300, 94001–94300, 100801–101100.
Do	J. De Leon	59901–60200.
Do	M. E. Norton	66601–66900.
Do	L. Devine	72301–72400.
M. C. Irvine	L. Forde	4701–5000, 17601–17900, 21301–21500.
R. F. Ball	E. C. Winston	5001–5400.
L. Archer	H. L. Cooke	5401–5700.
H. Starke	E. W. Pendleton	5701–5900.
W. A. Garrett	L. Forde	7101–7400.
Do	L. C. Royster	9501–9700.
Do	E. W. Pendleton	9701–9800.
Do	E. C. Winston	15201–15400.
Do	M. Gay	15401–15500.
Do	B. McRae	20201–20400.
Do	J. L. Johnston	20401–20500.
M. S. Nicholas	S. E. Hughes	7701–7900.
Do	M. Gay	10101–10400.
Do	E. W. Pendleton	22201–22400.
M. Allen	H. L. Cooke	7901–8200, 13201–13500, 17901–18200, 22601–22800, 25801–26200, 37201–37400, 41201–41400.
Do	S. E. Hughes	8201–8300.
Do	N. Palmer	18201–18300.
Do	A. S. Parry	100001–100300, 100401–100500.
Do	C. C. Veal	100301–100400.
V. M. Tyler	B. M. Payne	8301–8500, 14801–15000.
Do	M. F. Stevens	22901–23000.
Do	M. Pleasants	26201–26500, 36901–37200, 43601–43900, 56601–56700, 62301–62600, 65101–65400.
Do	M. Kirk	99801–99900.
M. E. Dudley	E. W. Pendleton	9801–9900.
Do	M. E. Norton	9901–10100, 16101–16300.
Do	L. C. Royster	16301–16400.
Do	M. Gay	19201–19500.
S. G. Sanxay	J. L. Johnston	10701–10800, 16001–16100.
Do	L. Macon	10801–11000.
Do	B. McRae	15801–16000.
Do	B. J. Clarke	23501–23600, 28001–28300.
Do	M. Dixon	38501–38800, 50101–50300, 51201–51500, 62901–63200, 66901–67200, 75001–75200.
J. Wilson	J. Douglas	12201–12400.
Do	E. C. Winston	12401–12500.
Do	J. B. Tiffey	14501–14700.
Do	J. L. Johnston	14701–14800.
Do	E. S. Read	23101–23300.
Do	E. Laurens	28301–28400.

Register of Confederate States Treasury Notes—Continued.

ACT OF FEBRUARY 17, 1864—Continued.

For Treasurer.	For Register.	Numbers of the notes signed.
		$10—A to H (1st series)—Continued.
J. Wilson	J. McGarr	28401–28600, 36601–36900, 43301–43600, 56501–56600, 64801-65100.
Do	E. S. Proctor	57001–57300.
Do	J. M. Connor	79301–79500.
E. S. Read	N. Palmer	12501–12700.
Do	L. Forde	12701–12900.
Do	B. Dabney	20701–20900.
Do	M. B. Kirby	20901–21000.
M. C. Waller	M. S. Apperson	13501–13700.
Do	M. B. Kirby	13701–13800.
Do	B. M. Abbott	19901–20000.
Do	E. A. Adams	20001–20200.
S. Lambert	B. M. Payne	20501–20700.
P. Savage	L. A. Norris	23001–23100.
Do	L. Macon	33101–33400, 53001–53300, 73601–73900, 77801–78100.
Do	A. Zealy	73901–74000.
Do	J. M. Connor	97701–97900.
N. Goodwin	M. Dixon	23301–23400, 32501–32700.
Do	M. B. Kirby	23401–23500, 32701–32800, 33701–34000, 39301–39600.
Do	E. Coffin	83201–83500, 96301–96600.
Do	S. E. Laval	86701–87000.
Do	J. Via	89001–89200.
Do	J. D. Treadwell	89201–89300.
A. Harrison	L. Devine	23601–23700, 28601–28900, 47601–47900, 50901–51200, 60801-61100.
Do	F. Rhett	71501–71700.
Do	J. Via	71701–71800.
Do	S. E. Laval	89301–89600.
Do	L. W. Elliott	96601–96900.
N. Semple	M. E. Norton	23701–23800, 26801–27100, 61901–62200, 74301–74500, 83001-83200, 91801–92000.
Do	B. Dabney	74501–74600.
Do	F. H. Marks	92001–92100.
M. Darby	C. Huger	23801–23900, 26501–26800, 37901–38100, 46501–46800.
Do	L. Henry	38101–38200.
Do	B. W. Tyler	55801–56000, 67701–68000, 76301–76500, 99401–99500.
Do	S. Southall	99501–99600.
E. A. Dennison	M. E. Gilliam	24201–24400, 31601–31900, 49001–49300, 53901–54200, 61601-61900, 78101–78300, 84001–84300, 98201–98500.
Do	M. E. Brady	87501–87600.
Do	L. W. Elliott	87601–87700.
Do	F. C. Jones	87701–87800.
A. Points	do	24401–24600, 27701–28000, 37401–37600, 42001–42100, 92801-93100.
R. Haynes	B. Dabney	24601–24700, 31901–32200, 39901–40100, 48701–49000, 73301-73500, 77501–77800, 80101–80200, 85401–85600, 87001–87100, 87801–88000, 97901–98200.
Do	A. Zealy	53601–53900.
Do	M. E. Norton	73501–73600.
S. McCants	M. Pleasants	24901–25000.
Do	E. S. Read	27101–27200, 27301–27400.
Do	E. Coffin	27201–27300, 40801–41000, 48501–48700.
Do	M. Kirk	56701–57000.
Do	M. F. Jarvis	79101–79300.
Do	M. E. Norton	79701–79800.
Do	M. J. Black	79801–79900.
E. M. Bell	M. F. Jarvis	25001–25100, 29801–30100, 36101–36400, 43901–44200, 59001-59300, 62601–62900, 66001–66300, 70501–70800, 85901–86200, 99601–99800.
Do	M. Dixon	70801–70900.
Do	M. Taylor	76701–76800.
L. Holmes	E. Laurens	25101–25200, 30401–30700, 44901–45000, 50301–50400.
Do	E. Davis	50701–50800, 55701–55800, 86601–86700, 95201–95500, 101101-101300.
Do	J. M. Connor	58501–58600, 62201–62300, 67401–67700.
Do	H. L. Cooke	101301–101400.
M. Wade	L. Henry	25201–25300.
A. Gray	E. Coffin	25301–25400, 30701–31000, 77301–77400.

Register of Confederate States Treasury Notes—Continued.

ACT OF FEBRUARY 17, 1864—Continued.

For Treasurer.	For Register.	Numbers of the notes signed.
		$10—A to H (1st series)—Continued.
A. Gray	M. Taylor	37601-37900, 45001-45300, 51501-51800, 60501-60800, 63401-63700, 68301-68600, 74001-74300, 80001-80100, 83701-84000, 98501-98800.
Do	M. Pleasants	77201-77300.
Do	S. Johnson	77401-77500.
J. Logan	F. Rhett	25401-25500, 33401-33700, 39101-39300, 47101-47400.
Do	V. Penrifoy	52001-52300, 59601-59900.
Do	N. Brisbane	70901-71100, 97401-97700, 101701-101800.
Do	L. Devine	71101-71200.
Do	H. E. Alexander	101801-102000.
M. Cooper	M. S. Apperson	25501-25600, 28901-29200, 40401-40600, 43001-43300.
Do	F. Rhett	54801-55000.
Do	M. Kirk	57601-57900, 81801-81900.
Do	M. E. Gilliam	64501-64800.
Do	L. Macon	81601-81800.
C. Morris	N. Brisbane	25601-25700, 34601-34800, 40601-40800, 50501-50600.
Do	M. B. Kirby	58601-58800.
Do	E. S. Proctor	78601-78700, 98901-99000, 99901-100000.
Do	H. E. Alexander	98801-98900.
S. Scott	E. Davis	25701-25800, 30101-30400, 38201-38500, 44401-44600.
Do	L. Macon	44601-44700, 66501-66600.
Do	S. Southall	57301-57600, 66301-66400.
Do	L. Henry	66401-66500.
Do	L. A. Norris	78501-78600, 78701-78800, 82501-82800, 96001-96300.
M. Wade	E. Matthews	27401-27500, 42601-42700, 71201-71500, 85101-85400, 88301-88500, 90601-90900.
Do	L. A. Norris	27501-27600.
Do	B. J. Clarke	27601-27700.
Do	F. C. Jones	41001-41100.
Do	M. B. Kirby	42401-42600.
Do	J. M. Connor	60201-60500.
E. Willis	J. De Leon	29201-29500, 41601-41700, 44201-44400.
Do	E. S. Proctor	56201-56300.
Do	J. M. Connor	65701-65900, 76101-76300.
Do	E. Laurens	65901-66000.
J. Ellery	M. Kirk	31001-31100.
Do	A. Kennedy	31101-31300.
Do	E. Matthews	50401-50500.
Do	E. Laurens	56001-56100, 61201-61300.
Do	B. W. Tyler	61101-61200.
S. Neill	M. Kirk	32201-32500.
Do	S. Southall	44701-44900.
Do	E. Laurens	51801-52000, 67201-67400, 70401-70500, 89901-90100.
Do	J. De Leon	58801-59000.
Do	L. Macon	69701-69800.
Do	M. E. Gilliam	70201-70400.
J. Gill	A. Zealy	34001-34300, 41901-42000, 42701-42900.
Do	L. Macon	42901-43000.
Do	L. Pelot	59301-59600, 65601-65700.
Do	M. B. Kirby	65401-65600.
Do	H. E. Bryan	90501-90600.
Do	B. J. Clarke	92101-92500.
N. Giles	L. Henry	34301-34600.
Do	E. S. Read	42101-42200, 45801-46200, 52601-53000, 69801-70100, 94301-94700.
Do	S. E. Hughes	70101-70200.
E. Kelly	A. P. Pellet	34801-35100, 41101-41200.
Do	L. Pelot	42201-42300, 45301-45600, 56101-56200, 58201-58500.
Do	J. De Leon	72401-72500, 72601-72700.
Do	B. W. Tyler	72501-72600.
Do	M. Gaither	81001-81200, 81901-82200.
Do	M. Kirk	81201-81300.
M. Reeves	L. Pelot	35101-35200.
Do	E. Matthews	35201-35300.
Do	M. Dixon	35301-35400.
Do	S. Southall	50001-50100.
Do	C. Huger	50801-50900, 55601-55700, 75701-75900, 83501-83700.
Do	M. B. Kirby	56301-56400.

Register of Confederate States Treasury Notes—Continued.

ACT OF FEBRUARY 17, 1864—Continued.

For Treasurer.	For Register.	Numbers of the notes signed.
		$10—A to H (1st series)—Continued.
M. Reeves	N. Brisbane	64001–64100, 69201–69300.
Do	L. Macon	64101–64200, 69601–69700.
Do	L. A. Norris	71801–72000.
A. B. Capron	M. Taylor	35401–35600.
Do	L. A. Norris	35601–35700, 41401–41600.
Do	S. E. Hughes	49701–50000.
Do	M. B. Kirby	55301–55600.
Do	M. A. Yates	63201–63400, 69501–69600, 73001–73200, 99201–99300.
Do	M. E. Gilliam	73201–73300.
Do	C. C. Veal	99301–99400.
S. Wise	L. Pelot	36001–36100.
Do	E. Matthews	38801–39100, 53301–53600.
Do	L. A. Norris	47901–48200.
Do	L. Devine	69301–69500, 75401–75500, 76501–76700.
Do	M. E. Gilliam	75201–75400.
Do	S. E. Hughes	78301–78500.
Do	M. E. Norton	78901–79100.
M. Selden	A. P. Pellet	36401–36600, 42301–42400, 75901–76100, 78801–78900, 80701–81000, 93401–93700, 102601–102900.
C. Hix	B. J. Clarke	40101–40400, 49301–49700, 63701–64000, 68901–69200, 74601–74900.
Do	M. Kirk	74901–75000.
M. Kingman	S. Southall	45601–45700, 75501–75700.
Do	L. Macon	45701–45800, 56401–56500.
J. Ambler	M. Kirk	47401–47600.
Do	E. Matthews	50601–50700, 68101–68300.
Do	L. A. Norris	57901–58200.
Do	E. C. Winston	68001–68100.
Do	S. A. Doar	85601–85800.
Do	L. Michel	85801–85900.
Do	A. Zealy	89601–89900.
E. C. Trescot	E. S. Proctor	64201–64400.
Do	M. B. Kirby	64401–64500.
M. S. Gist	S. Johnson	72701–72900.
Do	M. E. Gilliam	72901–73000.
Do	L. Devine	76801–76900.
Do	L. Pelot	80401–80700, 91501–91800, 101401–101700.
E. McCully	H. C. Thomas	79501–79700, 88801–88900, 90901–91200.
O. McGowan	S. Johnson	79901–80000.
Do	F. C. Jones	84801–85000.
Do	S. Southall	85001–85100.
Do	L. W. Elliott	90401–90500.
H. Moise	S. Johnson	80201–80400.
F. Stocker	J. Via	81301–81500.
Do	S. K. Wells	81501–81600, 87201–87400.
Do	S. A. Doar	87401–87500.
Do	S. K. Wells	93101–93300.
Do	M. Kirk	93301–93400.
A. Caldwell	H. C. Thomas	82801–83000.
Do	S. Johnson	87101–87200, 90201–90300.
Do	J. D. Treadwell	90301–90400, 91201–91400, 100501–100800.
Do	B. Dabney	91401–91500.
F. Waties	E. C. Winston	84301–84400.
Do	N. E. Wingate	84401–84500, 94701–94900.
Do	F. H. Marks	94901–95000.
M. Carrington	S. Southall	86501–86600, 90101–90200, 95501–95700.
M. Boyd	S. A. Doar	92501–92800.
M. Dargan	C. C. Veal	93701–93900.
Do	L. W. Elliott	93901–94000.
S. Fuller	H. E. Bryan	95001–95200.
J. Jacobs	M. E. Brady	95701–96000.
J. Gott	M. E. Cullen	99001–99200, 102001–102300.
M. Godwin	M. Taylor	102301–102400.
Do	C. Percival	102401–102500.
Do	C. C. Veal	102501–102600.

Register of Confederate States Treasury Notes—Continued.

ACT OF FEBRUARY 17, 1864—Continued.

For Treasurer.	For Register.	Numbers of the notes signed.
		$10—A to H (2d series).
N. Giles	E. S. Read	1-400, 48801-49100, 64001-64400, 76901-77300, 92301-92500.
Do	H. E. Alexander	14601-14900.
Do	N. E. Wingate	14901-15000.
Do	A. S. Parry	19001-19400.
Do	B. W. Tyler	26701-27000.
Do	J. D. Treadwell	30101-30400.
Do	M. E. Harper	42401-42600.
Do	H. C. Thomas	42601-42800.
Do	M. E. Hamilton	48701-48800.
M. Wade	E. Matthews	401-700, 50501-50800, 61001-61200, 82701-82800, 82901-83000.
Do	L. W. Elliott	41301-41600.
Do	M. A. Yates	61201-61300.
Do	L. Michel	82801-82900.
F. Waties	N. E. Wingate	701-1000, 12301-12600, 40701-41000, 59001-59300, 74501-74800, 81801-81900, 88801-89100.
Do	E. C. Winston	29701-30000.
Do	M. Taylor	48401-48700.
S. Fuller	H. E. Bryan	1001-1300, 10101-10300, 17901-18200, 36101-36200.
Do	R. King	36201-36300, 43601-43800, 51601-51900, 63101-63400, 74201-74500, 81901-82000, 85701-85900, 88701-88800, 95401-95700.
N. Semple	M. E. Norton	1301-1600, 12001-12300, 20001-20300, 39501-39800, 49601-49900, 81801-81900, 87501-87700, 95701-95900.
Do	L. Pelot	95901-96000.
S. Scott	L. A. Norris	1601-1900, 31301-31600, 39201-39500, 51001-51300, 59301-59600, 71901-72300, 96101-96500.
Do	H. L. Cooke	67601-67700.
Do	E. Davis	72301-72400.
H. Balaguer	K. P. Howell	1901-2200, 16501-16700.
Do	E. Davis	42801-43000, 55901-56000.
Do	N. Brisbane	45301-45400, 55701-55800.
Do	H. Barnwell	55801-55900.
Do	S. Huard	58401-58700, 81401-81500, 85101-85400.
Do	L. Devine	81501-81600.
J. Gill	B. J. Clarke	2201-2600, 9701-10100, 51901-52300, 60101-60500, 69901-70000, 79601-79900, 84301-84600.
Do	J. M. Connor	38801, 39100.
Do	S. A. Doar	39101-39200.
Do	M. Taylor	84601-84700, 86801-86900.
Do	E. S. Read	86501-86800.
K. Nelson	L. Devine	2601-2700.
Do	H. E. Alexander	2701-2900.
Do	M. A. Mobley	23301-23500.
Do	R. King	35201-35400.
Do	L. Archer	45101-45200.
Do	L. A. Norris	54901-55000.
Do	M. Dixon	55001-55100.
Do	H. C. Thomas	65601-65900, 78301-78400.
Do	E. Davis	78401-78600, 91401-91700.
Do	M. Taylor	88601-88700.
E. McCully	H. C. Thomas	2901-3200, 16201-16500, 24001-24200, 27001-27300, 43301-43500.
Do	H. E. Bryan	43501-43600.
Do	A. S. Parry	52601-52900.
Do	H. Barnwell	60501-60600.
Do	J. De Leon	60601-60700.
Do	B. W. Tyler	60701-60800.
Do	M. F. Jarvis	73901-74200.
Do	E. Matthews	81601-81700.
Do	M. J. Black	89101-89400.
N. Goodwin	E. Coffin	3201-3500, 13501-13800, 20301-20600, 27801-28100, 33301-33500, 43801-44100, 52301-52600, 64401-64600, 71001-71300, 88001-88200.
Do	M. A. Yates	64601-64700.
Do	M. F. Jarvis	88201-88300.
E. A. Dennison	M. E. Gilliam	3501-3800, 13201-13500, 22401-22700, 27501-27600, 34301-34600, 41901-42200, 53501-53800, 63401-63700, 70001-70100, 76301-76500, 86201-86500, 90601-90900, 98001-98300.
Do	J. D. Treadwell	27601-27800.

Register of Confederate States Treasury Notes—Continued.

ACT OF FEBRUARY 17, 1864—Continued.

For Treasurer.	For Register.	Numbers of the notes signed.
		$10—A to H (2d series)—Continued.
E. A. Dennison	S. A. Doar	76501-76600.
J. Ambler	A. Zealy	3801-4100, 11301-11600, 19401-19700, 25501-25800, 33501-33800, 41001-41300, 52901-53200, 65901-66200, 78801-79000.
Do	M. E. Harper	79001-79100.
H. Moore	A. M. Foran	4101-4200, 66501-66700, 71601-71900.
Do	M. E. Hamilton	4201-4400, 36001-36100.
Do	M. A. Yates	16701-16800.
Do	E. Davis	96601-96700.
A. Harrison	J. Via	4401-4700.
Do	L. Devine	14101-14400, 33801-34000.
Do	L. W. Elliott	34001-34100.
Do	C. C. Veal	61601-61900.
Do	H. E. Bryan	77301-77600.
V. M. Rind	F. C. Jones	4701-4900.
Do	M. A. Yates	4901-5000, 53201-53500.
Do	F. E. Bernard	15001-15300, 41601-41900, 65301-65600, 70101-70300, 70401-70500, 81001-81100.
Do	H. Heriot	22801-23100.
Do	M. Kirk	28401-28700.
Do	H. E. Alexander	70301-70400.
Do	E. Coffin	92001-92200.
Do	H. Barnwell	92201-92300.
P. Savage	H. Heriot	5001-5300, 12601-12900.
Do	E. S. Proctor	19701-19900.
Do	L. Macon	19901-20000, 32401-32700, 50801-51000.
Do	L. Devine	61901-62100.
Do	C. C. Veal	62101-62200.
Do	S. Johnson	75101-75300.
Do	E. Coffin	75301-75400.
Do	A. Zealy	88301-88600.
M. Reeves	C. Huger	5301-5400, 15801-16000, 67401-67500, 79101-79400, 91201-91400.
Do	B. W. Tyler	5401-5500.
Do	H. Barnwell	44601-44700.
S. R. Simons	C. C. Veal	5501-5700, 9501-9700.
Do	H. E. Alexander	17201-17300, 28901-29100.
Do	M. Taylor	17301-17600.
Do	J. A. Acosta	44401-44600, 56501-56700, 83301-83600.
A. S. Stuart	F. H. Marks	5701-5900, 8601-8900, 21601-21900, 24901-25200, 30701-31000, 38301-38500, 49301-49600, 62801-63100, 68101-68200, 75701-76000, 81701-81800, 85401-85500, 85601-85700, 91701-92000.
Do	M. F. Jarvis	85501-85600.
H. Moise	S. Johnson	5901-6100.
Do	H. E. Bryan	45401-45500, 55501-55700.
Do	M. A. Yates	55401-55500.
A. B. Capron	do	6101-6400, 15501-15700, 23101-23300, 34801-35000, 56201-56300, 78601-78800, 92501-92700.
Do	A. Zealy	15701-15800.
Do	K. P. Howell	28101-28400.
Do	M. A. Mobley	56001-56200.
A. Gray	M. Taylor	6401-6700, 22101-22400, 31601-31800, 89401-89700.
M. Dargan	L. W. Elliott	6701-6900, 56701-56900.
Do	M. E. Cullen	36901-37200.
R. Haynes	B. Dabney	6901-7000, 8101-8400, 18901-19000, 26201-26500, 34601-34800, 43001-43300, 53801-54100, 66201-66500, 76601-76700, 76801-76900.
Do	E. Coffin	76701-76800.
M. Darby	B. W. Tyler	7001-7100, 8901-9200.
Do	F. Rhett	21301-21500.
Do	B. Dabney	21501-21600.
Do	C. C. Veal	45001-45100.
Do	J. De Leon	49101-49300, 62601-62800, 76201-76300.
Do	E. C. Winston	62501-62600.
Do	M. J. Black	68001-68100, 76001-76200.
M. Carrington	S. Southall	7101-7200, 24201-24300.
Do	R. King	30001-30100.
Do	M. E. Hamilton	59901-60100.
J. Jacobs	M. E. Brady	7201-7400, 47601-47900, 56901-57200, 83001-83300.

Register of Confederate States Treasury Notes—Continued.

ACT OF FEBRUARY 17, 1864—Continued.

For Treasurer.	For Register.	Numbers of the notes signed.
		$10—A to H (2d series)—Continued.
K. Korff	L. Arthur	7401–7500, 17601–17800.
Do	S. A. Doar	7501–7600.
Do	A. S. Parry	14401–14600, 17801–17900.
Do	H. Heriot	81101–81200.
C. Morris	E. S. Proctor	7601–7800, 16001–16200, 28701–28900.
Do	H. E. Bryan	39801–39900, 40001–40100.
Do	C. Huger	39901–40000, 56301–56500.
Do	M. Gaither	92901–93000.
Do	E. Davis	96501–96600.
O. McGowan	K. P. Howell	7801–7900.
Do	L. Arthur	24301–24400, 25201–25500, 35801–36000, 40501–40700, 60801–61000, 69401–69700, 93001–93100.
J. Wilson	J. McGarr	7901–8100, 70601–70900, 81201–81500, 93801-94100.
Do	M. A. Yates	36301–36600.
Do	H. L. Cooke	70901–71000.
Do	A. M. Foran	81501–81600.
Do	M. B. Kirby	94101–94200.
M. Allen	A. S. Parry	8401–8600.
Do	S. A. Doar	18201–18600.
Do	R. King	24401–24600.
Do	L. A. Norris	24601–24800.
Do	H. E. Bryan	82401–82700.
Do	J. D. Treadwell	93101–93200.
Do	M. B. Kirby	93201–93500.
L. Sims	L. Arthur	9201–9300.
Do	M. A. Yates	9301–9400.
Do	E. S. Proctor	9401–9500.
Do	C. C. Veal	24801–24900, 37701–38000.
Do	J. A. Acosta	44301–44400.
Do	M. J. Black	59601–59900.
Do	E. C. Winston	67701–67800.
Do	H. Barnwell	73501–73700, 73801–73900, 84701–85000.
Do	A. S. Parry	73701–73800, 85001–85100.
L. Holmes	J. Via	10301–10600.
Do	F. Rhett	49901–50200.
Do	L. Michel	67201–67400, 79401–79600, 81701–81800.
E. Kelly	L. A. Norris	10601–11000.
Do	F. H. Marks	44701–44900.
Do	H. C. Thomas	44901–45000.
Do	B. W. Tyler	54101–54500, 82001–82400.
M. Selden	A. P. Pellet	11001–11300, 18601–18900, 30501–30700, 33001–33300, 62201–62500, 69001–69300, 90901–91100.
Do	B. Dabney	30401–30500.
Do	E. S. Proctor	69301–69400.
Do	M. B. Kirby	91101–91200.
A. Caldwell	J. D. Treadwell	11601–12000, 23501–23800, 38501–38800, 51301–51600, 74801–75100, 87701–88000.
Do	M. Dixon	31001–31300.
M. Cooper	M. Kirk	12901–13200.
Do	A. M. Foran	32701–32900.
Do	H. E. Alexander	32901–33000.
Do	C. C. Veal	81601–81700.
L. C. Minor	E. C. Winston	13801–14100, 20601–20900.
Do	H. E. Alexander	26501–26700.
M. Boyd	S. A. Doar	15301–15500, 37501–37700, 47301–47600, 79901–81100, 94801–95100.
M. S. Gist	L. Pelot	16801–17200, 29201–29600, 58101–58400, 67801–67900, 72701–73100, 83901–84100.
Do	M. E. Hamilton	84101–84300.
J. Logan	N. Brisbane	20901–21100, 21201–21300, 31801–32100, 50201–50500, 65001–65300, 77601–77900.
Do	E. Coffin	21101–21200.
Do	S. A. Doar	70501–70600.
J. H. Angel	S. Southall	21901–22000.
Do	M. Gaither	22001–22100.
Do	M. A. Mobley	35601–35800, 61301–61600, 81201–81400.
Do	E. Matthews	54701–54800.
Do	J. De Leon	54801–54900.

Register of Confederate States Treasury Notes—Continued.

ACT OF FEBRUARY 17, 1864—Continued.

For Treasurer.	For Register.	Numbers of the notes signed.
		$10—A to H (2d series)—Continued.
M. A. Dewees	E. C. Winston	22701-22800, 27301-27500.
Do	M. Gaither	34101-34300, 42201-42400, 63701-63800.
Do	S. E. Laval	54501-54700.
Do	J. D. Treadwell	63801-64000.
Do	A. S. Parry	69701-69800, 75401-75500.
Do	A. Zealy	75501-75700.
Do	M. J. Black	85901-86200.
Do	H. E. Bryan	90301-90600.
S. Neill	E. Laurens	23801-24000, 29601-29700, 35001-35200, 40101-40300, 45501-45600.
A. Miller	S. E. Laval	25801-26200, 35401-35600, 45201-45300, 45601-45800.
A. Points	E. S. Read	29101-29200.
Do	H. E. Bryan	36601-36900.
Do	E. C. Winston	45801-46100, 66701-67000, 67101-67200, 96001-96100.
Do	M. Gaither	67001-67100.
C. White	F. Rhett	32101-32400.
Do	M. J. Black	46101-46400, 96701-97000.
Do	H. L. Cooke	46401-46500.
Do	M. E. Gilliam	97001-97100.
J. Gott	M. F. Jarvis	37201-37500.
Do	M. E. Cullen	47901-48200, 68601-69000.
Do	E. Coffin	57201-57300.
Do	L. W. Elliott	57301-57400.
Do	C. Huger	57401-57500.
F. Stocker	N. Brisbane	38001-38300.
Do	S. K. Wells	58701-59000, 73101-73500.
S. G. Sanxay	M. Dixon	40301-40500, 48201-48400, 57501-57800, 83601-83900, 97501-97800.
M. Banks	L. A. Norris	44101-44200.
Do	M. Dixon	44201-44300.
Do	M. E. Harper	55101-55400, 64701-65000, 78001-78300, 86901-87200, 89701-90000.
V. M. Tyler	M. Kirk	46501-46800, 93501-93800.
Do	E. S. Proctor	71301-71500.
Do	M. B. Kirby	71501-71600.
E. M. Bell	M. F. Jarvis	46801-47100, 57801-58100.
L. Armstrong	M. E. Hamilton	47101-47200.
Do	H. Barnwell	47201-47300.
M. Godwin	M. A. Yates	67501-67600.
Do	M. B. Kirby	68201-68500.
Do	L. Devine	68501-68600.
M. Ringgold	E. Davis	67901-68000.
Do	C. Huger	81101-81200.
Do	F. E. Bernard	98301-98400.
Do	L. Henry	98401-98500.
M. Kingman	K. P. Howell	69801-69900, 80901-81000, 92701-92900, 95101-95400.
E. Willis	J. M. Connor	72401-72700, 94501-94800.
R. Macmurdo	E. Coffin	77901-78000.
S. J. Adams	H. C. Thomas	87201-87500, 90001-90300.
G. Loyd	H. E. Alexander	94201-94400, 97801-98000.
Do	M. A. Yates	92401-92500.
E. Baker	M. B. Kirby	97101-97400.
Do	E. Matthews	97401-97500.
* * * *	* * * *	* * * * * * *
		$10—A to H (3d series).
F. Stocker	S. K. Wells	1-300, 37001-37300, 80301-80600.
Do	J. M. Connor	11701-12000.
Do	L. Devine	12001-12100.
Do	C. Percival	23001-23100.
Do	A. M. Foran	23101-23200.
Do	H. Heriot	45301-45400.
Do	L. Pelot	45401-45500.
Do	L. Michel	45501-45600.
Do	S. A. Doar	64301-64600.
A. S. Stuart	F. H. Marks	301-600, 10201-10500, 19101-19400, 29701-30000, 38701-39000.

Register of Confederate States Treasury Notes—Continued.

ACT OF FEBRUARY 17, 1864—Continued.

For Treasurer.	For Register.	Numbers of the notes signed.
		$10—A to H (3d series)—Continued.
A. S. Stuart	S. A. Doar	45901–46200.
M. Darby	J. De Leon	601–700, 38501–38700, 62301–62500, 74901–75000.
Do	M. Gaither	74801–74900.
H. Balaguer	S. Huard	701–1000, 8501–8800, 10001–10200, 17401–17700, 28501–28800, 34601–34900, 43201–43500, 54201–54500, 61001–61300, 66501–66800, 79701–80000, 92801–93100.
C. Morris	B. Dabney	1001–1300, 9401–9700.
Do	M. E. Hamilton	20001–20200.
Do	J. De Leon	20201–20300, 29201–29400.
Do	L. Courtney	88901–89200.
J. H. Angel	H. E. Bryan	1301–1400, 94701–94900.
Do	R. King	1401–1500, 58201–58300.
Do	L. Pelot	1501–1600.
Do	M. A. Mobley	7901–8100, 13001–13200, 25901–26200, 33001–33200.
Do	L. Henry	8101–8200, 33201–33300.
Do	F. C. Jones	58301–58400.
Do	E. S. Proctor	88201–88500.
Do	F. Rhett	94901–95000.
A. Caldwell	J. D. Treadwell	1601–1900, 51201–51500, 62001–62100, 65901–66200.
Do	F. Rhett	24901–25200.
Do	H. L. Cooke	51501–51600.
E. Kelly	B. W. Tyler	1901–2200, 23501–23900, 65501–65900, 97201–97400.
Do	E. S. Read	46501–46600.
Do	C. Percival	46601–46700.
Do	S. Huard	46701–46800.
Do	M. Taylor	91601–91900.
E. McCully	A. S. Parry	2201–2500, 22001–22300, 39301–39600, 52701–53000, 66801–67100.
Do	M. Dixon	11401–11700.
Do	L. W. Elliott	43801–43900.
Do	M. F. Jarvis	43901–44000.
Do	V. Penrifoy	44001–44100.
Do	E. Davis	95601–95900.
J. Logan	N. Brisbane	2501–2700, 13801–14000, 20301–20600, 31001–31300, 47401–47700, 51701–52000, 64601–64900, 73101–73400, 82801–83100, 92501–92800.
Do	L. Pelot	2701–2800.
Do	H. Heriot	14001–14100.
Do	M. A. Yates	39601–39900.
F. Waties	N. E. Wingate	2801–3100, 9701–10000, 10801–11100, 23201–23500, 30701–31000, 47101–47400.
Do	H. Barnwell	91101–91200.
P. Savage	L. Macon	3101–3300, 15201–15500, 53301–53600, 66201–66500.
E. M. Bell	M. F. Jarvis	3301–3600, 9101–9400, 20601–20900, 44901–45300, 60301–60600, 84301–84700, 88501–88800.
Do	M. E. Brady	60601–60700.
Do	M. B. Kirby	88801–88900.
M. Reeves	M. A. Yates	3601–3700.
Do	M. E. Harper	15501–15600.
Do	C. Huger	18501–18700, 37301–37500, 67701–67900.
Do	H. L. Cooke	18701–18800.
N. Giles	E. S. Read	3701–4000, 12101–12400, 22601–22900, 32601–32900, 37501–37900, 47701–48100, 57801–58200, 63201–63600, 91201–91600, 97801–98200.
Do	L. Devine	4001–4100.
Do	E. Davis	12401–12500.
Do	M. E. Harper	22901–23000.
Do	B. J. Clarke	41801–42200.
M. Banks	M. E. Harper	4101–4400, 42701–42800, 54501–54800, 67901–68200.
M. A. Dewees	H. E. Bryan	4401–4600, 14401–14700, 23901–24200, 40201–40500, 48901–49200, 56901–57200, 69001–69300, 75601–75900, 80601–80900.
Do	M. B. Kirby	4601–4700.
S. J. Adams	H. C. Thomas	4701–5000, 41501–41800, 55101–55400, 68201–68500.
E. A. Dennison	M. E. Gilliam	5001–5300, 15001–15200, 24201–24500, 40501–40700, 49501–49800, 57201–57500, 68701–69000, 75901–76200, 81401–81700.
Do	C. C. Veal	40701–40800.
A. Gray	M. Taylor	5301–5600, 14901–15000, 41301–41500, 69501–69600, 71301–71600.

Register of Confederate States Treasury Notes—Continued.

ACT OF FEBRUARY 17, 1864—Continued.

For Treasurer.	For Register.	Numbers of the notes signed.
		$10—A to H (3d series)—Continued.
A. Gray	M. Kirk	14701-14900.
Do	B. W. Tyler	26201-26400.
A. Harrison	A. Zealy	5601-5900.
Do	L. Macon	41001-41300.
Do	S. A. Doar	67101-67400.
V. M. Rind	F. E. Bernard	5901-6200, 15901-16200, 26701-27000, 32301-32600, 42201-42500, 48601-48900, 55701-55800, 69901-70200.
Do	L. Henry	55801-56000.
Do	F. Rhett	93101-93200.
K. Nelson	A. M. Foran	6201-6500, 25201-25500, 42501-42700, 48501-48600, 55401-55700, 69601-69800.
Do	M. E. Norton	69801-69900.
Do	L. Arthur	93401-93600.
L. Armstrong	E. Coffin	6501-6600.
Do	J. De Leon	6601-6700, 17101-17400.
Do	H. Heriot	42801-43000.
Do	M. E. Brady	74201-74400.
Do	S. E. Hughes	74401-74500, 87001-87300.
J. Gott	M. E. Cullen	6701-6900, 10501-10800, 18801-19100, 28801-29200, 36201-36600, 76201-76600, 82101-82400.
Do	L. Pelot	82401-82500.
Do	M. Taylor	89801-89900, 90001-90200.
Do	S. Huard	89901-90000.
L. Sims	M. Gaither	6901-7000.
Do	H. Barnwell	21701-22000, 35801-36100, 44501-44800.
Do	L. A. Norris	36101-36200.
Do	J. M. Connor	44801-44900.
Do	N. E. Wingate	62801-63100.
Do	H. L. Cooke	63101-63200.
Do	L. Courtney	78201-78500.
Do	M. E. Norton	90901-91100.
M. Allen	B. J. Clarke	7001-7300.
Do	M. B. Kirby	7301-7400.
Do	M. Dixon	16601-16900.
Do	H. C. Thomas	16901-17000.
Do	M. A. Yates	27301-27400, 27601-27700, 50301-50600.
Do	L. Macon	27401-27600.
Do	E. Coffin	33301-33700.
Do	A. Zealy	50201-50300.
Do	M. Kirk	50601-50900.
Do	F. C. Jones	58501-58800, 70901-71300, 77201-77600, 95901-96300.
Do	M. E. Brady	58801-58900.
M. Carrington	M. E. Hamilton	7401-7600.
Do	R. King	16401-16500.
Do	E. Coffin	18301-18400.
Do	M. A. Yates	18401-18500.
Do	J. De Leon	74001-74200.
N. Semple	M. E. Norton	7601-7900, 22301-22600, 34001-34300, 53601-53900, 61701-62000, 65201-65500, 96301-96600.
Do	H. E. Bryan	92201-92300.
Do	A. M. Foran	92301-92400.
Do	J. De Leon	92401-92500.
L. Holmes	L. Michel	8201-8500, 19401-19700, 28201-28500, 35201-35500, 56301-56600, 72501-72800, 77901-78200.
Do	M. Taylor	96601-96900.
M. Dargan	L. W. Elliott	8801-9100, 12701-13000, 31301-31600, 91901-92200.
Do	M. A. Yates	24601-24900.
M. S. Gist	L. Pelot	11101-11400, 21301-21600, 31601-31900, 36601-37000.
Do	M. E. Harper	21601-21700.
Do	R. King	31901-32000.
Do	E. Coffin	83101-83400.
Do	F. Rhett	95501-95600.
J. Ambler	J. De Leon	12501-12700.
Do	H. C. Thomas	27001-27200.
Do	M. A. Yates	39001-39300.
Do	A. Zealy	46801-47100, 57501-57600, 67401-67700, 93601-93900, 98201-98400.
S. Scott	H. C. Thomas	13201-13500.

Register of Confederate States Treasury Notes—Continued.

ACT OF FEBRUARY 17, 1864—Continued.

For Treasurer.	For Register.	Numbers of the notes signed.
		$10—A to H (3d series)—Continued.
S. Scott	L. A. Norris	25501–25900, 30301–30700, 39901–40200, 44101–44500, 53901–54200, 61301–61700.
Do	M. F. Jarvis	63601–64000.
M. Selden	M. Gaither	13501–13800, 27901–28200.
Do	B. Dabney	38201–38500, 52401–52700, 70201–70400, 71901–72200, 82501–82800.
S. Fuller	R. King	14101–14400, 20901–21000, 30001–30300, 37901–38200, 49801–50100, 56001–56300, 64001–64300.
Do	M. Kirk	59401–59700.
N. Goodwin	E. Coffin	15601–15900, 32101–32300, 58901–59000, 69301–69500, 94301–94400, 95201–95300.
Do	R. King	32001–32100.
E. Willis	M. E. Hamilton	16201–16400.
Do	J. M. Connor	35501–35800, 45601–45900, 58401–58500, 78901–79200, 90201–90400.
Do	M. Taylor	94401–94700.
M. Ringgold	M. Kirk	16501–16600.
Do	M. E. Harper	27201–27300.
Do	J. A. Acosta	50101–50200, 54801–54900, 55001–55100.
Do	L. Henry	40801–41000, 54901–55000, 68501–68700, 95301–95400.
Do	J. McGarr	95401–95500.
V. M. Tyler	M. E. Hamilton	17001–17100.
Do	R. King	71601–71900.
C. White	M. J. Black	17701–18000, 75301–75500, 78501–78900, 89201–89500.
Do	C. Percival	75501–75600.
Do	M. E. Hamilton	97401–97800.
J. Jacobs	M. E. Brady	18001–18200, 43501–43800.
Do	M. B. Kirby	18201–18300.
H. Moore	E. Davis	19701–19900, 27701–27900, 79501–79700, 90401–90600.
Do	L. Macon	19901–20000.
J. Gill	B. J. Clarke	21001–21300, 48101–48500, 52001–52400, 93901–94300.
R. Haynes	B. Dabney	24501–24600.
Do	M. Gaither	33801–33900, 49201–49500, 56601–56900, 80901–81100.
Do	L. Macon	72801–73100.
Do	J. D. Treadwell	81101–81200.
J. Wilson	J. McGarr	26401–26700, 59001–59200, 72201–72500.
Do	E. Davis	57601–57800.
Do	L. Courtney	59201–59400.
Do	M. B. Kirby	76901–77200.
M. Wade	E. Matthews	29401–29700, 34901–35200, 81201–81400.
K. Korff	J. De Leon	33701–33800.
Do	H. Heriot	43001–43100.
Do	M. Taylor	43101–43200.
Do	L. Courtney	62501–62800.
Do	M. E. Hamilton	79201–79500, 90601–90900.
M. Kingman	K. P. Howell	33901–34000, 51601–51700, 84701–84900.
S. McCants	C. Percival	34301–34600, 62101–62300, 74501–74800.
G. Loyd	H. E. Alexander	46201–46500, 53001–53200, 64901–65200, 77601–77900.
Do	L. Courtney	53201–53300.
A. Points	E. C. Winston	50901–51200, 59701–60000, 70401–70600.
M. Cooper	C. C. Veal	60001–60300, 84901–85200, 86601–87000.
S. G. Sanxay	M. Dixon	60701–61000, 76601–76900, 80001–80300.
A. Miller	S. E. Laval	70601–70900, 84001–84300, 85001–86300.
O. McGowan	L. Courtney	73401–73700.
Do	L. Arthur	83401–83700, 87601–87900.
E. C. Trescot	V. Penrifoy	73701–74000, 83701–84000, 93201–93400.
Do	S. Johnson	86301–86400.
Do	J. D. Treadwell	86401–86500.
Do	E. C. Winston	86501–86600.
S. Neill	F. Rhett	75001–75300, 85501–85800.
Do	M. A. Yates	87901–88200.
E. Baker	H. Heriot	81701–82100.
M. Boyd	S. A. Doar	85201–85500, 87301–87600, 96901–97200.
S. R. Simons	J. A. Acosta	85801–85900.
H. Moise	S. Johnson	89501–89800.
A. B. Capron	M. A. Yates	95001–95200.
* * * *	* * * *	* * * * * * *

Register of Confederate States Treasury Notes—Continued.

ACT OF FEBRUARY 17, 1864—Continued.

For Treasurer.	For Register.	Numbers of the notes signed.
		$10—A to H (4th series).
* * * *	* * * *	* * * * * * *
		$10—A to H (5th series).
* * * *	* * * *	* * * * * * *
		$10—A to H (6th series).
* * * *	* * * *	* * * * * * *
		$10—A to H (7th series).
* * * *	* * * *	* * * * * * *
		$10—A to H (8th series).
* * * *	* * * *	* * * * * * *
		$10—A to H (9th series).
* * * *	* * * *	* * * * * * *
		$10—A to H (10th series).
* * * *	* * * *	* * * * * * *
		$5—A to H.
M. Cooper	M. S. Apperson	1-200, 22601-22900, 30401-30700, 42801-43000, 49101-49300, 53601-53800.
Do	A. Kennedy	201-300.
Do	Y. Penrifoy	15201-15500.
Do	M. B. Kirby	17301-17600.
Do	M. Kirk	43001-43100.
Do	B. W. Tyler	49301-49400.
Do	F. Rhett	53801-53900, 76701-76800.
Do	M. A. Yates	59701-60000.
Do	M. Gaither	76601-76700.
Do	L. Macon	76801-76900.
M. Kingman	M. Pleasants	301-600.
Do	J. De Leon	7401-7700.
Do	S. Southall	20101-20400, 33001-33100, 33201-33300, 38601-38900, 49701-49900, 58201-58400.
Do	M. B. Kirby	33101-33200.
Do	L. A. Norris	49901-50000.
Do	A. Zealy	58401-58500.
A. Harrison	L. Devine	601-900, 25101-25400, 45701-46000.
Do	L. W. Elliott	89201-89400.
J. Wilson	J. McGarr	901-1200, 1501-1800, 9701-10000, 14901-15200, 17001-17300, 21601-21900, 36301-36600, 39401-39700, 49401-49700, 54701-55000, 58801-59100, 65801-66100, 82601-82900, 84801-85100.
Do	S. E. Hughes	21901-22000.
Do	M. Kirk	55001-55100.
S. McCants	L. Henry	1201-1500, 8001-8200, 20801-21100, 30701-30800, 30901-31000, 40901-41100, 50301-50500.
Do	J. M. Connor	8201-8300, 58601-58700.
Do	B. Dabney	30801-30900.
Do	M. E. Gilliam	41101-41200.
Do	M. Dixon	50501-50600.
Do	L. Devine	53001-53300.
Do	M. Taylor	58501-58600, 58701-58800.
Do	M. E. Norton	73501-73600.
Do	M. J. Black	81701-82000, 84501-84800.
J. Ellery	B. W. Tyler	1801-1900.
Do	A. Kennedy	8801-8900.
Do	F. C. Jones	14301-14400.
E. M. Bell	M. F. Jarvis	1901-2200, 9201-9500, 15901-16200, 23201-23500, 32001-32300, 44201-44500, 53901-54200, 83501-83800, 87101-87400.
Do	L. Macon	23501-23600.
Do	B. J. Clarke	67301-67600.
E. Willis	M. A. Yates	2201-2400.

Register of Confederate States Treasury Notes—Continued.

ACT OF FEBRUARY 17, 1864—Continued.

For Treasurer.	For Register.	Numbers of the notes signed.
		$5—A to H—Continued.
E. Willis	E. S. Proctor	8301-8400, 16501-16700.
Do	B. W. Tyler	8401-8500.
Do	J. M. Connor	15501-15700, 16701-16800, 24101-24400, 31001-31300, 40601-40900, 50601-50900, 63601-63900, 83201-83500, 85701-86000, 92201-92400.
J. Gill	A. Zealy	2401-2700, 7701-8000.
Do	M. Dixon	14601-14900.
Do	L. Pelot	28601-28800, 34601-34900, 40301-40600, 50901-51200, 54401-54700, 59401-59700, 62001-62300.
Do	M. E. Norton	73001-73100.
Do	E. Coffin	73101-73200.
Do	B. J. Clarke	87701-88100.
C. Morris	N. Brisbane	2701-2900, 9501-9700.
Do	E. S. Proctor	23901-24100, 39201-39400, 54201-54400, 60001-60200, 67901-68100.
Do	L. Devine	29601-29800.
Do	S. E. Hughes	51201-51400.
L. C. Minor	E. C. Winston	2901-3200, 26001-26200, 26801-26900, 31701-32000, 43601-43900, 62301-62600, 71401-71700, 75101-75400.
Do	M. E. Norton	10901-11200.
J. Logan	V. Penrifoy	3201-3500, 25401-25700, 31401-31700, 45401-45700.
Do	B. J. Clarke	55701-56000.
Do	N. Brisbane	62601-62800, 79101-79400.
Do	M. E. Gilliam	62801-62900.
Do	N. Brisbane	91001-91200.
S. Neill	E. Laurens	3501-3700, 16801-17000, 26201-26400, 61801-62000, 67601-67800, 82001-82200.
Do	S. E. Hughes	26401-26500, 45001-45200.
Do	A. P. Pellet	31301-31400.
Do	M. E. Norton	67801-67900.
Do	E. Davis	82201-82300.
Do	E. Coffin	90401-90500.
Do	J. A. Acosta	90501-90700, 96101-96300.
Do	S. Johnson	96301-96400.
E. Kelly	L. Pelot	3701-4000, 10701-10900.
Do	J. De Leon	23601-23900, 37901-38100, 41501-41700, 63901-64100, 68101-68300, 86001-86400.
Do	M. Norton	38101-38200.
Do	M. B. Kirby	41701-41800.
Do	M. E. Gilliam	60901-61200.
Do	E. Coffin	68301-68400.
Do	B. W. Tyler	94301-94600, 96401-96800.
S. G. Sanxay	M. Dixon	4001-4300, 11201-11500, 34301-34600, 42201-42500, 56901-57100, 64501-64800, 70301-70600.
Do	E. S. Read	57101-57200.
A. Gray	M. Taylor	4301-4600, 12901-13200, 27201-27500, 36101-36400, 42501-42800, 77301-77600, 81101-81400.
L. Holmes	E. Davis	4601-4800, 10001-10100, 22901-23000, 23101-23200, 33301-33500, 44801-45000, 52201-52500, 56301-56500, 70601-70800, 80401-80700.
Do	F. C. Jones	11501-11700.
Do	S. E. Hughes	23001-23100, 97701-98000.
Do	M. Norton	56501-56600.
Do	M. Kirk	73301-73400, 83901-84200.
Do	L. Michel	97101-97400.
J. Ambler	L. A. Norris	4801-5100, 10101-10400, 11701-12000, 26501-26800, 34001-34300, 43901-44200.
Do	A. Zealy	64801-65100, 68901-69200, 72701-73000, 77601-77900, 91901-92200.
M. A. Dewees	S. E. Hughes	5101-5400.
Do	M. A. Yates	69201-69300.
Do	B. W. Tyler	76301-76600.
Do	M. A. Mobley	93001-93200.
P. Savage	L. Macon	5401-5700, 35201-35500, 46701-47000, 69701-69900.
Do	M. Dixon	68401-68700.
Do	J. M. Connor	69601-69700.
Do	M. Norton	89401-89700.

Register of Confederate States Treasury Notes—Continued.

ACT OF FEBRUARY 17, 1864—Continued.

For Treasurer.	For Register.	Numbers of the notes signed.
		$5—A to H—Continued.
R. Haynes	B. Dabney	5701-6000, 25701-26000, 34901-35200, 44501-44700, 68701-68900, 73201-73300, 76901-77100, 88701-88900, 92401-92700.
Do	M. A. Yates	44701-44800.
V. M. Rind	V. K. Davies	6001-6300, 13501-13800, 19001-19300, 69901-70100, 72201-72500, 77901-78200.
Do	M. E. Gilliam	19301-19400.
Do	E. Coffin	70101-70200.
Do	F. E. Bernard	93501-93800.
S. Wise	M. Kirk	6301-6600.
Do	E. Mason	14401-14600.
Do	M. B. Kirby	28301-28600.
C. Hix	B. J. Clarke	6601-7000, 13801-14100, 18201-18600, 36601-36900, 38501-38600, 47601-47900.
Do	L. Macon	18601-18700.
M. Wade	E. Matthews	7001-7200, 24401-24700, 35501-35800, 47201-47400, 64101-64500, 87401-87700.
Do	M. Kirk	10401-10700.
M. Reeves	C. Huger	7201-7400, 61601-61800, 67101-67300, 74801-75100, 78801-78900, 90101-90400.
Do	M. E. Gilliam	12001-12200, 27701-27800.
Do	L. Macon	12201-12300.
Do	M. A. Yates	27501-27700.
Do	E. Laurens	33801-34000.
Do	F. Rhett	45201-45300, 78901-79000.
Do	M. Kirk	45301-45400.
Do	M. Taylor	52801-53000.
V. M. Tyler	M. Pleasants	8501-8800, 17601-17900, 22001-22300, 29301-29600, 39701-40000, 48801-49000, 55101-55400, 59101-59400, 65501-65800.
Do	M. Kirk	78201-78500, 97401-97700.
Do	C. Percival	82901-83200, 85101-85400.
S. Scott	S. Southall	8901-9200, 16201-16500.
Do	A. Zealy	24701-25100, 33501-33800, 43301-43600, 51401-51700, 56601-56900.
Do	B. W. Tyler	51701-51800.
Do	L. A. Norris	78501-78800, 89801-90100.
E. A. Dennison	M. E. Gilliam	12301-12600, 69301-69600, 76001-76300, 88901-89200.
V. K. Davies	M. E. Norton	12601-12900.
A. B. Capron	M. E. Gilliam	13201-13300.
Do	M. A. Yates	13301-13500, 38201-38500, 46401-46700.
E. C. Trescot	E. Mason	14101-14200.
Do	L. Devine	14201-14300.
Do	N. Brisbane	19801-20100, 29801-30100, 38901-39200.
Do	V. Penrifoy	48501-48800, 52501-52800, 57601-57900.
M. Darby	B. W. Tyler	15701-15900, 22301-22400, 22501-22600, 28801-28900, 30101-30400, 55401-55700, 61501-61600, 62901-63200, 66801-67100.
Do	S. E. Hughes	22401-22500.
N. Goodwin	E. Coffin	17901-18200, 36401-36700, 47401-47600, 48301-48400, 75401-75700, 94001-94300.
R. Macmurdo	F. Rhett	18701-19000, 36701-36900.
Do	B. W. Tyler	47001-47200.
M. Selden	A. P. Pellet	19401-19700, 29001-29300, 47901-48100, 51801-52200, 57301-57600, 70201-70300, 71901-72200, 79401-79700, 90801-91000.
Do	M. E. Gilliam	19701-19800.
Do	B. W. Tyler	48201-48300.
Do	J. De Leon	90701-90800.
A. Points	F. C. Jones	20401-20800, 32701-33000, 41301-41500, 82301-82600, 84201-84500.
Do	M. E. Gilliam	41201-41300.
Do	M. Jones	66101-66400.
Do	H. E. Bryan	95301-95600.
M. Allen	H. L. Cooke	21101-21500, 32301-32700, 41801-42200, 66401-66800.
Do	S. E. Hughes	21501-21600.
Do	M. Gaither	83801-83900.
N. Semple	M. E. Norton	26901-27200, 35801-36100, 48401-48500, 61201-61500, 80701-80900.
N. Giles	M. E. Gilliam	27801-28100.
Do	L. Devine	28101-28200.
Do	S. E. Hughes	28201-28300, 28901-29000.

Register of Confederate States Treasury Notes—Continued.

ACT OF FEBRUARY 17, 1864—Continued.

For Treasurer.	For Register.	Numbers of the notes signed.
		$5—A to H—Continued.
N. Giles	E. S. Read	36901-37300, 46001-46400, 57201-57300, 60201-60600, 63201-63600, 71001-71400, 74101-74500, 79701-80000.
Do	J. D. Treadwell	80001-80100.
M. Godwin	M. B. Kirby	40001-40300, 50001-50200, 53301-53600, 57901-58200, 65301-65500.
Do	L. Devine	50201-50300.
M. S. Gist	S. Johnson	43101-43300, 48101-48200.
Do	M. F. Jarvis	56001-56200.
Do	E. S. Read	56201-56300.
Do	F. Rhett	60601-60800.
Do	A. Zealy	60801-60900.
Do	L. Devine	65101-65300.
Do	M. J. Black	73401-73500, 75701-75900.
Do	M. Kirk	75901-76000.
Do	M. E. Brady	79001-79100.
A. Caldwell	S. Southall	70801-71000, 77101-77300.
F. Waties	N. E. Wingate	71701-71900, 74501-74800, 80101-80400, 86501-86700.
Do	J. M. Connor	86401-86500.
E. McCully	H. C. Thomas	72501-72700, 73601-73700.
Do	E. S. Read	89701-89800.
F. Stocker	A. S. Parry	73701-73800.
Do	S. E. Laval	73801-73900.
Do	S. K. Wells	81401-81700.
M. Carrington	A. S. Parry	73901-74000.
Do	S. Southall	74001-74100.
M. Boyd	S. A. Doar	80901-81100, 91401-91600.
J. Gott	M. E. Cullen	85401-85700, 98001-98400.
J. Jacobs	M. E. Brady	86701-87100.
M. Dargan	L. W. Elliott	88101-88400, 96801-96900.
L. Sims	L. Macon	88401-88700.
J. H. Angel	H. E. Alexander	91201-91400.
S. Fuller	R. King	91601-91900.
M. Banks	M. E. Harper	92701-93000.
K. Nelson	H. C. Thomas	93201-93300, 93401-93500.
Do	S. E. Laval	93301-93400.
M. Ringgold	E. Davis	93801-94000.
O. McGowan	L. Arthur	94601-94800.
H. Moore	A. M. Foran	94801-94900, 95201-95300.
L. Armstrong	H. Barnwell	94901-95000, 95601-95800.
A. Miller	S. E. Laval	95001-95100.
Do	H. C. Thomas	95101-95200.
S. R. Simons	J. D. Treadwell	95801-95900, 96001-96100.
Do	S. Johnson	95901-96000.
Do	J. A. Acosta	96901-97100.
H. Balaguer	S. Huard	98401-98500.
		$5—A to H (1st series).
A. B. Capron	M. A. Yates	1-300.
V. M. Rind	F. E. Bernard	301-500, 15101-15400, 25701-26000, 47101-47400, 60601-60900, 75101-75400, 84301-84600.
Do	M. F. Jarvis	501-600.
Do	J. M. Connor	9601-9900.
Do	M. Taylor	9901-10000.
Do	E. Coffin	34701-35000.
Do	A. S. Parry	81301-81600.
L. Holmes	L. Michel	601-700, 18301-18600, 37001-37300, 64401-64700, 83601-83900.
Do	S. Johnson	701-800.
Do	J. De Leon	41301-41600.
M. Boyd	S. A. Doar	801-900, 26801-27000, 65201-65300.
Do	A. S. Parry	901-1000.
Do	L. Devine	65001-65100.
Do	E. Davis	65101-65200.
L. Armstrong	E. Coffin	1001-1100.
Do	M. E. Cullen	1101-1200.
Do	M. B. Kirby	35001-35200.
Do	F. Rhett	35201-35300.
Do	J. M. Connor	83001-83100.

Register of Confederate States Treasury Notes—Continued.

ACT OF FEBRUARY 17, 1864—Continued.

For Treasurer.	For Register.	Numbers of the notes signed.
		$5—A to H (1st series)—Continued.
L. Armstrong	M. A. Yates	83101-83300.
H. Moore	A. M. Foran	1201-1400, 3601-3800.
Do	E. Davis	69001-69300, 85301-85600.
M. Carrington	M. E. Hamilton	1401-1600, 44001-44200, 53501-53700, 65901-66100.
Do	E. S. Proctor	88701-88900.
E. McCully	E. Matthews	1601-1700.
Do	S. Johnson	1701-1800.
Do	M. J. Black	2701-3000.
Do	A. S. Parry	13701-14000, 18001-18300, 33901-34200, 45601-45900, 59001-59300, 71601-71900.
Do	M. A. Yates	78001-78300.
Do	J. McGarr	89501-89600, 89701-89800.
Do	C. Percival	89601-89700.
A. Harrison	M. E. Hamilton	1801-1900.
Do	A. Zealy	6201-6500.
Do	M. Dixon	12501-12800.
Do	M. E. Harper	45401-45600, 46601-46700.
Do	L. Courtney	57701-58000.
Do	M. A. Yates	72801-73100.
Do	L. Devine	79301-79600.
G. Loyd	do	1901-2000.
Do	L. Macon	5701-5800.
Do	J. De Leon	5801-5900.
Do	A. M. Foran	36601-36700.
Do	H. E. Alexander	39701-39900, 60301-60500, 74801-75000, 91401-91700.
Do	B. W. Tyler	39901-40000.
Do	E. Coffin	60501-60600.
Do	A. P. Pellet	75001-75100.
M. Kingman	K. P. Howell	2001-2300, 39401-39700, 51201-51300, 76501-76800, 82201-82300.
J. Wilson	H. E. Alexander	2301-2400.
Do	C. Percival	2401-2600.
Do	M. B. Kirby	2601-2700.
Do	J. McGarr	40301-40600, 63801-64100, 83301-83600.
S. Fuller	R. King	3001-3300, 15701-16000, 20401-20700, 43101-43400, 55701-56000, 72501-72800, 88901-89200.
Do	E. S. Proctor	78301-78600.
N. Semple	M. E. Norton	3301-3600, 19501-19800, 27601-27800, 30601-30900, 42901-43100, 58001-58300, 71001-71300, 90401-90700.
Do	E. Davis	27801-27900.
M. Wade	E. Matthews	3801-4000, 11901-12200, 21801-22100, 29001-29300, 42701-42900, 52001-52300, 69701-70000, 86201-86500.
C. Morris	H. E. Bryan	4001-4300.
Do	E. Davis	17201-17300.
Do	M. Kirk	17301-17400.
Do	M. B. Kirby	17401-17500, 28401-28600.
Do	L. Courtney	42401-42700.
M. Gist	L. Pelot	4301-4600, 20701-21000, 37301-37700, 41701-42100, 51901-52000, 56501-56600, 65301-65600, 68001-68400, 89201-89500, 95801-95900.
Do	E. Davis	56301-56400.
Do	E. Coffin	56401-56500.
Do	H. L. Cooke	56601-56700.
Do	L. Devine	65601-65700.
J. Logan	N. Brisbane	4601-4900, 10001-10200, 24901-25200, 49101-49400, 59301-59600, 91701-92000.
Do	J. D. Treadwell	10201-10300.
J. Jacobs	M. E. Brady	4901-5100, 37701-37900, 54301-54600, 73901-74100, 92001-92300.
Do	L. Henry	5101-5200, 10801-11000.
Do	H. L. Cooke	10701-10800.
Do	F. Rhett	37901-38000.
H. Balaguer	S. Huard	5201-5500, 19801-20100, 29901-30000, 40601-40900, 54901-55200, 67001-67300, 90101-90400.
J. H. Angel	M. A. Mobley	5501-5700, 20101-20300.
Do	M. E. Harper	20301-20400.
Do	M. Taylor	60901-61200.
Do	C. C. Veal	66101-66200, 74101-74200.

Register of Confederate States Treasury Notes—Continued.

ACT OF FEBRUARY 17, 1864—Continued.

For Treasurer.	For Register.	Numbers of the notes signed.
		$5—A to H (1st series)—Continued.
J. H. Angel	S. E. Laval	66201–66300.
Do	A. M. Foran	66301–66400.
Do	C. Percival	74201–74300.
Do	M. E. Brady	74301–74400.
Do	A. S. Parry	95201–95500.
P. Savage	do	5901–6200.
Do	L. Macon	11601–11900, 23401–23700, 57001–57300, 93101–93300.
N. Giles	E. S. Read	6501–6900, 16001–16300, 23701–24100, 32801–33200, 46701–47100, 59901–60300, 69301–69700, 78601–79000, 90701–91100, 98101–98300.
Do	E. Coffin	16301–16400.
M. Dargan	L. W. Elliott	6901–7200, 36701–37000, 88401–88700, 97301–97500.
Do	S. Huard	56001–56100.
Do	M. B. Kirby	56101–56300.
Do	K. P. Howell	65701–65800.
Do	E. C. Winston	65801–65900.
Do	C. Percival	77701–78000.
A. Gray	M. Taylor	7201–7500, 14601–14800, 22801–23100, 35301–35600, 49401–49700, 80601–80900.
Do	M. A. Yates	80401–80500.
Do	E. Laurens	80501–80600.
N. Goodwin	E. Coffin	7501–7800, 33201–33500, 63001–63200, 74601–74700, 94901–95200.
Do	M. Dixon	25501–25700.
Do	J. A. Acosta	74701–74800, 79901–80100.
F. Stocker	S. K. Wells	7801–8100, 12201–12500, 19201–19500, 21001–21300, 30001–30300, 43401–43700, 56701–56900, 70301–70500, 92301–92600, 97501–97800..
Do	J. De Leon	54001–54300.
Do	L. Devine	56901–57000.
S. R. Simons	H. Barnwell	8101–8400.
Do	J. A. Acosta	83901–84100, 97201–97300.
F. Waties	N. E. Wingate	8401–8700, 23101–23400, 53701–54000, 59601–59900.
Do	M. A. Yates	45101–45400.
Do	H. Barnwell	71301–71600, 91101–91400.
Do	R. King	76801–77100.
E. M. Bell	M. F. Jarvis	8701–9000, 22101–22400, 29301–29600, 52301–52500, 70601–71000.
Do	C. Percival	22401–22500.
A. S. Stuart	F. H. Marks	9001–9300, 11001–11300, 17701–18000.
Do	M. B. Kirby	44201–44500.
K. Nelson	E. Davis	9301–9600.
Do	A. M. Foran	15401–15700, 26001–26300, 27901–28200, 34201–34400, 36301–36600, 45901–46200, 61201–61500.
Do	M. E. Norton	74401–74600.
Do	L. W. Elliott	79601–79900.
Do	S. E. Hughes	84601–84900.
Do	M. A. Yates	96201–96500.
L. Sims	H. Barnwell	10301–10700, 21501–21800, 29601–29900, 31001–31300, 44501–44800, 53201–53500.
Do	L. Devine	30901–31000.
Do	J. A. Acosta	68401–68700.
Do	S. Huard	70001–70100.
Do	S. E. Laval	70101–70200.
Do	J. De Leon	70201–70300.
Do	N. E. Wingate	77101–77400, 89801–90100.
S. Scott	L. A. Norris	11301–11600, 26301–26600, 40901–41300, 77401–77700, 94601–94900, 95901–96000.
Do	S. Johnson	67301–67600.
Do	E. Coffin	67601–67700.
A. Caldwell	J. D. Treadwell	12801–12900, 13001–13100, 27001–27200, 30401–30500, 55501–55700, 68701–69000.
Do	E. Coffin	12901–13000, 28901–29000.
Do	E. Davis	28601–28900.
Do	J. De Leon	30301–30400, 30501–30600.
M. A. Dewees	M. Gaither	13101–13400.
Do	H. E. Bryan	25201–25500, 31901–32200, 48001–48300, 61801–62100, 87801–88100.

Register of Confederate States Treasury Notes—Continued.

ACT OF FEBRUARY 17, 1864—Continued.

For Treasurer.	For Register.	Numbers of the notes signed.
		$5—A to H (1st series)—Continued.
E. A. Dennison	M. E. Gilliam	13401-13600, 28201-28300, 31601-31900, 48301-48600, 61501-61700, 88101-88400.
Do	E. Coffin	13601-13700.
M. Banks	M. E. Harper	14001-14300, 24101-24400, 62201-62500, 73101-73400, 81001-81300, 93601-93900.
S. J. Adams	H. C. Thomas	14301-14600, 24601-24900, 49701-50000, 51301-51600, 62501-62800, 73401-73700, 80701-81000, 93301-93600.
M. Selden	H. E. Bryan	14801-15100.
Do	M. Gaither	22501-22800.
Do	B. Dabney	43701-44000, 57301-57700, 85901-86200.
M. Allen	B. J. Clarke	16401-16800, 27201-27500.
Do	H. Heriot	27501-27600.
Do	H. L. Cooke	35901-36000, 38901-39000.
Do	F. Rhett	36001-36300.
Do	J. M. Connor	38701-38900.
Do	C. C. Veal	39001-39100.
Do	E. Coffin	50201-50500.
Do	M. E. Hamilton	50501-50600.
Do	F. C. Jones	63201-63600, 96801-97200.
A. Miller	S. E. Laval	16801-17100, 75801-76200.
Do	E. Davis	81901-82000.
J. Ambler	L. Henry	17101-17200.
Do	E. Coffin	24401-24600.
Do	M. E. Harper	32401-32600.
Do	L. Macon	47401-47700.
Do	A. Zealy	58701-59000, 71901-72200, 80101-80400, 93901-94200.
Do	F. C. Jones	82601-83000.
M. Reeves	R. King	17501-17600.
Do	M. E. Harper	17601-17700.
Do	H. Heriot	32601-32700.
Do	M. Gaither	32701-32800.
Do	C. Huger	47701-48000, 52901-53200, 55201-55500, 72201-72500.
Do	S. E. Hughes	79001-79200.
Do	C. Percival	79201-79300.
S. G. Sanxay	M. Dixon	18601-18700, 42101-42400, 52501-52800, 85601-85900.
Do	M. B. Kirby	18701-18800.
E. Kelly	B. W. Tyler	18801-19100, 31301-31600, 44901-45100, 54601-54900, 58301-58700, 75401-75600, 81601-81900, 94201-94500.
Do	H. Heriot	19101-19200.
Do	E. C. Winston	44801-44900.
Do	L. Devine	94501-94600.
M. Ringgold	H. L. Cooke	21301-21400.
Do	S. Johnson	21401-21500, 28301-28400.
Do	L. Henry	32201-32400, 48901-49100, 62101-62200, 73701-73800.
Do	M. B. Kirby	73801-73900, 92901-93000.
Do	S. Huard	93001-93100.
O. McGowan	L. Arthur	26601-26800.
J. Gill	B. J. Clarke	33501-33700, 33801-33900, 46201-46500.
Do	L. Pelot	33701-33800.
Do	L. Devine	46501-46600.
Do	S. Johnson	95501-95800.
E. Willis	J. M. Connor	34301-34700, 38001-38300, 40001-40300, 92601-92900, 97801-98100.
Do	B. J. Clarke	67701-68000.
R. Haynes	B. Dabney	35601-35700.
Do	M. Gaither	38501-38700, 48601-48900, 61701-61800, 64701-65000.
Do	J. D. Treadwell	87301-87500.
E. Baker	B. Dabney	35701-35800.
Do	L. Henry	35801-35900.
Do	M. B. Kirby	41601-41700.
Do	H. Heriot	66901-67000, 84901-85300.
K. Korff	do	38301-38500.
Do	M. Taylor	52801-52900.
Do	M. E. Hamilton	87501-87800.
V. M. Tyler	M. Kirk	39101-39400, 50601-50900, 76201-76500, 82301-82600.
Do	E. C. Winston	64101-64200.
Do	J. De Leon	64201-64300.
Do	L. Michel	64301-64400.

Register of Confederate States Treasury Notes—Continued.

ACT OF FEBRUARY 17, 1864—Continued.

For Treasurer.	For Register.	Numbers of the notes signed.
		$5—A to H (1st series)—Continued.
H. Moise	F. Rhett	50001-50100.
Do	S. Johnson	50101-50200.
A. Points	E. C. Winston	50901-51200, 63601-63800, 75601-75800, 82001-82200, 96001-96200.
C. White	M. J. Black	51601-51900, 86901-87200.
Do	E. C. Winston	87201-87300.
M. Darby	J. De Leon	62801-63000.
J. Gott	M. E. Cullen	66401-66800, 86501-86900.
S. McCants	C. Percival	66801-66900, 84101-84300, 96501-96800.
		$5—A to H (2d series).
S. Fuller	R. King	1-300, 19701-20000, 60501-60800, 85201-85300.
Do	L. Arthur	30901-31200.
Do	B. J. Clarke	78301-78600.
Do	A. P. Pellet	85101-85200.
Do	L. Macon	85301-85400.
E. Baker	H. Heriot	301-700, 44901-45100, 73901-74300.
N. Semple	M. E. Norton	701-1000, 37901-38200.
Do	M. B. Kirby	11801-12100.
Do	H. E. Bryan	66001-66300.
Do	A. S. Parry	69701-70000.
M. Carrington	M. B. Kirby	1001-1200.
Do	E. C. Winston	13101-13300.
Do	J. McGarr	24301-24600.
Do	H. C. Thomas	52201-52400.
Do	E. Davis	71601-71800.
Do	C. Huger	71801-71900.
M. Darby	M. Taylor	1201-1400.
Do	J. De Leon	13301-13500, 54401-54600, 60301-60500, 84901-85100, 97201-97400.
S. G. Sanxay	M. Dixon	1401-1700, 13501-13800, 35701-36000, 45401-45700, 54601-54900, 58701-59000, 63701-63800, 90701-90900, 96901-97200.
M. A. Dewees	H. E. Bryan	1701-2000, 14101-14400, 31501-31800, 40901-41200, 95201-95500.
J. Jacobs	M. E. Brady	2001-2200, 17601-17900, 30601-30900, 52001-52200, 56901-57200, 74301-74600.
E. McCully	A. S. Parry	2201-2500, 9901-10000, 19101-19300, 22201-22500, 50701-51000, 81501-81800, 88801-89100, 93301-93600.
Do	M. E. Norton	28101-28400.
Do	N. Brisbane	42601-42900.
Do	M. E. Hamilton	69101-69400.
E. A. Dennison	M. E. Gilliam	2501-2800, 13801-14100, 32301-32600, 41201-41500, 53501-53800, 58101-58400, 75901-76200, 95501-95800.
M. Dargan	L. W. Elliott	2801-3100, 14701-15000, 31801-32100, 46001-46300, 64501-64800, 76701-77000.
R. Haynes	L. Macon	3101-3400.
Do	B. J. Clarke	14401-14500, 14601-14700.
Do	J. D. Treadwell	14501-14600.
Do	E. S. Read	33001-33200.
Do	M. Gaither	33201-33300, 46601-46700, 53801-54100, 58401-58700.
Do	M. E. Harper	64801-64900.
Do	H. E. Bryan	76201-76500.
L. Sims	N. E. Wingate	3401-3700, 15601-16000, 38201-38600, 43701-44000, 62201-62600, 72801-73200, 77601-78000, 84201-84600.
Do	L. Pelot	3701-3800.
Do	F. E. Bernard	55701-55900.
A. Harrison	S. Huard	3801-4000.
Do	L. Devine	4001-4100, 18901-19100, 25501-25700, 39401-39700, 48601-48800.
Do	H. C. Thomas	48801-48900.
Do	F. Rhett	67001-67300.
Do	H. L. Cooke	78601-78900.
F. Waties	H. Barnwell	4101-4400, 17301-17600, 39101-39400, 48001-48300, 73601-73900.
Do	M. Kirk	61101-61400.
J. Logan	N. Brisbane	4401-4700, 16701-17000, 36601-36900, 61701-62000, 74601-74900, 84601-84900, 96601-96900.

Register of Confederate States Treasury Notes—Continued.

ACT OF FEBRUARY 17, 1864—Continued.

For Treasurer.	For Register.	Numbers of the notes signed.
		$5—A to H (2d series)—Continued.
J. Logan	L. Arthur	47401–47700.
S. Scott	L. A. Norris	4701–5100, 18301–18700, 90301–90600.
Do	A. P. Pellet	90601–90700.
F. Stocker	S. K. Wells	5101–5400, 15301–15600, 37201–37500, 86101–86400.
Do	S. E. Hughes	55401–55700.
Do	E. Coffin	60801–61100.
Do	R. King	65701–66000.
J. Gill	J. D. Treadwell	5401–5700.
Do	S. E. Hughes	5701–5800.
Do	C. Percival	20501–20900, 71501–71600.
Do	B. J. Clarke	40301–40600, 48301–48600, 62801–63200, 71201–71500, 87001–87200, 87301–87400.
Do	L. A. Norris	80101–80200.
Do	A. Zealy	80201–80500.
Do	L. Michel	87201–87300.
M. S. Gist	L. Pelot	5801–6200, 21101–21300, 32601–33000, 47001–47400, 52701–53100, 59301–59700, 75201–75600, 94801–95200.
Do	C. C. Veal	21001–21100.
Do	M. Taylor	65301–65400.
Do	J. M. Connor	65401–65700.
N. Goodwin	E. Coffin	6201–6500, 11101–11400, 24601–24900, 28401–28700, 44601–44900.
V. M. Rind	F. Rhett	6501–6800.
Do	S. E. Hughes	27001–27400.
Do	M. J. Black	42301–42600.
E. Kelly	S. Huard	6801–7000.
Do	H. C. Thomas	7001–7100.
Do	B. W. Tyler	16001–16400, 44001–44300, 62001–62200, 79201–79500, 86901–87000.
Do	F. Rhett	36501–36900.
Do	J. D. Treadwell	67901–68200.
Do	M. Taylor	86701–86900.
M. Banks	M. E. Harper	7101–7400, 20201–20500, 25701–26000, 40001–40300, 83601–83900.
Do	E. S. Proctor	49701–49900.
S. J. Adams	H. C. Thomas	7401–7700, 20001–20200, 26001–26300, 39701–40000, 81501–81800, 83301–83600.
J. Ambler	A. Zealy	7701–8000, 81101–81400.
N. Giles	E. S. Read	8001–8400, 19301–19700, 26601–27000, 35301–35700, 68501–68900, 77001–77400, 91601–92000.
M. Ringgold	L. Henry	8401–8600, 21601–21800, 38601–38800, 49001–49100.
Do	L. W. Elliott	21801–21900.
Do	M. Gaither	48901–49000.
Do	L. Courtney	62601–62700.
Do	J. McGarr	62701–62800.
Do	M. E. Norton	66901–67000.
Do	C. Percival	77401–77600.
Do	M. Kirk	83901–84100.
Do	J. De Leon	84101–84200.
E. Willis	J. M. Connor	8601–8900, 21901–22200, 31201–31500, 45701–46000, 59701–60000, 75601–75900, 93901–94200.
M. Allen	F. C. Jones	8901–9300, 23601–24000, 27401–27800, 41901–42300, 51301–51700, 70501–70800, 81801–82200, 88401–88800, 92301–92700.
Do	C. Percival	70801–70900.
V. M. Tyler	M. Kirk	9301–9600, 23301–23600, 28901–29200, 44301–44600.
S. R. Simons	J. A. Acosta	9601–9900.
A. Points	E. C. Winston	10001–10200, 28701–28900, 51701–52000, 70001–70300, 82201–82500, 87701–88000, 92001–92300.
Do	J. De Leon	42901–43100.
L. Holmes	L. Michel	10201–10500, 29801–30100.
Do	M. A. Yates	24901–25200.
Do	M. E. Harper	43101–43400.
Do	M. B. Kirby	51001–51300.
Do	H. L. Cooke	70901–71200.
Do	M. E. Norton	82801–83100.
Do	L. Courtney	89701–89900.
Do	S. E. Hughes	89901–90000.
S. McCants	C. Percival	10501–10800, 93601–93900.

Register of Confederate States Treasury Notes—Continued.

ACT OF FEBRUARY 17, 1864—Continued.

For Treasurer.	For Register.	Numbers of the notes signed.
		$5—A to H (2 series)—Continued.
M. Boyd	S. A. Doar	10801–11100, 25201–25500, 30101–30300, 82501–82800, 89101–89400, 92701–93000.
A. Miller	J. McGarr	11401–11800.
Do	S. E. Laval	41501–41900, 50001–50400.
M. Wade	E. Matthews	12101–12300, 22501–22900, 33301–33500, 59001–59300, 68901–69100, 73201–73600.
Do	E. Davis	55101–55400.
J. Gott	M. E. Cullen	12301–12600, 22901–23000, 23101–23300, 34201–34600, 52401–52700, 64901–65300, 95801–96200.
Do	M. E. Norton	12601–12700.
Do	J. De Leon	23001–23100.
E. M. Bell	M. F. Jarvis	12701–13100, 34901–35300, 53101–53500, 64101–64500, 72201–72400.
Do	E. Coffin	72401–72500.
H. Balaguer	S. Huard	15001–15300, 34601–34900, 49101–49400, 57501–57800, 63801–64100, 78001–78300, 83101–83300.
K. Nelson	J. De Leon	16401–16500, 16601–16700, 74901–75200.
Do	M. E. Norton	16501–16600.
Do	A. Zealy	38801–38900.
Do	M. E. Brady	38901–39000.
Do	M. A. Yates	39001–39100, 49401–49600.
Do	L. Arthur	49601–49700.
Do	C. Percival	63201–63400.
Do	J. D. Treadwell	71901–72200.
Do	A. M. Foran	89401–89700.
A. Caldwell	J. D. Treadwell	17001–17200, 33901–34200, 46301–46600, 54101–54300, 61401–61700.
Do	E. Coffin	17201–17300.
Do	F. Rhett	54301–54400.
M. Selden	A. P. Pellet	17901–18000.
Do	B. Dabney	18001–18300, 36901–37200, 47701–48000, 57201–57500, 67301–67600, 69401–69700, 79801–80000, 85701–85900, 88001–88400.
Do	E. Davis	80001–80100.
P. Savage	L. Macon	18701–18900, 40601–40900, 57801–58100.
H. Moise	S. Johnson	20901–21000, 27801–28100, 93001–93300.
Do	M. Kirk	43401–43700.
C. Morris	L. Courtney	21301–21600, 29201–29500.
O. McGowan	L. Arthur	24001–24300.
J. H. Angel	L. Pelot	26301–26400.
Do	E. C. Winston	26401–26500.
Do	B. W. Tyler	26501–26600, 32101–32300.
Do	M. B. Kirby	68201–68500, 72501–72700, 90901–91200.
Do	E. Coffin	72701–72800.
L. Armstrong	S. E. Hughes	29501–29700.
Do	J. McGarr	29701–29800.
Do	M. J. Black	50401–50700, 55901–56200.
Do	H. E. Alexander	94501–94800.
H. Moore	E. Davis	30401–30600, 63401–63700.
C. White	M. E. Hamilton	33501–33900, 45101–45400, 56501–56900, 96201–96600.
K. Korff	C. Percival	36001–36300.
Do	M. B. Kirby	49901–50000.
G. Loyd	H. E. Alexander	36301–36600, 46701–47000, 54901–55100, 60001–60300, 66301–66600, 79501–79800, 86401–86700.
S. Neill	L. A. Norris	56201–56500.
Do	F. E. Bernard	90001–90300.
Do	M. Kirk	94201–94500.
J. Wilson	J. McGarr	66601–66900, 78901–79200.
A. B. Capron	M. A. Yates	67601–67800, 80801–81100.
Do	A. P. Pellet	67801–67900.
Do	E. Laurens	87401–87500.
Do	C. Huger	87501–87700.
Do	S. E. Hughes	91201–91400.
R. Macmurdo	F. Rhett	70301–70500.
M. Reeves	C. Huger	76501–76700.
Do	E. S. Proctor	85901–86100.
A. Gray	M. Taylor	81401–81500, 85401–85700, 91401–91600.

Register of Confederate States Treasury Notes—Continued.

ACT OF FEBRUARY 17, 1864—Continued.

For Treasurer.	For Register.	Numbers of the notes signed.
		$5—A to H (3d series).
A. Caldwell	J. D. Treadwell	1-200, 6001-6100.
Do	M. Taylor	201-300, 5801-6000.
S. Scott	L. A. Norris	301-700, 13601-14000, 23401-23700, 34201-34500, 38101-38500.
Do	E. Coffin	23301-23400.
Do	M. A. Yates	34501-34600.
E. McCully	R. King	701-800, 30301-30400.
Do	A. S. Parry	801-900, 11001-11200.
Do	C. Percival	11201-11300.
Do	M. Dixon	19101-19400.
Do	S. E. Laval	30401-30500.
Do	J. D. Treadwell	30501-30600.
J. Logan	N. Brisbane	901-1200, 6101-6400, 15801-16100, 27801-27900, 34901-35100, 38501-38800, 39001-39300.
Do	M. Taylor	27601-27800.
M. Darby	L. Macon	1201-1400.
Do	J. De Leon	8101-8300, 20901-21100.
M. Banks	M. E. Harper	1401-1700, 6801-7100, 26401-26700, 36701-37000.
Do	M. Kirk	16701-17000.
H. Balaguer	S. Huard	1701-2000, 16101-16400, 19701-20000, 35501-35800.
A. Harrison	L. Devine	2001-2200, 7401-7700, 17001-17300, 25901-26100, 35801-36100.
F. Waties	H. Barnwell	2201-2400, 17901-18200, 27001-27300, 42701-42900.
G. Loyd	H. E. Alexander	2401-2600, 17601-17900, 36401-36700, 41201-41500.
J. Ambler	A. Zealy	2601-2900, 18201-18500.
M. Reeves	J. D. Treadwell	2901-3100, 7101-7200.
Do	E. Laurens	3101-3200.
Do	L. Henry	7201-7300.
Do	E. S. Proctor	16401-16600, 37901-38100.
Do	F. Rhett	16601-16700.
Do	L. Arthur	25701-25900.
N. Giles	E. S. Read	3201-3600, 8601-9000, 15101-15500, 24701-25000.
Do	E. S. Proctor	24601-24700.
A. B. Capron	A. S. Parry	3601-3900.
Do	M. A. Yates	9001-9300.
S. Neill	F. E. Bernard	3901-4200, 10701-11000, 20301-20600, 29401-29700, 41001-41200.
Do	E. Laurens	40901-41000.
K. Nelson	S. Huard	4201-4500.
Do	E. Coffin	11901-12100.
Do	L. Macon	12101-12200.
M. Dargan	L. W. Elliott	4501-4800, 15501-15800, 22301-22600, 30601-30900.
J. Jacobs	E. S. Proctor	4801-5000.
Do	M. E. Brady	14001-14300, 26101-26400, 32301-32500.
M. Gist	L. Pelot	5001-5400, 14701-15100, 23001-23300, 35101-35500.
Do	L. Henry	22901-23000.
E. Kelly	B. Dabney	5401-5600.
Do	S. Johnson	5601-5800.
Do	M. Kirk	25301-25400.
Do	B. W. Tyler	25401-25700, 30901-31300.
L. Sims	N. E. Wingate	6401-6800, 14301-14700, 21501-21900, 34601-34900.
M. Ringgold	L. Henry	7301-7400.
S. Fuller	R. King	7701-7900, 11601-11900, 24301-24600, 42101-42400.
M. A. Dewees	H. E. Bryan	7901-8100, 21101-21300, 32901-33200.
E. Willis	J. M. Connor	8301-8600, 21301-21500, 37001-37300.
M. Allen	F. C. Jones	9301-9700, 28001-28400, 39301-39700.
A. Points	E. C. Winston	9701-10000, 18501-18800, 28401-28800, 38901-39000.
L. Holmes	S. E. Hughes	10001-10300.
Do	E. Davis	10301-10400, 24101-24200.
Do	M. Kirk	24201-24300, 33401-33600.
M. Boyd	S. A. Doar	10401-10700, 29701-30000, 40701-40900.
Do	E. Davis	40601-40700.
F. Stocker	S. K. Wells	11301-11600, 20001-20300, 29101-29400, 40301-40600.
E. A. Dennison	M. E. Gilliam	12201-12500, 22601-22900, 33201-33400.
J. Gott	M. E. Cullen	12501-12800, 23701-24100, 33601-33900.
R. Haynes	M. Gaither	12801-13000.
S. G. Sanxay	M. Dixon	13001-13300.
C. White	M. E. Hamilton	13301-13600, 21901-22300, 31601-31900.
Do	M. A. Yates	31901-32000.
J. Wilson	H. E. Alexander	17301-17600.

Register of Confederate States Treasury Notes—Continued.

ACT OF FEBRUARY 17, 1864—Continued.

For Treasurer.	For Register.	Numbers of the notes signed.
		$5—A to H (3d series)—Continued.
J. Wilson	J. McGarr	18801–19100, 37301–37600, 39901–40300.
L. Armstrong	L. Arthur	19401–19700.
K. Korff	M. J. Black	20601–20900, 31301–31600.
J. H. Angel	M. A. Yates	25001–25300.
Do	L. Arthur	37601–37800.
Do	M. B. Kirby	37801–37900.
S. J. Adams	H. C. Thomas	26701–27000, 36101–36400.
M. Selden	B. Dabney	27301–27600.
R. Macmurdo	M. Kirk	27901–28000.
Do	J. D. Treadwell	38801–38900.
Do	A. P. Pellet	39701–39900.
H. Moise	B. J. Clarke	28801–29100.
Do	M. Taylor	41501–41800.
S. R. Simons	J. A. Acosta	30001–30300, 41801–42100.
E. M. Bell	E. Coffin	32001–32300.
E. Baker	H. Heriot	32501–32900.
C. Morris	L. Courtney	33901–34100.
Do	J. D. Treadwell	34101–34200.
E. C. Trescot	V. Penrifoy	42401–42700.
* * * *	* * * *	* * * * * * *
		$5—A to H (4th series).
* * * *	* * * *	* * * * * * *
		$5—A to H (5th series).
* * * *	* * * *	* * * * * * *
		$5—A to H (6th series).
* * * *	* * * *	* * * * * * *
		$5—A to H (7th series).
* * * *	* * * *	* * * * * * *
		$2—A to H.
* * * *	* * * *	* * * * * * *
		$1—A to H.
* * * *	* * * *	* * * * * * *

Issue of Confederate States Treasury Notes.

ACT OF MARCH 9, 1861.

Denomination and serial letter.	Numbers.	Amount by serial letter.	Amount by denomination.
$1,000.			
A—A	1-607	$607,000 00	$607,000 00
$500.			
A—A	1-607	303,500 00	303,500 00
$100.			
A—A	1-1606	160,600 00	
B—B	1-5798	579,800 00	
			740,400 00
$50.			
A—A	1-1606	80,300 00	
B—B	5798	289,900 00	
			370,200 00
Total			2,021,100 00

ACT OF MAY 16, 1861.

Denomination and serial letter.	Numbers.	Amount by serial letter.	Amount by denomination.
$100.			
B—B	1-4695	$469,500 00	
C—C	1-32460	3,246,000 00	
			$3,715,500 00
$50.			
B—B	1-51400	2,570,000 00	
Bb—Bb	1-39704	1,985,200 00	
C—C	1-32460	1,623,000 00	
			6,178,200 00
$20.			
B—B	1-9980	199,600 00	
C—C	1-19660	393,200 00	
Cc—Cc	1-39336	790,720 00	
Ccc—Ccc	1-86012	1,720,240 00	
D—D	1-109800	2,196,000 00	
			5,299,760 00
$10.			
A—A	1-126776	1,267,760 00	
B—B	1-12180	121,800 00	
C—C	1-32038	320,380 00	
			1,709,940 00
$5.			
B—B	1-22985	117,275 00	
Bb—Bb	1-49900	249,500 00	
F—F to I—I	1-3889	77,780 00	
			444,555 00
Total			17,347,955 00

ACT OF AUGUST 19, 1861.

Denomination and serial letter.	Numbers.	Amount by serial letter.	Amount by denomination.
$100.			
A—A	1-34000	}	
B—B to D—D	1-5203	} $5,481,100 00	
E	1-5202	}	
A^{C}—A to A^{K}—A	1-22918	18,332,800 00	
A^{1}—A to A^{8}—A	1-32946	26,356,800 00	
cA—A to fA—A	1-9344	}	
gA—A to kA—A	1-9410	} 10,552,000 00	
lA—A to oA—A	1-7626	}	
			$60,722,700 00

Issue of Confederate States Treasury Notes—Continued.

ACT OF AUGUST 19, 1861—Continued.

Denomination and serial letter.	Numbers.	Amount by serial letter.	Amount by denomination.
$50.			
A—A	1-34008		
B—B to D—D	1-5203	$2,740,950 00	
E—E	1-5202		
A^{D}—A	1-116207	6,067,250 00	
A^{E}—A to A^{L}—A	1-734		
A^{1}—A to A^{8}—A	1-33145	14,674,800 00	
A^{9}—A to A^{16}—A	1-3542		
A—A (Southern Bank Note Company)	1-14860	743,000 00	
1A—A1 to 4A—A4	1-239	47,000 00	
wA—Aw to zA—Az	1-81247	16,249,400 00	
wA—Aw to zA—Az, 2d series	1-25000	5,000,000 00	
			$45,523,200 00
$20.			
A—A	1-107878		
B—B to E—E and L—L to O—O	1-6458	4,337,880 00	
F—F to I—I and O—O to R—R	1-6353		
S—S and T—T	1-3264		
bA—A	1-103644	2,072,880 00	
BA—A	1-40328		
CA—A	1-43819	6,119,360 00	
DA—A to KA—A	1-27857		
LA—A	1-26822		
aC—C to aF—F	1-7893	631,440 00	
bB—B to tT—T	1-1511	543,940 00	
A^{D}—A to A^{L}—A	1-25516	4,191,360 00	
A^{C}—A and A^{M}—A to A^{U}—A	1-544		
A^{1}—A to A^{4}—A and A^{9}—A to A^{12}—A	1-21706		
A^{5}—A to A^{8}—A and A^{13}—A to A^{16}—A	1-21700	24,186,800 00	
A^{17}—A and A^{18}—A	1-2834		
A^{19}—A to A^{26}—A	1-107053		
19A—A to 26A—A	1-24097	3,855,520 00	
A^{1}—A to A^{8}—A, 2d series	1-8723	1,395,680 00	
A—A (*green*)	1-43732	874,640 00	
A—A (Southern Bank Note Company)	1-14860	297,200 00	
1—1 to 8—8, 1st series	1-18100	3,856,000 00	
1—1 to 8—8, 1st series (duplicates)	1-6000		
1—1 to 10—10, 1st series (remnants, $13,980)	18101-155640	27,521,980 00	
1—1 to 10—10, 2d series	1-100600	20,120,000 00	
1—1 to 10—10, 3d series (remnants, $1,320)	1-26032	5,207,720 00	
W—W to Z—Z	1-41062	3,284,960 00	
			108,497,360 00
$10.			
H—H to K—K	1-69600	2,784,000 00	
A—A to H—H (remnants, $210)	1-35826	2,866,290 00	
1—1 to 8—8, 1st series (remnants, $60)	1-61976	4,958,140 00	
1—1 to 8—8, 2d series (remnants, $350)	1-122488	9,799,390 00	
1—1 to 8—8, 3d series (remnants, $460)	1-6100	488,460 00	
1—1 to 10—10, 4th series (remnants, $860)	1-53131	5,313,960 00	
A—A and B—B (Southern Bank Note Company)	1-22000	588,600 00	
C—C (Southern Bank Note Company)	1-14860		
A9 to A16 (remnants, $340)	1-134588	10,767,380 00	
W—W to Z—Z (number *red*)	1-44679	1,787,160 00	
W—W to Z—Z (number *black*)	1-128600	5,144,000 00	
W—W to Z—Z, 2d series	1-12100	484,000 00	
Ab	1-7160	71,600 00	
A—A	1-10000	203,330 00	
A—A^{1}	1-10333		
I—I to P—P (remnants, $500)	1-79400	6,352,500 00	
			51,608,810 00
$5.			
A—A and B—B (Southern Bank Note Company)	1-22000	294,300 00	
C—C (Southern Bank Note Company)	1-14860		
A	1-10000	101,665 00	
A^{A}	1-10333		
Ab	1-7160	35,800 00	
H—H to K—K (number *red*)	1-25344	506,880 00	
H—H to K—K (number *black*)	1-34189	683,780 00	

Issue of Confederate States Treasury Notes—Continued.

ACT OF AUGUST, 19, 1861—Continued.

Denomination and serial letter.	Numbers.	Amount by serial letter.	Amount by denomination.
$5—Continued.			
W—W to Z—Z	1-31822	$636,440 00	
9A to 16A (remnants, $90)	1-168100	6,724,090 00	
9A to 16A, 2d series (remnants, $960)	1-291446	11,658,800 00	
9A to 16A, 3d series	1-2289	91,560 00	
A—A to H—H (remnants, $4,180)	1-82973	3,323,100 00	
1—1 to 8—8, 2d series	1-42333	1,693,345 00	
			$25,749,760 00
Total			292,101,830 00
Less notes stolen, destroyed, &c			140,000 00
Net amount issued			291,961,830 00

ACT OF APRIL 17, 1862.

Denomination and serial letter.	Numbers.	Amount by serial letter.	Amount by denomination.
$100.			
A—A and A—Ab to A—Az	1-2500	$2,000,000 00	
A—Aa to A—Az	2501-69900	53,920,000 00	
W—W to Z—Z	1-167600	67,040,000 00	
			$122,960,000 00
$2.			
1—1 to 10—10, 1st series	1-47000	940,000 00	
1—1 to 10—10, 2d series	1-62800	1,256,000 00	
1—1 to 12—12, 3d series (remnants, $2,400)	1-54200	1,303,200 00	
			3,499,200 00
$1.			
1—1 to 10—10, 1st series	1-51340	513,400 00	
1—1 to 10—10, 2d series	1-54200	542,000 00	
1—1 to 10—10, 3d series (remnants, $2,800)	1-87000	1,046,800 00	
			2,102,200 00
			128,561,400 00
Less 100's destroyed			320,000 00
Total issue			128,241,400 00

ACT OF OCTOBER 13, 1862.

Denomination and serial letter.	Numbers.	Amount by serial letter.	Amount by denomination.
$100.			
A—A to D—D, 1st series	1-124400	$49,760,000 00	
A—A to D—D, 2d series	1-27860	11,144,000 00	
			$60,904,000 00
$50.			
wA—Aw to zA—Az, 3d series	1-91200	18,240,000 00	
			18,240,000 00
$20.			
A—A to H—H, 1st series	1-88400	14,144,000 00	
			14,144,000 00
$10.			
A—A to H—H, 1st series	1-143900	11,512,000 00	
A—A to H—H, 2d series	1-65600	5,248,000 00	
A—A to H—H, 3d series	1-107000	8,560,000 00	
A—A to H—H, 4th series	1-66000	5,280,000 00	
			30,600,000 00
$5.			
A—A to H—H, 1st series	1-124600	4,984,000 00	
A—A to H—H, 2d series	1-173400	6,936,000 00	
A—A to H—H, 3d series	1-56200	2,248,000 00	
			14,168,000 00

Issue of Confederate States Treasury Notes—Continued.

ACT OF OCTOBER 13, 1862—Continued.

Denomination and serial letter.	Numbers.	Amount by serial letter.	Amount by denomination.
$2.			
A—A	1-100000	$200,000 00	
B—B to I—I, 1st series	1-61775	988,400 00	
B—B to I—I, 2d series	1-1100	17,600 00	
			$1,206,000 00
$1.			
A—A	1-110400	110,400 00	
B—B to E—E, 1st series	1-121200	484,800 00	
F—F to I—I, 1st series	1-126500	506,000 00	
B—B to I—I, 2d series	1-5000	40,000 00	
			1,141,200 00
Total			140,403,200 00
Less twos, 1st series, never issued		1,600 00	
Less ones, 1st series, never issued		800 00	
			2,400 00
Net issue			140,400,800 00

ACT OF MARCH 23, 1863.

Denomination and serial letter.	Numbers.	Amount by serial letter.	Amount by denomination.
$100—A—A to D—D.			
1863—April	1-26500	$10,600,000 00	
May	26501-64800	15,320,000 00	
June	1-53200	21,280,000 00	
July	1-24000	9,600,000 00	
August	1-38900	15,560,000 00	
September	1-29800	11,920,000 00	
October	1-47600	19,040,000 00	
November	1-63700	*a*25,480,000 00	
December	1-69600	27,840,000 00	
1864—January	1-91300	36,520,000 00	
February			
			$193,160,000 00
$50—wA—Aw—zA—Az.			
1863—April	1-53300	10,660,000 00	
May	53301-108600	11,060,000 00	
June	1-30300	6,060,000 00	
July	1-72400	14,480,000 00	
August	1-71000	14,200,000 00	
September	1-51500	10,300,000 00	
October	1-77000	15,400,000 00	
November	1-57500	*a*11,500,000 00	
December	1-73000	14,600,000 00	
1864—January	1-30100	6,020,000 00	
February	1-9600	1,920,000 00	
			116,200,000 00
$20—A—A to H—H			
1863—April	1-124700	19,952,000 00	
May	124701-192800	10,896,000 00	
June	1-71700	11,472,000 00	
July	1-89200	14,272,000 00	
August	1-70100	11,216,000 00	
September	1-98400	15,744,000 00	
October	1-31300	5,008,000 00	
November			
December			
1864—January			
February			
			88,560,000 00
$10—A—A to H—H.			
1863—April	1-36000	2,880,000 00	
May	36001-165700	10,376,000 00	

Issue of Confederate States Treasury Notes—Continued.

ACT OF MARCH 23, 1863—Continued.

Denomination and serial letter.	Numbers.	Amount by serial letter.	Amount by denomination.
$10—A—A to H—H—Continued.			
1863—June	1-116500	$9,320,000 00	
July	1-96900	7,752,000 00	
August	1-79500	6,360,000 00	
September	1-102600	8,208,000 00	
October	1-89900	7,192,000 00	
November	1-81200	6,496,000 00	
December	1-64400	5,152,000 00	
1864—January	1-61700	4,936,000 00	
February	1-69200	5,536,000 00	
			$74,208,000 00
$5—A—A to H—H.			
1863—April	1-147700	5,908,000 00	
May	147701-207400	2,348,000 00	
June	1-46700	1,868,000 00	
July	1-97400	3,896,000 00	
August	1-66600	2,664,000 00	
September	1-95700	3,828,000 00	
October	1-84000	3,360,000 00	
November	1-83100	3,324,000 00	
December	1-60200	2,408,000 00	
1864—January	1-63100	2,524,000 00	
February	1-165000	6,600,000 00	
			38,728,000 00
$2.			
A—A to H—H, 1st series	1-25900	414,400 00	
A—A to H—H, 2d series	1-53400	854,400 00	
A—A to H—H, 3d series	1-5100	81,600 00	
			1,350,400 00
$1.			
A—A to H—H, 1st series	1-135400	1,083,200 00	
A—A to H—H, 2d series	1-54800	438,400 00	
A—A to H—H, 3d series	1-14800	118,400 00	
			b 1,640,000 00
50c.			
A to I, 1st series	1-*149532	672,894 00	
A to I, 2d series	1-*53485	240,068 50	
			c 912,962 50
			514,759,362 50
a Add amount of $100's and $50's issued in November, 1863, record missing			3,200,000 00
b Add difference between $2,990,400, as above, and $3,023,520, the amount of twos and ones issued, as reported by the Register of the Treasury			33,120 00
c Add difference between $912,962.50, as above, and $915,758.50, the amount of 50-cent notes issued, as reported by the Register of the Treasury			2,796 00
Total			517,995,278 50
Less tens printed but never issued			24,000 00
Net issue			517,971,278 50

[NOTE.—The record of issue of fractional currency is missing. The numbers marked * indicate the highest number that has come under my observation.—R. P. T.]

Issue of Confederate States Treasury Notes—Continued.

ACT OF FEBRUARY 17, 1864.

Denomination and serial letter.	Numbers.	Amount by serial letter.	Amount by denomination.
$500.			
A—A to D—D	1-*37607	$75, 214, 000 00	$75, 214, 000 00
$100.			
A—A to D—D	1-98000	39, 200, 000 00	
A—A to D—D, 1st series	1-93600	37, 440, 000 00	
A—A to D—D, 2d series	1-*32561	13, 024, 400 00	89, 664, 400 00
$50.			
wA—Aw to zA—Az	1-97000	19, 400, 000 00	
wA—Aw to zA—Az, 1st series	1-95400	19, 080, 000 00	
wA—Aw to zA—Az, 2d series	1-96700	19, 340, 000 00	
wA—Aw to zA—Az, 3d series	1-*84595	16, 919, 000 00	
wA—Aw to zA—Az, 4th series	1-*44166	8, 833, 200 00	83, 572, 200 00
$20.			
A—A to D—D	1-100000	8, 000, 000 00	
A—A to D—D, 1st series	1-99300	7, 944, 000 00	
A—A to D—D, 2d series	1-99100	7, 928, 000 00	
A—A to D—D, 3d series	1-96200	7, 696, 000 00	
A—A to D—D, 4th series	1-95100	7, 608, 000 00	
A—A to D—D, 5th series	1-95100	7, 608, 000 00	
A—A to D—D, 6th series	1-96500	7, 720, 000 00	
A—A to D—D, 7th series	1-97200	7, 776, 000 00	
A—A to D—D, 8th series	1-96600	7, 728, 000 00	
A—A to D—D, 9th series	1-*52892	4, 231, 360 00	
A—A to D—D, 10th series	1-*67803	5, 424, 240 00	
A—A to D—D, 11th series	1-*78456	6, 276, 480 00	85, 940, 080 00
$10.			
A—A to H—H	1-143400	11, 472, 000 00	
A—A to H—H, 1st series	1-102900	8, 232, 000 00	
A—A to H—H, 2d series	1-*98500	7, 880, 000 00	
A—A to H—H, 3d series	1-*98400	7, 872, 000 00	
A—A to H—H, 4th series	1-*102258	8, 200, 640 00	
A—A to H—H, 5th series	1-*97263	7, 781, 040 00	
A—A to H—H, 6th series	1-*104630	8, 370, 400 00	
A—A to H—H, 7th series	1-*104586	8, 366, 880 00	
A—A to H—H, 8th series	1-*96433	7, 714, 640 00	
A—A to H—H, 9th series	1-*114015	9, 121, 200 00	
A—A to H—H, 10th series	1-*79481	6, 358, 400 00	91, 359, 200 00
$5.			
A—A to H—H	1-98500	3, 940, 000 00	
A—A to H—H, 1st series	1-98300	3, 932, 000 00	
A—A to H—H, 2d series	1-97400	3, 896, 000 00	
A—A to H—H, 3d series	1-*97397	3, 895, 880 00	
A—A to H—H, 4th series	1-*97405	3, 896, 200 00	
A—A to H—H, 5th series	1-*93932	3, 757, 280 00	
A—A to H—H, 6th series	1-*100026	4, 001, 040 00	
A—A to H—H, 7th series	1-*7698	307, 920 00	27, 626, 320 00
$2.			
A—A to H—H	1-*102799	1, 644, 784 00	1, 644, 784 00
$1.			
A—A to H—H	1-*74800	598, 400 00	598, 400 00
50c.			
A to I, 1st series	1-*105418	474, 381 00	
A to I, 2d series	1-*10939	49, 225 50	523, 606 50
			456, 142, 990 50

[NOTE.—The above sum of $456,142,990.50 does not represent the full amount of issues, the records being incomplete. The numbers marked * indicate simply the highest number that has come under my observation. In notes of $5 and upwards the entries represent an issue of $329,680,000.—R. P. T.]

Issue of Confederate States Coupon Bonds, Stock, &c.

LOAN OF FEBRUARY 28, 1861.

COUPON BONDS.

April 17 to November 1, 1861.	Denomination.				Amount.
	$1,000.	**$500.**	**$100.**	**$50.**	
April 17-30	592	2	1,082	765	$739,450
May 1	4,534	3,003	5,940	4,034	6,831,200
May 2-31	29	9	32	40	38,700
June	200	86	119	114	260,600
July	369	237	302	271	531,250
August	527	250	117	589	693,150
September	810	1,450	358	1,941	1,667,850
October	10	203	....	81	115,550
November	....	10	....	....	5,000
Total	7,071	5,250	7,950	7,835	10,882,750
November 1, amount exchanged for stock				$231,950	
January 24, 1865 (J. P. Benjamin), for stock				13,950	
					245,900
Total outstanding January 24, 1865					10,636,850

[NOTE.—The number of the last $1,000 bond issued is 7161. Nos. 4614 to 4653 (40), and 7078 to 7127 (50), were canceled.—R. P. T.]

Issue of Confederate States Coupon Bonds, Stock, &c.—Continued.

LOAN OF FEBRUARY 28, 1861.

STOCK.

Date.	$300,000.	$230,000.	$200,000.	$100,000.	$50,000.	$40,000.	$35,000.	$30,000.	$26,000.	$24,000.	$20,000.	$15,000.	$10,000.	$6,000.	$5,000.	$4,000.	$3,000.	$2,400.	$2,000.	$1,000.	$800.	$500.	$250.	$100.	$50.	Amount.
1861—April 17-30			1	5	1			1					2		12	4	2	1	6	763	1	155	1	274	287	$1,779,700
May 1																				29		5				31,500
May 2-31													1		2		3		4	18	3	17	2	57	24	73,300
June															4	1			1	52		27	2	30	4	95,200
July	1	1			2			3	1	1		2	15		11	3	6		4	168	6	28	28	115	38	1,250,200
August					1	1	1	1			10	1	10	1	5	2	6	2	8	54	5	30	10	63	8	630,000
September								2		1	1	4	7	2	14		7		21	53	5	85	8	116	9	492,550
October											1			1			1			7		5		12	2	39,800
December																									1	50
1862—January											1	1	3		11	2	1		9	22	1	28		58	8	192,000
July				1							3				2		5		1	19		8		15		211,500
1863—January											11	3	7		6	6	8		11	27	1	11	2	16	1	470,450
July											2	2	7		9	4	6		4	125	5	9		29	2	363,500
1864—January				4							4		8		15	5	7		5	21	6	12		30	1	720,850
July													4		8	1	8		8	13	1	9		9	4	143,400
1865—January											3	1	2		5	3	4		9	2	1	1		9	1	166,250
March 1													1				1					1		4	1	13,950
Total	1	1	1	10	4	1	1	7	1	2	36	14	67	4	104	31	65	3	91	1,373	35	431	53	837	391	6,674,200

RECAPITULATION.

Total value of certificates issued		$6,674,200
Certificates erroneously issued	$3,650	
Transfer certificates	2,317,400	
		2,321,050
Net stock outstanding March 1, 1865		4,353,150

Issue of Coupon Confederate States Bonds, Stock, &c.—Continued.

LOAN OF MAY 16, 1861.

COUPON BONDS.

Date.	Denomination.		Amount.
	$1,000.	$500.	
1861—September 17–30	110	....	$110,000
October	144	7	147,500
November	268	1	268,500
December	93	8	97,000
1862—January	44	25	56,500
February	29	27	42,500
March	52	12	58,000
April	47	10	52,000
May	3	10	8,000
June 30	9	219	118,500
	799	319	958,500

STOCK.

Date.	No. of certificates ($100 to $500,000).	Amount.
September 1, 1861, to March 20, 1865	1–3551	$12,235,600
Less amount of transfers	....	3,870,400
Net issue	....	8,365,200
Less amount of certificates redeemed	....	237,100
Stock outstanding March 20, 1865	....	8,128,100

Issue of Confederate States Coupon Bonds, Stock, &c.—Continued.

LOAN OF AUGUST 19, 1861.

COUPON BONDS.

Dates of redemption.	Denomination.				Amount.
	$1,000.	$500.	$100.	$50.	
1864—January					
July	927	700	598		$1,336,800
1865—January	671	381	449		906,400
July	993	742	614		1,425,400
1866—January					
July	1,093	831	594		1,567,900
1867—January	1,000	866	358		1,468,800
July	1,199	901		926	1,695,800
1868—January	1,094	1,132	628		1,722,800
July	1,283	957	727		1,834,200
1869—January					
July	593	1,005	8,884		1,983,900
1870—January					
July	1,491	1,126	877		2,141,700
1871—January	1,600	1,080	916		2,231,600
July	1,488	1,207	2,294		2,320,900
1872—January					
July	1,600	1,307	2,012	1,110	2,510,200
1873—January	1,832	1,388	846		2,610,600
July	1,901	1,397	1,094		2,708,900
1874—January					
July	2,064	1,408	1,187	998	2,936,600
1875—January	1,950	1,600	1,234	3,614	3,054,100
July	2,176	1,650	1,752		3,176,200
1876—January					
July	2,302	1,784	2,414		3,435,400
1877—January	2,512	1,831	1,454		3,572,900
July	2,598	1,933	1,513		3,715,800
1878—January	2,702	1,971	1,769		3,864,400
July	2,800	2,115	1,615		4,019,000
1879—January					
July	2,919	2,576	1,399		4,346,900
1880—January	3,099	2,484	1,798		4,520,800
July	3,296	2,431	1,901		4,701,600
1881—January					
July	3,457	2,621	2,000	2,059	5,070,450
Total	50,640	39,424	40,927	8,707	74,880,050

Less bonds redeemable:		
July, 1864, returned by T. S. Metcalf, depositary	$370,300	
July, 1866 ....do ....do	23,900	
Jan., 1867, canceled and exchanged	1,000	
Jan., 1868 ....do ....do	24,500	
Jan., 1875, returned by T. S. Metcalf, depositary	34,800	
July, 1881 ....do ....do	2,850	
		457,350
Net issue		74,422,700

Issue of Confederate States Coupon Bonds, Stock, &c.—Continued.

LOAN OF AUGUST 19, 1861.

STOCK.

Date of redemption of stock.	Oct. 22, 1861, to May 31, 1862.	June 1, 1862, to Sept. 30, 1862.	Oct. 1, 1862, to Nov. 30, 1862.	Dec. 1, 1862, to Jan. 31, 1863.	Feb. 1, 1863, to May 31, 1863.	July 1, 1863, to Sept. 30, 1863.	Oct. 1, 1863, to Nov. 30, 1863.	Jan. 1, 1864, to May 31, 1864.	July 1, 1864, to Nov. 30, 1864.	Jan. 1, 1865, to Mar. 23, 1865.	Total issue.	Amount of transfers.	Net issue.
1864—January	$502, 700	$328, 400	$621, 450	$59, 500	$43, 300	$71, 650	$39, 750				$1, 666, 750	$448, 550	$1, 218, 200
July	3, 350				50						3, 400		3, 400
1865—January	226, 050	109, 900	167, 550	1, 100		85, 400	3, 500	$5, 150			598, 650	110, 650	488, 000
July	24, 200										24, 200		24, 200
1866—January	43, 650	72, 000	42, 800	396, 350	1, 104, 500	30, 050	42, 250	77, 650	$23, 050	$50, 450	1, 882, 750	325, 200	1, 557, 550
1867—January	214, 800	450			800	100	5, 350	14, 500	5, 500	2, 000	243, 500	80, 200	163, 300
1868—January	72, 200	7, 300		700			10, 000	10, 500	9, 500	500	110, 700	32, 500	78, 200
1869—January	46, 350	55, 500	93, 500	65, 200	2, 165, 250	303, 200	143, 450	306, 250	53, 300	43, 700	3, 275, 700	1, 356, 900	1, 918, 800
1870—January	11, 250	104, 700	116, 250	193, 700	1, 699, 150	64, 250	49, 950	251, 550	57, 900	58, 400	2, 607, 100	531, 100	2, 076, 000
July					4, 000						4, 000		4, 000
1872—January	1, 351, 700	571, 250	696, 550	264, 800	126, 100	145, 600	111, 850	152, 450	58, 000	82, 700	3, 561, 000	1, 157, 650	2, 403, 350
1873—July					7, 650	4, 000			500	500	12, 650	6, 500	6, 150
1874—January	4, 300	558, 900	65, 050	636, 000	1, 972, 650	262, 850	71, 100	451, 900	67, 200	94, 250	4, 184, 200	1, 375, 800	2, 808, 400
1876—January	7, 500	73, 850	455, 350	1, 428, 450	1, 607, 800	216, 150	62, 800	284, 650	115, 100	116, 750	4, 368, 400	1, 040, 650	3, 327, 750
1879—January	1, 750	191, 100	406, 750	3, 595, 750	263, 150	190, 800	70, 550	561, 250	87, 150	121, 900	5, 490, 150	1, 332, 600	4, 157, 550
1881—January	807, 000	2, 474, 050	1, 872, 850	909, 650	253, 000	117, 950	133, 000	330, 000	204, 400	233, 450	7, 335, 350	2, 443, 300	4, 892, 050
July				14, 650							14, 650		14, 650
Total	3, 316, 800	4, 547, 400	4, 538, 100	7, 565, 850	9, 247, 400	1, 492, 000	743, 550	2, 445, 850	681, 600	804, 600	35, 383, 150	10, 241, 600	25, 141, 550

Issue of Confederate States Coupon Bonds, Stock, &c.—Continued.

LOAN OF AUGUST 19, 1861—Continued.

STOCK.

Date.	1864.		1865.		1866.		1867.		1868.		1869.		1870.		1872.	
	Jan.	July.	Jan.	July.	Jan.	July.	Jan.	July.	Jan.	July.	Jan.	July.	Jan.	July.	Jan.	July.
October 22, 1861, to May 31, 1862	245	2	113	17	21	......	90	......	52	......	35	......	22	......	739	......
June 1, 1862, to September 30, 1862	174	......	46	......	30	......	......	......	2	......	38	......	42	......	372	......
October 1, 1862, to November 30, 1862	216	......	102	......	34	......	......	......	......	......	46	......	66	......	392	......
December 1, 1862, to January 31, 1863	73	......	1	......	247	......	......	......	3	......	35	......	151	......	78	......
February 1, 1863, to May 31, 1863	23	......	......	......	572	......	5	......	......	......	536	......	498	1	76	......
July 1, 1863, to September 30, 1863	25	......	10	......	26	......	1	......	......	......	82	......	39	......	27	......
October 1, 1863, to November 30, 1863	16	......	3	......	36	......	4	......	2	......	32	......	22	......	84	......
January 1, 1864, to May 31, 1864	......	......	5	......	49	......	8	......	7	......	72	......	82	......	112	......
July 1, 1864, to November 30, 1864	......	......	......	......	15	......	4	......	4	......	21	......	26	......	22	......
January 1, 1865, to March 23, 1865	......	......	......	......	19	......	1	......	1	......	14	......	26	......	26	......
Total	772	2	280	17	1,049	......	113	......	71	......	931	......	974	1	1,928	......

Date.	1873.		1874.		1876.		1877.		1879.		1881.		Amount.
	Jan.	July.	Jan.	July.	Jan.	July.	Jan.	July.	Jan.	July.	Jan.	July.	
October 22, 1861, to May 31, 1862	......	......	2	......	6	......	88	......	3	......	258	......	$3,321,300
June 1, 1862, to September 30, 1862	......	......	214	......	16	......	......	......	60	......	746	......	4,547,400
October 1, 1862, to November 30, 1862	......	......	37	......	236	......	......	......	183	......	730	......	4,538,100
December 1, 1862, to January 31, 1863	......	......	247	......	460	......	......	......	1,145	......	308	2	7,565,850
February 1, 1863, to May 31, 1863	......	6	687	......	389	......	......	......	80	......	88	......	9,249,200
July 1, 1863, to September 30, 1863	......	1	95	......	71	......	......	......	78	......	68	......	1,492,000
October 1, 1863, to November 30, 1863	......	......	27	......	25	......	......	......	47	......	50	......	743,550
January 1, 1864, to May 31, 1864	......	......	97	......	87	......	......	......	94	......	102	......	2,445,850
July 1, 1864, to November 30, 1864	......	1	33	......	46	......	......	......	33	......	30	......	681,600
January 1, 1865, to March 23, 1865	......	1	43	......	48	......	......	......	32	......	46	......	804,600
Total	......	9	1,482	......	1,384	......	88	......	1,755	......	2,426	2	35,389,450

Issue of Confederate States Coupon Bonds, Stock, &c.—Continued.

LOAN OF DECEMBER 24, 1861.

SIX PER CENT. CALL CERTIFICATES.

Date.	Issued.	Redeemed.	Outstanding.
To October 13, 1862	$57,526,570	$6,049,400	$51,477,170
November 1, 1862	3,891,000	2,000,000	53,368,170
December 1, 1862	2,270,900	4,467,000	51,172,070
January 1, 1863	5,318,400		56,490,470
Total	69,006,870	12,516,400	

LOAN OF APRIL 12, 1862.

COUPON BONDS.

Date.	Denomination.		Amount.
	$500.	$100.	
May 16, 1862, to March 3, 1864	5,560	381	* $2,818,100

STOCK.

Date.	No. of certificates.	Amount.
February 2, 1863, to November 1, 1864	1–129	$448,550
Less amount of transfers		44,100
Net issue		404,450

LOAN OF FEBRUARY 20, 1863.

EIGHT PER CENT. COUPON BONDS.

Date.	Denomination.			Amount.
	$1,000.	$500.	$100.	
March 2, 1863, to July 1, 1864	49,510	58,917	26,996	$81,668,100

EIGHT PER CENT. STOCK.

Date.	No. of certificates.	Amount.
February, 1863, to January 1, 1864	1–5362	$17,026,300
January 1, 1864, to January 1, 1865	5363–6258	3,886,500
January 1, 1865, to March 8, 1865	6259–6381	459,300
Total issue		21,372,100
Less amount of transfers		6,459,300
Net issue		14,912,800

* This amount includes $9,200 (eighteen $500 and two $100) issued under the provisions of the act of April 27, 1863.

Issue of Confederate States Coupon Bonds, Stock, &c.—Continued.

LOAN OF FEBRUARY 20, 1863—Continued.

SEVEN PER CENT. COUPON BONDS.

Date.	Denomination.			Amount.
	$1,000.	**$500.**	**$100.**	
April 6, 1863, to July 31, 1863	34,361	33,031	33,066	$54,183,100

SEVEN PER CENT. STOCK.

Date.	No. of certificates.	Amount.
February, 1863, to January 1, 1864	1–5724	$14,872,350
January 1, 1864, to January 1, 1865	5725–6247	1,736,400
January 1, 1865, to March 23, 1865	6248–6309	179,250
Total issue		16,788,000
Less amount of transfers		4,029,900
Net issue		12,758,100

LOAN OF MARCH 23, 1863.

COUPON BONDS.

Date.	Denomination.			Amount.
	$1,000.	**$500.**	**$100.**	
Six per cent.				
March 23, 1863, to February 6, 1865	15,046	2,404	4,923	$16,740,300
Four per cent.				
March 23, 1864, to December 21, 1864	18	6	13	22,300
Total	15,064	2,410	4,936	16,762,600

[NOTE.—Pencil entries would seem to indicate that of above six per cent. bonds, seven hundred and sixty-seven of $1,000, fifty-three of $500, and fifty-five of $100 were issued under eighteenth section of act of February 17, 1864; but other records of issues of bonds under that section confuse real facts.—R. P. T.]

SIX PER CENT. STOCK.

Date.	No. of certificates ($100 to $50,000).	Amount.
March 23, 1863, to February 24, 1865	1–1613	$5,023,800
Less transfers		745,700
Net issue		4,278,100

Issue of Confederate States Coupon Bonds, Stock, &c.—Continued.

LOAN OF APRIL 30, 1863.

COUPON BONDS.

Date.	Denomination. $1,000.	Amount.
July 28, 1863, to November 21, 1864	8,372	$8,372,000

LOAN OF FEBRUARY 17, 1864.

FOUR PER CENT. REGISTERED BONDS (*second section*).

(May 3, 1864, to March 1, 1865.)

Denomination.	No. of bonds.	Amount by series.	Amount by denomination.
$5,000.			
1st series	815	$4,075,000	
2d series	62	310,000	
			$4,385,000
$3,000.			
1st series	190	570,000	
2d series	50	150,000	
			720,000
$1,000.			
1st series	2,269	2,269,000	
2d series	256	256,000	
			2,525,000
$500.			
1st series	2,890	1,445,000	
2d series	256	128,000	
			1,573,000
$100.			
1st series	8,842	884,200	
2d series	1,116	111,600	
			995,800
Total issue			10,198,800
Less amount of transfers			14,900
Net issue			10,183,900

SIX PER CENT. COUPON BONDS (*sixth section*).

Denomination.	No. of bonds.	Amount by series.	Amount by denomination.
$10,000.			
1st series	100	$1,000,000	$1,000,000
$5,000.			
1st series	200	1,000,000	1,000,000
$1,000.			
1st series	9,300	9,300,000	
2d series	10,900	10,900,000	
3d series	10,800	10,800,000	
4th series	10,100	10,100,000	
5th series	11,200	11,200,000	
6th series	* 9,577	9,577,000	
7th series	* 7,100	7,100,000	
8th series	*10,200	10,200,000	
9th series	* 9,800	9,800,000	
10th series	*11,200	11,200,000	
11th series	*12,200	12,200,000	
			112,377,000

Issue of Confederate States Coupon Bonds, Stock, &c.—Continued.

LOAN OF FEBRUARY 17, 1864—Continued.

SIX PER CENT. COUPON BONDS (*sixth section*).

Denomination.	No. of bonds.	Amount by series.	Amount by denomination.
$500.			
1st series	9,500	$4,750,000	
2d series	10,000	5,000,000	
3d series	* 4,876	2,438,000	
4th series	*10,700	5,350,000	
5th series	*10,700	5,350,000	
6th series	* 8,000	4,000,000	
7th series	* 9,200	4,600,000	
			$31,488,000
$100.			
1st series	9,500	950,000	
2d series	* 9,400	940,000	
			1,890,000
Total			145,755,000

[NOTE.—The records (incomplete) show an issue of $69,882,800 to January 31, 1865. The numbers marked * indicate the number of bonds received by the register of the Treasury from Mr. S. G. Jamison, chief Treasury-Note Division at Columbia, S. C., up to March 18, 1865.—R. P. T.]

FOUR PER CENT. CALL CERTIFICATES (*seventh section*).

Date.	Denomination.		Amount.
	$100,000.	**$50,000.**	
To February 7, 1865	444	422	65,500,000

[NOTE.—The above statement shows the *highest number* sent by the register to the depositaries. The dates are those of the register's letters transmitting the securities.—R. P. T.]

TWENTY YEARS SIX PER CENT. BONDS (*twelfth section*).

Date.	Denomination.			Amount.
	$1,000.	**$500.**	**$100.**	
To January 31, 1865	4,000	3,500	2,500	6,000,000

[NOTE.—The above statement shows the highest number of bonds of different denominations received by the register of the Treasury from Mr. S. G. Jamison, chief Treasury-Note Division at Columbia, S. C., the date being that of the last letter of the register acknowledging receipt.—R. P. T.]

Issue of Confederate States Coupon Bonds, Stock, &c.—Continued.

LOAN OF FEBRUARY 17, 1864—Continued.

SIX PER CENT. NON-TAXABLE CERTIFICATES (*fourteenth section*).

(July 1, 1864, to January 31, 1865.)

Denomination.	No. of certificates of each denomination.	Amount.
$10,000	190	$1,900,000
$5,000	921	4,605,000
$1,000	24,210	24,210,000
$500	12,410	6,205,000
$100	11,250	1,125,000
		38,045,000

[NOTE.—The face value of non-taxable certificates issued to April 1, 1865, amounted to $45,166,100. March 30, 1865, $100 certificates numbered up to 13811 were sent by register to Mr. J. H. Lindsay, depositary at Greensborough, N. C.; and April 1, 1865, $1,000 and $500, certificates numbered up respectively to 31460 and 24650, were transmitted to Mr. J. R. Snead, depositary at Macon, Ga., making a grand total of $45,166,100 actually issued from the Treasury.—R. P. T.]

FOUR PER CENT. COUPON BONDS (*eighteenth section*).

Date.	Denomination.		Amount.
	$1,000.	**$500.**	
To February 8, 1865	15,061	2,405	$16,263,500

STOCK (*eighteenth section*).

Date.	No. of certificates ($20,000 each).	Amount.
To February 8, 1865	1–1602	$32,040,000

[NOTE.—The above statement shows the *highest number* sent by the register to the depositaries. The dates are those of the register's letters transmitting the securities. See in connection with these tables note on issues under act of March 23, 1863.—R. P. T.]

LOAN OF JUNE 13, 1864 (amendatory act of May 16, 1861).

COUPON BONDS.

Date.	Denomination.			Amount.
	$1,000.	**$500.**	**$100.**	
August 24, 1864, to March 25, 1865	2,120	73	75	$2,164,000

Issue of Confederate States Coupon Bonds, Stock, &c.—Continued.

LOAN OF JUNE 14, 1864 (amendatory of section 12 of act of February 17, 1864).

Date.	Denomination.		Amount.
	$1,000.	**$500.**	
To February 10, 1865	3,000	2,000	$4,000,000

[NOTE.—The above statement shows the highest number of bonds of different denominations received by the register of the Treasury from Mr. S. G. Jamison, chief of Treasury-Note Division at Columbia, S. C., the date being that of the last letter of the register acknowledging receipt.—R. P. T,]